THE NORTON

Field Guide
to Speaking

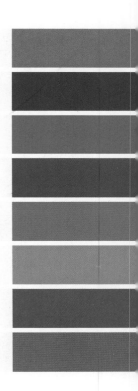

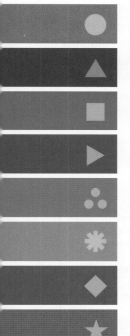

THE NORTON

Field Guide to Speaking

SECOND EDITION

Isa N. Engleberg
PRINCE GEORGE'S COMMUNITY COLLEGE, PROFESSOR EMERITA

John A. Daly
UNIVERSITY OF TEXAS, AUSTIN

Susan M. Ward
DELAWARE COUNTY COMMUNITY COLLEGE

W. W. NORTON & COMPANY
Independent Publishers Since 1923

W. W. NORTON & COMPANY has been independent since its founding in 1923, when William Warder Norton and Mary D. Herter Norton first published lectures delivered at the People's Institute, the adult education division of New York City's Cooper Union. The firm soon expanded its program beyond the Institute, publishing books by celebrated academics from America and abroad. By midcentury, the two major pillars of Norton's publishing program—trade books and college texts—were firmly established. In the 1950s, the Norton family transferred control of the company to its employees, and today—with a staff of five hundred and hundreds of trade, college, and professional titles published each year—W. W. Norton & Company stands as the largest and oldest publishing house owned wholly by its employees.

Editor: Elizabeth Pieslor
Developmental Editor and Project Editor: Michael Fauver
Editorial Assistant: Joseph Payne, Anthony Cardellini
Media Editor: Katie Bolger
Associate Media Editor: Jessica Awad
Media Editorial Assistant: Juliet Godwin, Felicia Jarrin
Director of Production, College: Jane Searle
Ebook Production Manager: Sophia Purut
Market Research and Strategy Manager, Communication and Media: Trevor Penland

Sales and Market Development Specialists, Humanities: Heidi Balas, Emily Frankenberger, Sarah Purnell, Ryan Schwab
Design Director: Rubina Yeh
Designers: Anna Palchik and Jen Montgomery
Director of College Permissions: Megan Schindel
Text Permissions Manager: Patricia Wong
Photo Editor: Thomas Persano
Copyeditor: Jude Grant
Proofreader: Debra Nichols
Indexer: Caryn Sobel

Composition: MPS Limited
Manufacturing: Transcontinental—Beauceville

W. W. Norton & Company, Inc., 500 Fifth Avenue, New York, NY 10110
wwnorton.com
W. W. Norton & Company, Ltd., 15 Carlisle Street, London W1D 3BS

1 2 3 4 5 6 7 8 9 0

Contents

Part 5   Engaging Your Audience   303

★ Part 8   Special Speaking Occasions   463

Notable Speakers

Each Notable Speaker presentation is fully annotated to call attention to the most important speaking strategies and skills in a particular chapter and is followed by a series of reflection questions.

 Greta Thunberg 14

 Susan Cain 205

 David Epstein 398

 Monica Lewinsky 27

 Yassmin Abdel-Magied 225

 Ron Finley 458

 George W. Bush 69

 Jordan Raskopoulos 246

 Dr. Ronald A. Crutcher 478

 Meghan Markle 86

 ShaoLan Hsueh 279

 Courtney Britt 478

 Zach Wahls 106

 Rita Pierson 333

 Berta Cáceres 497

 Malala Yousafzai 119

 Kyle Martin 346

 Bill Nighy 505

 Sebastian Wernicke 171

 Mileha Soneji 385

 Oprah Winfrey 512

Full video version of the Notable Speaker available in the Norton Ebook.

Excerpted video version of the Notable Speaker available in the Norton Ebook.

How to Use This Book

The Norton Field Guide to Speaking provides the practical advice you need to become an effective speaker, along with the flexibility to find specific advice that works best for you. Here are some of the ways you can find what you need in the book:

1 Read the book in order or as it's assigned to you by an instructor. As you do, you'll encounter **color-coded cross references**, which indicate that a topic is described in detail elsewhere in the book. Turn to those pages whenever you need more guidance. In the **ebook**, you can click on the reference to go directly to that section.

> **THE CENTRAL IDEA**
>
> Whether you use chunking, mind mapping, or some other method to start organizing your ideas and supporting material, you will eventually determine the key ideas that reflect your **PURPOSE STATEMENT ▲ (115–17)**. Now it's time to write out your *central idea*.
>
> Your **central idea** (sometimes called the **thesis** or preview statement) summarizes your overall message and tells the audience what your main points will be—it describes specifically what you intend *to* say.

Color-coded cross references may refer to a specific section within a chapter—sometimes the same chapter you're already reading. Others cover broader topics and direct you to a complete chapter.

> **Writing Your Purpose Statement**
>
> Once you know why you're speaking and have a grasp of your general objective, you should write a **purpose statement** that, at least preliminarily, specifies the goal of your presentation. A well-written purpose statement is a reality check that ensures you can achieve your goal in a time-limited presentation to a particular audience. "My purpose is to tell my audience all about my job as a real estate agent" is too general

2 **A Brief Guide** provides a preview of the concepts and advice in each chapter, making it easy to find the information you need.

1.4 Ethics and Free Speech

🔍 **A BRIEF GUIDE TO THIS CHAPTER**

- **Ethical communication** (p. 44)
- **Using sources ethically** (p. 48)
- **Using generative AI ethically** (p. 50)
- **Freedom of speech** (p. 55)

The ancient Roman rhetorician Quintilian gave aspiring speakers this advice: "The orator must above all things study morality and must obtain a thorough knowledge of all that is just and honorable, without which no one

---

3 **Norton InQuizitive**, a low-stakes learning tool, helps you learn and practice key concepts from each chapter and includes direct links to relevant pages in the ebook. If your instructor assigns InQuizitive activities, you can keep answering questions to improve your grade.

🐰 **INQUIZITIVE**

Chapter 3.1: Choosing a Topic

📄 Page 127 | 3.1.1. Consider Your Interests and Values

Fill in the blank to complete the following statement about choosing a topic.

Complete the passage by filling in the blank(s). Drag the word(s) below to fill in the blank(s) or use your keyboard to choose word(s) from the dropdown menus.

Considering your beliefs and values as a source for a topic involves thinking about what ⬚

| applies to your coursework + | interests you + | makes you happy + | guides your actions + |

You can also use InQuizitive on your own to review course material. See if you can reach the target score for each chapter, and then refer to the activity report to determine which learning objectives you already have a firm grasp of and which you might want to read again (or for the first time).

Like the ebook, you can access InQuizitive by registering the code inside the front cover of your print book or by purchasing at digital .wwnorton.com/nfgspeaking2.

4 At the back of the book is a combined **Glossary** / **Index**, where you'll find full definitions of key terms and topics, along with a list of the pages where you'll find more detail. You can read the glossary entries for key terms wherever they appear in the text of the ebook by hovering your cursor over them.

Preface

We welcome you to the Second Edition of *The Norton Field Guide to Speaking*. Based on valuable feedback from instructors who adopted the First Edition, general and specialized reviewers, and a wise publisher, we began our revision on the first word of the preface and ended with the last sentence in the final chapter.

The Norton Field Guide to Speaking's Second Edition builds on the goals of the previous edition: to provide supportive guidance for students and new instructors as well as the flexibility experienced faculty members want. We cover all major types of presentations assigned in college courses along with practical how-and-why advice that helps students make informed decisions as they prepare and deliver presentations in a variety of contexts today.

Just as there are field guides for bird watchers, gardeners, and even specialized accountants, this field guide is—obviously—for speakers. A field guide differs from a traditional textbook in that it helps readers identify valuable information in an easily accessible, browsable form. We have drawn inspiration from *The Norton Field Guide to Writing*—one of the most respected and popular English composition textbooks on the market for the last 20 years. *The Norton Field Guide to Speaking* contains eight major parts, each distinguished by a color and an icon. Color-coded cross references help students find the information and guidance they need when they most need it, which keeps the chapters short, focused, and easy to read. New outlines at the start of every chapter, new tables, a combined Glossary / Index, and bulleted lists make this edition even easier to use and navigate.

Some of the most significant differences in this edition are the contributions of Susan Ward, our third coauthor. Susan is an experienced, award-winning educator and professor whose expertise in areas such as online teaching and online presentation speaking expanded our knowledge base. She knows her stuff and knows how to teach it. Her work as a faculty development trainer enriched the instructional ancillaries that accompany this textbook. We welcome and applaud her valuable contributions, participation, goodwill, and good humor in the book-revision process.

Oh, and who is Norton? W. W. Norton is one of the largest and most respected independent and employee-owned publishers in the United States, and they entered the communication discipline with the publication of this textbook. Along with their reputation for independence comes their stability, their steadfastness, and the freedom to publish "books that live."

Distinctive Features in *The Norton Field Guide to Speaking*

Introductory textbooks in every academic discipline cover similar material. The best textbooks combine must-know subject matter with distinctive features that address learner needs. *The Norton Field Guide to Speaking* includes five distinctive features that we believe will prepare students to speak effectively and ethically in a variety of contexts.

UNIFIED PERSPECTIVE: THE RHETORICAL SITUATION

The Norton Field Guide to Speaking presents a set of six core elements that characterize every presentation's rhetorical situation: occasion, speaker, audience, purpose, content, and delivery. Your ability to succeed as a speaker depends on how well you think critically and make strategic decisions about each of these elements, so we introduce them in Chapter 1.1. We provide more detailed information in chapters dedicated to each element and

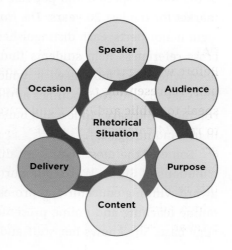

help students return to those essential elements with color-coded cross references throughout the rest of the book.

PRESENTATIONS, NOT JUST PUBLIC SPEAKING

Presentations occur every day and everywhere, in private and public settings, in various places and times with different purposes. Presenters speak to friends and family members, colleagues and managers, students and scholars, customers and salespeople, and wedding and workshop attendees. Public speaking is a specific kind of presentation that occurs when you address a *public* audience in community, government, or organizational settings.

You will make more presentations than public speeches over the course of your life. That's why we've titled this book *The Norton Field Guide to Speaking* and why we use the word *presentations* rather than *public speeches* throughout. The core principles and essential skills in this text are designed for all kinds of *speaking* situations—that is, any time you create and share verbal and nonverbal messages with a group of people. Whether you're preparing to speak before a city council, in an oral communication course, during a team discussion, or at a wedding ceremony, this book contains the advice and strategies to help you speak effectively and confidently.

PART 5: ENGAGING YOUR AUDIENCE

Before writing the First Edition, the authors asked hundreds of individuals, representing two distinct groups—professionals who frequently speak to public audiences and introductory public speaking students—to rate 24 commonly identified skills used by effective speakers. Both groups rated the ability to "keep an audience interested" as the *most important*. This result was a revelation for both of us. Inspired by this response, we prepared a unique Part 5: Engaging Your Audience, which addresses this topic. We know of no other book that devotes relevant, researched attention to this skill area as *The Norton Field*

Guide to Speaking. We thank the hundreds of anonymous individuals who helped us focus on what matters most to most speakers.

Part 5 includes four chapters designed to help speakers capture and keep their audience's interest from start to finish. "How can I not be boring?" asked one of our students. In response, these chapters do more than describe *what* to do; they tell you *how* to do it, with practical advice on the following strategies:

- Using expressive and vivid language to bring a presentation to life (**Chapter 5.1: Language and Style**)
- Telling effective stories, one of the most powerful ways to engage and impress an audience (**Chapter 5.2: Telling Stories**)
- Gaining, maintaining, and enhancing audience interest in several ways, such as limiting your presentation's length and using appropriate humor (**Chapter 5.3: Generating Interest**)
- Conducting an effective question-and-answer session as well as how to ask—as a speaker or audience member—clear, purposeful, and fair questions (**Chapter 5.4: Question-and-Answer Sessions**)

STRATEGIES FOR INFORMATIVE SPEAKING

Whereas most public speaking textbooks provide a wide range of persuasive strategies in a substantial chapter on persuasive speaking, the same cannot be said about strategies for informative speaking. Most textbooks offer little more than recommendations for organizing such speeches along with a series of tips for success. We don't think that's enough.

Students should also have a wide range of strategies for informative speaking. After all, skilled speakers would use one set of strategies for describing the anatomy of a fire ant and another set for explaining the basic principles of string theory. So, in Part 6: Speaking to Inform, we highlight distinct types of informative speaking and provide guidance based on whether a presentation reports new information or explains complex ideas.

NOTABLE SPEAKER FEATURES

Throughout the book, in addition to advice and guidance, we include 20 Notable Speaker features. Much more than a list of sample speeches, these features highlight recorded presentations—easily found online—by a diverse group of skilled presenters. While some of the speakers are well known, others are worth knowing as exceptional presenters.

Each presentation is annotated with time-stamped commentary, identifying how it exemplifies key strategies and skills of a particular chapter. These annotations—rhetorical analysis in miniature—help students appreciate and understand what works and what (occasionally) does not work in these examples. Each presentation is followed by a list of reflection questions that can be used for classroom discussion, individual assignments, or group activities, and new interactive video versions are now embedded directly into the ebook.

What's New

There is something new in every chapter of *The Norton Field Guide to Speaking*—including new examples, updated advice, and easy-to-reference tables. As the saying goes, "Make new friends, but keep the old." We kept and updated essential content *and* incorporated new material that addresses the realities of speaking today. In response to feedback from users and reviewers, we enriched and relocated six chapters, created an inviting new design, and added new advice on topics like generative AI, online presentations, and using respectful and inclusive language—all while keeping explanations brief and without increasing the total page count of the text. Rather than presenting a laundry list of every revision, here we present the major changes to this Second Edition.

A NEW LOOK

We updated the look and layout of *The Norton Field Guide to Speaking* to be more inviting for students and instructors alike. A new font and slightly larger trim size allow for more space on each page, making the text easier to read. New tables, charts, and photographs summarize and illustrate key information in an easy-to-reference format. New Brief Guides at the start of each chapter preview the key concepts and advice that students will encounter. And the new cover incorporates the icons from each part of the text, representing the multiple and interconnected components of the speechmaking process.

NOTABLE NEW AND UPDATED CHAPTERS

- **Chapter 2.1: Occasion (new).** In writing the Second Edition, we decided to create a new chapter on occasion to address the question "Why am *I* speaking on *this* occasion?" With this addition, the text now provides a chapter for each element of the rhetorical situation, strengthening the rhetorical perspective and better preparing students to prepare for any speaking situation.
- **Chapter 2.2: Audience (updated).** The First Edition included a chapter titled "How to Survey an Audience" in the final part of the book. Given that some instructors include this method in units on audience analysis, we moved the material to Part 2 and appropriately adjusted its content.
- **Chapter 3.4: Framing and Outlining (new).** In our many years of teaching, we have found that students often find extemporaneous speaking to be a challenge. While many instructors advise the use of full-sentence outlines, we prefer an alternative, less linear method—the speech framer—for strategically structuring a presentation's content. To give both these techniques more significance and visibility, we now cover framing and outlining in a single chapter. The result is more comprehensive and easy-to-use coverage, allowing students and instructors to choose what works best for them.
- **Chapter 4.4: Presentation Aids (updated).** The chapter on presentation aids has been enhanced and now appears in Part 4: Delivery. We emphasize the essential design principles based on the recommendations of professional designers as well as delivery strategies recommended by speaking experts.
- **Chapter 4.5: Online Presentations (new).** This chapter has undergone a major transformation to acknowledge the realities of presentation speaking today. Online speaking, once considered a special occasion, has become far more commonplace. As a result, we've rewritten the chapter and moved it to Part 4: Delivery, emphasizing what is different about the nature of speaking online and how to best prepare for this type of delivery.

- **Chapter 5.1: Language and Style (updated).** Language choices are instrumental in making presentations more engaging, worthwhile, and memorable. This edition now includes a section on respectful and inclusive language to help students choose words that invite every audience member to listen. We discuss the differences between person-first and identity-first language, plus advice to help speakers consider race and culture, gender, and ability when making language choices.
- **Chapter 5.4: Question-and-Answer Sessions (new).** As with online presentations, we no longer treat question-and-answer sessions as special occasions. Many presentations incorporate Q&As—they are one of the most significant ways to focus audience attention and enhance speaker credibility. We enriched the chapter by addressing common concerns about this often-neglected component of a presentation and moved this chapter to Part 5: Engaging Your Audience, where it belongs.

THE ROLE OF GENERATIVE AI IN SPEECHMAKING

Whether you encourage students to use it or you have classroom policies against its use, generative AI has arrived and has the potential to significantly impact many parts of the speechmaking process.

To help students understand the consequences and benefits of using generative AI as they prepare for their presentations, we have added a significant new section, "Using Generative AI Ethically" to Chapter 1.4: Ethics and Free Speech. Here, we explain the nature of generative AI, provide criteria for deciding *if* and *how* to use it, and list best practices for using it ethically.

In addition, we have added new advice and sample prompts to three chapters to help students use and be aware of generative AI in key areas where it offers the greatest potential benefit for student speakers:

- **Chapter 3.1: Choosing a Topic.** A new section explains how generative AI can help a speaker generate and refine potential presentation topics, along with cautions about using AI for this purpose.
- **Chapter 3.2: Research and Supporting Material.** A new section explains the differences between using established internet resources and using generative AI during the research process, with a suggested prompt to help students

use generative AI to develop research questions that can help to guide their research process using established catalogs, databases, and search engines.

- **Chapter 4.4: Presentation Aids** cautions students to check the authenticity and accuracy of any video, image, and audio to ensure they are not using AI-generated deepfakes in their presentation aids.
- **Chapter 5.4: Question-and-Answer Sessions** offers a suggested prompt designed to help students predict possible Q&A questions with the help of generative AI.

NEW NOTABLE SPEAKERS

We are particularly proud of the Notable Speaker features available in the textbook and the supplementary Speech Library available online. The presentations by 20 notable speakers are attached to chapters where their strategies and skills match the chapter's purpose and pedagogy. References to these speakers are also noted in the margins of other chapters when they exemplify a particular strategy or skill. All the presentations are real: credible speakers in front of specific audiences on a specific occasion with a unique purpose supported by valid, relevant content.

Five new Notable Speakers have been added to the Second Edition:

- **George W. Bush (Chapter 2.1: Occasion).** Former president George W. Bush's Ground Zero speech, as it is known, demonstrates how matching a specific purpose with the occasion enhances the impact and memorability of the presentation and its message.
- **Sebastian Wernicke (Chapter 3.3: Organizing Content).** With a healthy dose of humor, Dr. Sebastian Wernicke uses data about TED talks to explain the components of the ultimate TED talk while using his own presentation as an example of how to the organize content of a presentation.
- **Jordan Raskopoulos (Chapter 4.2: Vocal Delivery).** In this dynamic presentation, Australian singer, comedian, and actress Jordan Raskopoulos demonstrates the components of vocal delivery while she shares her personal experience living with high-functioning anxiety.
- **ShaoLan Hseuh (Chapter 4.4: Presentation Aids).** Tech entrepreneur and designer ShaoLan Hseuh demonstrates how the right presentation aids can

make all the difference in accomplishing the purpose of her presentation: to help people to learn to read Chinese . . . with ease.

- **Kyle Martin (Chapter 5.3: Generating Interest).** After experiencing a mere 15 seconds of excitement when he learned he was valedictorian of his 2019 high school graduating class, Kyle Martin generates audience interest with his energetic and expressive delivery and language as he challenges the audience to think about what happened in the sixteenth second, after his euphoria of being chosen as the commencement speaker.

Resources for Students

EBOOK

The Norton Field Guide to Speaking is available as an ebook—readable on all computers and mobile devices—and is included with all new print copies of the textbook. The content featured in the print book is enhanced by the digital format, as dynamic hyperlinks make the book's color-coded format and cross-refences even more convenient and easy to use. The Notable Speaker features are now embedded as videos in the ebook, along with the corresponding "What to Watch For" annotations, offering students the chance to watch, analyze, and learn before they move on to practicing the skills modeled by these speeches. Students can also quickly access relevant pages of the ebook within InQuizitive activities.

Offered at less than half the price of the print book, the ebook provides an active reading experience, enabling students to take notes, bookmark, search, highlight, and read offline. Instructors can even add notes that students can see as they are reading the text.

INQUIZITIVE

Included with all new print copies of the text, Norton's award-winning, easy-to-use adaptive learning tool personalizes the learning experience for students, helping them master—and retain—key learning objectives. Premade activities for each of the major chapters in the book start with questions about key concepts, proceed to application questions, and even include questions about the Notable Speaker videos from the textbook.

Offering a variety of question types, answer-specific feedback, and interactive gamelike features, InQuizitive motivates students to carefully read and engage with course content. As a result, students arrive better prepared for class, giving instructors more time for instruction, discussion, and activities and providing students a more solid foundation for working on their own presentations.

A robust activity report makes it easy to identify challenging concepts and allows for just-in-time intervention when students are struggling. The convenience of learning management system (LMS) integration saves time by allowing InQuizitive scores to report directly to the LMS gradebook.

SPEECH LIBRARY

In addition to the Notable Speaker examples in the book, a curated collection is available online and provides links to more than 25 sample speeches by a variety of presenters. This Speech Library also includes examples of student speeches so students have a chance to learn directly from their peers.

MLA AND APA STYLE GUIDES

In addition to Chapter 3.2: Research and Supporting Material, students have online access to *The Norton Guide to MLA Style* and *A Guide to APA Style*. These guides provide up-to-date information about how to format a variety of common sources used for presentations.

PLAGIARISM TUTORIAL

Though many students have had some level of instruction about plagiarism, they often still struggle with understanding what counts as plagiarism and how to avoid it. Norton's Understanding and Avoiding Plagiarism Tutorial is a valuable resource for students to demonstrate their understanding of plagiarism by completing activities and quizzes. With the Second Edition, the Plagiarism Tutorial has been updated to cover the use of generative AI in the public speaking course. It is an ideal companion for Chapter 1.4: Ethics and Free Speech.

Resources for Instructors

NORTON TEACHING TOOLS

With special contributions from the authors and instructors across the country, Norton Teaching Tools for *The Norton Field Guide to Speaking* provides support for teaching every chapter in the text. The Norton Teaching Tools site is searchable and can be filtered by chapter or by resource type, making it easy to find exactly what you need for your course, including:

- **Chapter Resources.** A variety of resources are available for each chapter, including chapter outlines, PowerPoint lecture slides, activities, suggestions for using the Notable Speaker features and Speech Library, and assignments for in-person and online classes, tips for tackling difficult concepts, and image files for each chapter.
- **Presentation Assignment Resources.** A set of common presentation assignments is accompanied by rubric templates, student models, and a curated Speech Library.
- **Guides for Teaching the Introductory Speaking Course In-person and Online.** A comprehensive guide to teaching the introductory speaking course offers syllabus and course design models, strategies for dealing with communication apprehension, and an introduction to culturally responsive teaching. In addition, a guide for teaching public speaking online provides recommendations for how to approach online course design when addressing the unique needs of teaching the course online.
- **Test Bank.** More than 750 questions for *The Norton Field Guide to Speaking* can be searched and filtered by chapter, type, difficulty, learning objective, and other criteria in Norton Testmaker, making it easy to construct tests and quizzes that are meaningful and diagnostic. Available online, without the need for specialized software, Testmaker allows easy export of tests to Microsoft Word or Common Cartridge files for the course LMS.

Your Norton representative can provide more information about all these resources. Visit wwnorton.com/find-your-rep to find your representative.

RESOURCES FOR YOUR LEARNING MANAGEMENT SYSTEM

Digital resources provided by Norton—including InQuizitive and customizable quiz questions using Norton Testmaker—can be integrated with your online, hybrid, or lecture courses so that all activities can be accessed within your existing LMS.

Acknowledgments

As we have traveled around the country—as active conference presenters, book authors, consultants, representatives of our institutions, and National Communication Association officers—we've met hundreds of instructors and students who helped us identify what students need to know to improve their speaking skills.

OUR REVIEWERS

We offer special thanks to the instructors from across the country who reviewed the Second Edition of *The Norton Field Guide to Speaking* in various draft stages: Frances E. Brandau (Sam Houston State University), Stephen Brown (Tarrant County College), Ferald J. Bryan (Northern Illinois University), Thomas Damp (Central New Mexico Community College), Carlos de Cuba (Kingsborough Community College), Zachary Frolich (Texas Christian University), Katherine Fulton (Iowa State University), Laura Glasbrenner (Mineral Area College), Paul T. M. Hemenway (Lamar University), Margaret R. LaWare (Iowa State University), Laurie Sadler Lawrence (Florida State University), David Haldane Lee (New York City College of Technology), Gail Lewis (Queensborough Community College), Jermaine Martinez (Northern Arizona University), Laura McDavitt (Hinds Community College), Shellie Michael (Volunteer State Community College), Andrea Peck (Cuyahoga Community College), Hattie Pinckney (Florence-Darlington Technical College), Tonia Pope (Houston Community College), Angela Putman (Penn State Brandywine), Brandi Quesenberry (Virginia Tech), Theresa Russo (Central Piedmont Community College), Cynthia Sampson (Louisiana State University), Poppy Slocum (LaGuardia Community College), Justin Stanley (Johnson County Community College), Tia C. M. Tyree (Howard University).

We would also like to thank the nearly 50 instructors who completed a survey and reviewed our new coverage of generative AI for this edition. Your feedback helped us include the information and advice that would best support the wide range of ways instructors use, want to use, discourage, and prohibit generative AI in the classroom.

We also want to remember and thank again the instructors who reviewed the First Edition of *The Norton Guide to Speaking*. They led the way in ensuring that we met the needs of both instructors and students who teach and learn the art, science, and craft of presentation speaking: Jaye Atkinson (Georgia State University), Ferald Bryan (Northern Illinois University), Deanna Fassett (San Jose State University), Tonya Forsythe (Ohio State University), Brandi Frisby (University of Kentucky), Brandon Gainer (De Anza College), Liliana Herakova (University of Maine), Brittany Hochstaetter (Wake Technical Community College), Emily Holler (Kennesaw State University), Angela Hosek (Ohio University), Jennifer Mellow (California State University San Marcos), Shellie Michael (Volunteer State Community College), Elizabeth Nelson (North Carolina State University), Leslie Pace (University of Louisiana Monroe), Dennis Porch (Wake Technical Community College), Kendra Rand (University of Maine), Toni Shields (Ivy Tech Community College), David Simon (Northern Illinois University), Shelly Stein (Hillsborough Community College), Ruth Stokes (Trident Technical College), Dudley Turner (University of Akron), Victor Viser (Texas A&M University at Galveston), and Kylene Wesner (Texas A&M University at College Station).

OUR NORTON PUBLISHING TEAM

A textbook without a good editor can easily lose its focus, vigor, and strength. A textbook also needs an editor who is patient and offers an experienced, guiding hand. The Second Edition of a textbook needs a renovator and redecorator with eyes focused on the future—someone who knows how to preserve what's valuable and add what is needed. These qualities describe editor Elizabeth Pieslor, our friendly, fearless leader. She gracefully walks the line between the needs and wants of the authors and the realities of bookmaking. How on earth did she keep smiling and putting up with us when we were not at our best? Part of the answer is that she never lost her enthusiasm for our project and knew when and how to praise us when we were at our best. She is smart, insightful, encouraging, and wise. We shall keep Elizabeth close.

A special callout is in order for Pete Simon, our original editor, who inspired, nurtured, and built on our initial ideas to make *The Norton Field Guide to Speaking* a breakthrough resource for students and instructors and for anyone seeking to become a more engaging, effective, and ethical speaker. Pete is now the editor in chief of Liveright, an imprint of W. W. Norton.

Michael Fauver, our indefatigable developmental editor *and* project editor was a twofold gift when we worked on the First Edition. We were honored to work with him again as we made the transition to the Second Edition. Michael analyzed the ideas, research, and claims we made to ensure they were clear, accurate, appropriate, and consistent with other content. He questioned—with amazing restraint, patience, and good humor—apparent errors, debatable conclusions, the relevance and timeliness of the research and examples we used, and the specificity and style of our language. And, as project editor, he was the conscientious "traffic manager" between Norton's editorial and production departments. His exceptional contributions have made *The Norton Field Guide to Speaking* clearer, more valuable, and more beautifully stitched together than it otherwise would have been.

We also worked with what Michael Fauver rightly described as our "rock star" copyeditor and proofreader. Jude Grant and Debra Nichols did more than find errors no one else had seen; they asked questions that changed entire sentences, paragraphs, and chapters as well as identified inconsistencies from one chapter to another. We also thank them for suggesting the perfect word we'd been searching for.

Our media editor, Katie Bolger, and her predecessors, Joy Cranshaw and Erica Wnek, were with us from the very beginning of working on *The Norton Field Guide to Speaking.* Rather than waiting until we completed writing, they and other members of the Norton team began developing the media program in tandem with our efforts. The ebook, the innovative InQuizitive platform, and all the other resources that accompany this book reflect the Norton media team's forethought and professionalism.

The Norton Field Guide to Speaking has been reenvisioned by Jen Montgomery, guided by design director Rubina Yeh. Their work transformed and adapted the original design into a fresh and attractive textbook. We also extend our deep gratitude to Jane Searle, who managed the book's production even as she also manages Norton's entire production department; Patricia Wong, who cleared text permissions with gentle professionalism; and Tommy Persano, who researched and secured permissions for our many new photos and illustrations.

Knowing how challenging persuasion is in almost any context, we hold the marketing and sales team in great esteem. We thank Trevor Penland, our diligent marketing research and strategy manager, as well as the humanities sales and marketing development specialists who help Norton's traveling sales reps get our book in the hands of professors across the country: Heidi Balas, Emily Frankenberger, Sarah Purnell, and Ryan Schwab. We trust you all will enjoy meeting these folks and will realize, through them, that Norton is a perfect fit for the communication discipline.

We applaud and are grateful to Norton's leadership team, including President Julia Reidhead, director of the College Department Mike Wright, and editorial director Ann Shin, for taking a leap of faith when they entered the communication market at a time of extreme uncertainty throughout higher education. Norton chose to do so at a time when effective speaking is also more important than ever. We hope that they look back on that decision fondly in the years to come.

OUR STUDENTS

Finally, we thank the thousands of students who enrolled in our courses in person and online, including those who took our classes well before we wrote this book. You are the reason we do what we do. You are the measure of all things that matter in terms of promoting, learning, and demonstrating the value of effective and ethical communication.

About the Authors

ISA N. ENGLEBERG

Isa N. Engleberg is a professor emerita at Prince George's Community College in Maryland and was the vice president of advancement and planning. With more than 35 years of teaching experience in communication studies at all levels of higher education, she has authored 10 college textbooks and published dozens of articles and book chapters.

Isa has held numerous leadership positions in professional communication associations, including president of the National Communication Association and director of its Research Board. She has a BA from George Washington University, an MA from the University of Maryland, and an EdD from Boston University. She loves traveling in the United States and abroad and enjoys theatre, music, and art.

JOHN A. DALY

John A. Daly is a professor at the University of Texas at Austin, where he directs the professional communication skills course. He has edited both *Communication Education* and *Written Communication* and is a former president of the National Communication Association. His undergraduate degree is from the University of Maryland (where Isa Engleberg was his debate coach), his MA from West Virginia University, and his PhD from Purdue University.

John has also worked with hundreds of organizations worldwide helping them address and improve issues tied to communication and leadership. He has coached many well-known business and political leaders on their communication. John has worked with firms on six of the seven continents and hopes for an opportunity in Antarctica soon.

SUSAN M. WARD

Susan M. Ward is a tenured professor at Delaware County Community College and serves as the faculty fellow for the college's quality assurance program for online learning. In her 25 years of teaching, she has taught at four-year public and private universities as well as community colleges. Her research and presentations have focused on pedagogical topics, including competencies for introductory communication studies courses and teaching public speaking online.

Serving in various leadership roles representing community colleges, Susan is an active member of the National Communication Association and Eastern Communication Association. She holds three degrees in communication studies, including an MA from West Chester University and a PhD from Regent University. More importantly, she has two cats.

THE NORTON

Field Guide to Speaking

PART 1
Getting Started

Your voice matters. And how you use it matters. The chapters in this section will help you take your first steps as a speaker. We'll start with a big-picture overview of the entire **SPEECHMAKING PROCESS**, which gives you a roadmap for everything else in the book; we'll address the perfectly understandable—and manageable—phenomenon of **SPEAKING ANXIETY**; and we'll help you understand your **ETHICAL OBLIGATIONS** as a speaker and audience member, including **EFFECTIVE LISTENING** strategies.

Getting Started

1.1 Introducing the Speechmaking Process

Why read a book about speaking? In life, you'll likely be *asked* to speak, perhaps to testify at a hearing, give a toast at your brother's wedding, or deliver a report on Zoom. You may also be *compelled* to speak about something that matters to you, perhaps to request support for a cause you believe in or share a memory at a grandparent's memorial. Whatever the situation, you'll want to meet the moment with preparation, practice, and confidence. This book will help you do just that. Our goal is to help you develop your unique voice, use it confidently, and realize that *your voice matters*—to you, your friends and colleagues, and even to the world at large.

Effective Presentation Speaking

So how do you go about deciding what to say to your audience, and how to say it? To be an effective speaker, you need to make strategic decisions before and while you speak, considering the occasion for your presentation, your relationship to the audience, and your particular purpose.

More than two thousand years ago, the Greek philosopher Aristotle wrote *Rhetoric*, a public speaking handbook that describes the strategies and devices successful speakers use to express their views clearly and persuasively. Today we think of **rhetoric** as the art and craft of influencing how an audience thinks, feels, and behaves while and after we speak. Aristotle's insights still inform many of the speaking strategies we use in presentations today.

Why refer to *presentations* over *public speaking*? A **presentation** occurs any time a speaker creates meaning with verbal and nonverbal messages and establishes relationships with audience members. Presentations occur in many contexts. They can be used to teach classes, brief colleagues, summarize sales strategies, and coach middle-school soccer teams. **Public speaking** is a specific kind of presentation that occurs when a speaker addresses a public audience, like in community, government, or organizational settings. Public speeches are often used to campaign for votes, give sermons, dedicate monuments, and deliver public lectures.

You will likely make more presentations than public speeches over the course of your life. When employers are asked about the skills they seek in new employees, the ability to present ideas and information to colleagues and clients is near the top of the list. What they're looking for are good *presenters*, not necessarily dazzling public orators. Of course, if you decide to run for public office or become active in community issues, or if you become famous—as either an expert or a celebrity— you will give many public speeches. Rest assured, the principles and skills described in this book will be useful to you if such a future awaits. But most of us, most of the time, will make presentations in smaller, less public settings.

Throughout this book, we still use the phrase *public speaking* and the word *speech* when the situation warrants those terms. No matter the term or phrase, when you are *speaking to an audience*, you will need to make many critical decisions to ensure that you achieve your speaking goal.

Elements of the Rhetorical Situation

Effective presentation speaking is a rhetorical process. It includes a set of decisions that work together in each unique speaking situation to achieve a speaker's intended purpose. Every **rhetorical situation** includes six core elements that embody this process: your occasion, audience, purpose, content, and delivery—and you, the speaker.

As you prepare for your presentations, you'll find that each of these elements is multifaceted, and none are independent from the rest. The decisions you make about one will affect all the other decisions for your presentation. The chapters that follow will provide specific advice for helping you do just that, but let's start by taking a brief look at each element.

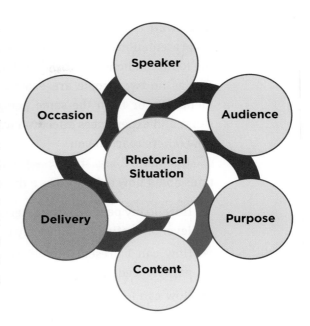

OCCASION

All presentations occur for a particular *reason*. They also happen at a specific *time* in a particular *setting*, using a particular *medium*. These four factors—reason, time, setting, and medium—constitute a presentation's occasion.

Based on the occasion, your audience will have certain expectations about what you'll say and how you'll say it. The norms and expectations of a toast will be quite different, for example, from those of a eulogy.

Chapter 2.1 **OCCASION ▲ (61–68)** explores the following questions to help you adapt your presentation for your occasion:

- Why am *I* speaking on *this* occasion?
- What does the audience expect for this occasion?
- What is appropriate for this occasion?
- Where will I speak and how many people will be there?
- When and for how long should I speak?
- What equipment and accommodation services will be available?

SPEAKER

All presentations require a speaker, so ask yourself, "Why am *I* here speaking to this audience on this occasion?" What do you bring to the occasion? Just as no two people are exactly alike, no two speakers communicate identically or from the same perspective. Your personal characteristics, skills, and experiences affect the way you speak to others and, as a result, how others react to you.

Chapter 2.2 **SPEAKER ▲ (72–85)** will help you answer the following questions about how to be seen as a trustworthy, likable, and dynamic speaker:

- How do my personal characteristics, traits, skills, attitudes, values, and level of confidence affect my credibility?
- How can I present myself as a competent speaker: knowledgeable, experienced, qualified, and well prepared?
- How can I demonstrate that I am a trustworthy speaker?
- What can I do to be a likable and dynamic speaker?

AUDIENCE

When you speak, the members of your audience—the people whose knowledge, beliefs, feelings, or actions you seek to influence—are not passive. They will react in a variety of ways to what you say, and their reactions will be shaped by their unique mix of attitudes, values, experiences, and characteristics. No two audiences are exactly alike, and they are the ones who will decide whether you are worth believing, admiring, and supporting.

Chapter 2.3 **AUDIENCE ▲ (88–105)** will help you answer the following questions to become an audience-centered speaker:

- How do I analyze my audience: who are they, why are they here, and what do they know?
- How do I analyze and adapt to the interests, attitudes, and values of my audience?
- How will the audience likely respond to what I say?
- What strategies should I use to adapt my presentation to my audience?
- How can I find common ground, respect audience diversity and differences, and be mindful of and responsive to audience feedback?

PURPOSE

What do you want your audience to know, think, believe, or do as a result of your presentation? That's your purpose. In short, your purpose is the desired outcome of your presentation; your purpose is not the same as your presentation's topic, subject matter, or occasion.

A speaker's purpose usually has an overarching goal: to inform and explain, persuade and influence, inspire and motivate, entertain and please. Effective speakers identify a more specific, relevant, and achievable purpose statement and use it to guide all other major decisions for their presentation.

Chapter 2.4 **PURPOSE ▲ (109–18)** will help you answer the following questions about determining and achieving your purpose:

- What is my general speaking objective: to inform, persuade, entertain, or inspire?
- What do I want my audience to know, think, believe, or do a result of my presentation?
- How will achieving my purpose benefit me *and* my audience?
- Is my purpose appropriate for my occasion, myself, and my audience?
- What is my purpose statement? Is it specific, achievable, and relevant?

CONTENT

Every presentation conveys a **message**—the ideas and information you want to share with your audience. Knowing your occasion, your credibility as a speaker, your audience, and your purpose, you can then decide what to include and how to organize your presentation.

Your presentation should include key ideas and relevant information that supports your purpose and is appropriate for your occasion and audience. You should also organize your ideas and information into a coherent and compelling message. To achieve those goals, you will have to decide which ideas, facts, information, arguments, quotations, definitions, examples, visuals, and stories you do or don't want to include in your presentation.

Part 3 CONTENT ■ (123–207) will help you answer the following questions about choosing a topic, finding and using appropriate supporting material, and organizing your presentation effectively:

- Where and how can I find appropriate and meaningful ideas and information for my presentation?
- How much and what kind of supporting material do I need?
- Is my supporting material valid, appropriate, believable, and engaging?
- Do I have a clear central idea and relevant key points?
- What is the most effective way to organize my presentation?
- What should I say in the introduction and conclusion of my presentation?

DELIVERY

Delivery is what audience members see and hear when you speak. It's how you use your voice, face, body, notes, and presentation aids to convey your message to your audience.

What medium or media will you use to transmit your message? In other words, what **channel** or channels will you use? Messages can be sent via all five senses—and electronically. Most presentations use sight and sound, and many use presentation aids. Speaking to a live audience in person is different from delivering to a live audience online. Recording and posting a presentation for later viewing requires different strategies than giving a real-time, in-person speech.

Part 4 DELIVERY ▶ (209–301) will help you answer the following questions about practicing your delivery, using presentation aids, and preparing to deliver a speech online:

- How can I improve my vocal delivery with appropriate volume, rate, pitch, and fluency?
- Should I deliver my speech memorized, from a manuscript, or using notes?
- How much should I practice?
- What level of eye contact, facial expressions, gestures, posture, and movement should I use?

- How should I design and use presentation aids?
- How can I adapt my delivery for an online presentation?

Putting It All Together: Self-Introductions

As we have said, the six elements of the rhetorical situation are interconnected and will guide all your decisions as you prepare for your presentation. To illustrate, let's consider one example of a type of presentation you'll often be asked to do and have probably done many times in your life: a self-introduction.

A **self-introduction** is just what its words say—you are introducing yourself to a group of people who may not know you well or at all. It requires a coherent message with little or no preparation and no time to practice. You may be called on to do this kind of presentation the first day of a class, at the first meeting of a new group, at the beginning of a public forum, or at a job interview. It's how you'll reply to a common prompt: "Tell us about yourself!"

How can you possibly create a great self-introduction with little notice? You may or may not have time to collect your thoughts and jot down a few ideas before speaking. However, when you know the elements of the rhetorical situation, you'll be able to prepare for any introduction on the spot.

Suppose your instructor gives you the following directions:

Select one letter of the alphabet and think of three words beginning with the same letter that describes who you are, your beliefs, your behavior, or something you like to do. For example: *M* for *mountains*, *motorcycling*, and *motivated*; *T* for *teaching*, *traveling*, and *talking*. After choosing a letter and three words, prepare a brief presentation to the class in which you

- State your preferred name (and anything interesting you would like to share about your name)
- Share the letter and the three words you chose and then briefly explain why you selected those words

You may write your three words on a small piece of paper to make sure you don't forget them.

The following table illustrates how you can consider each rhetorical element to prepare for a presentation in this situation.

Occasion	This presentation is occurring on the first day of class in which 20 students are enrolled, so each student has a limited amount of time to speak. Your classmates don't expect you to have rehearsed, and they won't expect your delivery to be superlative.
Speaker	What is it about you that best describes who you are? What three words accurately and memorably capture your uniqueness?
Audience	Given what you know about your classmates, what three words might they find interesting, unusual, and memorable? Are there any words that you should avoid using with this audience?
Purpose	Your purpose has been determined for you by your instructor: to help your classmates become acquainted with you and remember you.
Content	The three words you choose and the explanations you give for each one is the content of your presentation. For a clear and well-organized presentation, you might explain each word in turn before moving on to the next.
Delivery	Given the classroom setting, you should use a conversational voice that is loud enough for everyone to hear. Make a note to look at your audience and smile!

Here are two examples of this kind of presentation:

Hi. My name is Mike Robertson. The letter I chose is *R*: *rap*, *Rachel*, and *reading*.

My first word is *rap*. Not only do I like most rap music, but I also like writing rap music and lyrics. Here's a short verse from one. [He performs the verse.]

My second word is *Rachel*. She's my girlfriend and we've been together since our junior year in high school. If you met Rachel, you'd say, "Mike's a lucky guy."

My third word is *reading*. I'll read just about anything. Online news and blogs, social media sites, and books about music and history.

Notice how another student speaker makes different rhetorical decisions for her self-introduction:

> Good morning. My name is Jessica Nevins. It was hard to choose a letter, but I went with *N*. The three words are *Natovitz*, *nursing*, and *nature*.
>
> *Natovitz.* When my grandfather emigrated from Russia in 1909, his last name was Natovitz. Because Natovitz was hard to spell, difficult to say clearly, and not very American sounding, he changed it to Nevins.
>
> *Nursing.* I'm a nursing major hoping to become a registered nurse and then a nurse practitioner. A lot of friends and family members think I should become a doctor, but I think nursing suits my personality and lifestyle better.
>
> *Nature.* I love nature. Walking in the woods. Working in a garden. Watching wild birds at the feeder in my backyard. I also think we should do everything we can to preserve natural wonders and animal habitats. Someday I'll go on a safari.

Conclusion

Your voice matters. And how you use it matters. Your ability to speak effectively can land you a job, rally a group of friends to join you in a cause, and convince your organization to fund the summer college course you want to take. If you want to persuade other people that your ideas matter, you will need to speak up.

In all these cases, your success depends on how well you make decisions based on your rhetorical situation: your occasion, speaker, audience, purpose, content, and delivery. Reading this book will help. Speaking will help even more. Like many skills, speaking requires knowledge and practice. As you learn to think rhetorically and practice speaking, you will become a more confident, polished, and effective presenter. The following chapters provide advice and strategies to help you each step of the way. This may seem daunting, so we'll begin first with advice on addressing speaking anxiety. Read on!

Greta Thunberg

Greta Thunberg is a Swedish activist who, from a very young age, was moved by the enormity of the global climate crisis to become a public voice for her generation. Thunberg has been diagnosed with autism spectrum disorder and finds many aspects of social interaction difficult, but she felt compelled to speak out in order to persuade adults about the dangers of climate change. In August of 2018, at the age of 15, she skipped school for three weeks to protest in front of Sweden's Parliament House with a black-and-white sign reading "Skolstrejk för Klimatet" (School Strike for Climate). Her efforts grabbed the world's attention. That same year she spoke at a TEDx event in Stockholm, Sweden. In her talk, Thunberg makes a passionate case for why all of us need to be more concerned about climate change by asking us to act and not to rely on hope for change. Since then, Thunberg has received numerous honors, including *Time*'s Person of the Year (the youngest person to receive that honor), a place on Forbes' list of the World's Most Powerful Women, and three consecutive nominations for the Nobel Peace Prize. In 2018, she founded Fridays for a Future, an international movement of students calling for action to combat climate change.

Search Terms

To locate a video of this presentation online, enter the following key words into a search engine: Greta Thunberg The Disarming Case to Act Right Now on Climate Change Stockholm November 2018. The video is approximately 11:12 in length.

What to Watch For

[0:00–1:07] The *occasion* can be determined by considering the reason, time, setting, and medium for Thunberg's TEDx presentation. The reason for her presentation was to tell her story about fighting climate change, and it's likely that people gathered to hear her presentation because they are interested in fighting climate change as well. Speaking in an auditorium setting meant that Thunberg had to use a microphone to be heard, had to stand in a particular place on stage for the video recording, and had to follow specific guidelines of giving a TEDx talk, including abiding by a time limit.

[1:25–2:06] Thunberg's personal characteristics, attitudes, skills, and experiences affect who she is as a *speaker* and how her audience reacts to her. She explains that, as someone "with Asperger syndrome, OCD [obsessive-compulsive disorder], and selective mutism . . . I only speak when I think it's necessary." Drawing on these characteristics as a strength, she pointedly says, "Now is one of those moments." But what makes a teenager knowledgeable and qualified to speak about the climate crisis? Thunberg demonstrates her credibility by citing sources throughout her presentation that provide the necessary research to support her claims.

[2:25–5:20] Thunberg's *purpose* is to persuade her audience that action needs to be taken to address the climate crisis. Succinctly stated, Thunberg concludes, "Because if the emissions have to stop, then we must stop the emissions." She clearly identifies the benefits of her purpose for both the audience and her: "There are no gray areas when it comes to survival. Either we go on as a civilization or we don't. We have to change." To support her purpose, the *content* of her presentation conveys a message focused on key ideas and relevant information about the climate crisis. She provides an abundance of relevant information, including the situation in her own country, the recommendations of the Intergovernmental Panel on Climate Change, trapped greenhouse gases, extinction of species, the Paris Agreement, and managing the climate crisis in poorer countries.

[7:10–9:20] As in the case of most of her presentations to an *audience* of adults, Thunberg is keenly aware that *they* are the ones with the power to change the rules that govern how we respond to climate change. Focusing on their belief that climate change is important against the backdrop of their inaction about this belief, she argues that the climate crisis has already been solved "because we already have all the facts and solutions." She asks her audience why she should bother studying at school, given that "the most important facts given by the finest science of that same school system clearly means nothing to our politicians and our society."

[9:24–10:50] Thunberg's *delivery*—how she uses her voice, face, and body to convey her message to her audience—is direct, clear, and principled. By noting at the outset that she has Asperger syndrome and selective mutism, Thunberg contextualizes her speaking style so that the audience knows what to expect from her. As she addresses how "thirty years of pep talking and selling positive ideas" has not worked, she rolls her eyes and gives a nod that indicates it is time to do something different. She pauses after saying "And yes, we do need hope" and before saying "Of course we do." Lowering her volume and pausing here helps highlight the importance of the statement. Her hand gestures help emphasize the enormity of using "one hundred million barrels of oil every single day." Thunberg's delivery conveys that she knows why she is speaking—and she does so with poise rather than dramatics, with simple language rather than fancy words, and with absolute assurance that what she has to say must be said. This is especially clear in the precise final words of her conclusion: "Everything needs to change—and it has to start today."

EXERCISE

After reviewing Thunberg's speech, reflect on these questions:

1. Using the definition of the rhetorical situation, describe whether Thunberg delivered an effective presentation.

2. What expectations do you believe the audience had about Thunberg and what she would say based on the occasion?

3. How did Thunberg demonstrate to her audience that she shares similar questions and concerns about climate change?

4. How might it have altered her message if Thunberg had not mentioned her diagnoses of Asperger syndrome, OCD, and selective mutism? Do you believe it was appropriate for her to mention them?

5. Describe whether Thunberg's purpose was specific, achievable, and relevant.

6. What presentation aids could Thunberg have used to help the audience visualize key points from her presentation?

1.2 Speaking Anxiety

You may be asked to give a short presentation during the first week of your communication course. Perhaps you'll be asked to introduce yourself or to draw a random topic out of an envelope and speak about it for a minute or two. Whether you look forward to speaking or would do anything to avoid it, you'll probably feel some level of nervousness. After all, it will be the first time you've stood in front of your classmates to speak. What if you look uncomfortable or stumble over your words? What if you say the wrong thing?

Though it's common to feel nervous, it's certainly not fatal. In fact, a little bit of anxiety keeps you on your toes and can motivate you to spend time and effort developing and delivering an effective presentation. Reading this chapter can help too—a research study showed that reading about the nature, causes, and methods of managing anxiety made subjects less anxious than listening to relaxation tapes, reading self-help books, or doing nothing at all.[1] This chapter will help you understand why people get speaking anxiety and includes tips to help you reduce those fears and increase your speaking confidence.

Speaking Anxiety Is Very Common

Whether you call it stage fright or **speaking anxiety**, the apprehension you feel is one of the most common personal fears. Surveys consistently show that fear of speaking in front of a group is among people's most intense fears—sometimes ranked higher than their fear of death![2] In fact, 75 percent of the US population experiences some form of anxiety when faced with the prospect of making a presentation.[3] Even experienced musicians, actors, and athletes can experience high levels of anxiety before performing in front of an audience. Elvis Presley, who performed in hundreds of concerts during his lifetime, admitted:[4]

> I've never gotten over what they call stage fright. I go through it every show. . . . It's a new crowd out there, it's a new audience, and they haven't seen us before. So it's got to be like the first time we go on.

For an example of a confident public speaker who doesn't experience stage fright—but has high levels of anxiety in other speaking situations—see Notable Speaker: Jordan Raskopoulos, page 246.

You may feel just as nervous when speaking to a group of three people as others are in front of an audience of thousands. Those anxious feelings are perfectly natural in either setting. You might feel especially tense or uneasy before and as you begin speaking. That's normal too. In fact, thinking about what could go wrong can make you more nervous than actually delivering your presentation, and many speakers find that their anxiety subsides and their heart rate steadily declines less than a minute after they begin speaking.[5]

If you believe you're the only person feeling apprehensive about speaking, you may wrongly blame your nervousness for a poor presentation ("I was nervous; therefore, my talk went badly"). But nervousness doesn't predict whether a presentation succeeds or fails. Many nervous speakers deliver outstanding presentations. What matters is how you handle it. Successful speakers use their nervousness to make their presentations better.[6] Ultimately, it's not the anxiety that is important but how you choose to interpret it. Wouldn't you rather think of making a presentation as an exhilarating experience rather than a terrifying ordeal?

Sources of Speaking Anxiety (and How to Respond to Them)

Why are you feeling anxious? We've heard many reasons: "I could forget what I want to say." "My audience won't like me." "I'll make a huge, embarrassing mistake." The probability of any of these things happening is very small. But *imagining* them happening can create anxiety.

The reasons we feel nervous generally cluster into six categories. What follow are the most common sources of speaking anxiety and strategies for addressing each one:

The Source	The Strategy
Fear of the unknown	Make the unfamiliar familiar.
Fear of physical symptoms	Practice calming exercises.
Fear of failure	Convert anxiety into energy.
Fear of the spotlight	Focus on your audience.
Fear of rigid rules	Bend or break the rules.
Fear of evaluation	Prepare and practice.

FEAR OF THE UNKNOWN

Doing anything new or unusual can cause anxiety. Even if you know how to drive, for example, you might be anxious about driving in a new country with unfamiliar signs and rules. The same goes for speaking. Even experienced speakers may feel nervous speaking in a new location or in front of an audience that is very different from what they're used to. An important step to addressing this anxiety is to make something unknown into something familiar.

MAKE THE UNFAMILIAR FAMILIAR

- Learn more about the occasion and audience expectations.
- Practice until you feel more competent and confident.
- Know your message.

The more you learn about your **AUDIENCE ▲ (88–105)**, the less anxious you may feel. Talking to individual audience members can help take the edge off your anxiety. It may even give you some new ideas—a relevant story or an interesting fact—to share with the audience during your presentation.

Likewise, learn about your **OCCASION ▲ (61–68)**: consider how the time, place, setting, and medium may affect your speech. Get there early. Notice what might distract you or your audience. Is there a flickering light? Is the room warm or cool? Speak a few sentences of your introduction at the volume you intend to use in that room. Also, make sure any equipment you need is set up properly and working. The more you know about your setting, the more likely you will be comfortable and calm during your presentation.

If yours will be an **ONLINE PRESENTATION ▶ (282–301)**, make sure you are familiar with the technology. Practice how you'll use the microphone, look at the camera, and scan the chats for audience feedback while possibly also sharing your screen. Turn off notifications for your email or other messages. If you'll be using **PRESENTATION AIDS ▶ (260–78)**, make sure they are thoughtful, clear, and easy to read—most eyes will be on your slides, not on you, while you show them.

FEAR OF PHYSICAL SYMPTOMS

When you make a presentation, your palms may sweat, your pulse may speed up, your stomach may feel queasy, and your hands may shake. Inexperienced and highly anxious speakers often assume that their audience can see this happening. They may focus more on what their audience thinks of their shaky hands than what they want to say.

PRACTICE CALMING EXERCISES

- Trust that most of your symptoms are not visible.
- Do a set of relaxation exercises before speaking.
- Transform nervousness into extra energy and enthusiasm.

Experienced communication instructors, when asked about how anxious a student is, seldom accurately estimate the speaker's level of anxiety.[7] Though most symptoms of speaking anxiety aren't visible to your audience, they can feel obvious and distracting to you. Fortunately, you can reduce the intensity of these reactions by assuming that audience members will not notice your nervousness.

Develop a set of targeted exercises that relaxes your mind and body before you speak. Take deep breaths, relax tight muscles, and move around if you can. Nearly all performers—actors, musicians, dancers, and athletes of all kinds—have rituals that relax their bodies prior to a high-stakes challenge. Once *you* find a ritual that helps you relax, do it before every presentation. If nothing else, it takes your mind off worried thoughts.

Here's a technique that works for many speakers: Right before you speak, repeat a two-syllable word or phrase silently to yourself, syllable by syllable, deeply inhaling and exhaling each time. For example, try the word *relax*. Breathe in slowly while saying the sound "re" silently to yourself, holding the long "e" sound all the while you are inhaling. This should take two or three seconds. Then breathe out slowly, also for two or three seconds, as you say the sound "lax" silently to yourself. Hold the "a" sound while exhaling. Inhale and exhale "reee-laaax" four or five times. By the time you finish this 30-second relaxation exercise, your pulse should be slower, and, ideally, you will also feel calmer.

If repeating a word or phrase doesn't work for you, try a small yawn or quiet sigh right before you speak to relax your neck and throat muscles. Tensing and relaxing your stomach muscles before speaking can release stress from your body. Find the tension-reducing exercise that works for you, and you'll be rewarded with a calmer body, a calmer mind, and more confidence.

Then consider this: Aren't these feelings the same ones that occur when you are watching an action sequence of a movie or when you are buckling into your seat on a roller coaster? Feelings of anxiety and excitement are physically similar. Enlist those feelings as extra energy and enthusiasm. When you feel that rush of adrenaline and your heart beating faster and stronger, take those feelings as signs that you're revved up, eager, and ready to go. Instead of "Get me out of here," say, "Let's get this show on the road!"

FEAR OF FAILURE

Many nervous speakers believe their anxiety dooms them to failure. When we've asked students to share their goals for taking a speaking course— other than passing it with a good grade—an overwhelming number give answers related to fear of speaking. They want to "overcome anxiety," "stop being nervous," and "totally calm down." Professional speakers have a very different attitude and expectation. They admit that they're nervous and they accept that as normal. Instead, they transform worrisome, irrational, and nonproductive thoughts into positive statements.

CONVERT ANXIETY INTO POSITIVE ENERGY

- Accept nervousness as a common and normal response.
- Convert irrational beliefs into positive statements.
- Focus on your message and your audience to redirect your feelings.

Psychologists recommend a technique called **cognitive restructuring**, a method that challenges and changes unrealistic beliefs into realistic expectations.[8] Rather than thinking "I'll make mistakes," "I'll bomb," or "I'll forget what I want to say," experienced speakers focus on their message and remind themselves they will calm down once they begin speaking. Try to focus on positive thoughts, such as "I'm going to do a great job out there," "I'm a well-prepared speaker," "My message is important," or "Anxiety makes me work harder and do better."

Can positive statements like this really help? Sure! Positive self-talk helps you become more realistic about what you need to do and what will happen when you make a presentation. We promise: the speaking experience won't be as bad as you expect. You will survive, particularly if you discard the negative beliefs and unrealistic expectations that get in the way of successful speaking.

FEAR OF THE SPOTLIGHT

Most of us experience some anxiety when we are the focus of other people's attention. When all eyes are on you, that attention can make you more self-conscious than you otherwise might be. Psychologists call this reaction the **spotlight effect**, a tendency to overestimate the extent to which our behavior and appearance are noticed and assessed by others.[9] Whether you're standing under a real spotlight or not, it can help to focus more on your audience and less on yourself.

FOCUS ON YOUR AUDIENCE

- Engage audience attention and interests.
- Use positive, nonverbal cues to obtain similar reactions.
- Shift your attention away from yourself to the audience.

While you're speaking, your audience is listening to see how you'll address their needs and engage their interests—they're not looking to criticize your appearance or speaking skills. If they're absorbed in what you're saying and see how it affects their lives, they won't pay as much attention to your posture or pronunciation. Of course, your words, delivery, and appearance are important and you should aim to **PRACTICE YOUR DELIVERY ▶ (220–24)** for a polished and professional presentation. But if you find you're dwelling on your appearance and delivery *during* your presentation, that's the moment to refocus on your message and your audience.

Try shifting attention away from yourself and toward an audience member or two. It may be all that's needed to take the edge off your anxiety. Look at someone and nod your head. In many cases, they'll likely nod back. Pick someone else and smile at them. They'll probably smile back. Engage your audience as a group with a question or quick activity. Each of these actions, and others like them, mentally shifts your attention from yourself to others and reduces your anxiety in the process.

FEAR OF RIGID RULES

Although this book is filled with advice for how to become a more effective speaker, we're not suggesting these are rigid rules or unbreakable commandments that must be followed in every presentation. Knowing when—and when not—to follow these suggestions can help you feel more confident as a speaker.

BEND OR BREAK THE RULES

- Don't let rigid, unjustified rules control you.
- Dismiss rules that get in the way of achieving your purpose.
- Rely on being well prepared rather than focused on rules.

Some speakers may be nervous about violating a supposed rule of speechmaking. "Never," they were once told, "put your hands in your pockets or sit on the corner of a desk when you are speaking." Or "Banish filler phrases, like *um, uh, you know*, and *really*, from your presentation." While advice like this may be well-intentioned, always remember that connecting with your audience matters much more than following a set of rules. An occasional "um" or "uh" is natural and common in everyday speech. It can also make you sound thoughtful and relaxed.

Rigid rules trap us. Our advice: Focus instead on adapting your presentation to your occasion, audience, and purpose. Follow useful advice and recommendations, but don't let them control every decision you make.

FEAR OF EVALUATION

Fear of evaluation is a leading source of speaker anxiety. Does your audience believe you? Are they listening and interested? Do they find you persuasive and likable? Will this presentation accomplish your **PURPOSE ▲ (109–18)**? Will I get a good grade on this speech? Land the job offer? Meet my fundraising goal? We generally don't like to be evaluated by others, particularly if they have more status, power, or influence than we do. So how can you overcome this fear? Two words: *preparation* and *practice*.

PREPARE AND PRACTICE

- Spend enough time preparing your message.
- Make sure your message supports your purpose.
- Practice your delivery until you feel confident.

Researchers note that speaking anxiety affects the way speakers prepare presentations. Some anxious speakers don't prepare effectively because they don't know *how* to prepare. Rather than making orderly and well-informed decisions about a presentation, nervous speakers become lost in the process.[10] Consequently, they end up focusing on their fears rather than on what they need to say and do.

Giving yourself adequate time to prepare for your talk—**DOING RESEARCH ■ (139–43)**, choosing strong **SUPPORTING MATERIALS ■ (134–39)**, and **ORGANIZING ■ (152–70)** your key points—will reduce your speaking anxiety. Although it takes valuable time to **PRACTICE YOUR DELIVERY ▶ (220–24)**, the payoff is a confident and seemingly effortless presentation. Consider this: Would you be more nervous to deliver a presentation on a topic you don't know anything about or a speech that you thoughtfully researched and practiced on a topic that's meaningful to you?

Finally, practice the first minute of your presentation until you feel especially comfortable with it. Knowing you can get through your opening can help you feel more confident as you begin.

Conclusion

Speaking anxiety is complicated. There are no easy answers or magic bullets that guarantee a "cure." Whether you call it speaking anxiety, communication apprehension, or stage fright, it's entirely normal to get nervous at the thought of giving a presentation. Understanding why you experience speaking anxiety and using a few of the strategies recommended in this chapter can help you become a more confident speaker. Practice and experience helps even more. You may even find that framing nervousness as excitement can actually bring energy and enthusiasm to your presentations.

Over time, as you speak in a variety of rhetorical situations, you'll find it easier to project confidence in yourself and your message as a result. Until then, take a deep breath, focus on your goals, and start speaking!

Monica Lewinsky

In 1995—at the age of 22—Monica Lewinsky had spent more than a year working as a White House intern, during which time she had an affair with President Bill Clinton. Lewinsky faced intense media scrutiny when the matter became national news in January 1998. Although social media websites such as X (formerly Twitter) and Facebook did not exist at the time, the internet still provided a platform for the public shaming of Lewinsky. By 2005, she decided to escape the spotlight and move to London to pursue a master's degree in psychology. She maintained a relatively private life until October 2014, when she spoke about cyberbullying and internet shaming at a *Forbes* magazine "30 under 30" summit. Since her presentation at the summit and subsequent TED talk in 2015, Lewinsky has served as an ambassador for the antibullying organization Bystander Revolution, participated in a number of antibullying campaigns, and written about the #MeToo movement. In 2021, she created her own production company that aims to give a platform to others who have been silenced.

Search Terms

To locate videos of these presentations online, enter the following key words into a search engine: Monica Lewinsky first public speech Forbes; and Monica Lewinsky price of shame. The videos are approximately 25:31 and 22:31 in length.

What to Watch For

First speech: October 2014

[0:00–0:35] At the outset of the presentation, Lewinsky tells the audience that this is only her fourth time delivering a speech in public. She asks them to forgive her because she is nervous and emotional. Since anxiety is a common experience for most speakers, especially for those who don't have much experience speaking in public, it's not surprising that she is nervous.

[0:35–0:40] Since she has not given many public speeches, it is possible that she is experiencing fear of the unknown. In an effort to manage her anxiety, Lewinsky takes a deep breath before beginning her presentation. In the absence of her telling the audience that she is nervous and taking a deep breath, it's likely that the audience wouldn't be able to observe any outward signs of her anxiety because most symptoms of speaking anxiety are not visible.

[1:30–2:05] As a way of introducing herself to an audience who may know who she is but not know much else about her personal life, Lewinsky makes a humorous reference to all the rap songs she is mentioned in. The audience laughs at the reference, and Lewinsky pauses and thanks them for doing so. Focusing on the audience is an effective way of shifting the attention away from herself. This may help her feel less conspicuous.

[12:15–25:00] As Lewinsky reaches the midpoint of her speech, she appears more comfortable. While she may still be experiencing some anxiety, it is difficult from the audience's point of view to see her symptoms of nervousness.

Second speech: March 2015

[0:14–1:00] In March 2015, Lewinsky delivered a similar presentation at a TED talk event in Vancouver, British Columbia. Unlike her previous presentation, she begins this one without any mention of her nervousness. There is no way to know if she was experiencing the same level of anxiety as she did in October 2014.

[4:00–4:30] As the speech progresses, Lewinsky projects confidence by maintaining eye contact with audience members, using purposeful gestures, and speaking clearly. She mirrors the content of her message by using a kind and compassionate tone throughout the presentation. If she is experiencing any nervousness internally, it is not visible to the audience. The audience gives her a standing ovation at the conclusion of her presentation— a sign that her message and presentation achieved her purpose.

EXERCISE

After viewing both of Lewinsky's speeches, reflect on these questions:

1. In her 2014 speech, would you have known that Lewinsky was nervous if she hadn't told you?

2. Although we do not recommend telling an audience that you are nervous, was this a useful tactic for Lewinsky? Why or why not? How might doing so affect a speaker's credibility?

3. If at all, how did Lewinsky appear to use her nervousness to make her first speech more credible and effective?

4. Describe your reaction to Lewinsky's display of emotion about the possibility of her mother being prosecuted (7:20–7:30 in the first speech). Do you think it was appropriate? Did she need to say "sorry" before moving on?

5. How might preparation and practice have helped Lewinsky manage her anxiety between her first public address and her TED talk? What might account for a noticeable increase in her comfort level?

1.3 Listening

What is a chapter about listening doing in a book about speaking? If you doubt the importance of listening while speaking, watch how talented speakers keep their eyes on their audience to determine whether they are being understood. Watch them stop and say something in a different way if the audience seems confused or uneasy. Watch them smile when audience members nod their heads. An audience of good listeners is a gift to speakers who want to connect with them by sharing a meaningful message. And a speaker who listens well is a gift to an audience who wants their needs and interests to be considered. No matter how separate or remote a speaker is from the audience, they are partners in a communication event.[1] Listening is a two-way street.

What Is Effective Listening?

Listening is the process of receiving, constructing meaning from, remembering, and responding to spoken and/or nonverbal messages. Listening helps both speakers and audience members interact more effectively. If, as a speaker, you watch for and analyze your audience's reactions, you can adjust how you speak and motivate them to listen more attentively and remember what you've said. As an audience member, your ability to listen affects how you respond to a speaker's message. Communication is more successful and meaningful when both speakers *and* audiences commit themselves to listening attentively and responsibly.

Listening is our number one communication activity. On average we spend over half of our daily communication time listening—way ahead of speaking, reading, and writing.[2] Think about all the time you spend listening, whether you're with other people or on your own wearing earbuds. In a single day, you might listen to an interview on a podcast, a lecture by your instructors, a story from your friends, instructions on a YouTube video, lyrics in a song, and more.

Given the amount of time we spend listening, most of us aren't very good listeners. Immediately after listening to a short talk, most people can't accurately report 50 percent of what was said. But you can become a better listener. Like most complex skills, effective listening requires commitment and effort. And to learn to be an effective listener, it helps to identify—and avoid—poor listening habits.

POOR LISTENING

In a world filled with constant distractions, it's amazing that anyone can listen effectively. In the smaller world of presentation speaking, distractions can include loud and annoying sounds, an uncomfortable room, disruptive outside activities, and a speaker's delivery. It's difficult to listen to a speaker who talks too softly, too rapidly, or too slowly or who speaks in a **monotone voice**. Similarly, a noisy, fidgeting, nonresponsive, or noticeably critical audience can disturb and sidetrack a speaker.

But poor listening isn't always tied to distractions. All of us have developed a range of listening habits over the course of our lives. Here are some of the most common poor listening habits—the ones you should actively work to avoid:

- **Pseudolistening.** Faking attention or pretending to listen, particularly when your mind is elsewhere, you are bored, or you think it pleases the speaker. When you fake listening, you mislead the speaker into thinking that they've been heard and understood.
- **Selective listening.** Listening only to messages that you like and agree with or avoiding listening to information that is complex, unfamiliar,

or in conflict with your opinions. A selective listener may listen only to confirm prior beliefs or identify flaws in what a speaker says.

- **Superficial listening.** Paying more attention to how a speaker looks and sounds than to what they say. Superficial listeners often draw hasty conclusions about a speaker and their message before a speaker's presentation or idea is finished.

- **Defensive listening.** Assuming that a speaker's controversial or critical remarks are personal or unjust attacks. Defensive listeners primarily focus on how to respond to or challenge a speaker rather than trying to understand the speaker's message.

- **Disruptive listening.** Interrupting a speaker, exaggerating your nonverbal reactions, making distracting movements or noise, or noticeably withholding your attention during a presentation. Both the speaker and other audience members may become irritated or offended by disruptive listening.

- **Multitask listening.** Doing several things at the same time, such as listening while texting someone, whispering to someone next to you, reading a handout, or scrolling through your email.

- **The next-in-line effect.** Thinking about why you disagree with a speaker or silently rehearsing how you will challenge the speaker's claims instead of listening attentively to what a speaker is saying.

EFFECTIVE LISTENING

Of course, there's more to listening well than simply avoiding bad habits. Judi Brownell, a leading listening researcher, has identified six separate but interrelated skills that together constitute **effective listening**. Brownell's HURIER model—hearing, understanding, remembering, interpreting, evaluating, and responding—provides a clear and memorable description of effective listening.[3] Here are brief descriptions of the six listening skills and what you can do to improve each one:

- **Hearing.** Making clear, aural distinctions among spoken sounds and words. Make sure you're in the proper state of mind to listen, minimize distractions, and position yourself close to the speaker. If necessary, ask the speaker to repeat themselves or to speak in a louder voice.

- **Understanding.** Accurately grasping the speaker's intended meaning. You may need to ask the speaker to clarify, provide an example or definition, or rephrase what's been said in more precise terms. You can also state what *you* think the speaker is saying and then ask whether your understanding is correct.

- **Remembering.** Storing, retaining, and recalling information you have heard. One of the best ways to remember a speaker's message is to identify why you should care about what you're hearing. We remember things that are personally relevant and emotionally engaging much better than things that we perceive as disconnected from our lives. You can also write down essential ideas and repeat them silently to yourself as you record them.

- **Interpreting.** Understanding the meaning of what's being communicated beyond the literal, verbal message. Think critically about the speaker's **PHYSICAL DELIVERY ▶ (249–59)**—such eye contact, facial expressions, posture, appearance, and gestures—as well as their **VOCAL DELIVERY ▶ (229–45)**. Try to empathize with the emotions, values, and attitudes that the speaker is expressing through nonverbal cues.

- **Evaluating.** Analyzing and making a judgment about someone's message. Think critically about the validity of the speaker's **CLAIMS ◆ (408–11)** before criticizing, distinguish logical from **PERSUASIVE APPEALS ◆ (411–18)**, and monitor your own emotions and attitudes that could interfere with reasonable judgment.

- **Responding.** Providing appropriate and meaningful feedback that signals you have (or have not) heard and understood. Just as you can discern a speaker's intentions and meaning from nonverbal cues, you can communicate your own reactions nonverbally as clearly as you could verbally.

When and how you use these listening skills depends on whether you are the speaker or an audience member, whether you are speaking to a large or small group, whether the topic is controversial or not, and whether you have the flexibility to interact with the speaker or audience members during or after a presentation.

Shared Listening Responsibilities

As you work to improve your general listening skills, consider the responsibilities unique to the audience and to the speaker in any given speaking situation. Let's begin with the listening responsibilities shared by both audience members and the speaker. Three of the most important responsibilities are *overcoming distractions*, *"listening" to nonverbal messages*, and *listening with civility*.

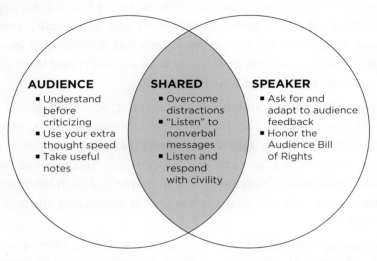

AUDIENCE
- Understand before criticizing
- Use your extra thought speed
- Take useful notes

SHARED
- Overcome distractions
- "Listen" to nonverbal messages
- Listen and respond with civility

SPEAKER
- Ask for and adapt to audience feedback
- Honor the Audience Bill of Rights

In presentation speaking, there are *shared* listening strategies and skills necessary for both the speaker and the audience as well as *distinct* listening strategies for each.

OVERCOME DISTRACTIONS

Distractions take many forms and can be caused by a speaker, an audience member, or outside interference. Depending on the circumstances and setting of a presentation, you may be able to take direct action to reduce behavioral noise. If an audience member is distracting, you could ask them to stop talking or moving around—after all, if they're distracting you, they're probably distracting others. If a presenter speaks too softly or uses visual aids that are too small, a conscientious audience member may ask the speaker to use more volume or further explain what is being shown.

When distractions are environmental, you are well within your rights as a speaker or audience member to shut a door, open a window, turn on more lights, and (of course) turn off cell phone sounds. In large facilities, you may need to ask permission to improve the group's surroundings. And during **ONLINE PRESENTATIONS** ▶ **(282–301)**, it's helpful for both speakers and audience members to close extraneous browser tabs, turn off notifications, and participate from a private, quiet location.

"LISTEN" TO NONVERBAL MESSAGES

Speakers and audience members don't put everything important into words. Often, you can understand a speaker's meaning or gauge audience members' reactions by noting and interpreting their nonverbal behavior.

Good listeners pay attention to the combined meaning of verbal and nonverbal messages, and they notice any mismatch between the two, such as if a speaker said, "I'm delighted to see you here today," while slouching and speaking in a dull voice.

A change in a speaker's **INFLECTION** ▶ **(239–40)** or volume may indicate "Listen up—this is important!" A presenter's sustained **EYE CONTACT** ▶ **(249–51)** may be a way of saying "I'm talking to you!" **FACIAL EXPRESSIONS** ▶ **(251–52)** can reveal whether a thought is painful, joyous, exciting, serious, or boring. Effective listeners pay attention to all aspects of a speaker's delivery.

In turn, effective speakers pay attention to audience members' nonverbal behaviors. Are listeners frowning in puzzlement or nodding their heads in agreement? What about their posture—are they sitting straight, leaning forward, and ready to engage, or are they slumping in their seats, looking like they hope to catch a nap? (It happens!) Is their full attention on the speaker, or are they preoccupied with their cell phones and tablets? All these nonverbal behaviors send messages about whether the presentation is on track or if changes are necessary to recapture the audience's attention and interest, and if we—as listeners and as speakers—fail to "listen" to each other's telling clues, we may be missing the intended meaning of a message.

LISTEN AND RESPOND WITH CIVILITY

For a successful presentation, both speakers and audience members must also listen respectfully to one another. In other words, they need to listen and respond with **civility**. In his book *Choosing Civility*, P. M. Forni defines civility as "being constantly aware of others and weaving restraint, respect, and consideration into the very fabric of this awareness."[4] In the context of presentation speaking, this can mean expressing empathy for a speaker who shares a personal story or being considerate of an audience who may hold very different beliefs than you do.

Listening to others with full attention is the hallmark of civility. It might seem easy, even enjoyable, to listen with civility when you completely agree with someone. But there's value, too, in listening with civility even when you disagree, as difficult as it may be. To cultivate a genuine, shared civility, we suggest two related strategies:

- *Be open to disagreement.* As a speaker it is your responsibility—even if your topic is controversial—to treat your audience with respect. If you advocate for something you know your listeners disagree with, you may be more effective if you listen to and respectfully acknowledge their point of view. And as an audience member, it's important to listen with the intent to understand, correctly interpret, and fairly evaluate what the speaker is saying. If you disagree after listening with an open mind, you still benefit from considering another person's point of view. In the words of author-scholar Roxane Gay: "Disagreement is wonderful. When someone disagrees, we try to reach common ground. That's good."[5]

- *Disagree without being disagreeable.* You can disagree with a speaker's message instead of disagreeing with the speaker. Try to empathize and understand even if you don't agree. As a speaker, you can share valid evidence and let facts do the talking. As an audience member, try to avoid criticizing, correcting, or dismissing what a speaker says; respond respectfully instead. Civility requires that both sides have the right to disagree without resorting to misinterpreting or disrespecting each other.

But what if your point of view is being attacked, even as you do your best to listen and respond with civility? What if—in disagreeing without being disagreeable—an audience's point of view has been continually dismissed or ignored?

Although listening and responding with civility means valuing empathy over anger, some studies show that there are circumstances where "outrage can serve as an important catalyst for collective action."[6] The upside of outrage is that it may encourage people to care, to sign petitions, or to volunteer. In fact, social psychologist Victoria Spring believes that expressing outrage has often been a way for marginalized groups to mobilize people to act. Arguably, listening and responding with civility isn't achieved with a one-size-fits-all approach to every speaking situation. The challenge is knowing when expressing empathy and/or anger will help or harm. The responsibility falls on all of us, as speakers and listeners, to hold ourselves to **ETHICAL COMMUNICATION** ● **(44–48)** standards wherever possible, even if we intensely disagree.

The Audience's Listening Responsibilities

What does it feel like to be a responsible listener in an audience? Ralph Nichols, the pioneer listening researcher, puts it this way:[7]

> Good listening is not relaxed and passive at all. It's dynamic; it's constructive; it's characterized by a slightly increased heart rate, quicker circulation of the blood, and a small rise in bodily temperature. It's energy consuming; it's plain hard work.

Although effective listening is neither easy nor instinctive, it is half the equation that constitutes effective communication. That alone makes it worth the effort to be a responsible listener, by *understanding before criticizing, using your extra thinking time*, and *taking useful notes*.

UNDERSTAND BEFORE CRITICIZING

Skilled listeners are open minded and make sure they understand a speaker before reacting to what they've heard. As a responsible listener, you should acknowledge that your feelings about and responses to other speakers are at least partly determined by *your* personal beliefs and experiences. Recognizing this perfectly human tendency will help you listen more thoughtfully and will put you in the right frame of mind to understand a speaker's message on its own terms. Use the **golden listening rule**: listen to a speaker as you would have them listen to you.

There are times when you may be offended or angered by what you hear. What should you do? As an effective listener, you should pause, maintain your concentration, and make sure that you accurately comprehend the speaker's message. In other words: *listen before you leap.* This doesn't mean you approve of or condone what someone says. Rather, you are deciding whether and how to react after determining if you've accurately understood the speaker's intended message.

USE YOUR EXTRA THOUGHT SPEED

Thought speed is the speed at which most people can think, as opposed to the speed at which they speak. Most speakers talk at a rate of 150 to 175 words per minute. If thoughts were measured in words per minute, most of us can think at three or four times the rate at which we speak.[8] Thus, for every minute we listen to another person's presentation, we have enough spare time to consider about 400 words' worth of thoughts.

So what do you do with all that extra thinking time? Poor listeners may use their extra thought time to daydream, have side conversations, take unnecessary notes, or plan how to confront a speaker. But effective listeners use that time to:

- Assess the speaker's CREDIBILITY ▲ (74–81), qualifications, and potential biases
- Identify the presentation's key points and summarize the CENTRAL IDEA ■ (156–57)
- Analyze the strengths and weaknesses of the speaker's SUPPORTING MATERIALS ■ (134–51) and PERSUASIVE STRATEGIES ◆ (437–57)
- Weigh the relevance and practicality of the speaker's remarks

TAKE USEFUL NOTES

Skilled notetakers recall messages better than non-notetakers. The key word is *skilled*. If you spend all your time taking notes or writing down almost every word you hear, you can't observe the speaker's nonverbal behavior or devote thinking time to assessing and responding to what the speaker says. Skilled notetakers select key words and phrases they want to remember or challenge. If speakers put almost every word they say on projected slides, don't be seduced into copying what's on the screen. Instead, listen to the speaker, read the slide (if you're given enough time to do that), and write down a short phrase to summarize the message in that portion of the talk.

When taking notes, use the method that works best for you. Some research demonstrates that we remember what we write more than what we type, because taking notes by hand helps you focus on the speaker and their message.[9] But some listeners prefer or need to take notes on a digital device. Use the method that will allow you to write and reference useful notes when you need them.

The Speaker's Listening Responsibilities

Listening to members of your audience goes beyond hearing and seeing their reactions before and after your presentation. As a speaker, effective listening also requires you to *ask for and adapt to audience feedback* and to *honor the Audience Bill of Rights*.

ASK FOR AND ADAPT TO AUDIENCE FEEDBACK

In face-to-face presentations, whether in-person or online, speakers can usually see, hear, and adapt to audience **feedback**, the verbal and nonverbal responses made by audience members as they interpret and evaluate the meaning and delivery of a presentation. Ask yourself, "Are audience members actively listening to me, or do I seem to be talking to a blank wall? Do they seem to understand what I am saying, or do they appear confused by my remarks?"

If audience reactions are difficult to see, hear, or interpret, ask them questions, such as "Let me make sure I'm explaining the different features in our new accounting system clearly. How could these features benefit your department or office?" Not only do questions help you ADAPT TO YOUR AUDIENCE ▲ (102–5), they also tell listeners that you are interested in their reactions.

You can also adapt to unforeseen problems—and pleasures—during your presentation. If you hear audience members whispering to each other rather than listening to you, pause briefly—the silence might help them refocus. If that doesn't work, ask members if they need clarification or more examples. If audience members are squirming in their seats, perhaps it's time to shorten your presentation or move on to a more interesting section. And if audience members are leaning forward and are highly focused, you may delight in how well you are doing—and carry on with more confidence.

ONLINE PRESENTATIONS ▶ (282–301) present unique considerations for adapting to audience feedback—you may or may not be able to see or hear your audience. If you can see them, there is a wealth of nonverbal behavior to observe, much as you would during an in-person talk. But if you can't see them, or you want another way to gauge their reactions to your speech, most virtual presentation platforms—such as Zoom or Microsoft Teams—include features that can help. For example, most platforms offer a chat feature where audience members can communicate with one another (and with you), allowing listeners to **ASK QUESTIONS ∴ (350–61)** and respond during your presentation. If possible, recruit a peer to monitor these messages for useful feedback. In other cases, you may be able to use a platform's live polling feature to solicit specific types of information from your audience. As with any presentation technology, you'll want to practice using these tools ahead of time.

In the case of televised, recorded, or time-delayed presentations, you cannot adapt to audience feedback in the moment and may have to wait until afterward to learn how people reacted. Your best option in these situations is to remember the central importance of your **AUDIENCE ▲ (88–105)** as you are preparing, practicing, and recording your presentation.

HONOR THE AUDIENCE BILL OF RIGHTS

Every audience member has the right to understand and evaluate a speaker's presentations. This right depends, in large part, on the speaker's ability to honor the audience's right to listen. In the following table, we present this Audience Bill of Rights in the context of the six elements of the **RHETORICAL SITUATION ● (6–11)**, and we provide advice for honoring each right as a speaker.

THE AUDIENCE BILL OF RIGHTS[10]

	Audience Right	Speaker Responsibility
OCCASION ▲ (61–68)	Listeners have the right to know why the speaker and topic have been chosen for this particular occasion. They also have the right to know, in advance, how long the presentation or session will last.	Briefly explain why *you* are speaking on this occasion. Provide the audience with a brief description of the presentation, including the length of time.
SPEAKER ▲ (72–85)	Listeners have the right to know enough information about the speaker's background, experiences, and expertise to decide whether the speaker is competent and credible.	Review what makes you a credible speaker. Provide the audience with a short biography ahead of time or discuss your credentials at the appropriate time during the presentation.
AUDIENCE ▲ (88–105)	Listeners have the right to be spoken to with civility and informed how the presentation speaks to their experiences, background, knowledge, attitudes, beliefs, and culture. They also have the right to ask questions and expect substantive answers.	Follow the guidelines for adapting your message to your audience. Demonstrate civility by showing empathy, respect, courtesy, maturity, and fairness, especially if your audience disagrees with you. Consider the best way to invite your audience to ask **QUESTIONS ∴ (350–61)**.
PURPOSE ▲ (109–18)	Listeners have the right to know the speaker's purpose—what the speaker wants them to think or do as a result of a presentation. They also have a right to know the reasons why the speaker has chosen this purpose and how they can benefit from its achievement.	Offer a clear **PURPOSE STATEMENT ▲ (115–17)** in the introduction of your presentation and/or propose a **VALUE STEP ✻ (367–69)**.
CONTENT ▪ (123–207)	Listeners have the right to understand and evaluate the ideas and information used to support the speaker's message. They also have the right to expect a clear, well-organized presentation.	Be intentional about selecting an **ORGANIZATIONAL PATTERN ▪ (157–66)** that makes sense for the message content. Provide clear **TRANSITIONS ▪ (168–69)** when moving from one major point to another.
DELIVERY ▶ (209–301)	Listeners have the right to see and hear a speaker and to be able to see every presentation aid used by the speaker, no matter where the aids are located.	Use well-practiced vocal and physical delivery to enhance and clarify the intended meaning of your message. Provide accommodation for audience members who may need closed captions or auditory explanations of **PRESENTATION AIDS ▶ (260–78)**.

Conclusion

We spend more time listening than we do speaking, reading, or writing. But most of us aren't always effective listeners. Effective listening is a complex process, requiring a variety of listening skills—hearing, understanding, remembering, interpreting, evaluating, and responding. Avoiding distractions and poor listening habits and learning to listen with civility require a conscientious commitment because they are the bedrock of effective listening.

Whether you are a speaker or an audience member, apply the golden listening rule by listening to others as you would have them listen to you. As an audience member, suspend your judgments and biases until you have understood and correctly interpreted a speaker's message. As a speaker, be aware of and adapt to the ways your audience is listening. The effort you devote to being a better listener will help you become a more effective, engaging, and memorable speaker.

1.4 Ethics and Free Speech

> ### 🔍 A BRIEF GUIDE TO THIS CHAPTER
>
> - **Ethical communication** (p. 44)
> - **Using sources ethically** (p. 48)
> - **Using generative AI ethically** (p. 50)
> - **Freedom of speech** (p. 55)

The ancient Roman rhetorician Quintilian gave aspiring speakers this advice: "The orator must above all things study morality and must obtain a thorough knowledge of all that is just and honorable, without which no one can either be a good man or an able speaker."[1] His enduring idea—*that a good speaker is a good person speaking well*—is as true today as it was then.

What Quintilian called morality we now more commonly refer to as *ethics*. **Ethics** is a system of principles that defines what is right or wrong, moral or immoral, about a belief or action. Ethical questions arise in every rhetorical situation when you make decisions about how to present yourself, interact with and adapt to your audience, and select strategies to achieve your purpose.

Ethics matters. And the very best speakers are committed to ethical decision making when developing and delivering their presentations. They speak honestly and keep the interests of audience members foremost in their minds. Remember that ethical decision making arises from *your* attitudes, beliefs, and values. Those ethical principles should guide how you approach every rhetorical situation and decision, including how you use and cite sources and how you use generative artificial intelligence (AI) responsibly.

For an example of a speaker committed to courageous expression of personal conviction, see Notable Speaker: Greta Thunberg, page 14.

Ethical Communication

If ethics is a system of principles, what are the principles that describe an ethical speaker? The National Communication Association (NCA)—the largest professional organization for communication scholars, educators, students, and practitioners—provides a useful place to start. The **NCA Credo for Ethical Communication** describes the obligations of an ethical communicator, whether they are interacting with one other person, a small group, or an audience of thousands.[2] The credo advocates freedom of expression; **LISTENING ● (30–42)** with civility, mutual respect, and fairness; and taking responsibility for the consequences of what you say. Let's explore these ethical principles of communication further, first as they apply to speakers and then as they apply to audience members.

THE ETHICAL RESPONSIBILITIES OF A GOOD SPEAKER

In a world where "fake news" seems to spread faster than real news, it can be challenging to tell the difference between ethical and unethical messages. This alarming trend runs counter to everything that matters in our homes, classrooms, communities, and democratic society. Fortunately, the very best speakers—those with a positive and enduring influence—are committed to ethical decision making as they develop and deliver their presentations. They speak honestly, verify their facts and evidence, and treat their audience with civility and respect.

To become a *good person speaking well*, you should apply the principles of ethical communication to every element in the **RHETORICAL SPEECHMAKING PROCESS ● (5–13)**. Audience members see ethical speakers as trustworthy, their messages as valuable, and their presentations as successful, even when they disagree. To become a more ethical speaker, consider the decisions you make about your rhetorical situation: your *occasion*; yourself as *speaker*; your *audience*; and your *purpose, content,* and *delivery*.

Ethical Decisions about the Occasion Consider your speaking **OCCASION ▲ (61–68)**. Does your presentation measure up to the occasion's reason, time, and place? Are you honoring your audience's expectations?

Credo for Ethical Communication

PREAMBLE

Questions of right and wrong arise whenever people communicate. Ethical communication is fundamental to responsible thinking, decision making, and the development of relationships and communities within and across contexts, cultures, channels, and media. Moreover, ethical communication enhances human worth and dignity by fostering truthfulness, fairness, responsibility, personal integrity, and respect for self and others. We believe that unethical communication threatens the well-being of individuals and the society in which we live. Therefore we, the members of the National Communication Association, endorse and are committed to practicing the following principles of ethical communication.

PRINCIPLES OF ETHICAL COMMUNICATION

- We advocate truthfulness, accuracy, honesty, and reason as essential to the integrity of communication.

- We endorse freedom of expression, diversity of perspective, and tolerance of dissent to achieve the informed and responsible decision making fundamental to a civil society.

- We strive to understand and respect other communicators before evaluating and responding to their messages.

- We promote access to communication resources and opportunities as necessary to fulfill human potential and contribute to the well-being of families, communities, and society.

- We promote communication climates of caring and mutual understanding that respect the unique needs and characteristics of individual communicators.

- We condemn communication that degrades individuals and humanity through distortion, intimidation, coercion, and violence, and through the expression of intolerance and hatred.

- We are committed to the courageous expression of personal conviction in pursuit of fairness and justice.

- We advocate sharing information, opinions, and feelings when facing significant choices while also respecting privacy and confidentiality.

- We accept responsibility for the short- and long-term consequences of our own communication and expect the same of others.

Regardless of whether the occasion is a classroom presentation, a work briefing, a wedding, an award ceremony, or a testimony at a public meeting, ethical speakers respect and adapt to what makes a speaking occasion unique.

Ethical speakers also make sure they don't exploit a speaking opportunity to achieve their private, contradictory goals. Would it be ethical for a political candidate to use a military funeral—where they are expected to speak with respect and gratitude for the deceased's sacrifice—to argue that a lack of adequate defense spending is somehow to blame for the deaths of military personnel? Regardless of the validity of their claims, it is unethical for speakers to take advantage of an emotional public occasion to advance their own personal agenda.

Ethical Decisions about Yourself as a Speaker The audience decides whether you are an honest, trustworthy, sincere, and competent SPEAKER ▲ (72–85). In other words, your audience will decide if you are a *good person speaking well*. Ask yourself, "Do I believe in my message, and does it align with my personal beliefs and values? Am I knowledgeable about my subject, and will my message benefit the audience? When I express my opinion, am I honestly and accurately describing other points of view, even as I make my own position as strong as possible?" If you can answer these questions with a yes, you are most likely demonstrating a commitment to ethical communication—and you'll be much more likely to achieve your purpose.

Ethical Decisions about Your Audience Apply ethical principles as you analyze and adapt to your audience. Are you committed to being an AUDIENCE-CENTERED SPEAKER ▲ (88–89)? Will you use what you know about your audience to help them, or will you manipulate and possibly harm them? Will you use RESPECTFUL AND INCLUSIVE LANGUAGE ∴ (318–22) that promotes listeners' appreciation and understanding, or will you speak in ways that may exclude them?

Making ethical choices about audience members begins with learning as much as you can about them—their knowledge, interests, attitudes, and values. But the more you know about your audience, the easier it is to tell them only what they want to hear. Ethical speakers resist this temptation by sharing a message that benefits all of their audience members, even if it isn't what their audience expected or wanted to hear. For example, an ethical politician may promise a group of parents that an increase in property taxes will be used only to improve public education and provide medical care for children—policies that polls confirm are popular. It would be unethical, however, if that same politician also promised businesses that the same increase would be used to reduce corporate taxes. Although changing your message as you move from one group to another may demonstrate that you are skilled at audience adaptation, it becomes unethical when the two messages contradict each other.

Ethical Decisions about Your Purpose Who will benefit if you achieve your **PURPOSE ▲ (109–18)**—you, your audience, or both you and your audience? It's fine to have private goals when you speak—goals that benefit you, such as getting a good grade in a communication course or getting a promotion at work—but your private goals should always complement your overall purpose or at least *not conflict with* it. If your private agenda undermines or contradicts your stated or publicized purpose, you may be headed down an unethical path. If you would be ashamed or embarrassed to reveal your private goal to an audience, you should question the honesty and fairness of your purpose.

Ethical Decisions about Your Content You will face many ethical choices when developing the **CONTENT ■ (123–207)** of a presentation. Are your **CLAIMS ◆ (408–11)** well founded and reasonable? Have you verified your **SUPPORTING MATERIAL ■ (134–51)** to make sure it is relevant, up to date, and accurate? If most experts disagree with you, can you support and justify your position with valid evidence? Are you using **STATISTICS ■ (147–49)** in a manner that is honest, clear, and understandable? Making ethical decisions about your content ensures that your presentation will be truthful and reasonable.

Ethical Decisions about Delivery While many speakers use their **DELIVERY ▶ (209–301)** skills to impress and persuade an audience, ethical speakers make sure not to use their delivery to distract or mislead an audience. If your delivery style springs from a genuine enthusiasm for the subject and an authentic belief in the value of your message, it is ethically appropriate. But when an emotional or dramatic performance is used to subvert the truth or to present a false argument, it is unethical. Ideally, your delivery should reflect and reinforce the other ethical decisions you have made about your presentation.

THE ETHICAL RESPONSIBILITIES OF A GOOD AUDIENCE

Audience members—not just speakers—have important ethical responsibilities in all rhetorical situations. First and foremost, **EFFECTIVE LISTENING ● (30–33)** is essential for making fair, well-informed judgments about speakers and their message. Listen for key ideas and information with an open mind and withhold evaluation until you fully understand a speaker's message. If, as an audience member, you don't or won't listen because you have decided, even before a presentation begins, that you don't like the message or the speaker, you will have made a conscious unethical choice.

Ethical audience members:[3]

- Allow a speaker to be heard even if they disagree with the speaker's view.
- Strive to understand and respect a speaker *before* evaluating and responding to their message.
- Provide honest feedback that allows speakers to adapt their presentations accurately and appropriately to audience responses.
- Think critically about the validity and consequences of a message.
- Follow the **GOLDEN LISTENING RULE ● (37–38)**. Ask yourself, "Would I want an audience to behave the way I'm behaving if I were the speaker?"

Using Sources Ethically

One of the most important ways to speak ethically is to explicitly acknowledge your sources—the facts, ideas, and opinions you use in a presentation—whether it's a quotation from an author, a fact in a news article, or an idea generated by AI. Using sources without acknowledging them is **plagiarism**, which occurs when you fail to document or give credit to the sources of your information, distort the information you use, and/or present source statements as your own. The word *plagiarism* comes from the Latin *plagium*, which means "kidnapping." In other words, it is taking or stealing something that belongs to someone else. People who've plagiarized have failed courses, lost elections, and been fired from jobs. And a good audience can usually tell when all or part of your presentation doesn't sound like you. Anytime you plagiarize, you also harm your credibility and are less likely to achieve your purpose.

AVOIDING PLAGIARISM

Most speakers don't intend to plagiarize, so it's especially important to know what counts as plagiarism in order to avoid it. Changing a few words of someone else's work is not enough to avoid plagiarism. If the ideas and most of the words are not yours, you are ethically obligated to tell your audience who wrote or said them and where they came from. We urge you to abide by the following guidelines:

- Provide an **ORAL CITATION** ■ **(150)** if a significant phrase or section was written by someone else, particularly if the source is not widely known or widely available. Identify the source with key words and in such a way that listeners can look it up on their own.

- Avoid using someone else's sequence of ideas and organization without acknowledging and citing the similarities in structure.

- Cite sources that provide information and data in a chart, table, or graph, as well as any photograph, video clip, music, or animation that was produced by someone else. Make sure to include a **WRITTEN CITATION** ■ **(150–51)** whenever these appear on screen.

- Exercise extreme caution when using audio and/or visual **PRESENTATION AIDS** ▶ **(260–78)** as well as supporting materials you didn't create on your own. These kinds of materials are protected by copyright laws, and as such, you could be liable if you use them without first seeking the explicit permission of the copyright holder. Without permission, you could be legally liable for violating copyright laws.

In 2016, plagiarism took center stage at the Republican National Convention in Cleveland, Ohio, where Melania Trump gave a speech to support her husband's candidacy for president. Although it was initially praised, the speech soon came under suspicion because key passages resembled portions of a speech that Michelle Obama gave at the Democratic National Convention eight years earlier. Review the two passages comparing Michelle Obama's 2008 speech and the one delivered by Melania Trump in 2016. What you are reading is a definitive example of plagiarism.

Michelle Obama's 2008 speech	Melania Trump's 2016 speech
"And Barack and I were raised with so many of the same values: that you work hard for what you want in life; that your word is your bond and you do what you say you're going to do; that you treat people with dignity and respect, even if you don't know them, and even if you don't agree with them.	"From a young age, my parents impressed on me the values that you work hard for what you want in life, that your word is your bond and you do what you say and keep your promise, that you treat people with respect.
"Because we want our children—and all children in this nation—to know that the only limit to the height of your achievements is the reach of your dreams and your willingness to work for them."	"Because we want our children in this nation to know that the only limit to your achievements is the strength of your dreams and your willingness to work for them."

Republican officials initially denied that the speech included plagiarized material, but those claims collapsed when Mrs. Trump's speechwriter, Meredith McIver, took the blame. This plagiarism overshadowed whatever positive impact Mrs. Trump's presentation had at the time she delivered it, and as a result, her speech is now remembered for all the wrong reasons.

Here's the bottom line: speak truthfully, and do not misrepresent someone else's work as your own. Otherwise, you risk undermining or destroying whatever credibility you may have established.

Using Generative AI Ethically

Now that we've covered the importance of acknowledging your sources, you may be wondering how this applies to information generated by a computer.

Let's consider a case study. A student, Maya, is putting together a presentation about the serious consequences of water temperatures rising above 100 degrees Fahrenheit off the coast of Florida. She's analyzed the speaking occasion and done her research by identifying valid facts and opinions. Now it's time to create the presentation. As she thinks about what to say and how to organize it, she asks ChatGPT, a generative AI tool developed by OpenAI, to provide some key ideas for her presentation. Within seconds she receives a clear, well-written summary of six significant harms—from health-related dangers to increases in the intensity of storms.[4] She's tempted to use four of them and will back up each harm with her views and the supporting materials she's collected.

Maya now faces several ethical decisions. Should she use the wording and content generated by AI without revealing her source? Does she run the risk of being caught and accused of plagiarism? Is it unethical to use generative AI if her instructor, college, or organization restricts its use? What if her college or class doesn't have a specific AI policy? Ethical questions like these aren't always straightforward, especially when it involves rapidly changing technology. To start considering these ethical questions, it helps to understand the nature of generative AI.

UNDERSTANDING GENERATIVE AI

Generative artificial intelligence (or **generative AI**) is a kind of machine learning algorithm that learns by searching and sourcing applicable available content, including text, images, and audio, to produce new content.[5] Generative AI entered the communication mainstream in the early 2020s with platforms such as OpenAI's ChatGPT, Google's Bard and Gemini, and Microsoft's Bing Chat and Copilot. By the time you read this book, there will be many more new and improved generative AI platforms and capabilities.

In this chapter, we refer to generative AI platforms that generally work in similar ways: you create a prompt or start a conversation that asks or describes what you want AI to generate, and the generative AI tool delivers a response gleaned from sources all over the internet, including journals, websites, databases, and social media. In doing so, the AI tool searches and sorts through vast amounts of information to deliver the information or new content that you request.

It may seem that generative AI is a more efficient version of doing an **INTERNET SEARCH** ■ **(141–42)**—and by the time you read this book, AI will likely be incorporated into your favorite internet search tool. But consider the key difference between *searching* for and *generating* the main ideas for a presentation. While a search tool helps you locate preexisting material from relevant sources, a *generative* tool creates new material by "reading" those sources, selecting the content to use, and presenting its findings in a way that mimics a human doing the work on your behalf. So, is it ethical to use the material that AI generated from a wide range of other sources? Should you cite generative AI and, if so, when?

ETHICAL DECISIONS FOR USING GENERATIVE AI

Let's return to three of the rhetorical elements that are most important when considering how to use generative AI ethically: your speaking *occasion*, yourself as a *speaker*, and your *content*.

Occasion: Using Generative AI in Academic Contexts The most important guideline for using AI ethically is to follow the policy or policies set by your instructor, college, or the institution hosting your presentation. If using generative AI is prohibited or discouraged, doing so in any capacity would be unethical and could be labeled as plagiarism. In some cases, you might be barred from speaking or receive an F on an assignment.

Answer the following questions before using generative AI in an academic context—even if you just plan to use it for brainstorming. If you don't know the answer to either of these questions, consult your syllabus or ask your instructor.

- Does your instructor or college have a policy for using generative AI as the basis for academic work?
- If permitted by your instructor or college, what are the acceptable circumstances and conditions for using generative AI?

Speaker: Generative AI and Your Ethics If permitted in your speaking situation, AI can be a helpful tool as you begin thinking about what to say—but only if you adapt any generated material to your audience and to your own ethics as a speaker.

The voice, language, and ideas generated by AI come from a wide range of sources—writers, thinkers, academics, social media users, editors, and even other AI chatbots. The material it generates does not come from *you*, speaking to *your audience* on a *particular occasion*. It doesn't incorporate your natural speaking style or your unique perspectives. You won't be as familiar with supporting material generated by AI as you would if you'd spent the time doing your own **RESEARCH ■ (134–51)**: finding, reading, evaluating, and summarizing your sources.

If you ask generative AI to produce an outline or manuscript, or if you use language generated by AI, you are crossing an ethical line by plagiarizing and saying words or ideas that don't reflect *you* and your personal ethics.

Content: Evaluating and Verifying Generated Material As an ethical speaker, it is your duty to **EVALUATE YOUR SOURCES ■ (143–47)**, and the same is true for anything generated by AI. Harvard University's Information Technology office puts it this way: AI-generated content can be inaccurate, misleading, entirely fabricated, or offensive, so be sure to carefully review any work containing AI content before you use or publish it.[6]

AI is notorious for producing **HALLUCINATED SOURCES ■ (142–43)** along with fully reliable ones, a concern that continues even as generative AI tools become more sophisticated. Upon releasing a powerful new version of ChatGPT in 2024, for example, OpenAI admitted that ChatGPT "'hallucinates' facts and makes reasoning errors."[7] So, if you use AI-generated text without verifying and citing the information it generates, you not only risk plagiarism, but you also risk losing credibility and spreading false information.

BEST PRACTICES FOR USING GENERATIVE AI ETHICALLY

Like any tool, there are proper and improper ways to use generative AI. Here are some best practices for using generative AI ethically:

- *Only use AI if permitted* by your instructor, college, workplace, or speaking situation.
- *Use AI as part of your overall process*, not as an ending point. You might, for example, **USE AI TO NARROW YOUR TOPIC ■ (131–32)** or to consider new and opposing viewpoints.

- *Track down the original source* for any information provided by generative AI. **ASK AI FOR CITATIONS** ■ **(142–43)**, and if AI cannot provide a source, seek out the original source on your own. Cite that source (not AI) in your presentation.

- *Verify all AI-generated content.* **EVALUATE** ■ **(143–47)** all information to make sure it is accurate, relevant, valid, and consistent with reputable sources. Consider an example of two lawyers who trusted ChatGPT to provide accurate information for a legal brief they submitted to a judge. They were fined $5,000 for including fake case citations and making "false and misleading statements to the court."[8]

- *Cite any AI-generated ideas*. Use an **ORAL CITATION** ■ **(150)** during your presentation and a written citation if required. All major source cit ation formats provide guidance about how to cite ideas generated by AI.

- *Be mindful of biases*. Generative AI reflects the biases that exist within the data it was trained on, which can reinforce inequalities and existing societal prejudices.[9]

- *Protect your credibility*. If an audience believes you are using generative AI without disclosing it, you may be seen as unethical and lose your credibility as a result.[10]

As we recommended earlier, you should avoid using someone else's sequence of ideas and organization without acknowledging and citing the similarities in structure. Recall Maya, the student researching a presentation on rising water temperatures off the coast of Florida. She would not want to use the AI-generated summary of six significant harms without citing it as a source. Since AI is compiling the work of others on your behalf, it counts as a "someone" who should be cited anytime you use AI-generated ideas, main points, or language.

And as an ethical speaker, you should not deliver a presentation written by AI as if it were your own. If you rely on AI to generate a full speech or outline the night before your presentation, you are committing plagiarism, you will risk spreading false information, and you will deliver a presentation that didn't come from *you*, for *your* audience, *your* occasion, and *your* purpose. Remember, *your voice*, not an AI chatbot's, is the voice that matters.

Freedom of Speech

Freedom of speech is more than an integral part of American life—it is enshrined in the US Constitution. As stated in the First Amendment:

> Congress shall make no law respecting an establishment of religion, or prohibiting the free exercise thereof; or abridging the freedom of speech, or of the press; or the right of the people peaceably to assemble, and to petition the Government for a redress of grievances.

The types of speech protected in the First Amendment are very broad. Even hate speech, for example—the sort of speech that overtly denigrates, insults, or demonizes other people based on their race, ethnicity, gender, or sexual orientation—is *legally* protected under the First Amendment as long as it isn't a direct and "true threat" that causes people to fear imminent physical harm. What the First Amendment doesn't protect are hate *crimes*, which are based on actions rather than expressions of an opinion.[11]

Your freedom to speak is not absolute—if you are met with hostility or heckling, with loud vocal objections, or censorship, your constitutional rights are *not* being violated. If you purposely lie, distort information, harm and harass others, and cause panic or injuries, you can be sued by those you maligned or unjustly attacked. If your statements about someone are false, unjustified, and/or harmful, you can be sued for **defamation**—that is, making a false statement that damages a person's reputation. If you say hateful or inflammatory things about a group or class of people, you may face hostility and harassment from vocal allies of the people you've targeted, as well as sharp criticism of your character and competence. If you harass, denigrate, and lie about someone, you may end up in court or facing a hefty fine.

In short, just because speech is free from *government* interference doesn't mean that unethical speech must be silently tolerated or that it is without consequences. And as speakers and listeners, we have the right to address unethical communication practices with forceful but well-reasoned and respectfully expressed criticisms when warranted. Consider the "heckler's veto," where a group of listeners take actions that cause a speaker to stop speaking or prevent a speaker from having the opportunity to speak. The heckler's veto has been used as a strategic weapon against hateful, inflammatory, and controversial speech on many college campuses in recent years.

In 2023, for example, students graduating from the City University of New York School of Law turned their backs when New York City mayor Eric Adams began his commencement address. Adams responded quickly by acknowledging their right to protest while also observing, "We're watching a clear lack of desire to even participate in healthy dialogue." In the short term, turning away (or away from) a speaker whose views or ideas are harmful, offensive, or hateful may seem like a victory. But remember that silencing speakers you vehemently disagree with by disinviting or heckling them is a tactic that can also be employed against other speakers whose ideas you support. It's also unethical.

The best protection of your right to free speech is to express your opinions respectfully, back up those opinions with legitimate facts and valid reasoning, and provide defendable responses to audience objections. But if reactions to your presentation are extreme, you may want to reassess the decisions you've made and the rhetorical strategies you've used. If you conclude that you have been truthful, fair, objective, and respectful—in short, that you have exemplified the qualities of an ethical speaker—you should take comfort in thinking about all the speakers who have come before you whose cause was just and whose ideas eventually prevailed despite attempts to silence them.

As an audience member, you may find it challenging both to defend everyone's right to speak and to productively oppose unethical communication. Understanding, thinking critically about, and responding to what people say—it's difficult work. It may not be as immediately gratifying as using incendiary language or disruptive tactics when someone speaks in a way that upset or offends you. But it is the more responsible, ethical, and, in the long run, more effective speechmaking strategy.

Conclusion

The NCA's Credo for Ethical Communication expresses what should be the guiding values of an ethical speaker in a democratic society. By keeping its principles in mind as you think about every rhetorical situation whenever you speak, you will better service your audience's interests as well as your own. One ethical obligation you have as a speaker is to build and maintain your credibility by using various sources and generative AI ethically. This means avoiding plagiarism by giving credit to the sources of your information. You also have ethical obligations as an audience member, the most fundamental of which is to listen well.

Freedom of speech is guaranteed by the US Constitution, but if an unethical speaker's message has unwarranted negative consequences, the speaker may be rebuked, sued, or found guilty of causing mental or physical harm. We agree with ethics scholar Ronald C. Arnett, who expresses hope for a time when we "emphasize the practical need for free speech and communication ethics working hand in hand as freedom and responsibility, and the conviction that the best and brightest ideas can be discovered together in conversation."[12]

PART 2
Fundamentals

Whenever you speak to a group of people—whether it's an introductory speech to your classmates, a presentation to colleagues about a new policy, a toast at a friend's wedding, or prepared remarks at a town council meeting—you should be aware of four fundamental elements: the **OCCASION**; you, as the **SPEAKER**; the **AUDIENCE**; and your **PURPOSE**. The other elements of the rhetorical situation are important, of course, but these four are fundamental—the beating heart of any speaking occasion. The following chapters focus on these elements and will help you make strategic decisions about a presentation before and as you speak.

Fundamentals

2.1 Occasion

> ## 🔍 A BRIEF GUIDE TO THIS CHAPTER
>
> - **Adapting to your occasion** (p. 62)
> - **Preparing for your occasion** (p. 64)
> - **Anticipating challenges** (p. 67)

When asked to make a presentation, what's the first thing you do? Do you write an outline? Create a slide deck? Craft a compelling introduction? Though these are important steps in speech preparation, first you need to ask, "What's the occasion?"

Your occasion can be as ceremonial as the inauguration of a US president or as routine as giving a status report at a staff meeting. Would you give the same presentation at a memorial service as at a pep rally? Of course not. By finding out *why* an audience will be assembled, you can make better decisions about what to say and how to say it.

Occasion can be the most important of the six elements of the rhetorical situation, so that's where we'll start. In this chapter, we introduce general steps for adapting to and preparing for the occasion—but occasion will come up again and again as we cover each step of the speechmaking process. In Part 8, **SPECIAL SPEAKING OCCASIONS** ★ **(463–525)**, we also offer brief guides for speaking at some of the most distinctive occasions, like giving a toast at a wedding or accepting an award at school. The advice in this chapter will apply to those special occasions—and will also help prepare you to speak at *any* occasion.

Adapting to Your Occasion

The **occasion** for a presentation involves four factors: the *reason* for the presentation, the *time* it will take place, the *setting* it will occur in, and the *medium* (in person, online, or recorded) that will be used. Analyzing these four factors may take no time at all or may require considerable research and strategic decision making. Every occasion will be different because they will never occur for the same reason, at the same time and place, and while using the same medium. So to determine the fundamental elements for any speaking occasion, ask:

- Why are *you* speaking on *this* occasion?
- What does the audience expect for this occasion?
- What is appropriate for this occasion?

WHY ARE *YOU* SPEAKING ON *THIS* OCCASION?

Are you speaking because you were required or invited to speak? As a student speaker, you may find yourself speaking to an audience of your classmates for an assignment. In your career, you might be required to deliver presentations to clients or coworkers. Or are you speaking because you *want* to speak? For example, you might volunteer to speak as part of a discussion about your favorite book, or you may excitedly step up to share a story about your grandmother at her 80th birthday party.

Whether you're asked to speak or want to speak, it's usually because you have experience, expertise, or perspective that will contribute something to your audience. For example, as the youngest employee at a marketing firm, you may be asked to speak about social media platforms that are popular with people your age. As the captain of your high school water polo team or valedictorian of your class, you may be invited to speak at a ceremony honoring a former coach or professor. Knowing why *you* are speaking on a particular occasion will help inform your understanding of your role as a **SPEAKER ▲ (72–85)**, including what to wear, what kind of language to use, what stories to tell, and what evidence to reference—in other words, how to build your credibility with an audience.

WHAT DOES THE AUDIENCE EXPECT FOR THIS OCCASION?

Your **AUDIENCE ▲ (88–105)** will also come to each speaking occasion with a set of expectations about you and the content of your presentation. For example, if you've been asked to give a toast at a wedding, guests expect to hear a sentimental and perhaps a humorous tribute to the couple. But if you're a divorce lawyer, your client will probably expect to hear compelling evidence of their spouse's shortcomings.

Your audience will also expect your **DELIVERY ▶ (209–301)** to match the needs of the occasion. Audiences attending a training session on CPR will probably expect a demonstration, whereas scholars at an academic conference may expect a speaker to read a manuscript at a lectern. Given the prominence of social media, many audiences now expect to hear short, crisp phrases when listening to presentations online. Think about what style of speech *you* would expect to hear on a particular occasion. Then try to match your speaking style to those expectations.

WHAT IS APPROPRIATE FOR THIS OCCASION?

Some occasions have specific rules of **protocol**, the expected format of a ceremony or the customs of a particular type of event. If you are attending for the first time a christening, a bar mitzvah, or a breaking of the daily fast during the month of Ramadan, you would want to know how to behave, when to arrive, what to wear, and whether you should bring a gift. The same is true for presentation speaking. Before you begin researching, writing, or practicing, make sure you know about any rules that may apply to the occasion.

Consider a student speech in a communication course. Before giving a presentation in your class, it is important to know the protocol your professor has established. You've likely been told the type of presentation to deliver (to inform or persuade), the length of the presentation (under six minutes, for example, so that everyone gets a chance to speak), and the requirements (turn in an outline with a list of the references, stand at the front of the class, use at least one presentation aid, etc.). If you do not adapt to this particular occasion and its rules, you may be disappointed by the reactions you receive from your audience and by a poor grade on your assignment.

Outside of a classroom setting, how will you know the appropriate protocol for a particular presentation? You can follow other examples if you've been to an event similar to the one where you'll be speaking. Or you can get more information from the person who invited you to speak or from people who have attended similar events. Consider asking:

- Is the occasion formal? Is there a dress code?
- Is there a preferred arrival time?
- Is an official speaker biography needed?
- Is the speaker expected to sit in a certain place on the stage?
- Is advanced submission of a manuscript or key points required?

Preparing for Your Occasion

After asking and answering questions about your role in, audience expectations for, and protocols of your presentation's occasion, you can prepare for the **logistics** of the occasion—the strategic planning, arranging, and use of materials and facilities. Even if you've been told that everything you need will be set up in advance, you still need to make sure that happens. Confirm answers to the following logistical questions as you prepare for each speaking occasion.

WHERE WILL YOU SPEAK?

Learn as much as you can about the site where you'll be speaking. Will you speak in an auditorium, at a backyard barbecue, in a classroom, or on Zoom? Will you stand on a stage or be in your bedroom looking at a camera? You may need to adjust the seating arrangements as well as the temperature, lighting, and sound system to match your own and the audience's needs. If you're planning to read from a manuscript in person, you may need a lectern—and if one isn't available, you might choose to memorize your presentation or use note cards instead. If you're speaking ONLINE ▶ (282–301), you'll have to consider lots of unique speaking logistics, like if you'll be able to see your audience, if you need to distribute the meeting link, and if you'll have use of a chat feature, for example.

HOW MANY PEOPLE WILL BE THERE?

Audience size matters for all presentation occasions. For example, if there are only 15 people in your audience, you probably won't have to worry about being seen or heard. But if there are 1,500 people, you'll probably need a microphone supported by a good sound system and appropriate lighting. Knowing the size of your audience also helps you figure out what kinds of presentation aids will work. If you're using a screen to project slides, videos, or a website, make sure the screen is large enough for everyone to see both the images and text clearly.

In a small presentation, you might invite audience members to ask questions throughout your presentation, but for a large audience you might ask them to submit questions ahead of time or to hold their questions until the end of the presentation. If you're presenting a webinar with more than a dozen or so people, consider asking for help with monitoring the comments for questions.

WHEN AND HOW LONG SHOULD YOU SPEAK?

Will you be speaking in the morning, during a busy workday, before a ceremony, or after a meal? Are you scheduled to speak for five minutes or for half an hour? Knowing the time and duration is essential for all presentations. After all, if you've prepared an hour's worth of material but discover that you have only ten minutes to speak, what do you cut?

The time of your presentation will impact everything from your delivery to your **LANGUAGE ∴ (305–22)**. Say, for example, you are scheduled to speak at 7 a.m. Because your audience may not be fully awake, adjust your speech so that it's crisp and clear—as well as kind and gentle to help them ease into the day. However, if you're scheduled for a 4:30 p.m. presentation, your audience may be tired, so a more energetic speaking style or more colorful language will help keep them engaged. And if you are scheduled to speak to an audience after a big meal or after another long speech, you may find that a short or humorous approach is the only way to compete with their desire to tune out or take a nap.

Know the duration of your speech—how long you are *scheduled* to speak—and **LIMIT THE LENGTH ∴ (336–37)** of your presentation accordingly. Time yourself when you **PRACTICE ▶ (220–24)**, keeping in mind that the actual presentation may take much longer. While you're speaking, you might ask someone to give you a signal when it's time to begin the conclusion. And when that signal comes, don't ignore it, even if it means skipping major sections of your message.

In general, try to speak for 20 minutes or less—just about the limit people can listen to and retain information.[1] If your occasion requires you to speak longer than 20 minutes, try one of these strategies to keep your audience engaged:

- Break up your talk with visuals or **DEMONSTRATIONS ✳ (381–82)**.

- Cover the basics in 15 minutes and then use the rest of the time to **ANSWER QUESTIONS ∴ (350–61)**.

- Insert short, personal **STORIES ∴ (323–32)** or anecdotes to help drive home your point and give the audience a pleasant respite.[2]

WHAT EQUIPMENT WILL BE AVAILABLE?

Though it's common for speakers to use presentation aids, you can't assume your speaking location will be set up to display them. If you plan on using a slide deck, ask if a projector and screen are available. Should you bring your laptop, or will there be a computer on-site that you should use? If you need audio, ask about how the sound system is set up and how it connects to your computer. Do you need to bring any special cables? You may need to request a table to display certain **PRESENTATION AIDS ▶ (260–78)** so the audience can see them properly. And the type of microphone available will determine whether you can move around during your presentation or if you'll need to stay in one place.

WHAT ACCOMMODATION SERVICES WILL BE PROVIDED?

To ensure that you and everyone in your audience can focus on your presentation, confirm what accommodation services will be provided. Start by asking about the accessibility of the facility and available interpreting services. Do not hesitate to ask for any accommodation that you may need as a speaker, like the height of a lectern or a particular type of lighting. Will you need a quiet place to gather your thoughts before you speak? If you have difficulty with steps, ask for a ramp or other guidance for getting on and off the stage. Is it possible to display real-time captioning of your presentation—whether in person or online? It is always a good idea to design your presentation with accessibility in mind—even if you do not know if an audience member will need it.

Anticipating Challenges

It *is* possible to be heard by an audience of a thousand people without a microphone. It *is* possible to describe a procedure if your demonstration video malfunctions, but only with careful logistical planning and preparation. Communication consultant Dorothy Leeds puts it this way: "You must be your own stage manager" because "you're the one who's ultimately in charge of your speaking situation. Do your best to control the environment, and you will control how your audience receives the words you've worked so hard to shape."[3]

Of course, no matter how meticulously you've planned and prepared, you may run into logistical issues that you cannot control. Despite repeated reminders and promises, you may discover that your presentation room has no chairs, lectern, table, and/or whiteboard or has poor lighting. Here are some practical steps you can take to anticipate and overcome common logistical challenges:

- *Arrive early.* Like a sharp-eyed stage manager, show up at least 30 minutes before you speak and check out the facility, or log on to the online speaking platform weeks or days before you speak.

- *Test the equipment.* Never assume that everything is in working order. Well before you speak, make sure that each piece of equipment works properly. Turn on every machine. Boot up your computer and click through a few slides (and don't forget to backtrack to the beginning of your presentation before you begin to speak!). Test your camera. Do you need pens or pointers? Do you need batteries for a remote? Did you bring the power cord for your laptop?

- *Make a backup plan.* Always be prepared to deliver an altered version of your presentation in case your audiovisual equipment doesn't work. How would you explain a part of your presentation that relies on showing your audience a chart if the projector is not working? If you plan to read notes from a digital device, do you have a hard copy in case you need it? If you're presenting online, can you "call in" to the meeting using a phone number in case your microphone or camera fails?

By arriving early and preparing a backup plan, logistical issues won't derail your presentation. If the unexpected happens, stay positive. Don't call attention to the problems in a way that may impact your credibility—blaming your ancient laptop or lack of technical knowledge may make you feel better, but it may also cause the audience to question your competence and confidence as a speaker. But if you're prepared and can communicate your message despite technological setbacks, your audience may even find you more credible as a result.

Conclusion

Why is my audience assembling at this time and in this place, either in person or online, to hear me speak? That's your occasion. Your answers will help you understand your role as a speaker, the audience's expectations, and the protocol for the occasion. Only then can you create a worthy message that is adapted to your audience and delivered effectively. Consider how your presentation will be impacted by the logistics of the occasion, including the site, audience size, time and duration, available equipment, and accessibility services.

In a perfect world, your speaking situation would always be under control, and nothing would ever go wrong. Since this is not likely to be the case, take a hands-on role in controlling the speaking situation to the best of your ability. Plan and prepare for the logistics beforehand and make a backup plan if your occasion or location is different than you expect. No matter what happens, you are still a credible speaker who has a worthy message to share!

George W. Bush

George W. Bush became the nation's 43rd president in January of 2001. On September 11, 2001, just nine months into his first term, the nation experienced the worst terrorist attack on US soil, which killed close to three thousand people and injured thousands more. President Bush faced the monumental task of both mourning with the nation and rallying them to be strong and courageous in the face of such incomprehensible acts of evil. His Ground Zero speech, as it is known, was delivered only three days after the attacks while workers were still combing through the rubble in search of survivors. Whereas Bush had been criticized as "missing in action" immediately following the tragedy, his impromptu Ground Zero speech was a fitting match for the occasion.

Search Terms

To locate a video of this presentation online, enter the following key words into a search engine: Bush 9/11 Ground Zero speech National Archives. The video is approximately 2:18 in length.

What to Watch For

When Bush hears the crowd chanting "USA!" "USA!" "USA!," he climbs to the top of a rubble pile at the site of the 9/11 attack in New York City. In his role as president and commander in chief, citizens expected him to speak to the nation. Given the occasion, a respectful and emotionally charged speech was appropriate.

The impromptu nature of the speech meant that there was no logistical planning. When the audience shouts that they can't hear him, the president grabs a bullhorn and climbs to a higher position so that his audience can both see and hear him. He had no sophisticated sound equipment, no manuscript, no lectern, no special lighting, and no time to prepare.

[0:00–0:52] The occasion of the speech was to provide emotional support to the hundreds of exhausted firefighters, police, medical personnel, and volunteers who had been working around the clock to rescue victims and clean up the wreckage. Speaking to emergency workers assembled around the rubble pile and those watching from home, President Bush immediately acknowledges that "America today is on bended knee in prayer for the people whose lives were lost here, for the workers who work here, for the families who mourn."

[0:53–1:20] The immediate audience at Ground Zero wanted both comfort and toughness from the president. The larger viewing audience wanted to see a strong leader taking charge. The audience cheers as President Bush provides words of comfort: "I can hear you! The rest of the world hears you." He follows with toughness by promising "And the people who knocked these buildings down will hear all of us soon."

[1:21–1:44] As the crowd erupts in chants of "USA! USA! USA!," the president takes a significant pause to let the momentum of the chant build. In the absence of a set protocol for how to handle such an unprecedented event, he allows compassion and empathy to guide his thoughts and delivery. He nonverbally displays this emotion by putting his arm around a firefighter, whom Bush had asked to stand next to him during the speech.

[1:45–1:55] President Bush concludes with a note of gratitude for the hard work the emergency workers have been engaged in. The immediate audience—firefighters, police, medical personnel, and volunteers—needed a short, rousing endorsement and tribute from the president. A brief speech was an appropriate choice since many of the workers had not slept but a few hours over the course of the previous three days. The president had already delivered a longer address to the nation on the day of the attacks, and others followed in the days and weeks after the attacks.

[1:56–2:18] As President Bush steps down from the pile of rubble, an American flag is handed to him. He pauses to wave it in the air before leaving. This small act is one last important nonverbal message that he stands in solidarity with the workers. The large audience of television viewers saw an intense and powerful president taking charge of an embattled scene.

EXERCISE

After viewing Bush's speech, reflect on these questions:

1. Considering the content and delivery expectations of his audience, how does Bush demonstrate empathy both verbally and nonverbally throughout the speech?

2. Do you think Bush should have spoken longer? Why or why not?

3. Explain how protocol played a role in why Bush was not wearing a suit and tie even though he was president of the United States.

4. What role might protocol have played in Bush placing his arm around the shoulder of the firefighter?

2.2 Speaker

🔍 A BRIEF GUIDE TO THIS CHAPTER

- **An effective speaker's core values** (p. 72)
- **Developing speaker credibility** (p. 74)
- **Restoring speaker credibility** (p. 82)

When you write something to be read by other people—an essay, a short story, or a report—the words on the page are front and center. But when you speak to an audience, *you*, the speaker, are the focus of attention. Whether you address a handful of people or thousands, your audience will respond to *you*—your gestures, tone of voice, and personality—as much as they will judge the content of your message.

An Effective Speaker's Core Values

A great **speaker** connects with their audience. When audience members believe they're listening to a person whom they trust and admire, they are much more likely to listen with interest and understanding.

There is no formula or list of dos and don'ts that will make an audience believe and trust you. But we know that successful speakers who make a genuine connection with audience members are guided by a set of core values: *a belief in their message, an openness to feedback,* and *a commitment to ethical communication.*

BELIEVE IN YOUR MESSAGE

Who are you? What are your interests, passions, values, capabilities, limitations, and experiences? By considering what *you* can bring to your speaking occasion, you can prepare a presentation that reflects who you are, on a topic that you care about. In doing so, you are more likely to be comfortable as a speaker and, in turn, make your audience more comfortable with you. In short, if you believe in your message, your presentation will be more effective, more exciting, and more gratifying to deliver!

If, on the other hand, you appear to be motivated by a self-serving goal or not motivated at all, your listeners may not like or listen to your message. If you deliver a presentation generated by AI or speak about a topic that doesn't interest you, your presentation will probably sound impersonal and insincere—it won't reveal your strengths or who you are.

BE OPEN TO FEEDBACK

Effective speakers welcome and are open to **FEEDBACK ● (39-40)** about their presentations. Honest feedback can come from a trusted friend during the preparation process or in practice sessions. Openness to feedback is just as important during a presentation, given that audience members may show nonverbal signs of interest, agreement, and encouragement—or boredom, annoyance, and confusion. Attentive speakers use feedback to analyze, understand, and adapt aspects of their presentations that help them empathize and connect with their audience.

COMMIT TO ETHICAL COMMUNICATION

Recall from our discussion of **ETHICS ● (43-57)** how the Roman rhetorician Quintilian described an ideal speaker: *a good person speaking well.* This simple but noteworthy phrase claims that a good speaker is both effective and ethical—committing to truthfulness, fairness, responsibility, and respect for others. They are also committed to being fair and open-minded about differences and disagreements. A commitment to ethical communication is more than doing the right thing; it can also affect whether audiences believe you and your message. Seen from the audience's point of view, one unethical comment or presentation can diminish your credibility and negatively affect how audiences respond to you in the future.

Developing Speaker Credibility

Speaker credibility is the extent to which an audience believes you and what you say. Listeners pay more attention to, remember more from, and are more likely to agree with speakers they perceive as credible. However, just because you think you are knowledgeable and believable doesn't mean that your audience sees you that way. You can try to shape an audience's perceptions of your credibility, but whether or not they perceive you as credible is entirely up to them.

Speakers often enter a room with some amount of credibility. Your classmates, coworkers, and friends, for example, have known you for a while by the time you make a presentation. What you have done and said before will have already shaped your credibility. On some occasions, a speaker's credibility may be established or strengthened when someone introduces them. Other speakers have a distinguished reputation that precedes them, thus establishing their credibility before they speak. Whether or not people know you beforehand, your audience will decide whether you are believable. Your credibility is not a given; it is solely based on the perception of your audience.

To understand how speaker credibility emerges from audience perception, it helps to recognize four major qualities that contribute to credibility—and the strategies that can help you enhance them. These four dimensions are *competence*, *trustworthiness*, *likability*, and *dynamism*. Keep in mind that these are not either-or characteristics. For example, it's not a question of whether or not you're trustworthy, but the *degree*

THE FOUR DIMENSIONS OF SPEAKER CREDIBILITY			
Competence	**Trustworthiness**	**Likability**	**Dynamism**
Experienced	Ethical	Audience centered	Energetic
Well prepared	Honest	Friendly	Confident
Qualified	Fair	Kind	Stimulating
Up to date	Respectful	Empathetic	Bold
Knowledgeable	Reliable	Sociable	Assertive

of trustworthiness your audience ascribes to you. Equally important, you should not simply focus on one or two of these dimensions, such as competence or likability, while ignoring the other two. Speaker credibility is multidimensional. It represents a combination of several characteristics that an audience identifies in a speaker.[1]

1. COMPETENCE

Competence refers to a speaker's perceived expertise and abilities. Competent speakers are seen as well prepared, knowledgeable, and qualified to speak about their topic.

If a speaker is a recognized chef, renowned brain surgeon, celebrated musician, or professional athlete—in short, a person famous for a particular talent or pursuit—an audience is likely to see that speaker as competent as long as they speak about topics within their known areas of expertise.

While most of us can't rely on fame or renown to demonstrate our competence, you can use some of the following strategies to demonstrate to an audience that you're qualified to speak on your topic.

Research Your Subject If you are not an expert or well informed about the topic of your presentation, research is how you acquire the knowledge you need to be seen as competent. **DOING RESEARCH** ▉ **(134–51)** can be a serious and intense process of reading, writing, and thinking, but it doesn't always need to be. Sometimes it can be as simple as considering what you already know about a subject and what you can learn from people in your life. It's not realistic to know everything about a topic, nor will your audience expect you to, but you should know enough to assure your audience that you have done your homework.

Begin your research as soon as you know you're scheduled to speak. The initial research process can guide you toward new and interesting information and different viewpoints about your topic. But if you cram your planning and research into the day before a presentation, especially if you are speaking on a topic that isn't familiar, you won't be adequately prepared, and your audience may question your credibility.

Plan for Questions Perceptions of your credibility and competence are often determined by how well you answer audience questions during and after a presentation. Studies suggest that audience evaluations of a speaker are significantly and positively affected by how well the speaker responds to questions and objections.[2] An engaging **QUESTION-AND-ANSWER SESSION** ⁝ **(350–61)** can boost your credibility—and even restore it if your presentation doesn't go as planned. If you plan to answer questions from the audience, be sure to do the following:

- *Prepare, predict, and practice.* Prepare in advance, predict possible questions and issues that may arise, and practice answering those questions.
- *Link your answers to your message.* Use audience questions as a bridge to your purpose, key ideas, and conclusions.

Use Appropriate Language Pay attention to the **LANGUAGE** ⁝ **(305–22)** and terminology that is frequently used when discussing a particular subject. If some of the terms are new to you, practice them until you feel comfortable saying them. When it's time to deliver your presentation, you can enhance your credibility by using and explaining these concepts in a manner that seems natural and well informed. But don't overdo it or your audience will get lost in specialized jargon. Will they know that *starboard* is the right side of a ship when facing forward? Will they know the exact meaning of *microbe, meme,* or *meunière*? When in doubt, define the specialized terms you use. Audience members who already know the meaning of these words will feel like experts, and those who don't will have learned a new and useful term.

Highlight Your Experiences You may not be an expert or have deep knowledge of your topic, but you may have direct experience with it. Including a personal observation or telling a **STORY** ⁝ **(323–32)** that supports your purpose can enhance the audience's perception of your competence. Students who played esports, studied anime in depth, shoed horses, or worked as a fashion model in Paris, for example, have delighted and impressed their classmates with memorable personal stories.

Cite Reputable Sources Our increasing access to information and opinions also increases our exposure to unreliable and biased sources. Think critically about your supporting materials. **EVALUATE YOUR SOURCES** ■ **(143–47)** for reliability and accuracy and only use information and opinions that you are confident are valid, up to date, reputable, and relevant. When making your presentation, cite your sources clearly and, if necessary, describe their expertise and trustworthiness as a way of enhancing *your* credibility.

To boost your competence, tell your audience what efforts you made to be well prepared. For example: "After reviewing a dozen books on this subject published during the last five years, I was surprised to learn that none of the authors addressed . . ." or "I spoke, in person, to all five of our county commissioners. They all agree that . . ."

Practice Your Delivery and Project Confidence If you hesitate as you speak, shuffle through your notes looking for a piece of information, or stumble over terminology, audience members may doubt your competence. Speakers with strong vocal and physical delivery are more likely to feel confident and be seen by their audience as highly competent. To most listeners, confidence implies competence. **PRACTICE YOUR DELIVERY** ▶ **(220–24)** until you are confident it will achieve its purpose.

2. TRUSTWORTHINESS

Are you a fair, honest, and reliable speaker? When you present an argument, is your evidence unbiased and your conclusions justified? In other words, are you a trustworthy speaker? An audience's perception of your **trustworthiness**—your perceived honesty, integrity, and good character—reflects your commitment to being an **ETHICAL SPEAKER** ● **(43–57)**. When you demonstrate ethical choices as a speaker, you are taking the necessary steps to earn your audience's trust. When you don't, listeners won't believe what you say, or they will have doubts about you, your motives, and your message.

If your listeners don't trust you, it won't matter that you consider yourself an expert, have prepared thoroughly, or are a technically skilled speaker. Perceived competence in your subject and obvious oratorical skill won't make up for an impression among your listeners that you are untrustworthy or dishonest. Here are some ways to demonstrate your trustworthiness to your audience.

Emphasize Your Good Reputation Generally, we trust people who are reliable. If you are often late for class or your job, or if you fail to meet your obligations to your classmates or coworkers in other ways, they may not trust you as much as you wish when it's your turn to give a presentation. Cultivate a reputation for reliability—be on time, follow through on your commitments, and do what you say you're going to do. In situations where your reputation precedes you, having a good reputation will encourage listeners to trust you when you speak.

Acknowledge and Respect Other Viewpoints When presenting your own opinions and perspectives, it is tempting to ignore or unfairly downplay opposing viewpoints or facts that contradict your message. But by LISTENING ● (30–42) to and acknowledging and respecting objections to your message, you demonstrate that you're not ignoring inconvenient truths. If you fairly summarize both your own perspective and those that differ, you show that you're not just focused on "winning" but that you have also thought carefully about the issue. This does not mean you have to agree with other viewpoints. In fact, explaining how and why you support your perspective while acknowledging opposing viewpoints will demonstrate that you are knowledgeable, fair, respectful, and confident—a perfect combination of credibility dimensions. Even more, doing so can keep your audience interested because it's unexpected.

3. LIKABILITY

Are you someone your listeners would like to know? When you interact with audience members before, during, and after speaking, are you friendly, warm, and considerate? If so, you are demonstrating the qualities of **likability**. Think about how likability affects your everyday life. If people show you kindness when you are facing a serious problem, or if they do small favors to show they care about you, don't you feel gratitude and fondness for them? Don't you listen to them more attentively and care about what they say, think, and feel? A similar dynamic applies when audiences perceive a speaker to be likable.

If you are extroverted and speak conversationally and confidently, you will probably come across as a likable speaker. If you are shy or introverted, you might enhance your likability by demonstrating your empathy, kindness, and concern for others in a manner that feels natural to you. Likability is not about changing your personality; it's about being **AUDIENCE CENTERED ▲ (88–89)** in a manner that is true to who you are.

For an example of a self-described introvert who is a likable and successful speaker, see Notable Speaker: Susan Cain, page 205.

There are several ways for a speaker to enhance their likability—but keep in mind that you don't have control over the biases that may be held by audience members. Think, for example, about women who have run for high-profile political offices. Some voters did not like them even though they were well qualified and highly competent. These voters unfairly judged assertive and confident women as violating stereotypical expectations about how women should behave. Unfortunately, it can be uniquely challenging for women to come across as both competent *and* likable to some audiences. Women may be expected to communicate warmth, empathy, humor, sociability, and sensitivity to be seen as likable and, at the same time, must demonstrate their strength of character and expertise—a tall order for any speaker.

What follows are strategies that can help enhance your likability—but only if you feel comfortable and confident using them.

Ask Questions Posing appropriate, friendly **QUESTIONS TO YOUR AUDIENCE ⁚ (343–44)** can be a powerful way to enhance your likability.[3] When you ask a good, relevant question, you communicate that you are interested in what they know, believe, and care about. Good questions—for example, "Now that you have heard my story, how many of you have been in a similar situation?"—demonstrate respect for the audience and a sincere desire to listen to and adapt to their answers. And questions need not be serious or even planned. Here's a playful example: if you hear some applause when you mention having lived in Ann Arbor, ask for a show of hands of members who lived or went to college in Michigan and then say, "Go Blue!" Then ask the rest of the audience to please forgive you for calling out your home team.

Project Friendliness and Openness Some speakers unintentionally allow their anxiety to overshadow their interactions with listeners. If you give audience members the impression that you are anxious or distant, you may diminish your overall credibility. Assuming the situation is appropriate, interact with audience members before, during, and after your presentation. Being genuine and authentic is the hallmark of likability. Smile (if appropriate), remember people's names, listen to their questions and concerns, maintain direct eye contact, thank the audience, and accept their compliments sincerely.[4] Most listeners will reflect this kind of positive energy right back at you.

Be Different A speaker who goes against the grain can make listeners want to learn more. Do you speak a different language at home and at school? Were you the only one in your high school class to play the tuba? What was that like? Have you abandoned using social media? Tell the audience why, without making them feel guilty about being active on social media. Whatever makes you different from others, consider making that difference a part of your presentation. Doing so increases the chances that your listeners will perceive you as someone they want to know better.

Tell a Story about Overcoming Adversity Just about everyone loves to root for the underdog. **TELLING A STORY ∴ (323–32)** about a serious setback that you've faced—a chronic illness, discrimination, job loss, failure at school, the death of someone close to you—can, if it is relevant to your message, greatly increase your audience's sympathy for and interest in you. If a story of adversity in your own life isn't quite right for the occasion, telling another person's story can both arouse audience sympathy for that person and cause them to see you as more compassionate and likable.

Respect Those Who Disagree Make it clear that you can be respectful and empathetic, even if you disagree with another person's views on a certain issue. If you show your listeners that you share many of the same opinions, values, and/or behaviors, even as you stake out your own claims—they may like you all the more for it. Barack Obama, after winning his second presidential term in 2012, said this about his opponent, Mitt Romney:[5]

> We may have battled fiercely, but it's only because we love this country deeply and we care so strongly about its future. From George to Lenore to their son Mitt, the Romney family has chosen to give back to America through public service and that is the legacy that we honor and applaud tonight. In the weeks ahead, I also look forward to sitting down with Governor Romney to talk about where we can work together to move this country forward.

For an example of a speaker who exemplifies most of these principles of likability, see Notable Speaker: Ron Finley, page 458.

If you want to be seen as likable in the eyes of your audience, don't fake concern or empathy if you don't feel it yourself. They will know. While the aforementioned strategies can help shape your audience's opinion of you, they can only do so if they are genuine. If you playact likability, your efforts will probably fail.

4. DYNAMISM

Great speakers are usually dynamic speakers. **Dynamism** is the ability to motivate and engage audiences with a high level of energy, enthusiasm, vigor, and commitment. It can arouse listeners' emotions and inspire them. Put another way, dynamism is the transfer of your enthusiasm and motivation to your audience.

Dynamism often has more to do with how you deliver a presentation than what you say; following advice to improve and practice your DELIVERY ▶ (209–301) can in turn boost your dynamism. But dynamism alone without competence, trustworthiness, and likability can actually reduce your credibility as a speaker. Speaking with too much energy and intensity can frighten or exhaust your audience, who may then question your motives. Instead of overdoing it, work toward using a strong, expressive voice and natural gestures to be a more dynamic speaker, and as a result, more credible in the eyes of your audience.

Restoring Speaker Credibility

A high level of speaker credibility is the gold medal of speechmaking. If your audience judges you as a credible speaker, they'll appreciate, respect, and like you. They'll also trust and listen to what you say. But any speaker can lose or damage their credibility if they exploit their audience's trust and fail to follow the standards of **ETHICAL COMMUNICATION ● (44–48)**.

You may have heard of Elizabeth Holmes, an American entrepreneur, inventor, and celebrity. Holmes relied on her background and perceived credibility to become a self-made billionaire—the youngest woman in the world to do so. After founding a blood-testing company, Theranos, at the age of 19, Holmes convinced wealthy investors and reporters that her company would reduce inefficiencies in our health care system, potentially saving lives and dollars on a massive scale.

Although Theranos sounded too good to be true, people believed Holmes because she seemed to be competent, trustworthy, likable, and dynamic. She had a great life story to tell. Although her presentations lacked specifics and clear descriptions, she used lofty language, imprecise scientific information, and elegant delivery to convince her audiences. But she soon lost all credibility when investors, law enforcement, and the public learned that her statements were exaggerated. "Everything about Theranos—from its promise for a healthier future in which all people could easily access their health information to Holmes's low-pitch voice—turned out to be a lie."[6] She had persuaded huge audiences with false claims and was sentenced to more than 11 years in prison for investor fraud.

Most speakers who lack or lose credibility won't go to prison. But once an audience decides that you are not competent, trustworthy, or likable (even if you continue be dynamic), you have squandered your influence and reputation as a

Elizabeth Holmes was a highly credible and skilled persuasive speaker whose message was "too good to be true."

speaker. Quite simply, you won't be able to inform, persuade, entertain, or inspire an audience that doesn't believe you—if they listen at all. Once you've established credibility, you must also maintain it—and try to restore it if damaged.

MAINTAINING CREDIBILITY

Most of this chapter focuses on why and how to establish and enhance your credibility. But just because one audience perceives you as credible doesn't mean the next audience will do so. On a different occasion in front of a different audience—even with a similar presentation—you may need to use different strategies and skills for establishing and maintaining your credibility. For one audience, you may need to emphasize your experience and include the most current supporting material. For another, you may need to be friendly, kind, empathetic, and sociable.

Think of credibility as a physical skill. Tennis pros continue to practice under the critical eyes of a coach. Concert pianists practice the pieces they perform until the technique becomes instinctive. And credible speakers thoroughly prepare and constantly scan their audiences for signs that they are interested, engaged, and approving, or skeptical, annoyed, and scornful. Once you've been granted credibility by your audience, don't stop practicing the strategies and skills that will support it in every rhetorical situation.

RESTORING CREDIBILITY

Even highly successful speakers who strive to be ethical and credible make mistakes or misread an audience and, as a result, lose credibility. Although you cannot change what happened, you can develop plans to ensure it doesn't happen again. If you find yourself in a similar situation, consider the following strategies:[7]

- *Analyze what happened.* Did you misread audience characteristics and attitudes? Were you unprepared in terms of what you said and how you said it? Was your information dated or biased? Did you mistakenly assume the audience would believe you given your background and experiences? Did you say something offensive or disturbing? Determining why you lost credibility is the first step in restoring it.

- *Acknowledge your errors.* Don't blame the audience, deny a genuine error, or pretend it didn't occur. If possible, admit you made a mistake and apologize for it. If appropriate, explain what happened, why it happened, how you feel about it, and what you will do to prevent it from happening again.

- *Reinforce your credibility in all four dimensions.* Competence: Remind the audience of your credentials and expertise. Trustworthiness: Share examples of your honesty, integrity, and reliability. Likability: Express empathy and concern for the audience's unease. Dynamism: Practice what you'll say and how you'll say it.

- *Project a positive attitude.* Don't panic or go into hiding. Be composed, calm, steady, and accessible.

Depending on the situation, "restoring credibility requires patience and persistence," but "a loss of credibility doesn't have to be a permanent condition."[8] Instead, it can be an important lesson that emphasizes the value and benefits of putting the audience first if you wish to reestablish speaker credibility and achieve your purpose.

Keep in mind that you may not always know why a presentation didn't go as well as you thought it would. It may have nothing to do with your credibility. Even those of us who are experienced speakers find that we sometimes "click" with an audience but other times we don't. Sometimes we expect to hear cheers when we conclude but instead receive only polite applause. Our recommendation is that after every presentation, return to the six elements of the **RHETORICAL SITUATION** ● **(6–11)** and analyze how well you considered each one. There is always something to learn after you've spoken.

Conclusion

Effective speakers who make a genuine connection with audience members are guided by several core values and qualities. They have an accurate assessment of who they are, a genuine commitment to share what they think and know with an audience, and a belief that their messages matter. They also have a strong commitment to communicate openly, responsibly, and ethically.

Guided by core values, effective speakers also know that their credibility depends on audience perceptions of the four main dimensions of credibility: competence, trustworthiness, likability, and dynamism. The strategies and skills described in this chapter can enhance the extent to which audience members believe, trust, like, and appreciate you and your message. And even if your credibility dims or is damaged, it is not a time to hide, blame, or give up. Instead, it's time to analyze what happened and embark on a plan to restore it. With responsible planning and practice, you can shape people's perceptions of your credibility in a way that accurately and positively reflects who you are.

NOTABLE SPEAKER
Meghan Markle

Before becoming the Duchess of Sussex when she married England's Prince Harry, Meghan Markle was an actress and humanitarian. She became a UN Women's Advocate for Women's Political Participation and Leadership in 2015. In this role, Markle focused on ways to empower women throughout the world to become leaders in their communities. In her speech at the UN Women's Conference in 2015, she encouraged the world community to embrace equality for women.

Search Terms

To locate a video of this presentation online, enter the following key words into a search engine: Meghan Markle UN speech. The video is approximately 9:41 in length.

What to Watch For

[0:00–0:50] At the beginning of her speech, Markle conveys her appreciation for the opportunity to serve in the role of UN Women's Advocate for Women's Political Participation and Leadership. Her nonverbal communication conveys warmth, particularly as she touches her heart to express gratitude for the invitation to speak. She then offers an honest awareness of who she is by telling the audience, "I am proud to be a woman and a feminist."

[1:15–4:45] Markle tells a story about seeing a commercial when she was in elementary school that promoted dishwashing soap only to women. She recalls feeling "shocked," "angry," and "hurt" when two of her male classmates responded to the commercial by saying that women "belong in the kitchen." She uses the story to make a point about what it means to stand up for equality. Markle's use of a personal story highlights her experience and helps establish her competence, trustworthiness, and likability.

[3:35–3:45] To further enhance her likability, Markle smiles frequently and appropriately, uses a sincere tone of voice, and maintains eye contact even though she is using a teleprompter. Markle continues to engage the audience and show how deeply she cares about the participation of women in their communities and government.

[5:45–6:35] To establish her competence beyond her own personal experience, Markle cites statistics about gender inequality and the slow rise of female parliamentarians around the world. Doing so, she demonstrates that she has researched and thought seriously about the subject matter. By offering a heartfelt and directed "Come on!" in reaction to the statistics and examples, Markle demonstrates her belief that what she is speaking about matters.

EXERCISE

After viewing Markle's speech, reflect on these questions:

1. Which core value(s) of an effective speaker does Markle demonstrate most effectively?

2. Would Markle have seemed less authentic if she hadn't told the story about her fight to get Procter & Gamble to change its marketing slogan?

3. To what extent does Markle's marriage to Prince Harry and their relationship to the royal family affect your reactions to this 2015 speech?

4. How does Markle demonstrate that she cares about this topic? How does she demonstrate empathy throughout the speech?

5. Is Markle a dynamic speaker? Why or why not?

6. Before hearing her speak, what was your perception of Markle's credibility regarding women's rights? Did it change after hearing the speech? If so, why?

2.3 Audience

Just as every occasion and every speaker is unique, so too is every audience. Some audience members will find your message fascinating and valuable. And if you are highly in tune with your audience, listeners who don't have high expectations about you or your message may become more engaged and appreciative as they listen. Every audience has different characteristics and attitudes, and every accomplished speaker knows how to adapt to those differences. So can you. That's what this chapter is all about.

Audience-Centered Speaking

Presentations are more likely to succeed when you, the speaker, connect with the people to whom you are speaking (your **audience**) in a meaningful way. If members of your audience become better informed about a topic, are moved by what you said, or are persuaded to modify their behavior, it's probably because you effectively analyzed and adapted to your audience. **Audience-centered speakers** strive to understand audience characteristics, knowledge, interests, attitudes, and behavior and then adapt their presentations accordingly. They think critically about listeners' points of view and also understand and empathize with listeners' motivations and needs. This is true at every stage of the speechmaking process—from the moment you decide or are asked to speak, through the various stages of preparation and practice, and even while you deliver a presentation. How can you hope to persuade an audience member to eat less meat, for example, if you don't know how much meat they consume and their attitudes about their health, environmental consequences, and the treatment of animals? How can you help an audience celebrate if you don't know what they value? Or persuade audience members if you don't know their backgrounds and beliefs about your topic?

In this chapter, we show you how to become an audience-centered speaker. In other words, someone who spends considerable time and effort learning about their audience: who they are, what they know, what they care about, and how they behave. Let's begin with three universal recommendations that form the basis of this chapter:

- *Seek common ground.* Look for and rely on **common ground**—the knowledge, attitudes, values, beliefs, and behaviors you share with audience members. Finding and standing on common ground with your audience builds rapport and establishes trust. Ask yourself, "How can I identify and appeal to the things my audience and I have in common?"

- *Respect differences.* Identify and consider how you and your audience differ. **LISTEN WITH CIVILITY ● (35–37)** to your audience and respect diverse viewpoints. Think of differences of opinion as a way to learn about, adapt to, and build bridges between you and your audience. Ask yourself, "Is my presentation inclusive and respectful of my audience's diverse viewpoints and backgrounds?"

- *Be mindful of and responsive to feedback.* Be fully present when you're speaking—aware of where you are, what you're saying, who you're saying it to, and how they receive it. In other words, be *mindful.* Listen to your audience before, during, and after your presentation. Ask yourself, "Am I focused more on the audience and less on myself?"

Audience Analysis

Being an audience-centered speaker requires **audience analysis**—the work you do to understand, respect, and adapt to listeners before and during a presentation. This kind of research will help you plan what to say and how to say it to achieve your purpose. It can also bolster your confidence when you finally address your audience because, in a way, you're already familiar with them. And if audience members sense that you have planned your presentation for them specifically, they'll be much more likely to care about and connect with you and your message.

Adapting to your audience doesn't mean meeting and adapting to every person in an audience. If you try to please everyone all the time, you'll probably please no one (including yourself). Instead, audience analysis can help you direct your message toward a significant portion of your listeners or to key decision makers and people with influence—in other words, to your **target audience**. Inevitably, some audience members will be spectators. Although these audience members may be less interested or less motivated than your target audience and if you plan and prepare your presentation well, you can successfully connect with your target audience without losing the rest of your listeners.

Ask and answer the following questions to learn more about your audience:

- Who are they?
- Why are they here?
- What do they know?
- What are their interests?
- What are their attitudes?
- What are their values?

As you begin thinking about your audience, you'll discover that many of these questions can be answered immediately or easily—especially if you're speaking to classmates, family, or coworkers you already know or see regularly. In other cases, you may have to devote more time to learning about your audience. We'll provide strategies for finding this information further in this chapter. But first, let's explore how answering each question

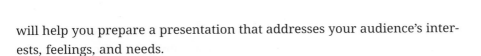

will help you prepare a presentation that addresses your audience's interests, feelings, and needs.

WHO ARE THEY?

The first question may seem an obvious one: Who will be in the audience? You don't need to know their names. Instead, look for **demographic information** about your listeners. This includes information about their occupations, places and types of residence, income, educational levels, political perspectives, organizational affiliations, social standing, and other unifying factors that may be more relevant to your presentation than demographic characteristics such as race, age, gender, ethnicity, nationality, religion, and citizen status.

Consider the demographic characteristics that bind members of your audience together. Are most of them young adults? Do most of them have roommates or children? Are they an audience of accountants, Lyft drivers, students, or marketing managers? Are they all taking the same class? Do they own or manage local businesses? Do they work together? Were they all alive at a time when an important historic or political event occurred?

Knowing these shared characteristics will help you prepare and deliver a presentation that resonates with the people in your audience. For example, if you're asked to speak about financial planning, the advice you give to a religious youth group will be different from advice to retirees at a monthly luncheon. Depending on whether your audience is British or American will impact how you use the term *football* in a sports-related presentation.

In some cases, the people in your audience may share a single demographic characteristic that isn't particularly relevant to your presentation. If you're commemorating an exceptional athlete at an end-of-season banquet for the women's basketball team, maybe the gender of your audience isn't the most relevant factor. What about the sport that they all play? Or the fact that they are all student athletes? Or that their parents are attending? These other characteristics of your audience may play a bigger role in shaping your presentation than their gender does.

As valuable as demographic information can be, it's important to recognize that every audience is made up of individuals with unique characteristics, motivations, values, and backgrounds. Avoid a "one size fits all" picture of your audience. You may see obvious surface similarities among them—such as their age, race, gender, and even appearance and style of dress—but if you stop there and fail to ask other questions, you will risk **stereotyping** your audience, which may lead to mistaken conclusions about their knowledge, attitude, beliefs, and values.

WHY ARE THEY HERE?

As much as you may want your audience to be there because they are interested in you and your presentation, this is not always the case. Determining why they're attending can help you meet your audience where *they* are rather than where *you* are.

Consider the following reasons for attending a presentation:

Reason for attending	Example
They are interested in the topic.	People who attend a presentation about their hobby
They are interested in the speaker.	Fans of a political candidate, comedian, author, or other public figure
They will be rewarded for attending.	Students who will receive extra credit for attending a guest lecture
They always attend.	Members of a campus club that meets regularly
They are required to attend.	Volunteers attending a mandatory training session

Each reason for attending presents a special challenge for a speaker. For example, a highly interested and well-informed audience demands a knowledgeable, well-prepared, competent speaker. On the other hand, an audience that is required or reluctant to attend a presentation may be pleasantly surprised by a dynamic speaker who makes a special effort to capture and maintain their interest.

WHAT DO THEY KNOW?

Figuring out what audience members know about your topic will help you match your presentation to your audience's level of understanding.

How much background material should you cover? Will they understand specific, topic-related terminology, or do you need to define essential vocabulary? For example, a speaker who worked on a cruise ship probably shouldn't use words such as *stern*, *aft*, *starboard*, *port*, *knots*, and *tenders* to classmates without explaining what these specialized terms mean. At the same time, if your content is too basic for a knowledgeable audience, they may become bored or question the value of your presentation. You wouldn't, for example, define a term like *meiosis* to an audience of biologists.

WHAT ARE THEIR INTERESTS?

Considering why your audience is attending your presentation and what they already know can help you gauge their interests. There are two types of audience interests: **self-centered interests** and **topic-centered interests**.

Self-Centered Interests Self-centered interests are focused on personal gain or loss. For example, a political candidate's position on tax increases can result in more or fewer taxes for audience members. A talk by a personnel director can provide information about how to get a more desirable job. A presentation by a classmate about how to change a tire may help every student who drives a car. In all these cases, the listener stands to lose or gain something as a result of the presentation or its outcome.

WIIFT ("WIIF-it") is a popular acronym used in sales training that stands for the question "What's in it for them?" It's a way of reminding salespeople to focus on customer characteristics, needs, interests, attitudes, and values rather than on WIIFM ("What's in it for me?"). Every speaker should also ask WIIFT. Why should this audience listen to you? What do they want? What do you have to offer them? If your audience sees no reason to listen, they won't.

Topic-Centered Interests Audience members also have topic-centered interests—subjects they enjoy hearing and learning about. Topic-centered interests can include hobbies, favorite sports or pastimes, or subjects loaded with intrigue and mystery. However, topic-centered interests often tend to be personal. A detailed description of the 1862 Battle of Pea Ridge may captivate Civil War buffs in the audience, but not other listeners. A presentation about the various characters in the Marvel Cinematic Universe may intrigue fans of superhero movies but may not interest those who prefer romantic comedies.

WHAT ARE THEIR ATTITUDES?

When you think about **audience attitudes**, try to determine whether the people in your audience agree or disagree with your position, how strongly they agree or disagree, and what you can do to influence their opinions and/or behavior.

Chapter 7.3
RHETORICAL STRATEGIES FOR PERSUASIVE PRESENTATIONS ◆ provides strategies for adapting to three basic audience attitudes.

There can be as many opinions in your audience as there are people. Some audience members will already agree with you before you begin to speak. Others will disagree no matter what you say. Some audience members will be indecisive or have no opinion. But if you've already thought about other aspects of your audience—who they are, what they know, and what their interests are—you may be able to predict what attitudes many audience members will bring with them to your presentation.

Suppose a speaker wants to persuade an audience that imposing longer jail sentences will benefit society. Consider the following spectrum of audience opinions:

AUDIENCE ATTITUDES: "LONGER JAIL SENTENCES WILL BENEFIT SOCIETY."				
Strongly agree	**Agree**	**Undecided**	**Disagree**	**Strongly disagree**
If people know they face longer jail sentences, they won't commit as many crimes.	Longer jail sentences may prevent some repeat offenders from committing crimes.	There are good reasons on both sides of the issue. *or* I don't care.	Longer jail sentences will unfairly impact poor defendants who can't afford good legal representation.	Longer jail sentences do not deter crime; they only create more-dangerous criminals.

Once you determine if audience members share the same attitude about an issue, you'll need to consider the many different reasons for that shared opinion before you start formulating **PERSUASIVE STRATEGIES ◆ (437–57)**. For example, audience members who oppose longer jail sentences may do so for various reasons. They may believe that jails are too crowded or inflict unnecessarily abuse. Or they might think rehabilitation is more important than punishment. When analyzing your audience's attitudes, think critically about *why* various audience members may have similar attitudes for different reasons.

WHAT ARE THEIR VALUES?

Values are the basic standards that guide and motivate our beliefs and actions. When analyzing an audience's values, consider the ideas and ideals that are fundamental to their lives—the principles that provide the foundation for everything they feel and do.

Universal Values We can safely assume that some values are universal: love, honesty, responsibility, respect, fairness, freedom, and compassion. An appeal to **universal values** will be welcomed by most audiences, no matter who they are or where they come from. The challenge is identifying the primary values of audience members and adapting your presentation to appeal to those values—without, of course, sacrificing your own.

Cultural Values Many values are particular to a cultural or organizational context. For example, the first principle in the Society of Professional Journalists' Code of Ethics is "Seek truth and report it." The motto of the US Marine Corps, *semper fidelis*, means being forever faithful and loyal to their country and to the corps. Although both groups may equally value truth and loyalty, you can probably see how speaking to an audience of journalists might be quite different from speaking to an audience of marines on a similar topic.

Researchers have investigated whether there are unique values that characterize a culture, which can be described and compared to other cultures.[1] One such value is the degree of individualism or collectivism

common to most members of a culture. **Individualism-collectivism** is a spectrum, describing a culture's preference for its members' personal independence at one end to collective interdependence at the other end.

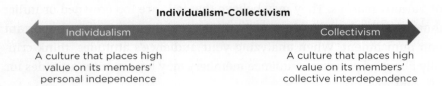

Individualism-Collectivism

Individualism — Collectivism

A culture that places high value on its members' personal independence

A culture that places high value on its members' collective interdependence

Many people in highly individualistic cultures (the United States, Australia, Great Britain, and Canada, for example) value personal achievement, autonomy, and freedom. People in collectivistic cultures (many Latin American and Asian countries, for example) are more likely to value group identity, group harmony, and collective action. These are broad cultural values, and their degree of importance can vary within cultures.

In general, audience members who value individualism may look for ways that a speaker's message can satisfy their personal needs, and they will be more responsive to speakers with an individualistic and confident speaking style. Those who lean more toward collectivist values will consider the ways that a speaker's messages may benefit their group, community, or nation, and they may be put off by speakers who talk about their own accomplishments and the benefits of competition and personal success. For example, audiences from collectivistic cultures are likely to think differently about being asked to wear a mask during a pandemic than audiences from individualistic cultures. Thinking critically about your audience's cultural orientation on this scale and being alert to the possibility of other audience members tilting in the opposite direction can help you make smart, audience-centered decisions as you plan your presentation.

Gathering Audience Information

Now that we've covered *what* to learn about your audience, we turn to *how* to do it. Before we go into more detail about the two most common ways to gather information about your audience—interviews and surveys—here are a variety of ways you can learn about your listeners:

- *Make a list of what you already know.* Do you have previous experience with this audience? What has an organizer told you?

- *Look online.* If you're speaking to a club, company, class, or other organization, look online for more information about them. Do they have a website with an "About" page that lists their mission, motto, or members? Is the organization on social media? Look for how the organization describes itself—rather than what outsiders say about them.

- *Revisit the occasion.* Is there an event related to your speaking occasion that will tell you more about who's attending? Is there publicity material or an invitation that can tell you more about the target audience?

- *Conduct an interview.* Try to speak with the organizer or the person who's asked you to speak. If you're speaking to an audience you know, try to meet one or several audience members ahead of time.

- *Conduct a survey.* In many speaking situations, you won't have access or permission to survey your audience beforehand. If you've used these methods to learn about your audience, you may not need to. But in some instances, like in a communication course, you might conduct a survey to learn about your audience's attitudes toward your topic.

INTERVIEWS

Before speaking, a private conversation with one or more audience members can provide valuable information to help you adapt your presentation to audience characteristics, needs, and attitudes. You might also interview the person who invited or assigned you to speak; they may know the audience better than you do. When conducting an interview, emphasize that your goal is to learn as much as you can in order to address *their* interests and needs.

Begin by asking general questions:

- What should I know about this audience?

- Do you think they'll be attentive and interested in my topic? Why or why not?

- What issues will be important to them?
- What are the demographics of the audience—not just age, gender, and race but also culture, work experience, educational level, and so on?

Listen for characteristics you may have in common with audience members. And remember that what you learn from a handful of interviews may not be representative of the audience as a whole. Some of the people you interview may be unwilling to give you honest answers—or they may give you the answers they think you want to hear. To minimize this response bias, avoid asking leading questions and keep the interview as brief as possible.

AUDIENCE SURVEYS

A **survey** is a research method that uses a series of questions to get useful information and insights about the characteristics, knowledge, attitudes, beliefs, and behaviors of a predetermined group of people. Corporations and politicians rely on surveys and polls to develop products, design ads, and craft public addresses. And some speakers use them to adapt a presentation to an audience.

A useful survey—with relevant questions—can provide information that will help you appreciate similarities and differences between your audience members—and between yourself and your audience.

Selecting Effective Question Types There are two general types of survey questions: open-ended questions and close-ended questions. Most surveys use both types of questions.

    Open-ended questions invite respondents to provide detailed answers by using probing words, such as *what* and *why*:

- If you have never donated blood, please give three reasons *why* you haven't.
- Explain *why* you signed up for this class.
- *What* are two characteristics you like most about your favorite professor?
- *What* social media platforms do you use most frequently?

Answers to open-ended questions are very valuable, but require more time and effort to answer. You can ask open-ended questions near the end of a questionnaire, so respondents have had time to think about the topic or ask them early so respondents aren't influenced by previous survey questions.

Close-ended questions force respondents to choose an answer from a limited list, such as multiple choice, ratings, or rank-ordering questions. These provide the clearest results and are the most common kinds of close-ended questions used in academic, marketing, and political research.

COMMON QUESTION TYPES FOR EFFECTIVE SURVEYS

Question type	Purpose	Example
Multiple-choice questions	Identifying measurable audience opinions, experiences, or attitudes in questions for which respondents select one single answer	What factor concerns you the most regarding the costs of higher education? a. Tuition fees b. Living expenses c. Textbooks and lab fees d. Transferring credits
Rating questions	Identifying an audience's level of agreement or disagreement with a series of statements, or the value they place on a series of items	On a scale of 5 (extremely important) to 1 (not at all important), rate the importance of each item in becoming an effective speaker. ____ Organizing a presentation ____ Memorizing a presentation ____ Adapting to an audience ____ Using presentation aids
Rank-ordering questions	Identifying the preferred order for multiple options in a list	Which fast-food chain provides the best customer service? Order them from best (1) to worst (4). ____ McDonald's ____ Burger King ____ Chick-fil-A ____ Five Guys

Writing Relevant Questions When drafting questions, always start with your PURPOSE ▲ (109–18). What is your goal, and what do you need to know about your audience in order to achieve it? Once you know the kinds of information you hope to gather, make sure your questions are specific and phrased to produce useful responses.

✗ **TOO GENERAL:**	Why do you support Robin Brown for mayor?
✓ **SPECIFIC:**	List three reasons that you believe make Robin Brown the best candidate for mayor.

A general question can give you a useless answer, such as "Because she is the best candidate" or "I dislike the other candidate." Asking respondents to list reasons why Robin Brown is the best (or worst) candidate will generate specific information you can use to improve your presentation.

✗ **TOO GENERAL:**	Do you exercise regularly? Yes____ No____
✓ **SPECIFIC:**	How often do you exercise for more than 20 uninterrupted minutes? _____ Rarely or never _____ Once or twice a month _____ Once or more a week _____ Daily

Even multiple-choice questions can be too general. For example, the question in the above left column does not specify what *regularly* means. Instead, write specific answer choices so the respondent can be specific with their answer.

Once you have written specific and useful questions, review each one to make sure your survey is *fair, neutral,* and *brief*:

1. *Fair.* Your questions should be just, honest, and accurate. Avoid yes/no questions, which can force respondents into a false choice.

✗ **UNFAIR:**	Are you against gun control?
✓ **FAIR:**	On a scale of 5 (extremely supportive) to 1 (not at all supportive), rate your support for gun control.

2. ***Neutral.*** Your questions should be unbiased, impartial, and objective. Avoid *leading questions* that seek predetermined or self-serving responses.

> ✗ **NOT NEUTRAL:** Why should you oppose the socialist medical plan advocated by our Senator?
>
> ✓ **NEUTRAL:** In one to three sentences, briefly explain your thoughts about the medical plan advocated by our Senator.

3. ***Brief and simple.*** Your survey should take less than 15 minutes to answer and should avoid overly complicated questions. The longer the survey, fewer people will complete it—leaving only the most impassioned respondents represented.

> ✗ **COMPLICATED:** List ten problems with the US Constitution and give an example or explanation to illustrate why you've listed each one.
>
> ✓ **BRIEF AND SIMPLE:** Rank the following six proposed changes to the US Constitution from most to least important.

Administering Your Survey Once you have prepared a set of good questions, distribute your survey and collect your responses. Make sure you leave yourself enough time to analyze the results so you can adapt your presentation accordingly.

1. ***Create a professional-looking questionnaire.*** Format your survey consistently so it is easy to read and includes a clear set of instructions.

2. ***Pretest your survey.*** Survey companies often pretest questions to find out if respondents will interpret their meaning as intended. If you don't have access to a few potential audience members, test your questions on friends, family members, or coworkers, then revise your questions to ensure you'll get the kind of information you need.

3. *Select distribution method.* Online surveying tools such as SurveyMonkey or Google Forms make it easy to deliver your survey and analyze the results, but it can be challenging to make sure your audience opens and completes the survey. If you're speaking to a classroom or workplace audience, you can alternatively hand out and collect a paper survey before your presentation—and set aside time to calculate and analyze the results.

Adapting Your Message to Your Audience

Once you have collected useful information about your audience—using a variety of methods—consider how your findings will impact your presentation. As an example, let's look at how audience analysis helped a student speaker adjust and refine her plans for a persuasive presentation about the effects of video game violence for an assignment in a communication course. She formulated a preliminary goal, then after speaking with several classmates and analyzing what she knew about her audience, she changed her goal to one that she believed would be more applicable to and effective with her audience.

Topic
The effects of video game violence

Preliminary Purpose
To warn my audience about the effects of video game violence

Audience Analysis
Who are they? The audience is composed of 25 college students, most of whom are between 18–25 years old. About half of them have younger siblings or cousins; a few are the parents of young children.

Why are they here? They are in this class because it is a general education requirement. Some will be presenting during the same class period, so they may be more focused on their own presentations rather than on listening to me.

What do they know? They have heard concerns about television and video game violence but may not be aware of the respected studies claiming that children are more likely to become aggressive and antisocial from such exposure.

What are their interests? All of them have played video games, and half play video games frequently (at least once a day). Most are interested in nonviolent games; some play violent games.

What are their attitudes? Some do not believe that video game violence is a major problem. The rest have strong opinions one way or the other: some believe that mediated violence is very harmful; others worry that controlling video game content would eliminate entertainment they enjoy. Those with children or younger siblings are more concerned about developmental effects of violent games.

What are their values? Most class members who are not currently parents say that they plan to raise families someday. A few already are parents. Everyone agrees that children should be protected from things that can harm them.

Revised Purpose

To urge listeners to adopt specific measures that significantly reduce children's exposure to violent video games, which research shows makes them more aggressive and antisocial

Notice the changes in the revised purpose. Rather than discussing the general effects of video game violence, she focused on how it makes children more aggressive and antisocial. She also decided to use strong validated studies to support her claims and recommendations.

Audience analysis and adaptation doesn't stop once you've settled on the **CONTENT** ■ **(123–207)** of your presentation or the **FORM OF DELIVERY** ▶ **(214–17)** you'll use. As you prepare for and practice your presentation, you may discover that you need more and better information about your audience. And, of course, adapting to your audience is just as important when you speak as it is when you are preparing.

MIDPRESENTATION ADAPTATIONS

Regardless of whether you are speaking to an audience you know well or are talking to an audience you've never met, you may want to ask the audience questions to analyze their reactions and modify your message as you speak. This is particularly true if your audience or their reactions are not what you expected.

For example, if an audience of developers unexpectedly bring their spouses to your product launch presentation how would you acknowledge and adapt to them? You might ask for a show of hands to identify if the spouses are unfamiliar with the new product—or if they've already used it! Unexpected attendees can end up being an asset in your presentation, but only if you ask. If your audience members seem restless, bored, or hostile, how can you adjust to that negative feedback? If they are fully engaged and attentive, can you take advantage of their enthusiasm and more fully connect with *their* expectations?

Here's a famous example of midpresentation adaptation in a speech that many people assume was fully prepared in advance. Martin Luther King Jr. was delivering what is now called the "I Have a Dream" speech. As he spoke, the audience was attentive, but not fully engaged or inspired. Then, the great gospel singer Mahalia Jackson (who often accompanied King at rallies and had heard many of his sermons) changed the course of his address. Jackson cried out, "Tell them about the dream, Martin! Tell them about the dream!" King then began speaking about "the dream" he'd described in previous speeches and sermons. His body language transformed from lecturer to preacher. Clarence B. Jones, one of King's advisers and speechwriters, recalled what happened after Jackson's callout: "I have never seen him speak the way I saw him on that day. It was as if some cosmic transcendental

Midpresentation adaptations have come to define some of the most famous speeches in history.

force came down and occupied his body. It was the same body, the same voice, but the voice had something I had never heard before."[2]

Like Martin Luther King Jr. did in this example, you should pay attention to audience reactions, like questions, restlessness, or facial expressions. By observing audience reactions as you speak, you can modify—substantially or modestly—what you're saying in ways that help you achieve your purpose. If your audience seems to be losing interest, try to listen and adapt. How you respond and modify your presentation accordingly is the difference between getting out what *you* want to say and truly connecting with audience needs, interests, and concerns. It is the difference between making a speech and achieving your purpose.

Conclusion

The presence of a living, breathing audience makes speaking different from most other forms of communication. Audiences make presentations unpredictable and potentially anxiety producing—and also one of the most personal, exciting, and empowering ways to communicate.

Audience-centered speakers have a good sense of who their audience is, how audience members think, what they value, what they want, and what they need. The time and energy you spend learning as much as you can about your audience, analyzing what you've learned, and then adapting your presentation accordingly is the heart of speechmaking. Your analysis helps you find common ground, respect differences, and appropriately adapt to feedback. And it's essential for achieving your purpose.

Zach Wahls

In 2011, the Iowa House Judiciary Committee conducted public hearings about a proposed constitutional amendment to ban gay marriage in the state. Zach Wahls, then a 19-year-old college student and the son of lesbian parents, spoke against the amendment during a public hearing before the committee. His presentation went viral and attracted national media attention. As a result of his speech, he was invited to speak to a variety of groups and eventually wrote a best-selling book, *My Two Moms*. A prominent LGBTQ activist, his advocacy work includes cofounding and leading Scouts for Equality, which campaigned for ending discrimination against LGBTQ people in Boy Scouts of America. He delivered a prime-time speech at the Democratic National Convention in 2012 and was elected to the Iowa Senate in 2018, then reelected in 2022.

Search Terms

To locate a video of this presentation online, enter the following key words into a search engine: Zach Wahls speaks about family. The video is approximately 3:00 in length.

What to Watch For

[0:00–0:10] In his opening, Wahls seeks common ground with his audience by telling them, "I'm a sixth-generation Iowan and an engineering student at the University of Iowa." In essence, he is one of them—he comes from the same place that they come from and attends a university that some of them likely attended. After establishing that he is an Iowan, Wahls reveals a unique fact about himself: he "was raised by two women."

[0:40–1:09] As a mindful speaker, Wahls doesn't ask for special treatment. He is asking to be understood. He emphasizes the normal, everyday values of his lesbian parents by highlighting things that they and his audience share in common, such as experiencing joy about a baby being born (love), spending time with family on vacations (relationships), and standing by family during difficult times (commitment). Based on these shared values, Wahls argues that his family is like any other family because they don't expect other people to solve their problems. What they do expect is to be treated fairly by their government.

[1:10–1:39] Wahls confronts his topic head-on by posing a question that was asked by his classmates and professors at times in some of his classes: Can gay people even raise kids? In response, he highlights how well he has done as a child of same-sex parents. He mentions his various achievements not to elevate himself but instead to demonstrate the good job that his parents did raising him. He again seeks to establish common ground by noting that the committee chairman would likely be proud of Wahls if Wahls were his son.

[1:40–1:50] Aware that many in the room have no firsthand knowledge about same-sex parenting, Wahls notes that no one has ever independently recognized that he was raised by a gay couple. Returning to common ground, he points out that neither his family nor the committee members' families "derive [their] sense of worth from being told by the state: 'You're married. Congratulations.'"

[2:02–2:30] Offering one reason his audience should listen to him, Wahls argues that legislators have an opportunity not to write discrimination into the state's constitution. The benefit for his audience is establishing a precedent whereby all Iowans are treated equally—something that Wahls argues is relevant to everyone in the audience.

[2:50–3:00] The last line of his presentation is a summation of his purpose statement. Here he reminds his audience that his parents' sexual orientation is not related to the content of his character. This idea echoes a famous line from Martin Luther King Jr.'s most famous speech, "I Have a Dream," thus making clear that the issue of marriage equality is as fundamental and important as the civil rights struggles of the 1960s.

EXERCISE

After viewing Wahls's speech, reflect on these questions:

1. What do you think Wahls did before his presentation to prepare to speak to this particular audience?

2. Do you believe that members of his audience were likely to be persuaded by his argument that his family was no different from their families? Why or why not?

3. What else could Wahls have done, if anything, to establish common ground with his audience?

4. In analyzing his audience, how might Wahls have answered these questions: "Who is in this audience—legislators, staff, media, journalists, supporters, detractors?" and "What does my audience think about gay marriage and families?"

5. Write a purpose statement for Wahls's presentation.

2.4 Purpose

A BRIEF GUIDE TO THIS CHAPTER

- The power of purpose (p. 109)
- Determining your purpose (p. 110)
- Writing your purpose statement (p. 115)

Have you ever listened to a speaker who didn't seem to know or care why they were speaking? Did you lose interest, leave, or let your mind drift to your to-do list? Even if you were interested in the subject and the speaker was dynamic, you may have become indifferent, confused, and even irritated because the presentation lacked a clear *purpose.*

Ask yourself, "What do I want my audience to know, think, feel, or do as a result of my presentation?" Your **purpose** is the answer to that question— it is the outcome you seek as the result of making a presentation. Purpose is *not* the same your topic or the subject matter of your presentation. For a talk about recycling, for example, it's the difference between "I support the state's recycling laws to protect the environment" and "Recycling is costly and ineffective." Each purpose requires different approaches and content.

The Power of Purpose

When it comes to measuring your success as a speaker, nothing is more fundamental than determining your purpose. When clearly defined, your purpose is quite literally the standard against which your success as a speaker is measured. Speaking without a purpose can jeopardize your credibility and the outcome of your presentation. More important, defining a clear purpose will help you achieve something meaningful as a result of what you say.

Think of your purpose as a tool that lets you prepare more quickly and effectively for your presentation. A clear purpose will help you in the following ways:

- *It guides your rhetorical decisions.* Revisiting your purpose as you make strategic decisions about key elements of the **RHETORICAL SITUATION** ● **(6–11)** makes these decisions fall into place more easily.

- *It shows respect for your audience.* Having a distinct purpose and making that purpose clear to your audience demonstrates that you are an **AUDIENCE-CENTERED SPEAKER** ▲ **(88–89)**—someone who has their best interests in mind, who seeks to share something of value, and who can clearly communicate a meaningful message. If you don't demonstrate a clear purpose, your audience may feel that you're wasting their time.

- *It calms your nerves.* If you momentarily forget what you're saying because of noise, distractions, or symptoms of **SPEAKING ANXIETY** ● **(18–26)**, a well-defined purpose can remind you why you're speaking and help you get back on course.

- *It makes the best use of your time and energy.* There's only so much time to prepare for a presentation, and having a clear purpose from the start helps you manage your time more effectively. You can, for example, limit your research only to material that will directly support your purpose and focus on **ORGANIZATIONAL PATTERNS** ■ **(157–66)** best suited to your purpose.

Determining Your Purpose

So how do you determine what you want your audience to know, think, feel, or do as a result of your presentation? To make this determination, start by asking yourself *why* questions like:

- Why am *I* speaking?
- Why am I speaking *about this topic*?

- Why am I speaking *to this audience*?
- Why am I speaking *in this setting*?
- Why am I speaking *on this occasion*?

Consider this exchange between a student and a communication instructor:

STUDENT: I've been asked to give a talk to new students in our department.

INSTRUCTOR: Why have you been asked?

STUDENT: I've been very involved. Between classes and extracurricular activities, I practically live in the department!

INSTRUCTOR: Not to mention that you're a pretty good speaker. But why you? Why not a faculty member?

STUDENT: I know the kinds of questions students have. New students probably feel more comfortable asking me a question than they would asking a professor.

INSTRUCTOR: What will you talk about?

STUDENT: I don't want to talk about the official stuff! They can get that in the catalog and the department handbook.

INSTRUCTOR: So what are they going to learn from you that they can't get from the handbook?

STUDENT: I guess I can give new students the inside scoop—the unwritten rules, the unofficial tips.

INSTRUCTOR: Congratulations! There's your purpose. Can you think of a title that describes both your purpose and your topic?

STUDENT: How about "A Student's Unofficial Guide to Surviving the Communication Department"?

INSTRUCTOR: Good. That's a presentation they'll appreciate.

By continually asking yourself *why* you are speaking, you can focus on what you want to—and are best suited to—accomplish in your presentation.

When you ask yourself why you are speaking, you may start to think of some **private goals** that you want to achieve. For example, the student speaker just mentioned has a clear speaking purpose: to "give new students the inside scoop." But they may also want to impress faculty members or use the speaking opportunity as a way to meet new students.

While a presentation should have only one *purpose*, it may have several private *goals*. In a communication course, a speaker's private goals frequently relate to academic ambitions: getting a good grade, for example, or securing a future recommendation from their instructor. In a work setting, a speaker's private goals might include demonstrating professionalism, impressing colleagues, or getting a promotion. These private goals are not the same as the speaker's purpose.

If your private goals don't conflict with or undermine your public purpose, there is nothing wrong with using a speaking opportunity to achieve them. There *is* something wrong if pursuing these goals deceives your audience or contradicts your speaking purpose. Making sure your private goals align with your speaking purpose is an essential component of **ETHICAL COMMUNICATION** ● **(44–48)**.

GENERAL SPEAKING OBJECTIVES

Before you determine your overall speaking purpose, you should identify the **general objective** of your talk. There are four general speaking objectives:

- To inform
- To persuade
- To entertain
- To inspire

Most of the time, the rhetorical situation will determine your general objective and will help you make appropriate decisions about the content and delivery of your presentation. For example, a toast is usually inspiring.

A sales presentation is persuasive. And a presentation to introduce a speaker can be all four. Knowing your general objective will guide your initial decision making. If your audience expects to be entertained, for example, a detailed statistical analysis or a series of complex arguments will not amuse them.

Speaking to Inform An **informative presentation** seeks to report new information, clarify difficult terminology, explain complex phenomena, or overcome confusion and misunderstanding. Informative presentations tend to be noncontroversial and concentrate on sharing or explaining information. Here are some examples:

Part 6 **SPEAKING TO INFORM** ☀ provides detailed strategies for informative presentations.

- *Report new information:* The new plagiarism and AI policies on campus
- *Clarify difficult terms:* The differences between statistical validity and reliability
- *Explain a complex concept:* Unravelling string theory
- *Overcome confusion and misunderstanding:* Myths about gluten sensitivity

Speaking to Persuade A **persuasive presentation** strives to change people's attitudes (what they believe, think, or feel) or to change their behavior (what they do). Some persuasive presentations seek to strengthen or weaken an existing attitude toward an idea, person, object, or action; others are designed to change audience attitudes or behaviors altogether. Persuasive presentations occur in courtroom arguments, in religious services, in blood donation drives, around the dinner table, and in daily conversations. Here are a few examples of attitudes a persuasive speaker may seek to change:

Part 7 **SPEAKING TO PERSUADE** ◆ provides detailed strategies for persuasive presentations.

- *Idea:* The Electoral College is an unrepresentative process for electing a US president.
- *People:* Beyoncé is more talented than Jay-Z.
- *Object:* Electronic bicycles are dangerous vehicles.
- *Action:* Everyone should be an organ donor.

The main challenge of persuasive speaking is that human beings are generally reluctant to change their minds and behaviors and are slow to do so even when they're open to being persuaded.

Speaking to Entertain As the name implies, an **entertaining presentation** tries to amuse, interest, divert, or "warm up" an audience. An entertaining speech can ease audience tensions, capture and hold audience attention, defuse opposition, and stimulate action. Listeners remember effective humorous speakers positively, even when they aren't enthusiastic about a speaker's message. Here are some examples of entertaining speeches and their general purposes:

- *Stand-up comedy:* To make an audience laugh and perhaps provide social commentary
- *After-dinner speech:* To amuse audiences too full to move or absorb serious ideas
- *Retirement party roast:* To celebrate a coworker and to delight colleagues, friends, and family members

It requires a lot of work and critical thinking to give a speech of any kind, even more so when trying to USE HUMOR∴ (340–42) at the same time. More than almost any other type of presentation, you should PRACTICE DELIVERING ▶ (220–24) an entertainment speech with an audience of friends whom you can trust to be honest about what's working and what's not.

Part 8 **SPECIAL SPEAKING OCCASIONS** ★ provides brief guides to delivering some of the most common presentations to entertain and inspire.

Speaking to Inspire An **inspirational presentation** brings people together, creates social unity, builds goodwill, or arouses audience emotions. Inspirational speaking occurs in special contexts, takes many forms, and can tap a wide range of emotions. Here are some examples of inspirational presentations and their general purposes:

- *Toasts:* To invoke joy and/or admiration for a person or persons
- *Eulogies:* To honor the dead and comfort the grieving
- *Speaker introductions:* To introduce a speaker to an audience, creating interest in and enthusiasm for the speaker and their message

- *Award presentations:* To praise and explain the reasons an honoree is receiving a noteworthy award

Inspirational speaking also includes commencement addresses, sermons, dedications, and tributes, as well as accepting an award. The challenge of inspirational speaking is finding ways to appeal to audience emotions based on their characteristics, opinions, needs, and values.

Inform, Persuade, Entertain, *and* Inspire Regardless of the type of presentation you have been assigned or have chosen to make, there may be benefits to including components that inform, persuade, entertain, and inspire your listeners. For example, the primary purpose of a college professor's lecture usually is to *inform*. In order to inform, however, a good teacher also may try to *persuade* students that the information is valuable and relevant. Such persuasion can motivate students to listen and learn. The professor may also try to *entertain* students so that they will pay closer attention to an informative lecture. Highly skilled professors *inspire* their students to study, learn, and even choose a major or career in the discipline.

Writing Your Purpose Statement

Once you know why you're speaking and have a grasp of your general objective, you should write a **purpose statement** that, at least preliminarily, specifies the goal of your presentation. A well-written purpose statement is a reality check that ensures you can achieve your goal in a time-limited presentation to a particular audience. "My purpose is to tell my audience all about my job as a real estate agent" is too general and is probably an impossible goal to achieve in the amount of time you have to speak. Here's a better option: "My purpose is to increase audience awareness of two common strategies used by real estate agents to help first-time home buyers decide what type of home is best for them." In addition to specifying the goal of your presentation in one sentence, an effective purpose statement has three characteristics: it is *specific*, *achievable*, and *relevant*.

MAKE IT SPECIFIC

A general, vague, or confusing purpose statement won't help you prepare your presentation. Think of your purpose statement as the description of a destination. Telling a friend "Let's meet on campus" is too general and vague. "Let's meet at the coffee shop in the Student Center at 5:30 p.m. on Tuesday" is a clear and specific statement that will make sure that both of you end up in the same place at the same time. "Use the government's guidelines for reducing lead exposure from lead paint" is better than "Learn about the danger of lead paint." A specific purpose statement ensures that both you and your audience know where you're going.

MAKE IT ACHIEVABLE

A purpose statement should establish an achievable goal. Inexperienced speakers often make the mistake of trying to cover too much material or asking too much of their audience. A presentation is a time-limited event, and an audience can only absorb a limited amount of information during a single speech.

Similarly, changing audience attitudes about a firmly held belief can take months rather than minutes. What is the likelihood that a student speaker can convert a class to their religion during a ten-minute talk? Can a speaker persuade audience members at a rally to donate $500 to the campaign of an unknown political candidate?

Rather than seeking to convert the whole class to your religion, you may be more successful if you try to dispel some misconceptions about it. Instead of asking for $500 for a candidate's campaign, ask audience members to take home campaign flyers, to consider signing up as campaign volunteers, or to donate ten dollars. Achieving one small step in your presentation may be much more realistic than attempting a gigantic leap into unknown or hostile territory.

MAKE IT RELEVANT

Even if your purpose statement is specific and achievable, you may still have difficulty reaching your goal if your topic is irrelevant to your audience's needs or interests. The characteristics of different varieties of tree frogs may fascinate you, but if you can't explain why the topic is important and interesting to listeners, you may find yourself talking to a glassy-eyed audience. Political candidates, for example, usually focus their attention on the issues that matter to a particular audience.

Consider the following examples as you write a purpose statement that is specific, achievable, and relevant:

Ineffective purpose statements	Effective purpose statements
Appreciate why earthworms are valuable	Earthworms aerate soil, fertilize gardens, create compost, and can provide a rich source of food protein.
Learn how to take amazing cell phone photographs	Improve the quality of iPhone photographs by following the rule of three, using natural light (not flashes), and sliding the exposure meter.
Abolish the Electoral College because it's unfair and undemocratic.	The Electoral College does not reflect the popular vote: it cancels votes in winner-take-all states; gives more weight to whiter, more rural states; and lets candidates ignore states with fewer elector votes.
Understand the causes, symptoms, treatments, and prevention of depression.	The best treatments for anxiety and depression include antidepressant medications, cognitive behavioral therapy, and/or lifestyle changes.

Having a clear purpose statement is essential, but you shouldn't assume that once you've formulated it, it is set in stone. As you plan and prepare your presentation, you may realize that your purpose statement needs to be rethought. For example, if **AUDIENCE ANALYSIS ▲ (90–96)** shows that your purpose is inappropriate for your listeners, return to the *why* questions on pages 110–11 and revise your purpose. Or if, as you **RESEARCH ■ (134–51)** a topic, you discover that there isn't enough valid information to support your purpose statement, you may decide to change it. As with other elements of the rhetorical situation, thinking about your purpose requires you to be open to feedback and new information.

Conclusion

Purpose states your speaking goals and suggests ways to achieve them. It is the measure of success for your presentation, it guides rhetorical decision making, it demonstrates respect for your audience, it can reduce your speaking anxiety, and it makes the best use of your preparation time and energy. Developing a specific, achievable, and relevant purpose statement is not merely an academic exercise; it can also help you determine the outcome you seek as well as how to prepare and organize your presentation.

NOTABLE SPEAKER
Malala Yousafzai

As a 15-year-old living under Taliban rule in Pakistan, Malala Yousafzai (commonly referred to by her first name) gained international recognition for her work as an education rights activist. Because of her activism, she became the target of a Taliban assassination plot. On October 9, 2012, a gunman shot her in the head, leaving her unconscious and in critical condition. After a lengthy recovery, Yousafzai became an even more engaged activist. She is the recipient of numerous awards, including the International Children's Peace Prize and Pakistan's National Youth Peace Prize. In 2013, Yousafzai and her father established the Malala Fund to provide educational opportunities for girls around the world. A year later, at age 17, she became the youngest recipient of the Nobel Peace Prize. In 2020, she graduated with a degree in philosophy, politics, and economics from Oxford University and has continued her advocacy work. At the 2014 Nobel Peace Prize concert to honor her, Yousafzai spoke about the need to provide safe educational environments for girls.

Search Terms

To locate a video of this presentation online, enter the following key words into a search engine: Malala Nobel Peace Prize concert. The video is approximately 8:37 in length.

What to Watch For

[00:00–02:55] Yousafzai doesn't need to answer all the *why* questions for her audience because the reason is embedded in the occasion and event: She is the recipient of the Nobel Peace Prize. She is speaking to this particular audience because they have gathered to celebrate her as a Nobel laureate by hosting a concert in her honor. She does, however, directly address one question: Why is she speaking *on this topic*? She is speaking about educating girls because she believes that education is a right for all children.

[1:25–1:34] Greeted on stage by an extended standing ovation, Yousafzai's credibility is already well established. In this speech to inspire, her words and demeanor convey that she genuinely seeks to share something of value with her audience. She connects their desire for peace with her purpose by highlighting their shared vision as "peace-loving people."

[2:15–2:25] Yousafzai's purpose is evident early in the speech: "I simply ask that the right to learning should be given to every child. I ask for nothing else." She has left no room for confusion or vagueness about the destination she hopes to reach through her activism.

[4:00–4:45] Yousafzai's goal of giving every child access to education is an inspiring but difficult goal, one that cannot be accomplished in the time-limited event of her speech. What she can accomplish, however, is to motivate her audience to join the collective effort to advocate that every child receive an education. She is direct in her appeal and requests that the audience think about how they can help—how they can become activists as well.

[4:50–6:30] Yousafzai highlights the relevance of her purpose by arguing that caring about the future—something most people do—necessarily means caring about educating children. She pursues her purpose by humbly asking the audience to make the right to an education their goal as she has made it hers. By noting that she's only 17 years old and "not very tall and very small," she appeals to the audience's ability to commit to the objective as well—particularly those who are likely stronger, more powerful, and richer than she is. If, as a teenager, she can consider it her duty to advocate for the education of children, the audience can do the same.

EXERCISE

After viewing Yousafzai's speech, reflect on these questions:

1. One of the challenges of inspirational speaking is establishing your credibility as a speaker. How did Yousafzai's credibility influence her ability to inspire this audience?

2. Describe how Yousafzai adapted to the audience's needs as she stirred their emotions.

3. Yousafzai stated her purpose as "I simply ask that the right to learning should be given to every child. I ask for nothing else." In your own words, what is she asking her audience to know, think, feel, or do as a result of her presentation?

4. Although Yousafzai's general objective is to inspire her audience, to what extent and how did she also inform, persuade, and even entertain her audience?

5. Explain why or why not Yousafzai achieved her purpose.

PART 3

Content

Sometimes *what* you'll talk about—your **TOPIC**—will be chosen for you, and other times the choice will be yours to make. Once you have a topic, there's much more to think about and plan regarding your content, starting with **RESEARCHING** and choosing effective **SUPPORTING MATERIAL**. The next step is identifying and **ORGANIZING** your key points into a coherent message with the help of a **SPEECH FRAMER** or an **OUTLINE**. Then, it's time to create a strong **INTRODUCTION** and **CONCLUSION** that makes your presentation clear and compelling from start to finish.

Content

3.1 Choosing a Topic

"What should I talk about?"

Unlike students in a communication course, most presenters are required, invited, or compelled to speak because they are experts on a subject, passionate about a topic, or recognized leaders. For example, a cybersecurity expert might be asked to speak to a company about well-known phishing scams, or a football coach may be called to speak about teamwork during a halftime huddle. Whether by requirement or invitation, "What should I talk about?" isn't usually their first concern.

But in a speech course, you're not speaking because you're a leader or a recognized expert. You're speaking to demonstrate your ability to develop and deliver an effective presentation. Most likely, you'll get to choose your **topic**—the subject of your presentation. And if you can talk about anything, how do you choose what you'll talk about?

It's tempting to pick the first topic you think of or one that seems easy. You might be tempted to use a search engine or generative AI for a list of possible topics. But if you choose one randomly, without giving serious thought to your reasons for selecting it, your presentation may fall flat. You won't have a clear purpose, your delivery may be uninspired, and you may not know where to start when it comes to research. In short, if you don't care about your topic, why should your audience? To reach your full potential as a speaker, look for topics that align with your **OCCASION ▲ (61–68)** as well as the interests, abilities, beliefs, and values of you *and* your audience. In this chapter, we'll provide advice for doing just that.

Consider Your Interests and Values

As a **SPEAKER ▲ (72–85)**, *you* are the most important and readily available source for finding a worthy topic. Think carefully about your *interests*, *abilities*, *beliefs*, and *values*. Hiding in plain sight among these is a topic that you'll be able address with commitment and enthusiasm.

DRAW ON YOUR INTERESTS AND ABILITIES

Most people have something they enjoy doing above and beyond the daily grind—a sport, a hobby, a charitable activity, a political cause, music and other arts, or a subject they like learning about in their spare time. What do you look forward to doing when you've finished school-work, when the kids are at school or in bed, or when you've left work? What skills and talents do you have? Maybe there is something about your job that genuinely interests you and might interest an audience. Whatever these things may be, they can become the basis for an effective presentation.

One way to find a topic that reflects your interests and abilities is to complete a set of leading statements, such as:

- I've always wanted to know more about . . .
- If I had an unexpected week off, I would . . .
- I've always been good at . . .
- I've always wanted other people to understand or know more about . . .
- My favorite topic of conversation is . . .
- A lot of people don't know or are surprised to learn that I . . .
- If I didn't have to worry about money at all, I would spend most of my time . . .
- I've always wanted to be able to . . .

DRAW ON YOUR BELIEFS AND VALUES

Your beliefs and values guide how you think about what is right or wrong, good or bad, just or unjust, correct or incorrect. They also trigger emotions and guide actions. As with interests and abilities, your beliefs and values can lead to a compelling presentation topic—and one you'll want to talk about.

To come up with a list of core beliefs and values, try using the following leading statements:

- If I could make two new laws, they would be . . .
- I am happiest when . . .
- If I could give away a million dollars, I would . . .
- I am gratified when . . .
- I am shocked when people . . .
- The world would be a better place if . . .
- My proudest moment was when . . .
- I often become upset when I read, hear, or see a news report about . . .
- The greatest lesson I ever learned is . . .

When you complete these leading statements, you may not name a specific belief or value. For instance, you may say, "I am gratified when cooking a weekly meal at the Grace Food Pantry." The activity—cooking—is specific, but the value—helping people in need—is implied. You may be happy because you love to cook (in which case "cooking" should also be added to your list of interests!), but the overall implication is that your satisfaction and happiness are rooted in the act of helping others. In each leading statement, ask yourself: What is the belief or value expressed in my answer?

Another useful exercise is to link the **UNIVERSAL VALUES ▲ (95)** —love, honesty, responsibility, respect, fairness, freedom, and compassion—to an interest or concern of *yours*. Combining a value with an issue can help you find a meaningful topic. For example, "love" plus "marriage" might generate the idea "the role of love in arranged marriages" for one person. For another person, this combination might suggest "In marriage, love is

For an example of a speaker who uses her own beliefs, values, skills, and experiences to choose a topic that also adapts to audience traits, attitudes, and interests, see Notable Speaker: Mileha Soneji, page 385.

what you *do*, not just what you *feel*." Either of these (and countless other) statements might be a compelling presentation topic.

VALUE	+	ISSUE	=	PRESENTATION TOPIC
love	+	marriage	=	*Example:* The role of love in arranged marriages
honesty	+	politics	=	_____
responsibility	+	voting	=	_____
respect	+	religious beliefs	=	_____
fairness	+	prison sentences	=	_____
freedom	+	gun control	=	_____
compassion	+	refugees	=	_____

Use this list, or pair other issues with each of the universal values. For example, you might also pair the universal value of freedom with issues of religion, hate speech, the press, clothing, or incarceration.

Consider Your Audience

When choosing a topic, questions about your AUDIENCE ▲ (88–105) are more difficult to answer than questions about your own interests and values. Although your audience can differ in as many ways as there are listeners, AUDIENCE ANALYSIS ▲ (90–96) can help you identify and adapt a topic to their characteristics and attitudes. For instance, you decide that you want to talk about video games, but your audience is a group of retirees. Would they be interested in a presentation about the differences between first-person shooter and role-playing games? Or would this audience—many of whom are grandparents—be more interested in learning if there are cognitive benefits to educational video games for children and even for them?

Then there are subjects—often called **toxic topics**—that have the potential to turn an audience against you and your message. Only the most skilled speakers know how to approach such topics without turning their audience off. We classify toxic topics into three categories:

1. Topics selected by speakers who are *overzealous*

2. Topics that *overpromise*

3. Topics that *offend* an audience

Overzealous speakers may have the best of intentions, but in their zeal to share their enthusiasm for their chosen topic, they forget to accommodate their audience's characteristics and beliefs. A student with strong religious beliefs will be on safe ground if they speak about aspects of religious life that are especially meaningful to them. However, if they try to convert the audience to their religion by evoking the wrath of God, they may come across as overzealous. Despite their obvious passion, overzealous speakers are rarely persuasive.

Some topics *overpromise*—that is, they offer promises that cannot be kept. Would you believe a speaker who claims that you can double your money in a no-risk investment scheme or master public speaking with five secret tricks? If you pick a topic that promises something that audience members may regard as too good to be true, be careful how you introduce and develop your content. A thoughtful audience will be skeptical if you can't deliver what you promise.

Finally, some topics may *offend* or insult individual members or an entire audience. Talking about a controversial topic is fine if you are sensitive to the needs and values of your audience. But choosing a topic that is deliberately hurtful or that blames a specific person or group is almost always a bad idea—and isn't **ETHICAL** ● **(43–57)**. To claim that a certain country "deserves damage from natural disasters because they aren't taking action against climate change" is a toxic topic. But a presentation about why some countries don't or can't take action against climate change may be enlightening. If a controversial topic may be perceived by audience members as toxic, you should either refine and narrow the topic or avoid it altogether.

Be sensitive to your audience's background, attitudes, beliefs, and feelings when you choose a topic. If you are unsure about your choice of topic and you're able to do so, ask potential audience members if they'd interpret your topic as overzealous, overpromising, or offensive. If there is even a hint of a yes, reconsider your topic. But don't be afraid to stand by a topic that reflects your deep-seated values if you're confident you can adapt to your audience's values and feelings. After all, it's not that you should say only what an audience wants to hear; adapt what *you* want to say so that it resonates with your listeners.

Narrow the Scope of Your Topic

There's an old saying: "Don't bite off more than you can chew." For presentations, the saying should be: "Don't say more than your audience can digest." If a topic is too broad, you'll bury your listeners under mounds of information. If you had time to tell them just one thing about your topic, what would it be? Often, conveying a single important idea is enough to achieve a worthy purpose.

Here are a few examples of general topic areas that have been narrowed down into better-defined topics:

    ✗ **TOO BROAD:** The history of hip-hop

    ✓ **BETTER:**   Grandmaster Flash and the development of quick-mix theory, punch phrasing, and scratching in early hip-hop

    ✗ **TOO BROAD:** A review of Greek mythology

    ✓ **BETTER:**   The origins of the Greek goddess Aphrodite

    ✗ **TOO BROAD:** The effects of global climate change

    ✓ **BETTER:**   The "death" of the Great Barrier Reef

    ✗ **TOO BROAD:** Graphic narratives

    ✓ **BETTER:**   The power of graphic novels: *Maus* and *Fun Home*

Once you've narrowed your topic to a manageable scope, you should be able to further develop and refine your **PURPOSE STATEMENT ▲ (115–17)** into a single sentence.

START YOUR RESEARCH NOW

The time to start **DOING RESEARCH ■ (139–43)** is *now*—that is, as soon as you select and narrow your topic for a particular rhetorical situation. In most cases, doing research early will help you sharpen the scope and purpose of a presentation on a particular topic. In some situations, it may even point you toward a better topic. It will also help you find useful and appropriate **SUPPORTING MATERIAL ■ (135–39)** for a more narrowly focused topic.

In some cases, if you have extensive knowledge about a topic, or have thoroughly researched it for some other assignment, doing research may simply be a matter of reviewing what you know about the subject and selecting and **ORGANIZING** ■ **(152–70)** the information you need to support your presentation's purpose.

Ask Other People . . . or Generative AI!

If you're still at a loss for a topic or don't know how to refine it, ask other people for advice. Start with friends and family. Because they spend considerable time with you, they probably have an intuitive sense of the subjects that you're most interested in and informed about. At the very least, they can be a useful sounding board as you consider potential topics.

You may also turn to the internet, the largest repository of other people's ideas that the world has ever assembled. By using the search phrase "speech topics," you'll find dozens of sites that list thousands of options—but these ideas may not align with your values as a speaker and the nature of your audience, occasion, and purpose.

And, of course, there is **GENERATIVE AI** ● **(50–55)**, which draws directly from those online sources and—if permitted for use by your college, instructor, or workplace—can be a valuable resource, even more so than a general internet search.

To avoid generic outputs and produce more useful and interesting responses from generative AI, Ethan Mollick, an AI expert and professor at the University of Pennsylvania's Wharton School of Business, recommends prompts that establish a clear and specific AI persona.[1] Give it a try with the following prompt by replacing the words in brackets with details about your own presentation:

Before turning to generative AI, check with your instructor and review the ethical considerations of using generative AI in Chapter 1.4 **ETHICS AND FREE SPEECH** ●.

> I need to select a topic for [an informative presentation] I'm delivering [in my college public speaking course]. Act as a tutor or coach and ask me questions about myself as a speaker, my audience, and my purpose to help me choose an interesting and relevant topic for my presentation.

By engaging with generative AI in this way, you can narrow your topic to be more specific for your speaking situation, and it can help to spark ideas or viewpoints you hadn't already considered. From there, take some of the most compelling ideas as a starting place to do more **RESEARCH** ■ **(139–43)**.

In general, if you consult the internet or generative AI while you consider your topic:

- *Be wary of choosing popular or "best" topics.* Student speakers so often speak about euthanasia, abortion, and the death penalty that unless you take a unique or carefully adapted approach, most audiences will dread hearing more about these topics (and they may know more about them than you do).

- *Adapt the topic for your rhetorical situation* and pay special attention to the allotted time limit.

- *Consider unique or surprising angles* if you're compelled to speak about common persuasive topics. For example, you could give a presentation that compares the use of the death penalty in different countries and its cultural implications, or you could talk about wrongful conviction cases and their impact on both prisoners and their families.

In short, don't let AI or the internet have the final say about your topic. No matter how much information you provide about your presentation, generative AI cannot take all these elements into account—in fact, that's a uniquely human capability!

While it's perfectly acceptable to seek help when choosing your topic, do not buy or copy a speech written by someone else, whether a friend, a professional, a performer, an online source, or a generative AI. Beyond the ethical and legal problems associated with **PLAGIARISM** ● **(49–50)**, a presentation written by someone else or by a machine will not sound like you, reflect your interests and values, or help you connect with a particular audience.

Conclusion

Choose a topic by considering your interests, abilities, and values; weighing your audience's needs and expectations against your own; and confirming that your sense of purpose is clear. Support that topic with relevant and engaging research findings, and if your research turns up a better approach or topic, change course if you can. Doing all these things in response to the question "What should I talk about?" will transform a merely acceptable presentation topic into one with the potential to be memorable and even extraordinary for both you and your audience.

3.2 Research and Supporting Material

Once you've identified your purpose and approach to your topic, you may think the next step is to start writing or outlining your presentation and begin designing your presentation aids. Certainly, if you've given serious thought to the rhetorical situation, you should already know a great deal about what you want to say. But knowing what you want to say isn't enough. You also need to find and select relevant, varied, interesting, and valid *supporting material.*

Supporting material consists of the ideas, information, and opinions you use in a presentation to support your purpose. Well-chosen supporting material helps you inform, persuade, entertain, and/or inspire your audience. It can also enhance your credibility, substantiate your claims, and generate audience interest.

Whether you're an expert on the topic or learning as you research, you *always* need to verify and cite your sources during your presentation. This chapter will help you find, verify, use, and cite supporting material to make your presentation more interesting, impressive, and memorable.

Types of Supporting Material

To begin, let's look at a few of the most common types of supporting material and when you might use each type in a presentation.

FACTS

A **fact** is a verifiable observation, experience, or event known to be true. For example, this statement is a fact:

> *Top Gun: Maverick* was the highest-grossing domestic movie in 2022.

But the statement "I think the acting in *Black Panther: Wakanda Forever* was better" is not a fact; it's an **opinion**—an evaluation or judgment that is arguable, not settled. Most presentations—regardless of their purpose—include facts.

Facts can be something you know ("It rained every day last week") or information you've researched ("Taylor Swift's Eras tour increased local earnings in Los Angeles by $160 million"). Sometimes a little-known or unusual fact can spark audience interest, such as:

> Testing water in a city's sewage treatment plant can identify the kind and amount of illicit drugs being consumed.

Use facts in your presentation when you need to establish the accuracy of a statement—especially if your audience may not believe the statement is true. Facts can help validate your ideas, enhance your **CREDIBILITY ▲ (74–81)**, and provide a context for understanding your message.

STATISTICS

Statistics are numerical data gathered from research or experimentation, which can help you understand the extent of a characteristic or the frequency of an occurrence among a large population. Statistics are also used to analyze or make predictions, such as analyzing economic trends and predicting the outcome of a sporting event.

Statistics can be used in a presentation to show trends over time or to provide accurate comparisons. Numerical evidence often verifies facts, opinions, and claims. Surprising statistics can also generate audience interest. For example, to introduce a presentation about plastics in the ocean, you might say:

> According to the National Academy of Sciences, Engineering, and Medicine, at least 8.8 million metric tons of plastic waste enter the world's oceans each year—the equivalent of dumping a garbage truck of plastic into the sea every minute.[1]

TESTIMONY

Testimony refers to statements or opinions that someone has said or written, ranging from historical figures to experts alive today. Testimony from topic experts can be used to verify and add credibility to your claims—especially when you lack expertise about the topic. Eyewitness testimony, or a statement from someone who is not an expert but has firsthand experience, can also be used as evidence or to heighten emotion in your presentation. For example, in a presentation about skin cancer, you might offer expert testimony from a leading dermatologist alongside eyewitness testimony from a patient who is undergoing treatment.

DEFINITIONS

A **definition** explains or clarifies the meaning or meanings of a word, phrase, or concept. A definition can be as simple as explaining what *you* mean by a word or as detailed as a dictionary entry. When considering the LANGUAGE ∴ (305–22) that's appropriate for your audience, you may need to include a definition if you know your audience may not understand a particular word, phrase, or concept. In the following excerpt, a speaker uses two very different definitions of the same term—one from a music dictionary and the other from a musician's colloquial expression—to talk about the blues:

> A formal definition of the blues identifies it as a uniquely American musical form . . . characterized by expressive pitch inflections (blue notes), a three-line textual stanza of the form AAB, and a twelve-measure form. Well, that's okay for some, but I like an old bluesman's definition: "The blues ain't nothin' but the facts of life."

EXAMPLES AND STORIES

An **example** is a specific case or instance that can be used to clarify, empha-size, and reinforce key ideas. (This book uses a lot of examples!) Examples can be brief descriptions or detailed explanations. In a presentation about the value of taxpayer-funded scientific research, a speaker might provide several examples of everyday items and services that originated from research at NASA: memory foam used to make pillows and mattresses, camera technology in modern cell phones, artificial limbs, enriched baby formula, MRI and CT scans, and solar panels, to name just a few!

A specific type of example, the **hypothetical example**, is a fictional example that can be used to explain a complicated concept in simpler terms or to illustrate an idea when you can't find an example that will resonate with your audience and explain a **KEY POINT ■ (153–56)**. Some of the most persuasive hypothetical examples ask audience members to imagine them-selves in an invented situation, usually beginning with a phrase such as "Suppose you . . ." or "Imagine a situation where . . ." or "Picture this . . ." Notice how the following hypothetical example makes a point about high drug costs more memorable and compelling:

> Suppose you need the rheumatoid arthritis drug Humira, but—if you're uninsured—you can't afford the $84,000-a-year cost. For that amount of money, you could fly first class to Paris, stay at the Ritz Hotel, dine at the best restaurants, buy a one-year supply of Humira at local prices in France, fly back home, and finish with enough money to hire a registered nurse to administer the injection every two weeks and put almost $35,000 into savings. Crazy, huh? Perhaps. But what's really crazy is how the cost of pharmaceuti-cals can be so different in the United States compared to other countries. Since it first hit the market 20 years ago, Humira's price has increased by 500 percent in the United States, while European users now pay up to 90 percent less than they used to.[2]

Similar to hypothetical examples, **stories** are accounts of things that have happened or might happen. Audiences remember relevant, well-told stories, even when they can't remember much else about a presentation. Real stories about real people in the real world can arouse attention, create an appropriate mood, and reinforce important ideas. **TELLING STORIES ⸪ (323–32)** is one of the best ways to generate audience attention and support your key points.

ORIGINAL MEDIA AND OBJECTS

Sometimes the best supporting material is an object or an original creative work, such as a song, photograph, model, excerpt from a novel, or piece of equipment. Used as supporting material and incorporated as **PRESENTATION AIDS ▶ (260–78)**, they can reinforce your ideas in memorable ways. For example, rather than reading a scholarly quote about the blues, play a Howlin' Wolf or Muddy Waters recording. In a more technical presentation, a piece of sheet music for a blues song can show exactly what a three-line stanza and a twelve-measure form look like.

VARY THE TYPES OF SUPPORTING MATERIAL

For an example of a speaker who uses several types of supporting material, including a personal story, facts, data, and examples, see Notable Speaker: Meghan Markle, page 86.

Effective speakers don't rely on just one type of supporting material. Why? Because using only one type of supporting material can make a presentation seem dull. Most audiences will become bored by an unending list of statistics. They may become frustrated by a speaker who tells story after story, particularly if there's no clear connection among them. A presentation that is little more than a series of quotations by famous people may convince your audience that you have nothing original to say. Try using several types of supporting material to build credibility and give your presentation life and vitality.

Here's a passage from a presentation that uses six different kinds of supporting material:

Story ——•
Definition ——•
Fact ——•
Example ——•

The Ku Klux Klan had humble beginnings. Right after the Civil War, six former Confederate soldiers in Pulaski, Tennessee, created a circle of like-minded friends. They chose the name Kuklux, a variation of the Greek word *kuklos*, which means "circle." They added the term *Klan* because they were of Scotch-Irish descent. In 1915, D. W. Griffith's film *The Birth of a Nation*—originally titled *The Clansman*—quoted a line from *A History of the American People*

by Woodrow Wilson, who would later become president of the
United States. Wilson declared, ". . . at last there has sprung into   •——— Testimony
existence a great Ku Klux Klan, a veritable empire of the South, to
protect the Southern country." By the 1920s, the Klan claimed eight   •——— Statistic
million members. Today, there are between five thousand and eight
thousand Klan members in the United States, split between dozens
of different organizations that use the Klan name.[3]

Doing Research

To find supporting material for your presentation, you'll need to do
research—and start doing it early! In addition to providing supporting
material, **research** can also help you refine the focus of your presentation
and **NARROW YOUR TOPIC** ■ **(130–31)**. You might even uncover information
that will change your opinion about your topic or your overall **PURPOSE**
▲ **(109–18)**. For example, if you were doing research for a presentation on
how cities can save money by promoting digital reading and downsizing
libraries, you may discover that libraries provide countless other services,
including resources to combat illiteracy and assistance to those in search
of employment. As a result, you might change your presentation to one
that advocates making library services more visible and available to the
community.

Look for supporting material in a variety of places, including books,
speeches, plays, magazine articles, podcasts, television shows, courtrooms, interviews, and social media platforms—the possibilities are
almost limitless! To find the supporting material best suited for your
presentation, utilize *library catalogs and databases* as well as *online
search engines*.

USING THE LIBRARY

Perhaps the *best* place to start your research is your college library or a
comprehensive public library—both the physical library and the library's
online catalog and databases. A librarian can help you navigate all the
library's resources, so come prepared with your topic and a set of questions in hand.

The Catalog An inventory of all the material the library owns, the catalog includes print and electronic material, books, encyclopedias, films, and more. You can search the catalog by author, subject, title, or publication. If you don't know where to begin, search by subject or keyword to find all available materials related to that topic. And if you're stuck, ask a librarian for help.

Databases Your library will also provide access to online databases, which are collections of newspapers, magazines, journals, and possibly even video and audio content. General databases provide scholarly and popular sources, and they're a good place to start. Subject-specific databases are helpful for researching topics that require specialized academic knowledge, such as PubMed Central (biomedical and life sciences), IEEE Xplore (electrical engineering and computer science), APA PsycInfo (psychology), and Project MUSE (humanities and social sciences). The best database to use will depend on the subject of your presentation. You could use an academic database to locate studies about the impact of mindfulness on stress levels, for example. A news database would be more helpful for up-to-date information about elections in your state.

USING THE INTERNET

The internet is often the first place people look to find supporting material. Internet research tools include search engines like Google, Bing, or DuckDuckGo, but they can also include Google Scholar, a search engine that will direct you to scholarly literature. Wikipedia, a free online encyclopedia, is also a helpful place to find other sources and get background information. Look at the bottom of any Wikipedia entry for a list of additional sources where you can continue your research. Although Wikipedia is maintained by editors to ensure accuracy, we recommend using the site as a starting point, not an end point.

The accessibility of the internet makes it an easy option for research—and possibly an unreliable one. Unlike the library catalog and databases, anyone with access to the internet can post their work without any verification. Be cautious and use the **SIFT METHOD** ■ **(145–47)** described later in this chapter to verify the credibility of sources you find online.

Internet Searches You can find almost anything on the internet. Learning how to search for useful information effectively will help find the best resources available. Let's say you're conducting research for a presentation about why people should support human rights. The search term *human rights* turn up more than 8 trillion results. You'll need to narrow that down! Fortunately, there are **Boolean operators**—words used to include or exclude information and make your search more specific.

- *Use AND to find sources that include all terms.* If you're looking for examples of human rights related to religion, search *human rights AND religion.*

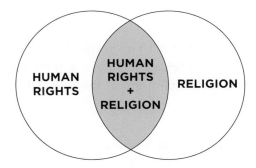

The results from a search for "human rights AND religion."

- *Use OR to find sources with either of those words,* like *human rights OR religion*

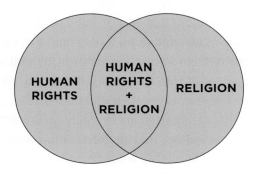

The results from a search for "human rights OR religion."

- *Use NOT to exclude a term.* Searching *human rights NOT religion* will return results that are about human rights but not religion.

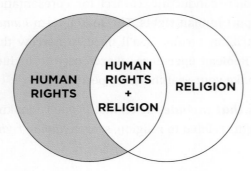

The results from a search for "human rights NOT religion."

- *Use quotation marks to find sources with a specific term.* Searching "human rights" will show results that include the term *human rights* as opposed to results that contain any of the words *human, rights,* or *human rights.*

Generative AI As you know, GENERATIVE AI ● (50–55) can process, in a matter of seconds, an incredible amount of information from the internet, third parties, and users in order to create new images, video, audio, and text. And, by the time you are reading this book, AI will probably be integrated into most search engines.

You may think of generative AI as a quick and effective shortcut for doing internet research and for reading and summarizing the supporting material you need for a presentation. But even if your instructor or speaking situation permits the use of generative AI, it may not be the best research tool for finding the most reliable supporting material. In addition to not always identifying the sources of the ideas and information it has gathered, generative AI has been known to create **hallucinated sources**,[4] generated content that is fictional, unsupported, or factually incorrect.

More importantly, identifying, reading, and understanding a range of supporting material is essential to becoming a confident and credible speaker. Relying on generative AI to read and summarize that information for you means that you'll miss this critical step. If during your presentation you refer to—or have to answer questions about—the sources and content you haven't actually read, your lack of competence and confidence will be on full display.

Although generative AI is getting more powerful and accurate every day, the technology has flaws—it can be wrong, and there can be legal and **ETHICAL ● (43-57)** issues that come with relying on AI to find your supporting material. Our advice is to use generative AI, if permitted, as a brainstorming tool to help guide your research process and consider new angles. Here's one example of such a prompt:

> For a [persuasive] presentation on [investing in e-bike infrastructure to improve safety and promote sustainability in rural college towns], please suggest three research questions to guide my initial research process.

When you have a clear direction for your research process, use the established and existing resources designed for that exact purpose: libraries, catalogs, databases, and search engines. And if, while using generative AI to brainstorm, you come across a story, quote, statistic, or other information that you'd like to use as supporting material, use your research skills to find the original source. You might even ask generative AI a follow up question, such as:

> That [statistic/quote/story/source] you provided could be useful for my presentation. Can you provide a source for that information? Can you provide other sources that say the same thing?

Once you have identified the original source, you'll need to read and evaluate the accuracy of that information by verifying it against other sources, which we will discuss next.

Evaluating Your Sources

Whenever you encounter new information, whether in the brainstorming phase or the research phase, you must evaluate all supporting material to ensure it's valid. By **valid**, we mean that the ideas, opinions, and information are well founded, justified, and true. This goes well beyond testing the accuracy of an AI response. It applies to any source, idea,

Which image is real and which one has been digitally altered? The image of the protest sign on the left has been edited to distort the meaning of the real photograph on the right. As generative AI makes it easy for anyone to create and share fake images, you must evaluate the accuracy of all supporting material you encounter.

and information you reference or use in a presentation. That includes all written material as well as audio, video, and images. No matter how and where you find supporting material, check its validity before adding it to your presentation. Failing to do so can seriously undermine your credibility as a speaker.

So how do you determine whether a source is valid? It may seem too easy to find information and too hard to evaluate everything you find. The massive amount of information from print and online sources is overwhelming. Even skilled researchers can find it difficult to differentiate between good and bad information or biased and unbiased sources. Two strategies (and the ones used by professional fact-checkers) can help you determine whether a source and its output is valid: *lateral reading* and using the *SIFT method*.

LATERAL READING

Lateral reading is "the practice of doing a quick initial evaluation of a website by spending . . . more time reading what others say about the source or related issue."[5] While lateral reading was developed to test the credibility of online sources, it can be used to determine whether any source is worth paying attention to or not.

When you locate a new source of information, search for other sources on that same topic. Look for consistencies or discrepancies in each. If a source claims something questionable or shocking, see if other sources make similar claims. If they do not, the original source is likely unreliable; use a fact-checking site to verify. You should also research the publication itself to determine if it has a particular agenda or exhibits some other kind of bias. Research the names of the authors to see if they are qualified to provide information and opinions about your topic.

THE SIFT METHOD

Mike Caulfield, a digital literacy expert at the University of Washington, has transformed the principle of lateral reading into four moves that you can use to initially evaluate the credibility and accuracy of online sources. He calls it the **SIFT method**, which stands for "stop, investigate, find, and trace."[6]

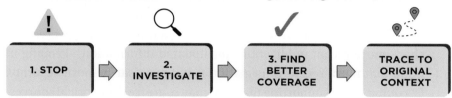

1. STOP ⇨ 2. INVESTIGATE ⇨ 3. FIND BETTER COVERAGE ⇨ TRACE TO ORIGINAL CONTEXT

1. Stop When you first land on a page, stop and consider the source: Do you recognize the information's source, and do you know if the site verifies its content and authors? Who is the author? In short, don't just assume that the information is correct. If you can't find an author's name and credentials, it's probably best to look for another source with an identifiable author. There are, however, exceptions when an online source identifies only the company or institution responsible for the message. Treat these sources as authors and check their legitimacy.

2. Investigate the Source Next, investigate the source to determine if it's *credible*, *unbiased*, and *up to date*.

- *Is the source credible?* Is the author or speaker a recognized expert, a firsthand observer, a scientist, or a respected journalist? Can you confirm that expertise, experience, or reputation by looking at several sources *other* than the one you're testing? Wikipedia is one easy tool to find more information about a source—its publication history, current circulation, and possible controversies. At this point, your goal is to determine if the publication is credible enough to consider as potential supporting material.

- *Is the source biased?* After testing the credibility of the publication, check for bias. A source with a consistent **bias**—a prejudice for or against something or an unreasonable partiality, opinion, or feeling—may express claims and opinions so slanted that they are neither objective nor fair. Check an author's biographical information, recent publications, website, social media account, or LinkedIn profile—and keep in mind that an author can be an individual or an organization. Does the author have agendas or interests that might cause them to make a strong or questionable claim?

- *Is the information recent?* Note the date of the information you want to use. When was the study conducted? When was the article published? If you find a source that is older but otherwise looks credible, check more recent publications for updated information—keeping in mind that more recent information is not necessarily more accurate. Of course, some supporting material may come from historical sources, but it's worth checking contemporary coverage for more recent findings on historical events, findings, and accounts.

3. Find Better Coverage If your source seems credible, look to see if other credible sources cite the same facts and make the same claims. A simple search of key terms will usually provide a quick overview of how the topic is viewed by other sources. As you look across other sources, check the credibility of each new source you encounter. To help, you might use fact-checking sites like FactCheck.org, PolitiFact, and Snopes. If you find inconsistencies, the source or claim you're investigating may not be credible. Consider if your personal viewpoints lead you to trust a particular source, even if other respected sources criticize its accuracy, truthfulness, and biases. This step can be especially effective when trying to recognize and avoid hallucinated sources produced by generative AI.

4. Trace to the Original Context Finally, examine the original context of the claim, quote, or media. Consider if the source is primary or secondary information.

A **primary source** is an original document or material that is produced from firsthand experience. Examples include an article from a researcher reporting the findings of their own research, an interview on a podcast, and the diary of someone who lived through World War I. Other primary sources include speeches, eyewitness accounts, and recordings or transcripts of statements and events.

A **secondary source** is a document or material that is created by someone who does not have firsthand knowledge of an experience or event. Secondary sources often describe, report, repeat, or summarize information from one or more other sources. Examples include a news article that summarizes someone else's scientific research and a description of an event by someone who was not there.

If possible, follow secondary sources of information back to their primary source. Look for hyperlinks in a source that direct you to the original. Perform a search on key terms used in the source. You can identify the original source of most photos by doing a reverse image search using a tool like Google Images or TinEye. Once you verify that the actual photo exists, confirm that it hasn't been cropped or altered in any other way. If there are differences between the primary and secondary sources, is there a valid explanation for those differences? Has the source or photo purposefully been removed or modified in a way that distorts or contradicts the original context?

To maintain your **CREDIBILITY ▲ (74–81)** and **ETHICS ● (43–57)** as a speaker, verify all sources—and don't take words or photos out of context to support your purpose, especially if it's not the original speaker or writer's intended meaning.

Evaluating Statistics

Many speakers consider statistical data to be the gold standard for supporting an argument—they can be very compelling and engaging! And yet unless you're presenting to statisticians, statistics can be hard for an audience to understand and easy for a speaker to manipulate. In fact, one of the best-selling books about statistics is called *How to Lie with Statistics*.

Imagine you were told that 100 percent of the physics professors at one college were Black and 100 percent of the physics professors at a neighboring college were White. What would you think, given only that information? You may wonder if a policy of educational segregation or discrimination was afoot. But what if you were then told that there is only one physics professor at each college? Is the statistic any less true? No. But is it meaningful? The use of a percentage figure in this case is misleading at best.

Before using statistical information in your presentation, ask the following questions:

- Is the statistical sample adequate?
- Do the statistics represent a mean or a median?
- Can you explain how the statistics support your claims?

IS THE STATISTICAL SAMPLE ADEQUATE?

Statistics are based on a **sample**, or portion of a population. To be adequate, a sample size must be large enough to stand in for the population as a whole. How large is large enough? If the methodology of a study is sophisticated and ethical, researchers can select a relatively small sample to draw conclusions about an entire population. For example, the typical sample size for a Gallup poll in the United States is 1,000 adults. This sample size is tiny compared to the population it's meant to represent—approximately 209 million adults—but because they use a widely respected methodology, Gallup's statistical results are generally seen as valid.[7]

An adequate sample should also be both random and representative to avoid **sampling bias**, which happens when some categories of individuals within the overall population are intentionally or inadvertently excluded from the sample. For instance, if a survey's sample is meant to represent all adults in the United States, that sample should include nearly the same number of women as men and the same percentages of different races and ages in the overall population.

DO THE STATISTICS REPRESENT A MEAN OR A MEDIAN?

Just about everyone is familiar with the concept of an *average*. In statistics, the words *average* and *mean* are used interchangeably. For example, if you add up the heights of all the students in your class and divide that sum by the number of students you measured, you will come up with the average—or mean—height in your class.

The term *median* refers to the figure that is at the midpoint between two extremes. If you create a list or chart of your classmates arranged from the shortest person (5'2") to the tallest person (6'4"), and that list has fifteen people on it, you'd look for the person right in the middle of the list—the eighth person. That person's height is not an average of the shortest and tallest nor the most frequent height. It's just the height that appears right in the middle of the list.

CAN YOU EXPLAIN HOW THE STATISTICS SUPPORT YOUR CLAIMS?

You might have heard the saying "The numbers speak for themselves." Sure, statistics may "speak," but they definitely don't *explain* themselves. If you use statistics in a presentation, you can and should explain them.

Here's an example of a how you might explain a statistic in a persuasive presentation:

> Today, 82.3 percent of Americans are classified as overweight or obese, if you're using the Body Mass Index (BMI) as a measurement of health.[8] But what does that really tell us? Not much. In her 2020 book *What We Don't Talk about When We Talk about Fat*, Aubrey Gordon explains that the BMI was never intended to diagnose obesity or measure individual health. Yet it has been used for decades to do so—often with serious consequences. In 1998, the National Institutes of Health redefined BMI categories so that the cutoff point between the normal and overweight categories was lowered. This meant 29 million Americans went to bed one night as "normal weight" and woke up the next morning as "overweight." What had changed about their individual health? Absolutely nothing. As Gordon notes, "Our oversimplified conversation about the BMI tricks us into believing that nearly every thin person is healthier than nearly every fat person."[9]

Citing Your Sources

All the supporting material used in a presentation should be documented and cited to enhance your credibility as a speaker. **Citation,** also known as **documentation**, is the practice of referring to the source of your supporting material in a presentation. In most college settings, you are required to cite your sources both during your presentation and in a written reference page.

If you cannot—or do not—cite your sources, you could fall into the trap of plagiarizing your source material unintentionally. The key to **AVOIDING PLAGIARISM** ● **(49–50)** is to identify the sources of your information in your presentation. If they're not your original ideas or images or most of the words are not yours, you must tell your audience who and where they came from.

CITE YOUR SOURCES WHILE SPEAKING

During a presentation, you should acknowledge the sources of supporting material out loud. Your **oral citation** should include enough information to allow an interested listener to find the original sources. As you prepare an oral citation, consider the following questions:

- *Who is being quoted or paraphrased?* Are they well known, or do you need to introduce them?
- *What are their credentials?* What degree, title, group membership, or accomplishments will communicate their experience and expertise?
- *From what publication or source* is the information taken? Will your audience recognize it?
- *What date* was the information generated, published, or last updated? Will this enhance the credibility of the source?

You may not need to list the credentials of a well-known person or organization, but the date the statement was made or published may be important. Generally, it's a good idea to provide the name of the person or organization, say a word or two about their credentials, and mention the source of the information. For example, "In an article posted on their website in June of 2023, the nonpartisan fact tank Pew Research Center analyzed how #BlackLivesMatter became a model of protest using social media."

CITE YOUR SOURCES IN WRITING

Always be prepared to provide a written list of the references you used to prepare your presentation—just as you would for a written report. In most speaking situations apart from the classroom, you will not be required to provide such a list. Even in those cases, keep a list of your references for your own use. If nothing else, it will remind you of which sources you used in the event that you are challenged about information or asked to repeat or to update your presentation.

Documentation follows one of several accepted formats, such as Modern Language Association (MLA) style, American Psychological Association (APA) style, or Chicago Manual of Style (CMOS). The documentation sections in their manuals provide models of how to format references, endnotes, and footnotes. If your instructor requires a written list of your references, make sure to ask which documentation format you should use.

If for your speaking situation it would be helpful to provide your audience with a complete bibliography of your supporting material, at the end of the presentation you could display a QR code on a slide or prepare a **HANDOUT ▶ (268–69)** to provide the complete reference list.

Conclusion

Savvy speakers begin collecting supporting material, including facts, statistics, testimony, definitions, examples, and stories, as soon as they know they'll be making a presentation. If they have a general idea about the topic they intend to cover, they'll begin researching a variety of resources. Good research helps you develop your presentation and fill in the blanks where you need additional material to support your purpose.

As you search for supporting material, remember that never before in history has there been so much information about so many subjects available to so many people. That's the good news. The bad news is that never before in history has there been so much false, misleading, and biased information about so many subjects available to so many people. Responsible speakers have an ethical obligation to understand the difference between facts and fiction as they choose appropriate supporting material for a presentation. Audience members, too, share that responsibility as they listen to a speaker.

3.3 Organizing Content

A well-organized presentation is easier to listen to and remember than a poorly organized one. If you've ever listened to a long-winded speech, you already know how difficult it is to understand a speaker who rambles and doesn't connect ideas. In fact, you may never want to hear that speaker again.

The **organization** of a presentation is the arrangement of its content into a structured, coherent message. Organization puts the major components of your presentation in an appropriate order and keeps you focused on the development of each idea. Not surprisingly, well-organized speakers are seen as more competent, confident, and persuasive than disorganized speakers. A thoughtful arrangement of ideas helps an audience understand and follow along.

Identifying Key Points and the Central Idea

Inexperienced speakers often feel overwhelmed by all the facts, ideas, opinions, and data that they've assembled during their RESEARCH ■ (134–51). So how do you make sense of it all? How do you select the information that will best support your PURPOSE ▲ (109–18)? Start by determining the *key points* and *central idea* for your presentation.

IDENTIFYING KEY POINTS

Key points are the main ideas or most important issues you want your audience to understand and remember. They are the basic building blocks of your presentation. To identify your key points, look for patterns or natural groupings of ideas and information. Two methods in particular—*chunking* and *mind mapping*—can help.

The Chunking Method **Chunking** is the process of recording and sorting the ideas and supporting material you've gathered so far. This simple method helps you identify your key points, then arrange and rearrange them until you've found a natural order.

Here's how it's done: During the research and planning stage of speech preparation, record each good idea and strong piece of SUPPORTING MATE-RIAL ▪ (135–39) on a single note card, sticky note, or virtual note. Put only one idea, point, phrase, example, statistic, quotation, or story on each card or note.

Once you have gathered and recorded your ideas and supporting material as separate notes, spread them out and look for relationships among them. You'll notice that some supporting material will back up specific ideas, some ideas will overlap or repeat one another, and some ideas and supporting material will prove to be unrelated to your topic or purpose. For each group of notes that belong together, create a unique category label, or key point. For instance, if you're preparing a presentation on flying cars, you might discover that you've chunked your ideas and supporting material into three key points:

1. *Technological development* of flying cars
2. *Infrastructure* required for using flying cars
3. *Benefits* of developing flying cars

If some of your notes don't fit into a distinct category with the others, keep them nearby in a pile of "leftovers." As your presentation develops, some categories might become more important and others less so, and these leftover ideas and supporting material may end up being relevant again.

The Mind Mapping Method Another method for identifying key ideas—**mind mapping**—produces a visual representation of potential key points and related supporting materials that clearly link to your topic and purpose.

The most common mind mapping method requires only a piece of paper and a writing tool. There are also dozens of mind mapping software tools available. The mind mapping steps that follow use the paper method.[1]

1. *Record your topic, ideas, and supporting material.* On a single, clean sheet of paper, write your TOPIC ▣ (125–33) in the middle of the page and circle it. Everything on your mind map should stem from this word or phrase. Experiment with the ideas that might become candidates for the key points in your presentation. Write down these ideas in the open spaces on the page. Then record the SUPPORTING MATERIAL ▣ (135–39) you wish to use near a relevant idea. You may find it necessary to add other ideas that capture the essence of the supporting material. Feel free to be messy. Neatness doesn't count. Initially, there are no bad ideas. What is important is that at the end of this initial step, you should have a one-page conglomeration of topic-related ideas and supporting material that you might include in your presentation.

2. *Connect related ideas.* Draw a circle around individual ideas and related supporting material. If two ideas are closely related, let your circles overlap or draw lines between those circles. Eventually, they may be combined into a single key point. Now examine ideas and supporting materials that aren't circled. Are they important? Do they support your purpose? If so, you may need to create a new idea or find more supporting material.

3. *Refine your mind map.* Critically analyze your mind map. Which ideas seem most significant and necessary as key points? Which ones can be discarded? If they're not important, cross them out. In some cases, you may want to redo your map to organize it further. In a second draft, you can concentrate on making sure that your mind map has adequate and appropriate supporting material for each key point.

The following figure is a mind map created by a student for a presentation about anger. The mind map is a hodgepodge of words, phrases, lists, circles, and arrows. After analyzing what was on her mind map, she identified and circled ideas and supporting materials for each of her key points and put them in a logical order. Given the large amount of interrelated material she found, mind mapping was a useful way to decide how much information she had time to include, identify her key points, and begin the organizational process.

CONSIDER THE RULE OF THREE

You may be tempted to include all your key points and supporting material in your presentation. Resist that temptation. Even the most attentive listeners in your audience will not remember everything you say. Ask yourself: Which key points are the most essential?

Generally, communication experts agree that an effective presentation should offer at least two key points and no more than five. Three key points is ideal, according to the **rule of three**. In fact, audience members frequently *expect* speakers to make three points in their speeches. This is a guideline, not an absolute, unbreakable rule—but in general, keeping the number of key points between two and five will ensure that your presentation remains interesting and memorable.

THE CENTRAL IDEA

Whether you use chunking, mind mapping, or some other method to start organizing your ideas and supporting material, you will eventually determine the key ideas that reflect your **PURPOSE STATEMENT ▲ (115–17)**. Now it's time to write out your *central idea.*

Your **central idea** (sometimes called the **thesis** or preview statement) summarizes your overall message and tells the audience what your main points will be—it describes specifically what you intend *to* say.

PURPOSE: To spread awareness about the ways we benefit from earthworms

CENTRAL IDEA: You may know that earthworms are helpful for fishing and gardening, but you may not know how they can enhance composting and provide a protein-rich meal.

Compare the preceding statements. Which would you rather say to an audience? That's your central idea. When you've finished your presentation, audience members should be able to remember and rephrase your central idea in their own words.

Writing down your central idea is a useful test to determine if you have, in fact, captured the core meaning of your message and previewed your main points. If it takes more than one sentence to state your central idea, you may be trying to do too much with your presentation, or you may not have a clear purpose or discrete set of key points.

The following example illustrates how topic, purpose, and central idea are different but closely related.

TOPIC AREA: Muzak

PURPOSE: To make the audience more aware of the purpose and power of Muzak

CENTRAL IDEA: The next time you hear Muzak playing, you will remember how pervasive it is, how it originated, and how it tries to lift your spirits and productivity.

Once you have drafted a central idea that captures what you want to say in your presentation, you can turn to the details of organization. Keep in mind that your initial central idea is not set in stone. As you organize your content or revise your presentation, you may find that you'll need to modify your central idea.

Patterns of Organization

In many cases, your topic, purpose, central idea, and key points will suggest an overall organization of your presentation. To explain how to make pasta, for example, there is a clear set of consecutive steps. If you're discussing Christopher Nolan movies, you might start at the beginning of his career and work your way forward. In other cases, the best arrangement may not be immediately apparent, so you might use one of the following common **organizational patterns** or come up with a new way to arrange and present your key points.

ARRANGE BY CATEGORIES

In **categorical arrangement**, you divide a large topic into smaller categories within that topic. For example, you could divide the topic of alcoholism into its symptoms and treatments, or you could devote your entire presentation to describing several treatments. Here's an example of a categorical arrangement for a presentation on anger:

TOPIC AREA: Common myths about anger

PURPOSE: To explain why anger can harm relationships

CENTRAL IDEA: Three myths about anger focus on an erroneous assumption, inappropriate expression, and a misattributed cause.

KEY POINTS: A. Myth: Anger and aggression are natural human instincts.

B. Myth: Forcefully expressing your anger is a healthy response.

C. Myth: Anger is caused by the action of other people.

SEQUENCE IN TIME

Time arrangement presents key points as a series of steps or points in time. Sharing recipes, instructions, and technical procedures often use a time arrangement, as do presentations about historical events. You also can use a time arrangement for a past-present-future pattern or for a before-after pattern.

TOPIC AREA: Conducting effective meetings

PURPOSE: To explain how to use meeting time effectively and efficiently

CENTRAL IDEA: Well-run meetings have a definite purposeful beginning, a well-organized middle, and a useful ending.

KEY POINTS: A. Purposeful beginning: Convene the meeting and share an agenda.

B. Well-organized middle: Follow the agenda.

C. Useful ending: Summarize next steps.

POSITION IN SPACE

If your information can be placed in different locations, you may want to use a **space arrangement** as an organizational pattern. In describing how to create a tidy living space, you might create key points for decluttering your bedroom, bathroom, and kitchen. Here's another example:

TOPIC AREA: Brain structure

PURPOSE: To explain how different sections of the brain are responsible for different functions

CENTRAL IDEA: A guided tour of the brain begins in the hindbrain, moves through the midbrain, and ends in the forebrain, with side trips through the right and left hemispheres.

KEY POINTS: A. The hindbrain

B. The midbrain

C. The forebrain

D. The right and left hemispheres

PRESENT PROBLEMS AND SOLUTIONS

Problem-solution arrangement describes a harmful or difficult situation (the problem) and offers a plan to solve it (the solution). In an **INFORMATIVE SPEECH ✳ (363–401)**, you may describe a problem that is simple and not controversial (a squeaking door, for example) and then describe how to solve it (lubricate the hinges). In a **PERSUASIVE SPEECH ◆ (403–61)**, the problem may be complex, controversial, and hard to solve, so you advocate a particular action to minimize or solve the problem. For example:

TOPIC AREA: Inactivity and health

PURPOSE: To recommend methods for reducing the detrimental effects of sitting too long

CENTRAL IDEA: Sitting for long periods of time can cause physical and mental health problems, but a schedule of simple physical activities can offset the harms.

KEY POINTS: A. Problem: Extended sitting can be harmful to physical health by, for example, increasing the risk of heart disease and cancer.

B. Problem: A sedentary lifestyle increases the risk of certain mental health problems, such as depression and dementia.

C. Solution: A regular schedule of simple physical activities, including standing up and walking, significantly reduces health risks.

SHOW CAUSES AND EFFECTS

A **cause-and-effect arrangement** either presents a cause and its resulting effect (cause-to-effect) or describes the effect that results from a specific cause (effect-to-cause).

In a *cause-to-effect arrangement,* you might claim that eating red meat causes disease and depression or that large classes and low teacher salaries explain a decline in test scores. In the following cause-to-effect arrangement, the speaker claims that using smartphones during class harms the learning process:

TOPIC AREA: Technology and learning

PURPOSE: To describe how using a smartphone during class negatively impacts learning

CENTRAL IDEA: Using smartphones during class distracts the student, disrupts the learning environment of others, and leads to lower test scores.

KEY POINTS: A. Cause: Using a smartphone during class distracts the student from focusing on what is being taught.

B. Cause: Using a smartphone during class disrupts the learning environment for other students.

C. Effect: Paying less attention during class results in lower retention of knowledge and test scores.

In an *effect-to-cause arrangement,* you describe a situation or behavior, create curiosity in your audience about its causes, and then explain why the situation or behavior exists. In the following effect-to-cause arrangement, the speaker identifies some of the causes of fatphobia:

TOPIC AREA: Health and well-being

PURPOSE: To understand why fatphobia persists in our culture

CENTRAL IDEA: Understanding the causes of fatphobia is the first step in combating its harmful effects.

KEY POINTS: A. Effect: Fatphobia leads to negative health outcomes for many people.

B. Causes:

1. The diet and fitness industry promotes thinness as the ideal body type and unhealthy methods to achieve it.

2. Myths persist that fat people are unhealthy and lack self-control. Doctors may prescribe losing weight, missing other underlying health issues.

3. Shaming to promote weight loss is rarely successful.

ARRANGE SCIENTIFICALLY

Scientists present claims by using the **scientific method arrangement**. When sharing the results of a scientific study or explaining the development of a theory—either your own or the work of a scientist—consider using an organizational pattern that follows the steps prescribed by journals that publish scientific research. Usually there are five basic sections in a scientific research report:

1. Explain the research question and why it is important.

2. Review previous research on the topic in question.

3. Describe the scientific methods used to study the research question.

4. Analyze and present the research results.

5. Discuss the implications of the research.[2]

The following example outlines a speech explaining the results of a study on the relationship between presentation anxiety and the preparation process:

TOPIC AREA: Presentation anxiety and the preparation process

PURPOSE: To explain why anxious speakers should study and learn how to prepare an effective presentation

CENTRAL IDEA: Learning effective preparation skills can reduce your level of speech anxiety and improve the quality of your presentation.

KEY POINTS: A. Research question: What is the relationship between speaker anxiety and preparation skills?

B. Review previous research.

C. Describe the research method.

D. Present the research results.

E. Discuss the implications of the research: learning effective preparation skills can reduce presentation anxiety.

TELL STORIES AND GIVE EXAMPLES

Sometimes a series of memorable **EXAMPLES AND STORIES** ■ **(137–38)** are so compelling and interesting that they can easily become the backbone of a speech. For example:

TOPIC AREA: Leaders and adversity

PURPOSE: To convince listeners that disabilities are not a barrier to success

CENTRAL IDEA: Many noteworthy leaders have lived exceptional lives with disabilities.

KEY POINTS: A. Elon Musk, the world's richest person, announced he was on the autism spectrum.

    B. Jan Scruggs, wounded soldier and founder of the Vietnam Veterans Memorial Fund, experienced PTSD.

    C. Harriet Tubman, abolitionist, lived with epileptic seizures.

COMPARE AND CONTRAST

A **comparison-contrast arrangement** shows your audience how individual things are similar to or different from each other. There are two basic ways to do this: *block* and *point-by-point* comparisons.[3]

    With a *block comparison*, you describe the relevant information about one item and then compare it to the relevant information about another item. For example:

TOPIC AREA: America's big cities

PURPOSE: To show that each of America's big cities is an excellent place to live, depending on your values

CENTRAL IDEA: Choosing to live in New York, Los Angeles, or Chicago depends on understanding the advantages and disadvantages of each one.

KEY POINTS:
A. New York: Advantages and disadvantages of the Big Apple

B. Los Angeles: Advantages and disadvantages of the City of Angels

C. Chicago: Advantages and disadvantages of the Windy City

Alternatively, when you do a *point-by-point* comparison, you focus on specific points of comparison between the things you are comparing. The following example compares types of animation, based on four points of comparison.

TOPIC AREA: Animation

PURPOSE: To recommend a way of evaluating different styles of animation

CENTRAL IDEA: Comparing drawing technique, versatility, character design, and cultural context can help you evaluate different styles of animation.

KEY POINTS: A. Drawing technique

B. Versatility

C. Character design

D. Cultural context

A different type of the comparison-contrast arrangement is called a *figurative analogy*. As a figure of speech, an **ANALOGY ∴ (312–14)** compares something unfamiliar with something more familiar, showing how two unrelated items have certain common characteristics. You can also use this framework to organize your speech. For example, drafting a fantasy football player isn't the same thing as predicting a student's success in college, yet the former provides a good analogy for thinking about the latter:

TOPIC AREA: Student success in college

PURPOSE: To identify the multiple factors that affect student success in college

CENTRAL IDEA: Predicting student success is like drafting a player for a fantasy football team: you must consider prior performance, coaching, and the environment.

KEY POINTS: A. Prior performance: A student's high school record = a player's NFL record

B. Coaching: A student's teacher and adviser = a player's coach

C. Environment: A student's learning environment = the player's home stadium

USE MEMORY AIDS

Journalists use the five Ws—who, what, where, when, and why—to remember the key questions they should answer in a news story. First-aid instructors teach the ABCs of first aid: open the airway, check for breathing, and check for circulation. In a presentation, you can use easily remembered letters, words, or phrases to organize your speech, help your audience follow along, and remember your key points.

TOPIC AREA:	Organizing a presentation
PURPOSE:	To provide an effective method for developing the key points of a presentation
CENTRAL IDEA:	The four Rs represent a series of critical thinking steps—review, reduce, regroup, refine—for generating a presentation's key points.
KEY POINTS:	A. Review
	B. Reduce
	C. Regroup
	D. Refine

OTHER ORGANIZATIONAL PATTERNS

In addition to these organizational patterns, there are patterns commonly used for specific professions and **SPECIAL OCCASIONS** ★ **(463–525)**. As we'll discuss in Part 7, there are also several unique **PERSUASIVE ORGANIZATIONAL PATTERNS** ◆ **(449–56)**, such as refuting objections, telling persuasive stories, and Monroe's Motivated Sequence.

Depending on your presentation, you may be able to adapt a common pattern or invent one of your own. Creative thinking can produce original patterns. For example, you might transform your key points into commonly asked questions. Think about how an audience might react to the following questions about the death penalty, as opposed to having the key points presented to them as statements:

Does the death penalty *deter* people from committing murder?

What *costs* more—life in prison or the legal process leading to execution?

Do victims' families have a right to *revenge* and emotional closure?

A creative organizational pattern can also generate interest with your audience. For example, Patricia Phillips, a customer-service expert, used excerpts from popular songs—"(I Can't Get No) Satisfaction" by the Rolling Stones, "Help!" by the Beatles, "Respect" by Aretha Franklin, "Don't Be Cruel" by Elvis Presley, and "Hit the Road Jack" by Ray Charles—to begin each major section of her training seminar. These well-known songs provided an upbeat way to move into each new section of the seminar.

Sequencing Key Points

Some of the organizational arrangements we've described (like scientific method arrangement) more or less dictate the order of your key points. Others (like comparison-contrast or telling stories) don't. The following general considerations can help you decide which key points should go first, next, and last.

STRENGTH AND FAMILIARITY

If one of your points is not as strong as the others or may be less familiar to your audience, place it in the middle position. For example, how would you order the stories in the presentation that focuses on Elon Musk, Jan Scruggs, and Harriet Tubman? Whereas most US audiences would be familiar with the first and third person, they may not recognize Jan Scruggs, a disabled Vietnam veteran who founded the Washington Vietnam Veterans Memorial Fund. Put the least familiar story in the middle of the presentation in order to start and end with better-known examples.

AUDIENCE ANALYSIS

Whether you "put your best foot forward" by leading with your strongest point or "save the best for last" will depend in part on your purpose and what you learn during AUDIENCE ANALYSIS ▲ (90–96) . If potential clients come to your sales presentation wanting information about pricing options, satisfy that need early on in your presentation. An audience motivated to hear something very particular shouldn't have to wait for it—and they might get distracted or interrupt you if they do. On the other hand, if an audience is not very interested in your topic, don't begin with your most technical, detailed point. You may be better off beginning with a point that explains *why* understanding the topic is important and then build up to your strongest point at the end.

Connecting Key Points

Connectives link one part of a presentation to another, clarify how one idea relates to another, and identify how supporting material bolsters a key point. Without connectives, a well-organized presentation can sound choppy and awkward. Connectives provide the "glue" that helps your audience follow, understand, and remember your message. There are four kinds of connectives: *internal previews, internal summaries, transitions,* and *signposts*.

INTERNAL PREVIEWS

When used in the introduction of a presentation, an **internal preview** reveals or suggests your key points to the audience. It tells them what you are going to cover and in what order. When used in the body of a speech, an internal preview describes how you are going to approach a key point. Here's how one student internally previewed his presentation about Taylor Swift:

> Why is Taylor Swift so popular? Some would say it's because of how the music industry has promoted her while others say that she has a keen awareness of what her fans want. Either or both reasons might be true. Let's begin by looking at . . .

INTERNAL SUMMARIES

Whereas an internal preview begins a section, an **internal summary** ends a section and helps reinforce important ideas. Internal summaries also give you an opportunity to pause in a presentation and repeat critical ideas or pieces of information. Here's an internal summary section on why Taylor Swift has a devoted fan base:

> Without a doubt, Taylor Swift has a devoted fan base because her lyrics are relatable, they support her fight for artists' rights, and she rewards them for being Swifties.

TRANSITIONS

The most common connectives are **transitions**—words, numbers, brief phrases, or sentences that help you lead your audience from one key point or section to another. They are bridges that help you get from one idea to the next. Transitions can be quite simple and consist of little more than a word or phrase, or they can be one or two complete sentences. They can help you move from one major section of a presentation to another. For example: "Now that we've established why Taylor Swift's fans are so devoted, it's time to consider how she has changed fandom."

COMMON TRANSITION WORDS AND USES		
Transition purpose	**Transition words**	**Examples**
Comparing	Similarly As with In the same way Just as	Just as smoking is banned on campus, so should . . .
Contrasting	Yet On the other hand Alternatively Whereas Otherwise	Yet it's important to remember . . . On the other hand, some people believe . . .
Illustrating and adding	For example As In addition Another reason Furthermore	In addition to her fan base, there is . . . Another reason she should be elected is . . .
Signaling a conclusion	Finally In conclusion As you can see	Finally, a responsible parent should . . .

Relying on these transitions alone won't add interest or variety to a presentation. Savvy speakers use a variety of transitional phrases and strategies to avoid repetition and heighten impact.

- *Bridge words* alert listeners that you are moving on to a new thought. Examples include "furthermore," "meanwhile," "however," "in addition," "consequently," and "finally."

- *Trigger transitions* use the same word or phrase twice to connect one topic to another. For example: "Now that we've explored common *characteristics* of Taylor Swift's fanbase, we can see how the *characteristics* of fandom have changed."

- *Questions* shift the audience's attention from one point to another. For example: "As we've discussed why Taylor Swift's fans are so devoted, you may be wondering, 'How has this devotion changed fandom as a whole?'"

- *Flashbacks* link a previous point to a new one. For example: "Earlier I mentioned that Taylor Swift's fans support her fights for artists' rights. Other artists support this fight as well."

- *Delivery transitions* use **PHYSICAL DELIVERY ▶ (249–59)** (movement, gestures) or **PRESENTATION AIDS ▶ (260–78)** to signal a transition from one thing to another. Examples include the "on one hand" and "on the other hand" gestures, moving one's body from one place to another in the room while describing a transition, or shifting from talking to using a visual aid.[4]

SIGNPOSTS

A final and important type of connective is the signpost. Just as most travelers like to know where they are, where they've been, and where they're going, audiences appreciate a speaker who uses connectives for similar reasons. **Signposts** are short, often numerical references that, like highway signs, remind listeners where they are and how far they have to go. A signpost can be as simple as "Let's begin by discussing how Taylor Swift's fans came to be known as 'Swifties.'" You might also begin each key point with a number, as in: "Third and finally, Taylor Swift rewards her fans for their devotion by including 'Easter eggs' in her lyrics, music videos, and social media posts." Making explicit how many points you will cover offers a preview for your audience and also signals your **CONCLUSION ■ (198–203)**.

For an example of a speaker who identifies, repeats, and rephrases three key points throughout a presentation, see Notable Speaker: David Epstein, page 398.

Conclusion

Making sure you have clear and coherent organization may not be the most exciting aspect of preparing your presentation, but it is among the most important. A coherent organizational structure helps you develop compelling and relevant key points that support your central idea in a way that enhances your audience's understanding and interest. A presentation that is organized badly—no matter how skillfully you deliver it—is much less likely to succeed.

Think of it this way: A speech without structure is like a human body without a skeleton. It won't stand up. Having structure won't necessarily make the speech a great one, but lacking structure will diminish any inspired thoughts because listeners are too busy trying to find out where they are in the presentation's progression.[5]

Sebastian Wernicke

Dr. Sebastian Wernicke clearly loves data—so much so that he is the Chief Data Scientist at One Logic, a company that helps organizations use data in meaningful ways. His TED talks are infused with a bit of humor, which may explain why his talk "Lies, Damned Lies and Statistics (about TEDTalks)" has been viewed more than two million times. He delivered the talk at the 2010 TEDActive program, which features workshops in a more casual and creative setting. Wernicke's presentation is a skillful explanation of how to use data to design the ultimate TED talk—and is also a helpful example of how to organize content for a presentation.

Search Terms

To locate a video of this presentation online, enter the following key words into a search engine: Sebastian Wernicke Lies, Damned Lies and Statistics. The video is approximately 5:42 in length.

What to Watch For

[0:00-0:51] Using a conversational style, Wernicke draws his audience in with a bit of humor about, of all things, statistics. Within just a few seconds of beginning, he states the purpose of the presentation—his goal—quite clearly: to teach his audience how to design the ultimate TED talk. He reinforces this goal by making it visual and adding a humorous secondary purpose statement—"the worst possible TED talk that they would still let you get away with." Using the rule of three, he describes specifically what he intends to say in his presentation (his central idea): what topic you should choose, how you should deliver the topic, and the visuals you should use on stage. Once again, he reinforces his point by making it visual.

[0:52–1:52] Wernicke has chosen a categorical arrangement, taking the larger topic of how to create the ultimate TED talk and dividing it into three smaller categories: topic, delivery, and visuals. He uses several connectives, such as a transition to move the audience into the first of those categories: "Now, with the topic. . . ." He then provides another connective—the internal summary—to reinforce which topics TED audiences connect with more and which topics they connect with less.

[1:53–3:16] Wernicke signals to his audience that he is transitioning to his next key point by asking a question: "How should you deliver your talk?" Using an internal preview, he tells his audience that he is going to give them three rules to obey when it comes to presenting their TED talk, and he clearly provides a signpost before talking about each one: "first of all," "secondly," and "finally."

[3:17–4:17] By saying, "Now, let's go to the visuals," he signals that he is moving onto his third key point. He continues to use bridge words and phrases to alert his audience that he is introducing a new supporting point. For example, the audience knows he is about to make a new point when he says, "And now the most important thing . . ."

[4:18–5:23] Wernicke makes it clear that he is concluding his presentation: "Now it's time to put it all together." He flashes back to the purpose statement, which is to help them design the ultimate TED talk. He calls for action by introducing them to TEDPad, a tool he created to help people create TED talks based on his statistical analysis of TED talk data. While this is a humorous call to action, it reinforces his use of statistics to help him accomplish his stated purpose.

While the slide with the three key points was displayed as he began the summary, there is an opportunity here for him to strengthen the conclusion by saying his central idea along with showing the visual. Before encouraging the audience to enjoy designing their own ultimate and worst possible TED talks, he could verbally remind them of his central idea: choosing the right topic, knowing how to deliver the topic, and using the right visuals on stage.

EXERCISE

After reviewing Wernicke's speech, reflect on these questions:

1. To what extent and how did Wernicke use any delivery transitions?

2. Is there another pattern of organization that would have worked well for his presentation? Explain why or why not.

3. Describe the effectiveness of his central idea. Could he have done anything differently to make it more effective?

4. Which key point used connectives most effectively? Which one could have used them more effectively?

5. Did you find it easy to remember Wernicke's key points after his presentation? Why or why not?

3.4 Framing and Outlining

Consider how a poet chooses the words for a sonnet or how a composer uses musical notes to write a song. In these examples, the creators arrange their work within a recognizable structure. Likewise, as a speaker, you can arrange your ideas in a framework that audience members will understand, appreciate, and remember. In this chapter, we focus on two methods for structuring your content—a *speech framer* and an *outline*.

You're probably familiar with outlines, which organize the components of a presentation in a specific order and format. Although outlines are helpful and often required by instructors, some presenters find that outlines constrain their thought processes and restrict the flow of their presentation.[1] The speech framer provides a useful alternative, giving you more flexibility with the contents of your presentation while also serving as the basis for a required outline. One or both of these methods can help you build a sound structure and reliable blueprint for your presentation.

Framing Your Presentation

The **speech framer**, is a visual framework that identifies a place for every component of a presentation's content.[2] We often begin structuring a presentation with a speech framer because, generally, it puts the introduction, key points and supporting material, and conclusion on a single page, and it's easy to modify. Think of it as a road map to your presentation.

SPEECH FRAMER TEMPLATE

Introduction:			
Central idea:			
Key points	1.	2.	3.
Supporting material			
Supporting material			
Supporting material			
Supporting material			
Connectives			
Conclusion:			

The speech framer works best when you are speaking **EXTEMPORANE-OUSLY ▶ (215)**, as opposed to using a manuscript or memorizing your presentation. It provides a set of well-prepared notes in a quick-to-reference format, making it easy to modify, move, add, and delete content before and as you speak. For example, if you discover that you have less time than you initially planned for, you can see your whole presentation at a glance and decide quickly which key points and/or supporting material you can shorten or eliminate. In this way, it encourages experimentation and creativity and serves as an efficient and adaptable set of speaking notes for any presentation.

Before using the speech framer, revisit your **MIND MAP ■ (154–55)** and review the probable key points of your presentation. Then identify an appropriate **ORGANIZATIONAL PATTERN ■ (157–66)** and select the **SUPPORTING MATERIAL ■ (134–51)** that you'll need to achieve your purpose. Finally, arrange your content into the speech framer template. As you can see in the template, the speech framer is designed to resemble a window, with each pane providing space for each component of your presentation.

The speech framer template has space for three key points and three pieces of supporting material for each point, and you can adjust the format to accommodate any number of key points and supporting material for your particular speech. For example:

- If you have four key points, add a fourth column to the frame.
- If you have three key points but do not have relevant supporting material for one of the points, delete that key point—or do more research.
- If there are three types of supporting material for one key point and two types for another, that's okay—just make sure all the supporting material is strong.

Although you can usually put most of a presentation's content on a one-page speech framer, there are some rhetorical situations where you may need more room than that. If, for example, your introduction is longer than usual or needs to be presented word for word along with your central idea, put those on the first page. A second page can cover the key points, supporting material, and connectives. If your conclusion doesn't fit on the second page, put it on a third page.

Outlining Your Presentation

Another method of organizing your presentation's content is to use an **outline**, which places the components of your speech in a specific order and with particular formatting conventions (indenting, numbering, and so on) to indicate the relative importance of, and the relationships among, those sections. Like the speech framer, an outline provides a road map for your presentation. And like the speech framer, you can only create an outline once you've identified your purpose, central idea, key points, supporting material, and a potential organizational pattern for your topic.

SPEECH FRAMER EXAMPLE: WHY AND HOW TO DEAL WITH ANGER

Introduction:	*[Ask the audience]* Have you ever been angry? Natural, human reaction. Soccer story.		
Central idea:	Understanding anger can help you avoid, manage, and respond appropriately to your own and others' anger.		
	Define anger: "Emotional response to unmet expectations" *[Connective to key point 1]*		
	Examples: Expected grade, promotion, honesty [Ask for more examples]		
Key points	**1. Anger myths**	**2. Your anger**	**3. Others' anger**
Supporting material	True or False? Anger can be helpful because it lets you vent your feelings. • <u>True</u>: Danger response • <u>False</u>: Angry people become angrier.	Admit you are angry. • No shouting • Control nonverbals: face, body, tone • (Ruth example)	Acknowledge. • "I understand how angry you are." • "I'd be just as upset if I were you." • "I should have . . ."
Supporting material	True or False? Anger is caused when someone upsets or hurts you. • <u>False</u>: You are responsible for your anger. • Don't blame others. (Ari example)	Avoid personal attacks. • Name-calling, threats, canceling • [Ask for more examples.]	Clarify. • "I don't think I said I'd write the report." • "How is this different from when we . . ."
Supporting material		Use "I" statements. • "I expected . . ." • "I don't understand . . ." • "I thought you said . . ."	Collaborate • "Let's work this out together." • Example: Asking Petra to mediate
Connectives	How to manage anger?	Responding to someone else's anger?	
Conclusion:	Understand anger myths, manage your anger, and respond appropriately to others' anger. Take responsibility for your feelings and behavior when you feel or face anger.		
	Carol Tavris (author of *Anger: The Misunderstood Emotion*) quote: Anger "requires an awareness of choice and an embrace of reason. It is knowing when to become angry...when to make peace; when to take action, and when to keep silent."		

Outlines vary in format and level of detail. If your speaking situation requires an outline, follow the two basic rules that apply to all outlines: *use numbers, letters, and indentations*; and *keep the outline consistent*.

USE NUMBERS, LETTERS, AND INDENTATIONS

Every part of an outline should be systematically numbered, lettered, and indented to signal the hierarchy of ideas in your presentation. Roman numerals (I, II, III, and so on) signify the largest major divisions at the top of the hierarchy. We recommend using a roman numeral I for your introduction, roman numeral II for the body, and roman numeral III for the conclusion since these sections are vital to a presentation's structure and success.

After using roman numerals to establish the major sections of your presentation, indented uppercase letters (A, B, C, and so on) identify the major sections in your introduction and the key points in the body of your presentation. Further indented arabic numbers (1, 2, 3, and so on) indicate the next level down in the hierarchy of your outline. They are used to substantiate the key points with supporting material. If you need a fourth level, use lowercase letters (a, b, c, and so on). If you include subsections to a point, include at least two subsections—after all, you can't divide something into just one part. In other words, if there is a point A, there must be a point B; for every subpoint 1, there should be a subpoint 2. For example:

    I. **Introduction**

    II. **Body**

       A. **Key point 1**

          1. Supporting material

          2. Supporting material

       B. **Key point 2**

          1. Supporting material

          2. Supporting material

    III. **Conclusion**

KEEP THE OUTLINE CONSISTENT

Use a consistent writing style throughout your outline. For each key point (A, B, C), use a single word, phrase, or full sentence, but don't mix styles. You may need more detail when you get to the arabic-number level (1, 2, 3), but try to be consistent in style and grammar at each level. If you begin a subpoint with a verb, the subpoints that follow should also start with a verb. This will make your outline easier to read and will help you find precise language for each section when delivering your presentation.

✓ **CONSISTENT STYLE:** I. Myths about anger
                                                          II. Management of anger

✓ **CONSISTENT STYLE:** I. Understanding the myths about anger
                                                           II. Managing your anger

✗ **INCONSISTENT STYLE:** I. Myths about anger
                                                            II. Managing your anger

Using an Outline to Prepare

Outlines are not born fully formed, with every detail and subpoint in place. They begin with a few basic building blocks and grow from there. A **preliminary outline** can help you develop and arrange your key points and supporting material into a sketch of your presentation. It lets you try different ways of organizing your content into a coherent message. In its simplest form, a preliminary outline looks like this:

  I. **Introduction**
     A. **Attention-getter:** _____
     B. **Central idea:** _____
     C. **Preview of key points:** _____
  II. **Body of presentation**
     A. **Key point 1:** _____
        1. Supporting material: _____
        2. Supporting material: _____

   B. **Key point 2:** _____
      1. Supporting material: _____
      2. Supporting material: _____
   C. **Key point 3:** _____
      1. Supporting material: _____
      2. Supporting material: _____
III. **Conclusion**

A preliminary outline can be used to organize almost any presentation by filling in the blanks for each section. Depending on the topic and the rhetorical situation, you can easily modify this template by changing the number of key points and amount of supporting material you decide to include for each point.

It may take some time to draft your preliminary outline, even after you have your key points and supporting material selected. Keep in mind that the resulting preliminary outline is just that—preliminary. It includes your initial ideas and will probably change as you further develop your presentation and continue to do **RESEARCH** ■ **(134–51)**. Here is a preliminary outline for a presentation about anger:

Preliminary Outline: Why and How to Deal with Anger
I. **Introduction**
   A. **Attention-getter:** Personal story about my soccer team
   B. **Central idea:** Understanding and rejecting the myths about anger to help us deal with it more effectively
   C. **Preview of key points:** Refuting anger myths, managing anger, and responding to anger
II. **Body of presentation**
   A. **Key point 1:** Refuting anger myths
      1. Supporting material: Believing that anger is good
      2. Supporting material: Believing that anger is caused by others
   B. **Key point 2:** Managing anger
      1. Supporting material: Acknowledging your anger
      2. Supporting material: Avoiding personal attacks

      C. **Key point 3:** Responding to anger
         1. Supporting material: Identifying the source of anger
         2. Supporting material: Seeking resolution
  III. **Conclusion**

WRITING A FULL-SENTENCE OUTLINE

Some speakers (and students required to do so by their instructors) take the outlining process one step further, expanding their preliminary outline into a **full-sentence outline**, which may contain every idea, concept, and fact you include in a presentation, depending on how detailed you choose to make it.

Writing a full-sentence outline while preparing a presentation can help you assess whether you have the right number of key points, explanations, and significant supporting material. If you are using MANUSCRIPT DELIVERY ▶ (216), a full-sentence outline can be a helpful speaking tool because it clearly separates the major parts of a presentation into concise sections. However, if you are using EXTEMPORANEOUS DELIVERY ▶ (215), a full-sentence outline should not be used as your speaking notes, as it shares the disadvantages of manuscript delivery, such as poor eye contact, limited movement, and difficulty modifying content. That said, including some full sentences in your speaking notes can provide precise language and ensure the accuracy of full quotations, important statistics, or specific examples.

As you'll notice in the following example, a full-sentence outline includes almost all the presentation's content and comes close to a word-for-word script. Brackets are used to indicate references, and there is a full reference list at the end. If your instructor asks you to submit references, use the style and format they prefer.

Full-Sentence Outline: Why and How to Deal with Anger
I. **Introduction**
    A. **Attention-getter:** "Have you ever been angry or enraged?" All of us have. Everyone feels anger at some time—it's a natural human reaction but can be distressing and harmful.

I first noticed the negative effects of anger when I lashed out at a teammate on my soccer team. It was uncalled for and embarrassing. I was benched for the next 3 games.

B. **Central idea:** To deal with the causes and consequences of anger, begin by fact-checking your beliefs about anger, finding ways to manage your anger, and learning how to respond respectfully to anger expressed by someone else. Before I recommend methods for dealing with anger, let's begin by understanding what anger is.

C. **Definition of anger:** Anger is "an emotional response to unmet expectations." Here are some examples: discovering a friend has told a falsehood when you expect them to tell the truth; expecting but not receiving praise for good work; expecting an A on an exam but getting a C. [*Ask the audience for additional examples.*]

Transition: I hope this simple definition helps you understand the nature of anger and its causes so you can consider the consequences of expressing anger inappropriately and learn to respond to anger responsibly.

II. **Body of presentation**

A. **Key point 1:** Many of us believe common myths about anger, which prevent us from effectively dealing with anger. [Eifert et al.] Consider the following statements:

1. **True or false?** Anger can be helpful, particularly if you feel threatened. This is true *and* false. True: In some cases, anger can be a warning of imminent danger. False: Anger is rarely helpful; it often makes things worse. If you're quick to anger, you may regret it later.

2. **True or false?** Anger results when someone says or does something that upsets or hurts you. False: While you might blame people or events for your anger, *you* are the source of anger. If you blame others, you don't have to change how you behave—and you stay angry. [Tell the story about apologizing to Ari after accusing him of making a mistake.]

Transition: In addition to understanding the nature of anger, it's just as important to learn how to manage your anger and avoid making things worse.

B. **Key point 2:** Learn how to manage your anger appropriately and effectively. Identifying the causes and consequences of anger can help you respond appropriately to threatening situations. Here are three ways to manage anger effectively [Wilmot and Hocker]:

   1. **Admit you are angry.** Don't shout. Control your nonverbal behavior, such as frowning or sneering, clenching a fist, or raising your voice. Calmly state why you are angry. [Tell the story about working with Ruth on a project.]

   2. **Avoid personal attacks.** Don't resort to name-calling. Describe the problem as objectively as you can rather than ranting and raging at someone.

   3. **Use "I" statements instead of "you" statements.** Describe *your* feelings instead of the bad things someone did to you. Say, "I thought that you would . . ." instead of "Because you screwed up, everything's a mess."

Transition: Learning to manage your anger appropriately is only half of the equation. The other half is learning to manage *your* response when someone is angry with you.

C. **Key point 3:** Learn constructive responses to someone else's anger. [Wilmot and Hocker]

   1. **Acknowledge why they are angry.** "I understand how angry you are. Given that the report is due next week, I think I'd be just as upset if I were you. I should have made myself available to help when I said I would."

   2. **Clarify the issue or source of anger.** "I don't think I said I'd write the report. I said I'd give you my notes from the meeting."

   3. **Seek a collaborative approach to resolution.** "Let's sit down and try to solve the problem."

III. **Conclusion**

    A. **Summarize key points.** Remember that myths about anger may prevent you from dealing with it effectively. How can you express your anger in a way that may resolve the problem? And how might you respond to someone else's anger without making matters worse?

    B. **Conclude.** Take responsibility for your feelings and behavior when you face an unmet expectation or disappointment. I'll leave you with another quotation worth remembering. Carol Tavris, author of *Anger: The Misunderstood Emotion*, wrote: Anger "requires an awareness of choice and an embrace of reason. It is knowing when to become angry . . . when to make peace, when to take action, and when to keep silent."

References

Cahn, Dudley D., and Ruth Anna Abigail. *Managing Conflict through Communication*. 5th ed. Boston: Pearson, 2014. 187–98.

Canary, Daniel J., and Sandra Lakey. *Strategic Conflict*. New York: Routledge, 2013. 56–59.

Eifert, Georg H., Matthew McKay, and John P. Forsyth. *ACT on Life Not on Anger: The New Acceptance & Commitment Therapy Guide to Problem Anger*. Oakland, CA: New Harbinger, 2006. 15, 16, 19, 20, 21.

Svitil, Kathy A. *Calming the Anger Storm*. New York: Alpha, 2005. 14–15.

Tavris, Carol. *Anger: The Misunderstood Emotion*. New York: Simon & Schuster, 1982. 253.

Wilmot, William W., and Joyce L. Hocker. *Interpersonal Conflict*. 6th ed. Boston: McGraw-Hill, 2001. 251–53.

Creating a full-sentence outline requires a great deal of time and effort, including multiple revisions, during which you may discover sections that have either too many or too few ideas and information. Do you have enough supporting material? Do you need to revise your central idea based on the key points and supporting materials that are most compelling in your outline? Do your connectives logically lead your audience from one key point or section to another? Keep revising and adjusting until your outline is balanced, well organized, and well supported.

Presenting with a Speech Framer or Outline

Once you've organized and developed your presentation with a preliminary or full-sentence outline, you're ready to start practicing your speech. If you're **MEMORIZING ▶ (216)** your presentation or reading from a **MANUSCRIPT ▶ (216)**, you'll need to expand your outline to create a full script to memorize or read. But if you plan to deliver your presentation in a conversational or **EXTEMPORANEOUS ▶ (215)** style, you'll need a brief overview of your presentation that relies on keywords, helping you stay on track without reciting every word you've written. We recommend the speech framer or a speaking notes outline.

Following the same organization as in your preliminary outline, a **speaking notes outline** should include your key points, ideas, and citations, using important words and phrases instead of full sentences. For example, you might write "manage anger" instead of "Learn how to manage your anger appropriately."

In the following example, notice how the outline is well organized with short phrases to function as an effective set of speaking notes. Assuming you are well prepared and well rehearsed, you may need only a hint to remember some sections, such as [*Ask the audience*] or *Soccer story*.

See Chapter 4.1 **DELIVERY DECISIONS ▶** for advantages and disadvantages of using impromptu, extemporaneous, manuscript, and memorized delivery.

Speaking Notes Outline: Why and How to Deal with Anger

I. **Introduction**

    A. **Attention-getter:**

        1. [*Ask the audience*] "Have you ever been angry?"

        2. Natural, human reaction

        3. Example: Soccer story

    B. **Central idea:** Understanding anger > avoid, manage, and respond appropriately to your and others' anger

    C. **Define anger:** "Emotional response to unmet expectations"

        1. Examples: expected grade, promotion, honesty

        2. [*Ask for more examples*]

    D. **Preview:** Key points

        1. Dispelling anger myths

        2. Managing your anger

        3. Responding to anger from others

II. **Body of presentation**

    A. **Key point 1:** Anger myths [Eifert et al.]

        1. True/False? Anger is helpful > lets you vent. <u>Both</u>.

            a. True: Danger response

            b. False: Angry people become angrier.

        2. True/False? Caused when someone upsets/hurts you.

            a. <u>False:</u> *You* are responsible for your anger.

            b. Don't blame others.

            c. Example: Apology to Ari

    B. **Key point 2:** Your anger

        1. Admit you are angry.

            a. No shouting

            b. Control nonverbals: face, body, tone

            c. Example: Ruth story

        2. Avoid personal attacks.

            a. No name-calling, threats, canceling

            b. [*Ask audience for more examples.*]

        3. Use "I" statements.

            a. "I expected . . ."

            b. "I don't understand . . ."

            c. "I thought you said . . ."

    C. **Key point 3:** Others' anger

        1. Acknowledge.

            a. "I understand how angry you are."

            b. "I'd be just as upset if I were you."

            c. "I should have . . ."

        2. Clarify.

            a. "I don't think I said I'd write the report."

            b. "How is this different from when we . . ."

3. Collaborate.

    a. "Let's work this out together."

    b. Example: Asking Petra to mediate

III. **Conclusion**

  A. **Summarize key points**

    1. Understanding anger myths

    2. Managing anger

    3. Responding to anger

    4. Summary: You are responsible for your feelings and behavior when you feel or face anger.

  B. **Carol Tavris quote:** Anger "requires an awareness of choice and an embrace of reason. It is knowing when to become angry . . . when to make peace, when to take action, and when to keep silent."

Compare this speaking notes outline to the example speech framer on page 177. They include the same introduction, central idea, key points, definitions, supporting material, stories, and conclusion. Both methods result in a usable set of notes that organize your content into a coherent message. Use the option that will work best for you, your presentation, and your speaking occasion.

As with the speech framer, your speaking notes will naturally evolve as you prepare for and practice your presentation. Abbreviate ideas you can recall easily and add cues for the ones you tend to forget. Remember, your first draft should never be your final draft! And before you even start practicing, use the following tips to prepare speaking notes that will be a helpful and reliable reference as you deliver your presentation:

See Chapter 4.1 **DELIVERY DECISIONS ▶** for more advice on using notes effectively while you practice your delivery.

1. *Title your notes.* Select a title that best represents your purpose and put it at the top of your notes. Not only will it keep you focused on your overriding purpose as you speak, it will also help you describe your presentation to others. Consider the difference between a presentation titled "Anger Is a Natural Response" and one titled "Why and How to Deal with Anger."

2. *Insert time markers.* On your outline or speech framer, note the amount of time you expect to take on each section of your

presentation. Make sure the total adds up to the assigned (or desired) time limit! As you practice your presentation, if a section runs too short or too long, you may need to speak faster, cut some material, or even drop a key point. And if unexpected changes or disruptions cut into your speaking time, those time markers will help you decide how and where to accommodate those changes.

3. *Use delivery cues.* When preparing your outline, **MARK UP YOUR NOTES** ▶ **(220)** with delivery cues that tell you which words or phrases to emphasize with changes in **VOCAL QUALITY** ▶ **(231–41)** as well as when to pause and when to **GESTURE** ▶ **(252–55)** and **MOVE** ▶ **(256–57)**. Use symbols, **bold**, underlining, and ALL CAPS to emphasize important words or phrases.

4. *Include written references.* Depending on your expertise, topic, and the rhetorical situation, add **CITATIONS** ▪ **(149–51)** to your notes. In some cases (such as a communication course), you may be required to turn in both an outline and a set of references. Audience members may ask about your data, the background of someone you quoted, or how to learn more about the topic. Having a list of references will help you **ANSWER QUESTIONS** ⸬ **(355–56)** with credibility and confidence.

Conclusion

There are many methods for organizing the content of a presentation into a clear and coherent message. We recommend using the speech framer or an outline. The speech framer is a flexible framework that puts every component of your presentation on a single page that may be used as speaking notes. Many speakers only use the speech framer rather than an outline, and some use the speech framer as a foundation for an outline.

A preliminary outline is a beginning step or draft for organizing your content, and it usually changes as you learn more about the occasion, audience, and topic. It can be expanded into a full-sentence outline that contains almost all the content in your presentation, coming close to exactly what you intend to say. The speech framer and speaking notes outline can distill a full-sentence outline into a clear, simple, and useful set of notes you can use as you speak.

Regardless of the method you use to arrange the content of your presentation, there is one universal and abiding truth: organization matters. Structure your presentation using the method that works best in a particular rhetorical situation and supports your delivery style to ensure a clear, communicative, and memorable presentation.

3.5 Introductions and Conclusions

"You never get a second chance to make a first impression"—so the saying goes. Think about your own snap judgments. A single photo often makes the difference between swiping left or swiping right on a dating profile. If the first few minutes of a TV show bore you, you may switch to something else. Likewise, if the beginning of your presentation isn't interesting, your audience might tune you out or misunderstand what you're saying. If you're speaking online, they might even walk away or close the tab!

On the other hand, a good beginning can create a positive, lasting impression and pave the way for a presentation that achieves its purpose. Psychologists call this power of first impressions the **primacy effect**, or the tendency to recall the first items you see or hear in sequenced information. The primacy effect suggests that audience members are more likely to remember the beginning of a presentation because that's when their attention is usually at its peak.

Likewise, a strong conclusion ensures that your audience will remember you and your message. Psychologists describe the power of last impressions as the **recency effect**, or the tendency to recall the items you see or hear at the end of sequenced information. Because it comes last, the conclusion of your presentation is likely to stay with your audience long after you've finished. In short, the goodbye matters as much as the hello. What you say and do during your introduction and conclusion can determine the success of your presentation.

Introducing Your Presentation

Your introduction should connect *you*, your *audience*, and your *message*. It introduces you and your topic to the audience; it also introduces your audience to you. Your introduction gives the audience time to adjust, settle in, block out distractions, and focus their attention. At the same time, it gives you a chance to get a feel for the audience, calm down, and make any last-minute adjustments to what you want to say and how you want to say it.

There are five main goals of any introduction:

1. *Focus audience attention and interest.* Your introduction should ENGAGE YOUR AUDIENCE ∴ (303–61) by using compelling supporting material, vivid and powerful language, and expressive delivery.

2. *Connect with your audience.* Thorough AUDIENCE ANALYSIS ▲ (90–96) will help link your message to the audience's characteristics, attitudes, needs, and interests. Give audience members a good reason to listen to you by explaining WHAT'S IN IT FOR THEM? ▲ (93).

3. *Put* you *in your presentation.* Link your expertise, experiences, and personality to the purpose and content of your presentation. An audience's initial impression of you, the SPEAKER ▲ (72–85), can be just as important as what they think about your message.

4. *Set the mood.* The emotions you express with your DELIVERY ▶ (209–301) and the tone of your LANGUAGE ∴ (305–22) can be positive and upbeat, respectful and sober, playful and amusing, or urgent and serious. It all depends on your purpose.

5. *Preview the message.* In most speaking situations, your introduction should give your audience an **INTERNAL PREVIEW** ■ **(167)** of your message. You can state your central idea, if appropriate, and briefly list the key points you will cover. However, in some persuasive or celebratory speeches, you may not want to reveal your central idea or key points at the beginning of a presentation.

You may not be able to achieve all five goals in every presentation. Just remember this: the single most important goal of any introduction is to focus audience attention and interest on you and your message. And there are endless ways to do just that! What follows are just some of the many effective ways to begin a presentation.

USE AN INTERESTING STATISTIC OR EXAMPLE

If you anticipate a problem gaining and maintaining your audience's attention, an unusual, dramatic, or unexpected **STATISTIC** ■ **(135–36)** or **EXAMPLE** ■ **(137–38)** can help focus their eyes, ears, and minds on you and your message. Here's an example:

> How much did Bob Iger, the CEO of the Walt Disney Corporation make in 2023? Counting salary, incentives, and bonuses, he made $31.6 million.[1] That's $607,000 a week. If he worked five days a week, he would only earn about $121,400 a day. Poor Bob! He's not even close to the 25 wealthiest people in the United States.

QUOTE SOMEONE

Rather than trying to write the perfect beginning yourself, you may find that someone else has already done it for you. As you research your topic, you may uncover a dramatic statement or eloquent phrase that is an ideal beginning for your presentation. A well-chosen quotation can overcome audience doubts, especially when the quotation is from someone who is highly respected or an expert source of information.

When quoting someone, make sure you identify the writer or speaker with an **ORAL CITATION** ■ **(150)**. In some cases, you need to state only the name of the person you are quoting. In other cases, you may need to provide more information about the person, circumstances, or publication. Consider this example, in which a speaker quotes Warren Buffett:

> Warren Buffett is the sixth-richest person in the United States. His net worth is more than $133 billion. When asked about the skill that was most important in improving and ensuring his success, he said, "You can improve your monetary value by 50 percent just by learning . . . public speaking." Let's take a closer look at why he is so adamant about the value of this skill and why you should heed his advice.

Depending on the length of the quotation and how well you've practiced the opening, you may be able to quote someone without looking at your notes. Otherwise, you can refer to your notes as a way of showing that you want to quote your source accurately.

TELL A STORY

Some speakers begin presentations with **STORIES ∴(323–32)** about their personal hardships or triumphs. Others share stories they've read about or heard from others. The following example comes from a student presentation:

> When I was fifteen, I was operated on to remove the deadliest form of skin cancer, a melanoma carcinoma. My doctors injected ten shots of steroids into each scar every three weeks to stop the scars from spreading. I now know that it wasn't worth a couple of summers of being tan to go through all that pain and suffering. Take steps now to protect yourself from the harmful effects of the sun.

An introductory story doesn't have to be personal or tragic—but it should be brief. Think of the lessons to be learned from your favorite books and films, from television characters, and from the biographies or autobiographies of important or historical figures. There are stories everywhere—just make sure the one you choose to tell is relevant to your purpose.

ASK A QUESTION

ASKING A QUESTION ⸫ **(343–44)** can attract your audience's attention and interest because it encourages them to think about possible answers. Although a few listeners may be able to answer the questions you pose, many more will think to themselves, "I have no idea!" and will be intrigued to hear more from you.

Sometimes one question can lead to a more important one. For example, you might ask a question that will help the majority of your audience identify with one another, such as:

> How many of you have a driver's license and regularly drive a car? How many of you have experienced or know someone who's experienced a serious car accident?

Seeing hands go up or down causes the audience to look around. That curiosity can create interest in your topic, develop empathy, and stir emotion in audience members, who will then look to the speaker for more information.

ESTABLISH A PERSONAL LINK

Use your introduction to link your background to your audience. Although you may be very different, you likely have shared similar experiences. When Margaret Muller, a middle-school student with Down syndrome, made a presentation to seventh- and eighth-grade classes, here's how she began:[2]

> Today I'd like to tell you about Down syndrome. My purpose for talking about this is to be able to say, Yes, I have Down syndrome. Sometimes I have to work harder to learn things, but in many ways I am just like everyone else. I would like to tell people that having Down syndrome does not keep me from doing things I need to do or want to do. I just have to work harder.

REFER TO AN EVENT, PLACE, OR OCCASION

An obvious way to begin a presentation is to refer to the place where you are speaking or the **OCCASION** ▲ **(61–68)** for the gathering. Your audience's memories and feelings about a specific place or event can conjure up the emotions needed to capture their attention and interest.

When Martin Luther King Jr. made his famous "I Have a Dream" speech on the steps of the Lincoln Memorial, his first few words echoed Abraham Lincoln's Gettysburg Address ("Four score and seven years ago"). Here's how he began: "Five score years ago, a great American, in whose symbolic shadow we stand, signed the Emancipation Proclamation."

Important events that occur shortly before a presentation or in the recent past can connect you with some of what your audience knows, thinks, and feels about an issue, as with this example:

> Dr. Larry Nassar, a physician who worked with the US Olympic Gymnastics Team, was accused of more than 250 sexual assaults against minors. In January 2019, he was sentenced to 40 to 175 years in jail for criminal sexual conduct—adding to a previous child pornography conviction of 60 years. Sadly, there are many sexual predators disguised as healers, teachers, soldiers, and business executives who have never been prosecuted or jailed.

ADDRESS AUDIENCE NEEDS

In a crisis, a speaker may need to address an immediate problem. If budget cuts require salary reductions, audience members will want the details. They won't want to hear a humorous story, a clever question, or an unusual statistic. When your listeners' jobs or futures are threatened, don't take up their time with a clever beginning. In fact, such introductions may even make the audience angry and damage your credibility. Get right to the point. Here's an example:

> As you know, our operating budget has been reduced by $2.7 million. It is important that you know this: All of you will have a job here next year—and the year after. There will be no layoffs. Instead there will be cutbacks in nonpersonnel budget lines, downsizing of programs, and, possibly, short furloughs.

This speaker went directly to the **CENTRAL IDEA** ■ **(156–57)** and previewed the **KEY POINTS** ■ **(153–56)** of their speech. After explaining that no one would be laid off, the speaker then described other measures that would offset the reduced budget.

MIX THE METHODS

Many speakers combine introductory methods to begin their presentations. For instance, this speaker offers a personal experience, statistics, and vivid examples as they begin their speech about funding medical research for Lou Gehrig's disease (amyotrophic lateral sclerosis, also known as ALS) among veterans:

Establish a personal link ———•

Use an example ———•

Use a statistic ———•

Ask a question ———•

Address audience needs ———•

> My grandfather died from ALS. He used to stumble a lot and had difficulty pronouncing words. It's a horrible disease. You can't walk or talk. You choke on food, you can't swallow. You often suffocate to death. Here is what's odd. Four of his friends also suffered from ALS. Given that only about six thousand people get diagnosed with the disease each year, what are the odds that five people who all knew one another get the same diagnosis? What did they have in common? One thing—they all served in the army. In fact, serving in the military makes you 60 percent more likely to get this horrifying disease. But no one knows why. Today I want to speak about why this is happening and what we, as individuals and a nation, can do about it.

Tips for Starting Strong

As important as introductions are, many inexperienced speakers don't prepare them with the care they deserve, thus setting themselves up to make fundamental errors at the very beginning of their presentations. The following tips will help you start strong by avoiding the most common introductory errors.

PLAN THE BEGINNING AT THE END

In most cases, don't plan the introduction to your presentation before you've developed the body of your speech. There are many decisions to make when developing a presentation; how to begin should not necessarily be the first. You must know your purpose before deciding how your introduction can support it. Even better, identify your **KEY POINTS** ■ **(153–56)** so you'll know how to preview them.

DON'T APOLOGIZE FOR LACK OF PREPARATION

Wouldn't it be strange if an actor walked on stage before a play and told the audience he hadn't really learned his lines or that his opening number would be a little rough? Why, then, should a speaker apologize for their presentation before it's even begun? Too often, speakers open with apologies or excuses: "I don't speak very often, so please excuse my nervousness"; "I wish I'd had a few more days to prepare for this presentation, but I just found out on Tuesday that I had to make it."

Comments like these do not accomplish very much and in fact can adversely impact your **CREDIBILITY ▲ (74–81)**. If your message is well delivered, excuses will only confuse your audience. Your introduction should not apologize for your level of preparation or the quality of your **DELIVERY ▶ (209–301)**. If you've practiced and are adequately prepared, you can begin with confidence.

AVOID SAYING "MY SPEECH IS ABOUT . . ."

Beginning statements such as "I'm going to talk about . . ." or "My topic is . . ." may be true, but they're unlikely to help you gain the audience's attention or interest. Even though "My speech is about . . ." may introduce your topic, it will not necessarily be engaging or make the important connection between you and your audience.

Nevertheless, like many rules, there are exceptions. "I'm going to talk about how I was surrounded by killer sharks and survived" would probably make even the most jaded audience listen. "My talk will be about the budget crisis and how it will affect your jobs" will likewise hold audience attention and interest. Middle-schooler Margaret Muller (see p. 194) starts by saying "Today I'd like to tell you about Down syndrome" for good reason. By openly and confidently addressing the one thing her classmates already knew about her—that she has Down syndrome— she appropriately establishes a connection with her audience in her introduction.

SET ACHIEVABLE GOALS

Don't overpromise what you can deliver in the introduction to your presentation. Our advice is simple: avoid offering impossible outcomes, like promising your audience that you will help them become more popular, lose weight, or get all A's. Your message is more likely to have a meaningful impact on your audience if you have an achievable goal.

USE HUMOR WISELY

USING HUMOR ∴ (340–42) in an introduction can be risky. Your audience may remember the humor but forget your message. And what if no one laughs? What if audience members are offended? But when used wisely, humor can energize your introduction. If it's appropriate and relevant to your purpose, humor can gain audience attention and provide a hint about the mood and direction of your talk.

KEEP IT SHORT

Generally, we recommend that your introduction take up no more than 10 percent of your speaking time. If it takes more time than that, make sure it's for a good reason. Otherwise, your audience may lose patience. There are, of course, times when your introduction will need to be longer. If you are facing a distrustful audience, for example, you may need more time to establish your credibility, generate a more hospitable mood, and reduce audience concerns about your message.

Concluding Your Presentation

Like your introduction, your conclusion should establish a relationship among three elements: *you*, your *message*, and your *audience*. It should also accomplish two major goals:

1. *Signal the ending.* As obvious as it may seem, your audience will appreciate knowing that you are wrapping up your presentation. If you signal that you are concluding your presentation, audience members are prompted to assess your message

and to think about their own interpretations and judgments about what you've said.

2. ***Summarize your message.*** Repeat the one thing you want your audience to remember at the end of your presentation. Don't use the conclusion to add new ideas or to insert something that you left out. Use the conclusion to reinforce your message.

There are almost as many ways to end a presentation as there are ways to begin one. The following are several of many ways to conclude your presentation and leave a strong, lasting impression on listeners.

END HOW YOU BEGAN

If you have difficulty deciding how to end your presentation, consider using the **bookending method**—that is, end the same way you began. If you begin your presentation with a quotation, end with the same or a similar quotation. If you began by referring to an event, ask your audience to recall it. If you began with a story, refer back to that story. For example:

> Remember the story I told you about two-year-old Joey, who had a hole in his throat so he could breathe, a tube jutting out of his stomach so he could be fed? For Joey, an accidental poisoning was an excruciatingly painful and horrifying experience. For Joey's parents, it was a time of fear, panic, and helplessness. Thus, it is a time to be prepared for and, even better, a time to prevent.

SUMMARIZE

A concluding summary reinforces your message, but it should be clear, logical, and brief. A summary can be a memorable way to conclude a presentation. For example, the following conclusion of a student's presentation on sleep deprivation sums up her major ideas clearly without labeling each key point with numbers or reciting them word for word. She ends with two short, but memorable sentences.

> Recognizing that you may be sleep deprived is the first step. The hardest thing to do is to alter your habits. Retraining yourself to

follow a normal sleep pattern isn't going to happen overnight. But once you discover that a few extra hours of sleep will help you feel more rested, relaxed, and revitalized, giving up that extra hour on the internet or watching TV will have been worth it. There is so much in life to enjoy. Sleep longer, live longer.

QUOTE SOMEONE

A memorable quotation can give your speech a dramatic and effective ending.

For example, on January 28, 1986, President Ronald Reagan addressed the nation a few hours after the fatal *Challenger* disaster that killed all seven crew members. Reagan ended his conclusion with a line from "High Flight," a sonnet written by John Gillespie Magee, a pilot with the Royal Canadian Air Force in World War II who died at the age of nineteen during a training flight:[3]

> The crew of the space shuttle *Challenger* honored us by the manner in which they lived their lives. We will never forget them, nor the last time we saw them, this morning, as they prepared for their journey and waved goodbye and "slipped the surly bonds of earth" to "touch the face of God."

TELL A STORY

Ending with a good **STORY ∴ (323–32)** can help audience members visualize the desired outcome of your presentation and remember your main ideas. A public speech by Marge Anderson, chief executive of the Mille Lacs Band of Ojibwe, uses a story to conclude:[4]

> I'd like to end with one of my favorite stories. It's a funny little story about Indians and non-Indians, but its message is serious. You can see something differently if you are willing to learn from those around you. Years ago, white settlers came to this area and built the first European-style homes. When Indian People walked by these homes and saw [windows], they looked through them to see what the strangers inside were doing. The settlers were shocked, but it made sense when you think about it: windows

are made to be looked through from both sides. Since then, my People have spent many years looking at the world through your window. I hope today I've given you a reason to look at it through ours.

SHARE YOUR PERSONAL FEELINGS

Putting yourself into the ending of a presentation by disclosing how you feel can touch the emotions of your audience and leave them with a strong memory of you, the **SPEAKER ▲ (72–85)**. Earlier in this chapter, you read the introduction to Margaret Muller's speech on Down syndrome to seventh and eighth graders. Here is how Margaret concluded:[5]

> I am not sad about the fact that I have Down syndrome. It is just part of me. I have a great brother (most of the time), and parents who love me a lot. I have wonderful friends who enjoy hanging out and having fun with me. I have teachers who help me keep on learning new things. I am glad to be a student at Lincoln Middle School, because it is a great school and almost everyone is really nice. Down syndrome has not stopped me from having a worthwhile life.

USE POETIC LANGUAGE

USING LANGUAGE ∴ (305–22) in a way that inspires and resonates is one of the best ways to ensure that your conclusion is memorable. If Martin Luther King Jr. had said "Don't worry, things will get better" at the end of his famous "I've Been to the Mountaintop" speech, his words would not have had the desired impact or become a well-known quotation. In his conclusion, he used lyrics from the "Battle Hymn of the Republic": "I'm not worried about anything. . . . 'Mine eyes have seen the glory of the coming of the Lord.'" Poetic words can make your conclusion sing.

You don't have to be a poet or a famously eloquent politician to conclude your presentation poetically. One of our students ended his presentation about respecting older people with a slightly reworded version of a short but poetic phrase by Francis Bacon: Old wood best to burn, old wine to drink, old friends to trust, and old people to love.

CALL FOR ACTION

A challenging but effective way to end a presentation is to **CALL FOR ACTION** ◆ **(454)**. Use a call for action when you want your audience to do more than merely listen—when you want them to *do* something.

Here is how Dr. Robert M. Franklin, president of Morehouse College, ended remarks delivered to a town hall meeting of students on his campus:[6]

> Morehouse is your house. You must take responsibility for its excellence. . . . If you want to be part of something rare and noble, something that the world has not often seen—a community of educated, ethical, disciplined Black men more powerful than a standing army—then you've come to the right place. . . . Up you mighty men of Morehouse, you aristocrats of spirit, you can accomplish what you will!

MIX THE METHODS

As with introductions, many speakers rely on more than one way to conclude a presentation. Note how this student speaker uses statistics and a personal story to end a speech on alcoholism:

Summarize ⟶
Bookend ⟶
Call for action ⟶

> As you now know, about one in eight adults—that's 12.7 percent of the American population—abuse alcohol or are alcoholics. Few, if any, of these people planned on becoming alcoholics. And many, like my sister, were well informed about the disease before falling victim. I've told you her story and alerted you to the role of denial in the hope that someday, if that doubt ever creeps into your mind and you find yourself asking whether you might have an alcohol problem, you'll remember my speech and take a harder, more objective look at that question. It didn't save my sister's life. But it could save yours.

Tips for Ending Effectively

Taking time to create a well-planned, well-delivered conclusion may be the last thing you want to worry about as you near the end of the preparation process. But we know that last impressions linger—the last thing you say can be just as important as the first. The following tips will help you plan a strong conclusion.

MATCH THE MOOD OF YOUR PRESENTATION

We often tell students, "Don't go for fireworks without a reason to celebrate." In other words, don't tack on an irrelevant or inappropriate ending. If you have given a serious speech about the need for better childcare, don't end with a tasteless joke about naughty children. If you have explained how to operate a new and complicated machine, you probably shouldn't conclude with flowery poetry. Match the mood and method of your ending to the mood and style of your presentation.

HAVE REALISTIC EXPECTATIONS

What if you issue a call for action and no one in your audience acts? Don't expect more from your audience than is reasonable. Only an inexperienced speaker would expect everyone in an audience to immediately sign an organ donation card following a presentation. Most audiences will not act when called on unless the request is carefully worded, reasonable, and possible. Don't conclude by demanding something from your audience unless you are reasonably sure that you can get it.

END WHEN YOU SAY YOU WILL END

How do you react when you hear a speaker say, "And in conclusion . . . ," and then take 10 minutes to finish speaking? A prolonged conclusion can frustrate an audience that expects the speech to end. The announced ending of a presentation—signaled by phrases such as "In conclusion" or "Let me close by"—should be used only when the ending of your speech will follow in less than a minute. When you say you are going to end, *end*.

Write Your Introduction and Conclusion

Unless you are very familiar with your audience and your topic, we recommend that you write your introduction and conclusion word for word with the expectation that you will change and improve the phrasing several times—even as you speak. Because the beginning and ending of a presentation matter so much, every word counts.

Instead of reading these sections from a manuscript, **PRACTICE ▶ (220–24)** your introduction and conclusion so often that you won't need detailed notes (unless you're including a long quotation or complicated set of statistics). You will probably be most nervous at the beginning of your speech, so knowing your introduction very well will also help you mask and minimize any **SPEAKING ANXIETY** ● **(18–26)** you may be feeling. As you close, delivering a well-practiced conclusion allows you to focus on your audience and "clinch" your message.

We are not recommending that you memorize and recite your introduction and conclusion. Rather, make sure you can begin and end your presentation with only a few notes, plenty of eye contact, and expressive delivery that reinforces the connection between you and your audience.

Conclusion

You already know that the first and last impressions you make on someone are important and long lasting. That's why you want to look and sound good at the start of a date, a job interview, or an important meeting. It's also why you want to leave a favorable impression when the date, interview, or meeting is about to end. And in presentations, a good first and last impression helps you achieve your purpose while enhancing your credibility as a speaker.

Keep in mind that introductions and conclusions are not the same. Their goals differ, as can the methods you use to achieve those goals. Well-crafted and skillfully delivered introductions gain audience attention and interest and help you connect with your audience, demonstrate your competence and credibility, set the appropriate mood, and preview your message. A well-crafted and skillfully delivered conclusion is the finale of a presentation. It lets the audience know you're about to sum it up, make a final appeal, and create a memorable moment.

NOTABLE SPEAKER
Susan Cain

After practicing corporate law for seven years, Susan Cain left her successful career behind to pursue her childhood passion for reading and writing. This passion led her to research and think critically about the general cultural preference for extroverts in the United States. As the self-described "Chief Revolutionary" of an organization she has called the Quiet Revolution, Cain has authored two best-selling books and led hundreds of workshops about the often overlooked power of introverts in everyday life. She took to the TED stage in 2012 to address the challenges faced by introverts living in a world favoring extroverts—a topic that she had written about in her book *Quiet: The Power of Introverts in a World That Can't Stop Talking*. The talk has been viewed more than 22 million times and was featured by the curators of the TED website on their homepage. In 2014, she was named one of the world's top 50 leadership and management experts by *Inc.* magazine.

Search Terms

To locate a video of this presentation online, enter the following key words into a search engine: Susan Cain introverts. The video is approximately 19:04 in length.

What to Watch For

[0:00–1:19] Cain focuses her audience's attention and interest by beginning her talk with a compelling story about her time away at summer camp as a young girl. She adds a visual component by holding a suitcase in her hand as she talks about how her mother packed her a suitcase full of books to take to camp. She continues to draw the audience into her personal experience by sharing the "R-O-W-D-I-E" cheer with them. This brings a touch of humor to the story and lightens the mood before she expresses the more serious point behind the story.

[1:34–2:06] Cain connects with her audience by contrasting her desire to read books while at camp with her counselor's desire that she should work hard to be outgoing. In doing so, she highlights experiences that some audience members will recognize at some level. An emotional tone in the message emerges as she moves the suitcase behind her to demonstrate hiding away a passion so that she could fit in with the other girls. She then tells the audience that she could have shared 50 similar stories with them—each one highlighting a time that she was told that she should try "to pass as more of an extrovert." In essence, she is asking the audience to connect with her human experience of not fitting in.

[2:31–4:02] She notes that "a third to half of the population are introverts," which is "one out of every two or three people" each of the audience members know—partners, children, and colleagues. From this foundation, she states her central idea: "When it comes to creativity and to leadership, we need introverts doing what they do best." To achieve this goal, she advocates a better balance between extroverts and introverts. This balance can be achieved if people accept and appreciate introverts' work-style preferences, such as more autonomy and less group work.

[13:21–15:54] As Cain prepares to end her talk, she returns to the suitcase. She pulls out several books from it and tells the audience that these books were written by some of her grandfather's favorite authors. Referencing the suitcase serves as a bookend to the beginning of the talk. The suitcase becomes a focal point of how books have affected her and how she wants her message to affect her audience. One of the lasting ideas she wants her listeners to embrace is the value of having time alone to think and to reflect. She reinforces her central idea by underscoring her belief that we are on the cusp of a cultural shift in how we understand and accommodate the unique skills of introverts.

[16:21–18:32] She ends the speech with a very clear call for action. She asks the audience to stop the "madness of constant group work," to unplug and get inside their own heads more, and to take a good look at what's inside their own "suitcase" and why they put it there. This last call to action is another clear reminder of how the suitcase serves as a centerpiece of making her message memorable.

EXERCISE

After viewing Cain's speech, reflect on these questions:

1. Did Cain effectively and appropriately incorporate herself into the introduction, body, and conclusion of her presentation?

2. Cain's introductory story was two-and-a-half-minutes long—about 25 percent of her speech. What did such a long introduction achieve?

3. Explain the role of the suitcase in her talk. Did it help her or distract you?

4. How successfully did Cain's speech demonstrate the primacy and recency effects?

5. How did the delivery of her last line—"So I wish you the best of all possible journeys and the courage to [in a quiet voice] speak softly"—help reiterate her central idea?

PART 4
Delivery

Whenever you speak to an audience, whether in person or through an audiovisual medium, your voice and your body play an important role in shaping your audience's impressions. The following chapters offer delivery strategies that can help you convey your ideas to your audience, such as improving your **VOCAL DELIVERY** and **PHYSICAL DELIVERY** skills, creating effective **PRESENTATION AIDS**, and adapting your delivery in **ONLINE PRESENTATIONS**.

Delivery

4.1 Delivery Decisions

What's more important—*what* you say or *how* you say it? In a speaking situation, you might have brilliant ideas and inspiring phrases, but they may not resonate with your audience if you speak too softly or monotonously, mumble, bury your head in your notes, use distracting movements, or generally lack energy or dynamism.

Delivery is the "how you say it" of presentation speaking. It is what audience members see and hear when you speak, whether in person or online. The elements of delivery include your voice, facial expressions, posture and body movements, and presentation aids; during online presentations, delivery also includes technical elements such as your physical background, microphone, and lighting.

Approximately two-thirds of the meaning we communicate to others is expressed through vocal and physical delivery.[1] If you haven't thought about and effectively practiced your delivery, you may leave your audience unimpressed and unmoved by what you say—that is, you've taken a crucial "speaking" element out of presentation speaking. You might as well send your audience a written memo! In other words, effective delivery is the nonverbal heart and soul of effective speaking. In this chapter, we look at the qualities of effective delivery as well as the decisions you can make to achieve those qualities.

The Qualities of Effective Delivery

Effective delivery has multiple components: a clear speaking voice at an appropriate volume, rate, and pitch; appropriate eye contact, gestures, and posture as well as meaningful facial expressions that complement your message. In addition to learning general delivery skills, you can (and should) try to create a personal and flexible delivery style that adapts to each **RHETORICAL SITUATION ● (6–11)**. After all, the delivery you use for a eulogy at a funeral should be very different from your delivery for a toast at a wedding.

Developing an adaptive delivery style requires an understanding of the four qualities that transcend individual speaking situations: *expressiveness*, *confidence*, *stage presence*, and *immediacy*.

EXPRESSIVENESS

Chapters 4.2 **VOCAL DELIVERY ▶** and 4.3 **PHYSICAL DELIVERY ▶** provide advice for specific kinds of delivery skills.

Expressiveness—a combination of the energy, variety, and vitality of your delivery—has a strong impact on audience attention. Expressiveness is more than enthusiasm. It's more than the sound of your voice, how you look, or how much you've practiced. It is an extension of who you are and what you care about. Put another way, expressiveness occurs when your vocal and physical delivery reveal and support how you genuinely think and feel about a subject.

If you care about your message and are sincerely interested in sharing your ideas with others, you are well on the way to being expressive. You'll be much more expressive if you know and care about your topic; your audience will know if you don't. Think of it this way: it's easy to read people who are expressive because their meaning and emotions are clear.

CONFIDENCE

Confident speakers are convincing. Research even shows that jury members are more likely to believe the testimony of confident eyewitnesses than of hesitant witnesses—even though confident witnesses are no more accurate when describing an event.[2]

Unfortunately, some speakers have important things to say but do not appear confident, which may lead an audience to ignore or dismiss their ideas. Other speakers have ordinary—or even harmful—ideas to communicate, but because they appear confident, audiences may accept and applaud

their message. For this reason, you must always consider your **ETHICS** ●
(43–57) and the needs of your audience, especially if you're a naturally
confident speaker. Politicians, corporate executives, celebrities, and bullies
are often confident, but they should not be trusted or admired because
of their confidence alone. Further, if you seem *too* sure of yourself or too
authoritative, your audience might question your motives. Unwarranted
or fake confidence can backfire.

So how do you project a sense of confidence that benefits you *and*
your audience? Believe in your message and use strategies to reduce
your **SPEAKING ANXIETY** ● **(18–26)**. Confidence is more likely to emerge
when you adequately prepare and practice your presentation.

STAGE PRESENCE

Stage presence is your ability to captivate, connect with, and command an
audience's full attention based on your talent, dynamism, and charm.[3] It
is about "owning" the stage. This characterization applies to great actors,
dancers, and musicians—and to great speakers.

Many people consider the late Steve Jobs, the genius inventor of Apple
products, to be an example of a speaker with stage presence. Though he
wasn't known to be especially personable, his delivery style made his presentations exceptional and memorable. He dressed differently than most
speakers (mock black turtleneck, faded blue jeans, gray sneakers, and round
rimless glasses), walked to the stage while maintaining eye contact with
his audience, rarely or never glanced at his notes, used expansive gestures
and an open posture, lovingly held up products, appeared both relaxed and
energized, and personified expressiveness as he moved around the stage.[4]

IMMEDIACY

The term **immediacy** describes delivery behaviors that help bring a speaker
and an audience closer together. Immediacy communicates warmth,
involvement, psychological closeness, availability, and positivity to an audience.[5] Although immediacy can be expressed with words, nonverbal immediacy (vocal and physical delivery) is more powerful: it has a significant
effect on audience engagement, motivation, and recall.

You can achieve nonverbal immediacy with a variety of methods,
but make sure your **VOCAL** ▶ **(229–45)** and **PHYSICAL DELIVERY** ▶ **(249–59)** are

consistent with your message. If, for example, your facial expressions and tone of voice communicate one emotion, but your words communicate another, the discrepancy might cause a rift between you and your audience, thereby reducing immediacy.

Researchers have identified several characteristics of nonverbal immediacy:[6]

- Close proximity to audience members
- Vocal variety in your volume, pitch, rate, and inflection
- Warm and expressive voice
- Smiling
- Direct face-to-face body orientation
- Direct and frequent eye contact
- Relaxed body posture, gestures, and movement

Forms of Delivery

To improve the quality of your delivery—your expressiveness, confidence, stage presence, and immediacy—you can start by considering which form (or forms) of delivery will best support your speaking situation. There are four major forms of delivery: *impromptu, extemporaneous, manuscript,* and *memorized* delivery. Each has advantages and disadvantages that depend on you, your audience, your occasion, and your purpose.

IMPROMPTU DELIVERY

See Chapter 8.1
**IMPROMPTU
SPEECHES** ★ for more advice on speaking with little or no preparation.

With **impromptu delivery**, you'll deliver a presentation with few or no notes—but this doesn't mean you won't be able to prepare ahead of time. For example, an author may not need notes to talk about their most recent work on a book tour, but they might research the location, occasion, and audience to adapt their approach for an upcoming speaking event.

Speakers use impromptu delivery for a variety of speaking occasions where they have little or no time to decide what to say. That doesn't mean they haven't thought about the subject. For example, an instructor may call on you to share your opinion about an assigned reading, your manager may ask you to summarize a project at work, or you may feel compelled to share your thoughts at a public meeting.

IMPROMPTU DELIVERY	
Advantages	**Disadvantages**
• Uses a natural and conversational speaking style	• Limits time to make decisions about the rhetorical situation
• Maximizes eye contact	• Can be awkward and ineffective
• Allows freedom of movement	• Makes speaking time difficult to gauge
• Allows adjustment to audience feedback	• Relies on little to no supporting material
• Demonstrates speaker credibility, knowledge, and skill	• Can erode speaker credibility
• Can exceed audience expectations	

EXTEMPORANEOUS DELIVERY

The most common and most powerful form of presentation speaking, **extemporaneous delivery** relies on notes or an outline to guide speakers through a well-prepared presentation. No other form of delivery offers as much freedom and flexibility while delivering a carefully planned message.

Most classroom lectures, business briefings, courtroom arguments, oral reports, and informal talks are delivered extemporaneously. Depending on your situation, you may need only a simple list of key points, or you may need a comprehensive **FULL-SENTENCE OUTLINE** ■ **(181–85)** .

EXTEMPORANEOUS DELIVERY	
Advantages	**Disadvantages**
• Seems spontaneous but is well prepared	• Increases likelihood of speaking anxiety about content not covered by notes
• Allows time to think critically about the rhetorical situation	• Encourages reliance on notes, which may hamper fluency and physical delivery
• Facilitates adjustment to audience feedback	• Can be difficult to choose appropriate words and speaking styles
• Allows more eye contact and audience interaction than manuscript speaking	• Can be difficult to estimate speaking time
• Receives generally positive response from audiences	
• Can include concise language for the central idea and key points	

MANUSCRIPT DELIVERY

Manuscript delivery involves reading a well-prepared speech aloud, word for word. Though precise, it's difficult to deliver an engaging presentation while reading from a manuscript.

Even if you'd prefer to speak extemporaneously, manuscript delivery is appropriate—and in some cases required—for legislative testimony, press statements, complex reports, scientific explanations, and synchronized multimedia scripts. And if the occasion is highly emotional—such as delivering a eulogy or accepting a prestigious award—you may need the support provided by a manuscript.

MANUSCRIPT DELIVERY	
Advantages	**Disadvantages**
• Allows careful attention to all the basic principles of effective speaking	• May result in dull delivery
• Allows speaker to carefully select and use appropriate speaking styles	• Can be difficult to maintain sufficient eye contact
• Can ease speaking anxiety	• Limits gestures and movement
• Allows speaker to stay within the time limit	• May result in an overly formal speaking style
• Allows for rehearsal of the same presentation every time	• Can be difficult to modify content and adapt to the audience and situation while speaking
• Ensures accurate reporting of content	• Can be disastrous if the manuscript is lost

MEMORIZED DELIVERY

In **memorized delivery**, you memorize your entire presentation. We discourage memorizing entire presentations, but it can be helpful to memorize your introduction, conclusion, or a few key sections.

If you memorize a speech, you need to spend extra time practicing physical delivery so your presentation doesn't come across as stilted or insincere. TED talks, for example, require speakers to memorize a presentation. With the help of coaches, they practice their delivery for months to ensure that it personifies expressiveness, confidence, stage presence, and immediacy.

MEMORIZED DELIVERY	
Advantages	**Disadvantages**
• Shares the preparation advantages of manuscript speaking	• Requires extensive time to memorize
• Shares the delivery advantages of impromptu speaking	• Can be disastrous if memory fails
• Maximizes eye contact and freedom of movement	• Can sound stilted and insincere
• Provides opportunity to craft language and vary language styles	• Can be difficult to modify or adapt to the audience or situation while speaking
	• Can lack a sense of spontaneity unless expertly delivered

MIX AND MATCH DELIVERY FORMS

There isn't a single best form of delivery. You might mix and match different forms at different points in your presentation. An impromptu speaker may recite a memorized statistic or a rehearsed argument, like a politician responding to anticipated questions from the press. An extemporaneous speaker may read a lengthy quotation or a series of statistics or deliver a memorized ending. A speaker reading from a manuscript may stop and tell an impromptu story using direct eye contact with the audience. During a memorized presentation, a speaker might insert an impromptu joke or rephrase an idea based on audience feedback.

If you are free to choose a form of delivery, how do you make that decision? You do it by experimenting with your options as you prepare and practice your presentation. This will help you determine which form or combination of forms is appropriate, most natural to you as a speaker, and most helpful for your rhetorical situation.

Using Notes Effectively

Regardless of the delivery form you select, be prepared to use notes. Excellent speakers feel incomplete without notes, even if they've practiced their presentation over and over. Winston Churchill, Great Britain's eloquent prime minister during World War II, was one such speaker. When asked why he always had notes for his speeches, even though he rarely used them, he replied, "I carry fire insurance, but I don't expect my house to burn down."

The look and scope of your notes will vary depending on your rhetorical situation and the form of delivery you decide to use. For impromptu delivery, you may have little more than six words written on a scrap of paper. In an extemporaneous presentation, you may use note cards or a **SPEAKING NOTES OUTLINE** ▪ **(185–88)** to guide you through your talk. A manuscript or memorized presentation requires a carefully prepared, word-for-word script that may include graphic cues to remind you when to pause, cue up a slide, and emphasize a particular word or phrase. You won't use your notes during a memorized presentation, but they should be nearby in case you need them.

While there are many ways to use your notes, one guideline rises above the rest: establish and maintain as much **EYE CONTACT** ▶ **(249–51)** as you can with your audience. Don't bury your head in your notes, manuscript, or phone.

To use notes effectively while looking up and engaging with your audience, make sure your notes are printed, written, or displayed in type large enough to be seen clearly at arm's length. Even if you want to read a full quotation accurately or share critical data, you can practice these sections enough to look at your audience while glancing at your notes. Create and test your note cards, outline, or manuscript during every practice session.

NOTE CARDS AND OUTLINES

Extemporaneous speakers often use note cards to record key points and some details about their supporting material. Think of each card as a PowerPoint slide. They should contain just enough information to trigger an idea or supply a vital piece of supporting material and its source. Put key words, rather than complete sentences, with large print on *only one* side of each card. To stay organized or rearrange key points at the last minute, number each card.

If you are using an outline, it can range from a larger list of key points and supporting material to a comprehensive, **FULL-SENTENCE OUTLINE** ■ **(181–85)** in which your presentation is written out word for word.

See Chapter 3.4 **FRAMING AND OUTLINING** ■ to learn how to create different kinds of outlines.

MANUSCRIPTS

If you decide to write major portions or the entirety of your presentation in manuscript form, make sure it's easy to read while you present. Double-space each line and use an easily readable font size. When reading from a printed manuscript, only print on the top two-thirds of the page, which allows you to keep your head up, maintain eye contact, and breathe easily. Set wide margins so you have space on the page to add any last-minute changes. Number each page and don't staple the pages together.

When reading a manuscript from a digital device, like a cell phone, tablet, or laptop, you won't lose your pages, but you can easily lose your place as you scroll. Viewing your manuscript as a PDF can replicate the experience of double-spaced print pages—but it can be challenging to add last-minute changes or markups. Using a device with a small screen may cause you to squint or hold the phone close to your face, reducing your immediacy with your audience. A larger screen makes your manuscript easier to read.

If you're using a printed manuscript, place it on the left side of the lectern and slide the pages to the right when it's time to go on to the next page. Don't let your manuscript hang over the front of the lectern. Some speakers put their manuscript in a three-ring binder to keep their pages in order while still allowing the freedom to gesture. If you're using a digital manuscript, angle your tablet upward or use an elevated laptop so it's easier to read while maintaining eye contact and gesturing. And make sure your device is charged! If you don't have a lectern or don't want to use one, it may be difficult to hold several pages of a manuscript or a tablet as you speak. In this case, it's worth considering if extemporaneous delivery would work better for your speaking situation.

MARKING UP YOUR NOTES

Many speakers mark up their speaking notes and manuscripts to help them with delivery, filling their pages with graphic cues as well as last-minute changes. Marking up your note cards, outline, or manuscript tells you which words or phrases to emphasize and when to pause, gesture, or move. The following figure shows a few of the cues we've seen on manuscripts.[7]

/	Short pause
//	Medium pause
///	Long pause
<	Speak louder
>	Speak softer
∧	Speak faster
∨	Speak slower
★	Key point or important sentence follows
☉	Make eye contact with audience
☺	Smile
◻❶	Slide 1
◻❷	Slide 2

Using too many symbols can make your notes unreadable. Use what you need—and invent your own!

Practicing Your Presentation

The best advice to improve your speaking is to *practice, practice, practice.* You may still feel nervous, but knowing that you've practiced and prepared, you can convert that nervousness into excitement. Although it takes time, the payoff is a confident and seemingly effortless presentation.

Practice tells you whether there are words you have trouble pronouncing or sentences that are too long to say in one breath. You'll notice **PRESENTATION AIDS ▶ (260–78)** that are out of order or inconsistent with your message (especially if you've revised your notes after making your slides). You may discover that your presentation is too long—and you'll still have time to make adjustments. You may realize that your audience can't hear you because your speaking voice isn't clear or loud enough. Practice helps prevent such surprises.

Students often ask, "How can I practice if I'm speaking extemporaneously? Won't my presentation be different every time?" Although it's true that each iteration of an extemporaneous presentation is slightly different, your note cards or speaking outline will guide you along the same path, with the same kind of introduction, content, key points, and conclusion.

The more you practice, the better you will recall word-for-word sections of your presentation. When you practice, you link the words you're speaking with your delivery, and by doing that, you create something like a "muscle memory"—a familiarity with your material that feels natural and unforced, much like the feeling you have when you finally achieve mastery of a physical skill, such as riding a bike or playing the piano.

HOW TO PRACTICE

Practice can take many forms. It can be as simple as closing your door and rehearsing your presentation in private or as complex as a video-taped dress rehearsal. At first, you may feel strange talking to yourself in private, watching a recording, or speaking in front of friends. It may help to remember that musicians rehearse alone, athletes practice alone, and actors recite their lines alone. Many also record themselves and rely on coaches for feedback.

Initially, practice is a solo activity. You might rehearse your presentation as you drive, while in the shower, or by yourself in the room where you will be speaking. Practicing alone helps you get more comfortable with your material, but it's harder to assess and know how to improve your delivery. Though it seems counterintuitive, we recommend that you don't practice in front of a mirror. Staring at yourself in a mirror as you are giving your presentation can be distracting and cause you to criticize yourself while you're speaking. Instead, recording your practice session with your phone, camera, or computer can help you observe what you are saying, how you sound, and what you look like as you are presenting. You might also enlist a friend, coach, or classmate to provide feedback and encouragement during a practice session.

Depending on how much time you have, the length and importance of your presentation, and your familiarity with your material, you can mix and match the three major ways to practice: *in private, recorded,* and *in front of others.*

When Practicing in Private

- *Simulate the real thing.* If you will be standing as you speak, stand when you practice. Use the same vocal and physical delivery you plan to use in your presentation.

- *Maintain eye contact.* Glance at your notes only occasionally. Use direct and frequent eye contact with an imagined audience.

When Recording Your Practice Sessions

- *Trust what you hear and see.* Listen for vocal clarity and expressiveness. Observe your appearance, stage presence, gestures, and movements. Though it may seem strange, remember this is how you'll look and sound to your audience.

- *Watch with a friend.* Because it can be difficult to watch yourself objectively, an honest friend's opinions may help erase some of your concerns and calm your nerves.

- *Make needed adjustments.* Consider specific aspects of delivery to practice. If needed, revise your content and organization.

When Practicing in Front of Others

- *Pick good listeners.* Friendly listeners can reassure you and give you an extra dose of confidence.

- *Listen to feedback.* Although they may not be speaking experts, they can give valuable advice, such as "I couldn't hear you" or "That explanation was hard to follow."

With each practice, think about how you'll adapt to unexpected events and conditions. What if you intend to tell a story about an audience member, but they don't show up? What if you have technical problems? Will you be able to speak without your visual aids, if necessary? What if you must shorten the presentation? What if a major news story breaks right before you speak? With practice, you'll be prepared to adapt on the day of your presentation as needed.

CREATE A PRACTICE PLAN

Generally, it helps to practice your entire presentation several different times rather than devoting one long session to the process. In addition, you should schedule shorter sessions where you practice portions of your speech, concentrating on your introduction, a single key point, or your conclusion. If you rehearse your entire presentation every time you practice, you'll become tired, bored, and frustrated, particularly when some sections go well and others need more practice.

As you practice your presentation, you may find it necessary to make revisions. For example, you may realize that the way you tell a **STORY** ⸭ **(323–32)** doesn't connect to your purpose or overall message. As a result, you may revise the story—or delete it. You may write several drafts of your notes before you find a level of detail that's most helpful to you. The first draft of your speaking notes is unlikely to be your best or final draft.

Schedule at least 3 complete run-through sessions but nowhere near 10 sessions. Too much practice can make you sound *canned*, or so well rehearsed that you no longer sound spontaneous and natural. Rather than prescribe the number of practice sessions, we offer this advice: keep practicing until you've improved the fine points of your presentation. Then stop. The following questions can help you develop a practice plan:

- Where will you practice the most? Will those spaces be available when you need them?

- How often will you rehearse? What days and times are you available? Will you have time to practice short sections and the entire speech?

- What technology will you use, and when can you practice using it?

See Chapter 4.4 **PRESENTATION AIDS** ▶ for advice on using presentation aids to complement your delivery.

Conclusion

The qualities of effective delivery—expressiveness, confidence, stage presence, and immediacy—develop as you practice your vocal and physical delivery skills. With practice, you can enhance your credibility and make your message more impactful and memorable.

First, decide which forms of delivery to use—impromptu, extemporaneous, manuscript, and/or memorized—depending on what will work best in the rhetorical situation. Fortunately, you can use one, two, three, and even all four forms of delivery in a single presentation, if appropriate. Then decide how to use speaking notes—as index cards, an outline, a manuscript, or none at all?

Practice every aspect of your presentation—not just your words or the sound of your voice. Whether you're practicing alone, in front of a recording device or in front of friends, practice as though an audience is present. Then reflect and adapt your delivery to heighten your expressiveness, confidence, stage presence, and immediacy when it's time for the real thing.

NOTABLE SPEAKER
Yassmin Abdel-Magied

An Australian immigrant born in Sudan who now lives in London, Yassmin Abdel-Magied is a writer, broadcaster, and social advocate. After working as a mechanical engineer for nearly a decade, Abdel-Magied became a full-time author and speaker. Her TED talk, "What Does My Headscarf Mean to You?" has been viewed more than two million times and was selected as one of TED's top ten ideas in 2015. During the talk, Abdel-Magied challenges perceptions of race and religion in a creative and thought-provoking manner. She points the audience toward meaningful ways that they can combat unconscious bias and serve as a mentor to people with different life experiences from their own. In 2018, Abdel-Magied received the Young Voltaire Award for free speech.

Search Terms
To locate a video of this presentation online, enter the following key words into a search engine: Yassmin TED talk. The video is approximately 14:01 in length.

What to Watch For

[0:00–0:14] We know that first impressions matter and can be the most important factor in determining audience opinions about a speaker. As a Muslim woman speaking to a predominantly non-Muslim audience, Abdel-Magied made a series of strategic decisions based on her analysis of audience characteristics and attitudes. Even before she utters her first word, she knows that the audience is evaluating her based on how she looks. She begins by asking the audience what they think when they see someone like her. The question introduces the role that unconscious bias plays in limiting opportunities for people who are different.

[0:44–1:19] Abdel-Magied demonstrates expressiveness, confidence, stage presence, and immediacy. Her voice, facial expressions, eye contact, and physical movements express warmth for the audience and the importance of the topic. The vitality, variety, and authenticity of her delivery is rooted in her desire to help the audience understand the meaning and consequence of unconscious bias as something that "we"—both her audience and Abdel-Magied herself—need to overcome.

[1:52–2:32] Throughout the presentation, Abdel-Magied's facial expressions—including a communicative ironic smile—convey how she feels. When reassuring the audience that she doesn't believe that "there's a secret sexist or racist or ageist lurking within" them, her facial gestures are a bit playful. Moments later, she uses a more serious facial expression as she talks about how bias is not an accusation but something that we need to identify in ourselves.

[2:50–4:05] Abdel-Magied projects a sense of confidence in her message throughout the presentation. Because she thoughtfully developed the message beforehand, she can present it here clearly and coherently, backed up by strong supporting material. She offers illustrations that clearly required adequate preparation in order to present them effectively. In one case, she discusses the lack of female musicians in orchestras and an experiment that was conducted to unearth the unconscious bias about men being better musicians than women.

[6:00–7:28] About midway through the speech, Abdel-Magied wonders aloud whether the audience members think they "have a good read" on her. With a photo of an oil rig behind her, she asks them if they would believe that she runs one of them. "Can you imagine me walking in and being like, 'Hey, boys, this is what's up—this is how it's done'"? Her stage presence—her ability to capture and keep the audience's attention—is solidified as she removes her abaya (the full-length outer garment worn by some Muslim women) to reveal the orange jumpsuit she wears on oil rigs. She tops off the wardrobe change by placing a hard hat on her head. By presenting herself in her work uniform, Abdel-Magied dramatically (and suddenly) alters her audience's impression of her.

[8:55–10:45] Abdel-Magied's vocal delivery also plays an important role in her speech. At the beginning of this segment, she slows down her rate and lowers her volume to signal a change in tone and direction. A slower rate emphasizes the importance of the message that follows, which is a description of ways that the audience can help combat unconscious bias.

Abdel-Magied also moves back and forth between standardized speech and the colloquial language of Australia. Consider how she speaks a mix of language styles: "If I see a Muslim chick who's got a bit of attitude, I'm like, 'What's up? We can hang out.'" And "Because, ladies and gentlemen, the world is not just. People are not born with equal opportunity."

[10:45–12:30] Although Abdel-Magied is confident throughout her talk, she does not act so confident that her message seems too polished to be believable. For example, while she maintains fairly consistent fluency, there are times when it appears that her breathing is a bit rapid, causing her to trail off at the end of a sentence or to pause in order to fill her lungs with air. When she removes her orange oil-rig uniform, Abdel-Magied struggles to get her feet out of the pant legs. Although it is a bit awkward to stand there with the uniform down around her ankles, she carries on as if saying, "I don't have time to worry about this. My message is more important."

[13:40–13:45] Despite having a remote in her hand during most of her speech, Abdel-Magied's gestures are a natural outgrowth of what she feels about the topic and what she has to say about it. Her gestures do not feel forced or fake but instead are an effective complement to the rest of her delivery. During the last line of the speech, she uses a wave-like gesture moving from one arm to the other to show that sometimes people are not who and what you think they are. And then, finally, she extricates herself from the pant legs.

EXERCISE

After viewing Abdel-Magied's speech, reflect on these questions:

1. What strategies did Abdel-Magied use to manage the audience's first impression of her before she spoke her first word? What, if any, alternative strategies would have worked as well?

2. To what extent did the combination of Abdel-Magied's vocal and physical delivery skills increase the impact and memorability of her message?

3. How do you think Abdel-Magied used practice sessions to improve her delivery skills? More specifically, what might she have done during these sessions to develop her expressiveness, confidence, stage presence, and immediacy?

4. How does Abdel-Magied's speech represent the importance of delivery as described in the chapter? Provide some specific examples (other than the ones already given).

5. In what ways, if any, could Abdel-Magied have improved the content and delivery of her presentation?

4.2 Vocal Delivery

🔍 A BRIEF GUIDE TO THIS CHAPTER

- **Breathing for speech** (p. 229)
- **Components of vocal quality** (p. 231)
- **Vocal clarity** (p. 241)

How often do you think about the sound of your own voice? Perhaps only now and then, perhaps only when you're speaking, perhaps not at all. Even though it may not cross your mind on a regular basis, the sound of your voice strongly influences how audiences respond to you and your message.

In this chapter, we provide advice for improving your **vocal delivery**, or how you use effective breath control, volume, rate, pitch, inflection, fluency, articulation, and pronunciation when you speak. Think of your voice as a musical instrument: its structure—or anatomy—dictates the kind of sounds you produce. And much like learning a musical instrument, you can improve the quality of your voice.

Breathing for Speech

Breathing for speech is the indispensable foundation of a clear and expressive voice. All the vocal sounds in the English language are made by exhaling air from your lungs. If you doubt this, try talking while breathing in! The key to effective breathing for speech is to control your outgoing breath, which improves the sound of your voice in five significant ways:

- **Strength:** Gives power to your voice, particularly across a large and crowded room.
- **Duration:** Allows you to say more with every breath.
- **Authority:** Helps you speak with a richer, more resonant, energetic, and persuasive voice.
- **Quality:** Improves the overall appeal of your voice.
- **Clarity:** Reduces vocal problems such as harshness, breathiness, and mumbling.

The first step in learning to breathe for speech is to note the differences between the shallow breathing you do unconsciously and the deeper, more purposeful breathing—sometimes called abdominal or diaphragmatic breathing—that produces a strong, sustained vocal quality. Whether teaching speakers, actors, or singers, voice coaches begin such training with abdominal breathing. Try the following exercise. Although you may find it strange and even challenging at first, your reward will be a stronger and more controllable voice.

1. Lie flat on your back on a flat, comfortable surface. Support the back of your knees with a pillow.
2. Place a moderately heavy hardbound book on the top part of your abdomen, right below your rib cage. The lower edge of the book should cover your navel.
3. Relax and breathe through your mouth. The book should move up when you breathe in and sink down when you breathe out.
4. Place one of your hands on the upper part of your chest as if you're reciting the Pledge of Allegiance. As you inhale and exhale, this area should barely move in and out.
5. Remove the book and replace it with your other hand. Your abdomen should be moving up when you breathe in and sinking down when you breathe out.
6. Once you're comfortable with step 5, try doing the same kind of breathing while sitting up or standing.

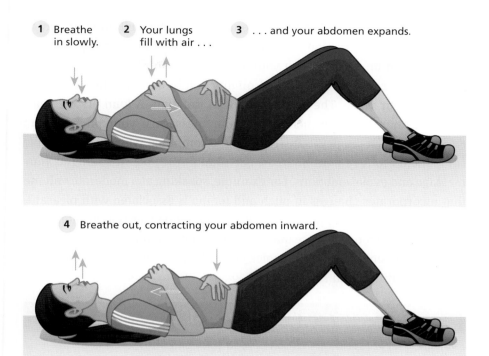

1 Breathe in slowly. **2** Your lungs fill with air . . . **3** . . . and your abdomen expands.

4 Breathe out, contracting your abdomen inward.

Abdominal breathing exercises can help you improve the quality of your voice.

Once you've learned how abdominal breathing feels, you can begin to add sounds. For example, try saying "ahh" with each exhalation. Then hold the "ahh" for five seconds. Now try counting out loud from one to five, holding the sound of each number for at least a full second. Next, use this breathing as you stand or sit up. Inhale right before you begin a sentence or phrase, then exhale to add force and volume to your voice.

When you're breathing correctly for speech, your voice will be clear, expressive, and more controlled. With practice, you will develop muscle memory for harnessing your breath effectively.

Components of Vocal Quality

There are entire books and programs of study devoted to improving the quality of your voice. In this chapter, we combine dozens of individual vocal qualities into five major components that are essential for effective presentation speaking: *volume*, *projection*, *rate*, *pitch*, and *fluency*. If you focus on improving these five components, you'll be well on your way to speaking in an expressive and confident voice that enhances your stage presence and immediacy with your audience.

The five components of vocal quality combine to create the unique sound of your voice. They do not work in isolation. A loud or soft voice won't communicate the meaning of your message if your pitch doesn't vary or you lack fluency. But when they're combined with skill, these five components convey more than a clear sound—they add meaning to your message and evoke emotions. For example, speaking at a moderate volume that incorporates changes in pitch and tempo is associated with pleasantness, liveliness, and happiness. Whereas a too-loud voice is associated with fear or anger, a too-soft voice may imply boredom, sadness, or uncertainty.[1] A warm and sincere-sounding voice can enhance immediacy and express specific meanings and emotions.

COMPONENTS OF VOCAL QUALITY	
Volume	Speaking in a soft or loud voice and other levels in between
Projection	Controlling vocal energy that gives clearness and power to your voice
Rate	Speaking slowly or rapidly, as measured by the number of words you say per minute
Pitch	Speaking at a variety of ranges from low to high
Fluency	Speaking smoothly without tripping over words or pausing at an awkward moment

VOLUME

If your audience can't hear you, you won't achieve your purpose. The loudness of your voice, otherwise known as **volume**, determines whether or not your audience will hear what you have to say. Here are some ways to ensure that your volume is appropriate for various rhetorical situations.

Evaluate and Adjust Your Volume One of the best ways to make sure that everyone in your audience can hear you is to PRACTICE ▶ (220-24) your presentation out loud, rehearsing the volume you intend to use in front of your audience. As you practice, make sure you are breathing correctly for speech and are using good posture to ensure that your airway is open.

In addition to practicing on your own, ask someone to listen to your practice session—someone you trust to give you honest feedback. If possible, practice in a room about the same size as the one where you will be speaking. Ask your listener to sit in a far corner and report your volume level. If you are not loud enough, increase your volume until your friend can hear you clearly. If no one is around to help you, place a recording device at the back of a room and experiment with different volumes until the voice you hear in the recording is clear and strong.

Speakers are rarely too loud. More often, they are not loud enough. Sometimes we ask soft-spoken students to repeat the first 10 seconds of their presentation in a louder voice. After they hesitantly respond in a slightly louder voice, we ask for more volume. And after that, we ask for an even louder voice. In bewilderment, students often say, "But I'm shouting!" We then ask the class for a verdict and the answer is always the same: "You're not shouting; your volume is just right." You can do the same activity with a friend who will tell you when your volume is "just right" for a presentation and its setting.

Sometimes speakers can't be heard for a simple reason: they barely open their mouths. If you don't open your mouth wide enough when speaking, your voice won't reach your audience because the sounds can't escape your mouth. To understand this phenomenon, try saying the tongue twister "Peter Piper picked a peck of pickled peppers" in three ways:

1. Say it as if your lips are almost glued together and your jaw is all but wired shut.

2. Say it with normal movement of your lips and jaw, as you would in a personal conversation.

3. Say it with more lip and jaw movement. Open your mouth almost as wide as you can.[2]

When you say this tongue twister in these ways, can you tell the difference? It's really quite simple: your voice will sound stronger and louder with a more open mouth.

Vary and Adjust Your Volume Listening to someone who speaks at the same volume throughout a presentation is tedious. In conversations, we unconsciously raise and lower our volume based on a word or phrase's importance and emotional mood. Varying your volume during a presentation makes it more pleasing and interesting to your listeners, and even more important, helps you emphasize some words and phrases more than others. For instance, you may vary your volume within a sentence in order to stress an important word. Consider the difference between "This is the ONLY time I'm free this week" and "This is the only time I'm free THIS week."

Master the Microphone In some rhetorical situations, you may be offered or expected to use a microphone. Don't say "No thanks" until you've considered the audience, the setting, and the advantages of amplification. Audience members with hearing disabilities and/or who rely on hearing devices will comprehend more of your presentation if you use a microphone. In a crowded or large space, amplification makes it possible for everyone to hear, listen, and understand.

If you're presenting in a hybrid setting—with attendees both online and in person—the audio output for online participants probably comes from a microphone. If you don't use the microphone in such cases, your online audience members may not be able to hear you. And when you're delivering a fully ONLINE PRESENTATION ▶(282–301) (using Zoom, for example), you must use a microphone.

Another reason to use a microphone is that it can help you convey subtle emotions and highlight important ideas, no matter the size of an audience or room. Speakers who know how to use a microphone can move from a gentle whisper to a powerful roar with ease.

Microphones present unique challenges. When speakers don't know how to use a microphone, the sound of their voice can be distorted, the letter "p" can make an annoying popping sound, and they may fumble with the equipment. To deliver your presentation effectively with a microphone, speak more slowly, articulate more clearly, and make sure the system can accommodate changes in your volume. If you speak too loudly, you may sound as though you are shouting (for real this time!)—and your audience will probably grimace in response to your artificially amplified volume. If you speak too softly or don't speak directly into the sensitive part of a microphone, it may not pick up everything you say.

If possible, test the microphone before the audience is in the room. Ask someone to sit at the back of the room and monitor your amplified voice. Can you speak at an audible and understandable volume without the microphone? If you can and want a more personal connection with your audience, you may not need a microphone. But if you do decide to use one, here are some strategies to keep in mind:

Hold a microphone below your mouth to amplify your voice most clearly and allow your audience to see your face.

- Determine whether the microphone can capture your voice from several angles and distances or whether you need to keep it close to your mouth.

- If you are using a stationary microphone, place it 5–10 inches away from your mouth. If you are using a handheld microphone, hold it *below* your mouth at chin level.

- If a microphone is clipped to your clothing or in a headset, test it and adjust it before your presentation. These kinds of microphones can produce distracting noises.

- Focus on your audience, not on the microphone. Don't tap it, lean over it, or keep readjusting it as a test.

- Keep in mind that a microphone will also amplify other sounds—coughing, shuffling papers, and tapping a pen or pointer.

- Stand or sit up straight when using a microphone. Don't hunch over it or bend your head down while speaking.

- Most important of all, speak the same way you would *without* a microphone. If you position your microphone properly, the dynamic characteristics and power of your voice will be fully projected.

PROJECTION

To *project* means "to extend, throw, or shoot something outward using a controlled force to reach a specific target." For speakers, **projection** describes a controlled vocal energy that gives clearness and power to your voice. To reach every audience member, even those farthest from you, you need to project your voice. Projection requires concentration, strong breath control, and a desire to communicate with your listeners. A projected voice is beamed to listeners. It does not just reach them; it penetrates them.[3] So, how do you project?

One simple technique can instantly improve your projection during a presentation: look directly at the people in the back row and deliberately think about making them hear you. The mere act of looking at and consciously thinking about these listeners will cause you to project your voice more effectively. What you will notice when you do this is that your volume alone won't do the trick.

To practice improving your projection before your presentation, ask a friend to sit at the back of the room or auditorium where you will be speaking. Then read a nonsense sentence in a loud and clear voice. Ask your listener to repeat the sentence back to you to test whether or not they heard you accurately. After a few tries, you will discover that merely speaking more loudly won't necessarily help your listener understand what you're saying. In addition to volume, you need to pronounce the consonants and vowels in the words more clearly and forcefully. Try to project your reading of the following sentences to someone sitting far away:

> Samuel Hornsbee threw a turkey at the dragon's striped Chevrolet.
> Twenty-seven squirrels sang chants for the Christmas-in-May ball.

Using nonsense sentences ensures that your listener cannot anticipate the correct words. When asked to write down or repeat what you have said, your listener won't be able to guess a logical ending to your sentence. But if you project with both force *and* clarity, your audience will be able to hear, understand, and even be amused by what you've said.

Later in this chapter, we examine how two other important factors, clear *articulation* and correct *pronunciation*, contribute to how well your words reach everyone in the audience.

RATE

We're sure you have heard speakers who spoke either too quickly or too slowly. How fast is too fast? How slow is too slow? Your rate of speech equals the number of words you say per minute (wpm) added to the number and length of pauses you use. Just as there are different driving speed limits for different roads and traffic conditions, your ideal speaking **rate** may change in different rhetorical situations. Your natural speaking style, the topic and mood of your presentation, the complexity of your vocabulary, and your audience's listening ability should affect how quickly or slowly you speak. Unlike projection and volume, you can practice speaking at different rates on your own. Let's use this paragraph as an example. It contains 150 words. Read it out loud in the kind of voice you would use before an audience. How long did it take you to read this?

75 seconds or more	Less than 125 wpm (too slow)
70–60 seconds	125–145 wpm (good range for a slower rate)
60–50 seconds	145–180 wpm (good range for a faster rate)
50 seconds or less	More than 180 wpm (too fast)

In **PERSUASIVE ◆ (403–61)** presentations, a quicker speaking rate can be effective, especially when the audience is engaged and actively listening. If you want to make a personal connection with your audience and ensure they understand your message, a slower speaking rate may be more effective. Slow talkers can be more persuasive because there is plenty of time for listeners to comprehend and agree with a message shared by a seemingly conscientious, **AUDIENCE-CENTERED SPEAKER ▲ (88–89)**.[4] You might use a slower speaking rate when your audience's listening ability and concerns demand it—for instance, when speaking to audience members who may have trouble hearing or understanding you, when giving step-by-step instructions, and when making an important point or explaining a complex idea.

Here are some tips for finding an appropriate and effective rate:

- *Monitor your speaking rate.* Time yourself when you practice. If you're much above 160 wpm most of the time, remind yourself to slow down.

- ***Practice in front of friends and record it.*** Let listeners interrupt and say, "What? I have no idea what you just said. Say it again—but slower."

- ***Repeat yourself when saying something important.*** Give your audience time to catch up.

Another aspect of your speaking rate is just as important as speaking fast or slow: How well and often do you pause? A pause is a meaningful period of silence within or between sentences and sections of a presentation. Effective speakers use breath control and vary the frequency and length of their pauses so that their presentation isn't choppy and monotonous. For example, Martin Luther King Jr.'s exceptional "I Have a Dream" speech opened at approximately 90 wpm but ended at 150 wpm and was punctuated by many dramatic and effective pauses along the way.[5] Now consider John F. Kennedy's "Ask not what your country can do for you—ask what you can do for your country." The enduring power of these words depends in large part on Kennedy's pause before the second half of the sentence. Without appropriate pauses, the meaning of your words may be difficult to understand and lose their impact.

Our advice: Speak at a rate that feels right for *you* and appropriate for the occasion as well as for your audience, purpose, content, and delivery. Make use of pauses to vary your rate and give your message dramatic power. Think of it this way: There's too fast, too slow, and just right. It's your job to figure out what's just right for you and the rhetorical situation.

PITCH

Just like the notes on a musical scale, **pitch** refers to how high or low your voice sounds. Anatomy determines pitch. Most men speak at a lower pitch than women do. Most adults speak at a lower pitch than children do.

Americans seem to prefer low-pitched voices, which can sound more authoritative and effective. To compensate for a high natural voice, some speakers push their voices down into a lower range of notes. However, overdoing this can limit the voice's expressiveness, make it sound harsh, and damage it by putting a strain on the vocal cords.

Optimum Pitch Instead of worrying about how to lower your voice's pitch in pursuit of a questionable cultural ideal, you should determine *your* **optimum pitch**, the natural pitch at which you speak most easily and expressively.[6] When using your optimum pitch, the muscles in your throat are closer to rest than any other time. Relaxed, expressive speaking will always be better received by an audience than an artificially low pitch that sounds strained or harsh. Speaking at your optimum pitch offers the following advantages:

- Your voice will be stronger and less likely to fade at the end of sentences.
- Your voice will not tire easily.
- Your voice will have greater intensity and clarity with less effort.
- You won't sound harsh, hoarse, breathy, or squeaky.
- You'll have "room to move" above and below the pitch, an absolute must for an expressive and energetic voice.

To find your optimum pitch, try singing "Happy Birthday." At what part of the song does your voice feel the most natural and the least strained? That's your optimum pitch, your baseline. Notice also how your voice unconsciously settles into a range of pitches you can actually sing, rather than gravitating toward the lowest or highest end of what's physically possible. This too is helpful to recognize because speaking often requires changing your pitch. (For example, does your pitch rise at the end of a sentence when you ask a question?) Try also singing "The Star-Spangled Banner" and notice just how wide its pitch range is—far wider than most people would use in a spoken presentation.

Inflection When we refer to the changing pitch within a syllable, word, or group of words, we're talking about **inflection**. Inflection makes speech expressive. Without inflection, you have what most people call a **monotone voice**, which occurs when there is little change in the pitch of sounds within words or the pitch of words within phrases and sentences.

Inflection helps you emphasize important and meaningful words or phrases. Even a small rise or drop in inflection can change the entire

For an example of a speaker whose inflection in pitch makes his vocal delivery expressive and interesting, see Notable Speaker: Ron Finley, page 458.

meaning of a sentence or the quality of your voice. Consider the following examples:

- *I* was born in New Jersey. (You, on the other hand, were born in Maryland.)
- I *was* born in New Jersey. (No doubt about it!)
- I was *born* in New Jersey. (So I know my way around.)
- I was born in New *Jersey*. (Not in New York.)

Changing the inflection of the words in this short sentence can produce four different meanings. Inflection is a key ingredient in making your voice more interesting, exciting, emotional, and empathetic.

FLUENCY

Fluency is the ability to speak smoothly without tripping over words or pausing at an awkward moment. As with so many other aspects of effective speaking, practice is the key to greater fluency. The more you practice your presentation, the more fluent you become. Even Barack Obama, an often eloquent and inspiring speaker, began his career as a less fluent presenter. As a young attorney, his speaking style was filled with too many "uhs" and "ers." By listening to other speakers and discovering what made them effective, he learned and practiced how to speak fluently.[7]

Lurking in the background of many presentations is a common fluency problem: **filler phrases**, a general term given to all the verbal interruptions, blunders, restarted sentences, and repeated words that fill space while we search for the next meaningful part of the sentence we're speaking. Filler phrases are quite common in our everyday speech, making up more than 5 percent of the words we use every day.[8]

The most common filler phrases are "um" and "uh." In fact, words similar to "uh" are universal speech fillers in every language on earth, and they seem to become part of our vocabulary before age three.[9] There is nothing wrong with an occasional "um" or "uh" in otherwise fluent speech. When used sparingly, "uh" and "um" can play a meaningful role in a presentation, signaling a significant word, phrase, or idea is about to be said. "Uh" usually appears more often before a short pause; "um," before a longer pause. Thus, an "um" is signaling a more important thought.[10] Eloquent speakers use them too, but their "ums" go unnoticed because they are fluent and confident.

In most presentations, it is perfectly okay to use a few of these short filler phrases—not five or six per sentence. Too many filler phrases, *you know*, *like uh*, *okay*, break up, *um*, your fluency and, *uh*, can drive your audience, *right*, *like*, crazy.

To determine if you overuse filler phrases, record one of your practice sessions or an actual presentation and count them. The result can surprise you and motivate you to use them less often. To break an excessive filler phrase habit, slow down and listen to yourself as you practice. At first, you will be less fluent, stopping at almost every phrase, correcting yourself. But you will soon recover your fluency and become a better speaker.

Vocal Clarity

A strong, well-paced, optimally pitched voice that is fluent and expressive may still not be enough to ensure the successful delivery of a presentation. The clarity of the words you speak and the way you pronounce those words will also influence your audience's impressions of your vocal delivery.

For an example of a speaker whose vocal delivery is clear and fluent, see Notable Speaker: Monica Lewinsky, page 27.

ARTICULATION

Articulation (or *diction*) is how clearly you make the sounds in the words of a language. Poor articulation is often described as "sloppy speech" or just plain mumbling. If friends ask, "What?" after you've said something in conversation, they are rarely asking you to speak louder; they are asking you to articulate.

Certain sounds account for most articulation problems. The most common culprits are combined words, "ing" endings, and final consonants. For instance, when read aloud by a speaker who isn't articulating properly, "First, I'm going to tell you what's the matter with saying and reading this sentence" might sound like "Firs, 'm gonna telya watsumata wi' sayin and readin thisenens." Many of us combine words—"what's the matter" becomes "watsumata"; "going to" becomes "gonna." Some of us shorten the "ing" sound to an "in" sound: "sayin" instead of "saying." And others leave off final consonants, such as the "t" in "first."

The final consonants that get left off most often are the ones that pop out of your mouth in a micro-explosion. Because these consonants—p, b, t, d, k, g—cannot be hummed like an "m" or hissed like an "s," it's easy to lose them at the end of a word. Although you can hear the difference between "Rome" and "rose," poor articulation can make it difficult to hear the difference between "rack" and "rag," "hit" and "hid," or "tap" and "tab," to give a few examples. Make a note of words ending with these consonants and practice articulating the final sounds correctly and audibly. And, without overdoing it, try to enunciate each word as you speak. It will force you to have better articulation.

PRONUNCIATION

Pronunciation refers to how you say words and the order in which you put all the sounds and stress for any particular word. There are often commonly accepted, or "correct," ways to pronounce words, and it can be embarrassing to mispronounce a common word. One of us heard a speaker give a presentation on the importance of pro*nun*ciation, but she undermined her effectiveness by referring to "pro*noun*ciation" throughout her presentation!

Finding a word's commonly accepted pronunciation is not difficult; if you're unsure, look it up in a dictionary. Online dictionaries can be especially helpful because they often give you an audio example of a person saying the word. If you know someone who knows how to pronounce a word (for example, your roommate is a biology major and you are planning to use several biology terms), ask them for help.

ACCENTS AND DIALECTS

If two people pronounce the same word differently, it doesn't always mean that one of them is mispronouncing that word. Differences in pronunciation and vocabulary may indicate that two people are speaking different dialects or accents of the same language. Do you say pop, soda, tonic, or soft drink? Do you like *pe*cans (PEE-cans) or pe*cans* (puh-CAHNS)?

To see an example of code-switching, watch Barack Obama's commencement speeches at the US Military Academy in West Point, New York, and at Hampton University in Hampton, Virginia, both from May 2010.

Some students, especially when speaking with an accent different from the majority of their audience, have asked us, "How can I get rid of my accent?" The honest answer is that there is no such thing as an unaccented language. In fact, what is commonly called **Standard American English** is nothing more than another accent. Granted, it is the accent that has been historically taught in schools and used by people in power, like politicians and corporate officers. Does that mean you should speak Standard American English when you give presentations in school and at work? No, not at all. As in all other ways, consider your rhetorical situation.

In some situations, you may find pressure or an expectation to use the dominant accent of your community or audience—or it may just work better for your purpose. This ability—called **code-switching**—describes how we modify our verbal and nonverbal communication in different contexts. If a person who speaks with a southern accent or Black English in some contexts decides to switch to Standard American English in other contexts, that's code-switching.[11]

President Barack Obama's introductions at two different commencement speeches, both delivered in May 2010, are useful examples.[12] While the occasion is the same—a graduation ceremony—he adapts to the differences between his two audiences by changing his speaking style. As their commander in chief, he uses a more formal tone when speaking to the graduates of the US Military Academy, conveying the seriousness of their commitment to defend and protect the United States. The decorum required of the cadets is mirrored in Obama's concise, crisp, and commanding word choices. In contrast, he uses a more casual tone as he begins his address to the graduates of Hampton University. As the first Black president speaking at a historically Black university, Obama's relationship with the graduates was more personal. An audience member shouts out, "I love you!" and he responds, "I love you back! That's why I'm here! I love you guys!" Would you expect the commander in chief to use such a casual tone when speaking to military graduates? Probably not.

Though you may choose to code-switch in some situations, your accent and dialect are part of *you*. Changing them to fit in with a particular audience is like denying part of who you are. If an audience understands you, you should not have to change the way you speak.[13] Your accent might help your audience connect with a particular aspect of your identity or lived experience. An accent can evoke a particular place, community, or cultural moment. In doing so, or in **code-meshing**, you might mix different languages and accents together or various purposes—whether in a presentation or daily conversation.[14] So how can speakers and listeners with different accents maximize vocal clarity and understanding? Let's look at a few tips.[15]

If you are speaking to an audience with an accent different from your own:

- Embrace your unique voice as part of your identity. Speak it with pride.
- Use an online pronunciation guide and practice saying difficult or important words.
- Read aloud from written material to practice your intonation.
- Speak clearly and avoid idioms or expressions your audience may not understand, or take time to explain them if they have special importance to your presentation.
- Use presentation aids to clarify important words and ideas.

If you are an audience member listening to a speaker with an accent different from your own:

- Be patient and attentive. Make an extra effort to **LISTEN ● (30–42)** to and understand the speaker.

- Avoid stereotyping the speaker based on their accent.
- Pay close attention to nonverbal behavior that communicates meaning.
- Avoid distractions that may impact your ability to hear the speaker clearly.

Conclusion

Everyone has a unique speaking voice. It's how you can recognize a good friend on the phone or a recording of a favorite singer. The same is true of speakers. Keep in mind that your voice is one of a kind. Don't try to sound like someone else or develop a "perfect" voice. Instead, work to improve the quality of the voice you have so that it works for the occasion and content as well as for you, your audience, and your purpose.

An effective, expressive voice requires the skilled application of breath control, volume, projection, rate, pitch, inflection, fluency, articulation, and pronunciation. You can't just hope your voice will improve. It requires time, effort, and practice to develop a natural-sounding voice that easily adjusts to your message and your audience in a variety of rhetorical situations.

Jordan Raskopoulos

As a well-known singer, comedian, and actress in Australia, Jordan Raskopoulos has spent a lot of time in front of audiences—both in person and online. She is a member of the award-winning comedy trio the Axis of Awesome whose musical parody "4 Chords" has more than 45 million views on YouTube. Beyond comedy and music, her interests include playing roller derby and the video game *Warhammer 40,000*, as well as serving as an ambassador for Twenty10, an organization that supports LGBTQIA+ youth. When she stepped on the TEDx stage in Sydney, Australia, in 2017, she used humor and surprising lack of stage fright to talk about her personal experience living with high-functioning anxiety.

Search Terms

To locate a video of this presentation online, enter the following key words into a search engine: Jordan Raskopoulos Ted Talk Anxiety. The video is approximately 14:20 in length.

What to Watch For

[0:15–0:44] Before she reaches center stage, Raskopoulos uses a loud, expressive, and confident voice that enhances her stage presence and immediacy with the audience. As she walks onto the stage, she shouts, "Come on, yeah, yes! Rock and roll! Come on, Sydney! Let's make some noise!" The audience responds with loud cheering and clapping. Continuing with a loud voice coupled with large gestures, she calls on the audience to vocalize their feelings: "Make some noise if you hate public speaking!"

[0:44–0:51] To draw attention to the seriousness of the issue, Raskopoulos begins to lower her volume when she says, "Make some noise if the idea of giving a talk in front of thousands of people . . ." However, to emphasize the fear that most people have about giving a talk in public, she raises her volume again as she finishes—"is your nightmare!"—and throws her arms in the air for emphasis.

[0:52–1:18] Raskopoulos surprisingly says that giving a talk in front of thousands of people does not bother her at all. In fact, she loves it because she knows the rules of the speaking situation. For example, she says and demonstrates that she can drop her volume a little bit and be more conversational. The result is that she and the audience feel as though they know each other a little bit better. Why? Because raising and lowering your volume is something we naturally do in conversations based on the importance of the words and the emotional mood. In a similar way, varying your volume while speaking to an audience makes your message more pleasing and interesting to them.

[1:33–1:50] Raskopoulos demonstrates how she uses vocal delivery to capture her audience's full attention by raising her "voice to a crescendo," letting silence "hang for three seconds," then by speaking "quietly, purposefully, and softly." By doing so, she displays mastery in using the microphone to move from a powerful yell to a much quieter volume.

[2:54–6:56] Her speaking rate picks up as she begins to list the ways in which people describe stage fright. A faster rate here helps the audience sense the anxiety beyond just hearing the descriptions. Her rate remains consistent as she describes her own anxiety culminating with the statement "I don't get stage fright. I get life fright." She pauses here and allows the audience a moment to process the contrast between what causes most people anxiety—stage fright—and what causes *her* anxiety—everyday life tasks. Her rate picks up again when she describes what happened when she signed up for a TED talk. The use of a faster rate here helps convey how overwhelming all of the tasks and interactions were for her as she went about preparing for the talk.

[7:13–7:40] Raskopoulos uses inflection to make her talk expressive and to emphasize important and meaningful words and phrases. For example, she places emphasis on the word "nothing" to explain how the outcome of her worrying a lot—even about a reasonable list of seven things to do—results in a failure to do anything.

EXERCISE

After reviewing Raskopoulos's speech, reflect on these questions:

1. Describe how Raskopoulos varied her the vocal qualities of volume, rate, pitch, and fluency during her presentation. How did her use of these variations affect the success of her talk?

2. Provide an example of how she used inflection (other than the one used in the above analysis of her speech).

3. Unlike most TED talk speakers, Rasko-poulos referred to her notes on a tiny piece of paper she held in her left hand. Was it distracting or reassuring to see a skilled speaker using notes? Why do you think she used it?

4. Did you notice any instances of code-switching? Provide an example to support your answer.

5. Assuming you are not Australian and from the same geographic region of the country as Raskopoulos, describe your experience listening to someone with an accent different from your own.

4.3 Physical Delivery

> ## 🔍 A BRIEF GUIDE TO THIS CHAPTER
>
> - **Eye contact** (p. 249)
> - **Facial expressions** (p. 251)
> - **Gestures** (p. 252)
> - **Posture and movement** (p. 255)
> - **Appearance** (p. 257)

The key to effective physical delivery is naturalness. However, being natural doesn't mean being unprepared or laid-back. Rather, it means being so well prepared and well practiced that your presentation is an authentic reflection of who you are and what you hope to achieve.

Your **physical delivery**—the way you position yourself in front of your audience, your eye contact and facial expressions, and the way you stand, move, and gesture—has a significant impact on the success of your presentation. Your physical delivery also tells an audience a great deal about how much you care about reaching them.

In this chapter, we identify five components of physical delivery: *eye contact*, *facial expressions*, *gestures*, *posture* and *movement*, and *appearance*. If you focus on improving these five components, you'll be well on your way to communicating expressiveness, confidence, stage presence, and immediacy through your physical delivery.

Eye Contact

Establishing and maintaining **eye contact**—a visual connection with individual members of your audience—is one of the most important and sometimes difficult physical delivery skills. When used effectively, eye contact initiates and controls communication, enhances your **CREDIBILITY** ▲ **(74–81)**, and provides a means of assessing listener **FEEDBACK** ● **(39–40)**. In short, if you don't look at your audience, they may have little incentive to look at *you*. When you establish eye contact with your audience, you also indicate that you are ready to begin speaking and that they should get ready to listen. Lack of eye contact can communicate a message too—that you don't care or want to connect with your audience.

Generally, the more eye contact you have with your audience, the better—especially when speaking in the United States. American audiences typically perceive speakers who use and maintain eye contact as strong and effective. But the value of eye contact is not universal. For example, in many Asian and African cultures, and in some Caribbean cultures, meeting another person's eyes directly can be perceived as rude or aggressive. When asked a question, Canadians are more likely to look up; Japanese are more likely to look down when answering. Some neurodivergent speakers may not make eye contact with the audience, and some neurodivergent audience members may not return the gaze of a speaker.[1] In **ONLINE PRESENTATIONS** ▶ **(282–301)**, when you look at images of your listeners, it may appear to them that you're looking down and not at them.

Effective speakers learn to adjust their eye contact to their **AUDIENCE** ▲ **(88–105)** and to their **RHETORICAL SITUATION** ● **(6–11)**. They sense when eye contact is appropriate, avoiding direct gazes at audience members who appear uncomfortable. If maintaining eye contact is possible and positive in your speaking situation, try the following strategies:

- Strive to look at your audience for at least 75 percent of your speaking time. If you are especially reserved, that percentage may be lower, but try to focus your eyes and attention on your listeners.

- Establish eye contact and connect with as many individual listeners as you can, but try not to jump rapidly from one person to another.

- Look at individual audience members the way you would look at someone familiar to you, holding eye contact for a few seconds or just long enough to finish a phrase or point.

- Move your gaze around the room, settle on someone, and establish eye contact. Then move on to another person. If someone in the audience avoids shared eye contact or seems uncomfortable, move your gaze to someone else.

- Look at audience members seated farthest away or off to one side as often as you look at those in the center and near you.

- To maintain eye contact without losing your place in a set of detailed **SPEAKING NOTES ▶ (217–20)** or a **MANUSCRIPT ▶ (219)**, try using the **eye scan**, in which you alternately glance at specific phrases or sentences in your notes, then look up at your audience and speak. Begin by placing your thumb and index finger on one side of your notes to frame the section you are using so you don't lose your place.[2] As you approach the end of a long phrase or sentence within that section, glance down and move your fingers to the next phrase to be spoken. Keep moving your fingers down as you move through your presentation.

These strategies provide a strong foundation for improving your eye contact and can replace some of the *bad* advice we've heard, such as look at a spot on the back wall, at groups of people in every section of the room, or only at your friends. These tactics have one thing in common: they don't work. If you fix your eyes on a clock at the back of a room, for example, you'll look like a zombie or a sleepwalker. If you look up and down every row, it will seem as though you're robotically taking attendance. There's really no secret to eye contact. Just look at individual people in your audience—eye to eye.

Facial Expressions

Regardless of why, where, when, and to whom you are speaking, listeners look at your face. Your **facial expressions** reflect your attitudes and emotional state, provide nonverbal feedback, and are a primary source of information about you and your message.[3] Despite the enormous significance of facial expressions, they can be difficult to control. Some people show little expression—they have a blank "poker face" most of the time. Other people are "like an open book"—there is little doubt about how they feel. It's difficult to transform a poker face into an open book—and vice versa.

Unless your topic is solemn or serious, a smile is a great way to start a presentation. A smile shows your listeners that you are comfortable and eager to share your ideas and information. Looking at a smiling speaker can also make audience members feel happy and positive, and they are more likely to smile at you in response.

If you don't feel comfortable smiling, don't force it—most listeners are likely to know if your smile is false.[4] In the end, the best advice is to let your face do what comes naturally. If you communicate your message sincerely and focus on your listeners, your facial expression will be appropriate and effective. As you become more physically confident while speaking, you'll also become more comfortable smiling.

Try to manage your emotional displays while you speak. For example, if someone asks you a question, you'll want to look confident as you answer. But when the answer to a question is clearly obvious to you and the rest of the audience, don't frown or roll your eyes. Your facial expression should make the questioner feel just as respected as other questioners.

During many presentations, there are points when you'll want to look thoughtful, sad, or happy. If you nod while talking, listeners will probably nod as well—and that can lead to them agreeing with the point you are making.

Gestures

A **gesture** is a body movement that conveys or reinforces a thought, an intention, or an emotion. Most gestures are made with your hands and arms, but the shrug of a shoulder, bending of a knee, and tapping of a foot are gestures too. Gestures can clarify and support your language, help you relieve physical responses to speaking anxiety, arouse audience attention, and function as a presentation aid.

We can't tell you how to gesture because you already know how to do it! You gesture every day—when you speak to friends, family members, coworkers, and even perfect strangers. Is this the same kind of gesture you need for a presentation? Of course it is! Too often, we've seen naturally graceful and energetic people become stiff as a stick when they speak in front of a group. Why? They become so worried about how they look and how to gesture that they stop doing what comes naturally. Sometimes we'll ask a student speaker who seems self-conscious or stiff a few easy questions at the end of a presentation, such as "Could you tell me more about this?" or "How did you first become interested in that?" In the blink of an eye, the speaker starts gesturing, moving naturally, and showing a lot of expression. The speaker has stopped thinking about how they look in order to answer a question.

EFFECTIVE HAND GESTURES

"What should I do with my hands?" is a question we're often asked. Our answer is deceptively simple: Do what you normally do with your hands. If you gesture a lot, keep doing what comes naturally. If you rarely gesture, don't try to invent new and unnatural hand movements.

In accepting an honorary degree from New York University, singer Taylor Swift lifts a finger to humorously accentuate that she's "technically" a doctor—one who can help in emergencies requiring a "catchy hook."

Effective gestures are a natural outgrowth of what you feel and what you have to say. Rather than thinking about your hands, focus on your audience and your message. In all likelihood, your gestures will join forces with your emotions in a spontaneous mixture of verbal and nonverbal communication.

If you still worry about your gestures or want to gesture more often, there are a variety of techniques that liberate your hands during a presentation. Begin by linking your gestures to a specific word, concept, or object. For example, introduce the number of key points in your presentation by holding up the correct number of fingers. Then lift one finger for the first point, two fingers for the second, and so on. If you are **DESCRIBING AN OBJECT** ✳ **(376–77)**, you can use your hands to trace its shape or size in the air. If you are telling a **STORY** ⸪ **(323–32)** in which someone scratches their head, points in a direction, or reaches into their pocket, you can do the same. If you're talking about alternatives, illustrate them first on one hand and then on the other. If none of these gestures come naturally or improve with practice, avoid them.

INEFFECTIVE GESTURES

Unless you have a lot of speaking or acting experience, it's difficult to plan your gestures. In fact, most preplanned gestures look artificial and awkward. When speakers try to choreograph their gestures in the same way they would a dance step, the results are usually ineffective and even comical.

While almost any natural gesture is acceptable if it is timely and appropriate, if your gestures fall into a pattern, your physical delivery can become distracting.

Also beware of **fidgets**—small, repetitive movements that act like physical **FILLER PHRASES** ▶ **(240–41)**. Constantly pushing up your eyeglasses, repeatedly tapping a lectern with a pencil, jingling keys in your pocket, playing with a necklace or tie, swaying back and forth, repeatedly hiking up your pants and tucking in your shirt, pulling on an earlobe or lock of hair, and playing around with a pointer are all fidgets. Not only can they annoy audience members, many of whom will focus on your fidget rather than on your message, they can also reduce an audience's perception of your **CREDIBILITY** ▲ **(74–81)**. One of the easiest ways to stop fidgeting is to record a video of your practice session and then watch it. Once you see how often you jingle your keys or sway back and forth, you'll never again want to distract your audience with those fidgets.

ADAPT GESTURES TO CULTURAL DIFFERENCES

People all over the world "talk" with their hands. The meanings of gestures, however, vary across cultures and contexts—both domestic and international. While students in the United States may not think twice about a professor who puts their hands in their pockets or holds them behind their back during a lecture, we know from a colleague who taught at Bangkok University in Thailand that these gestures can make some Thai listeners uncomfortable because they violate a cultural norm of keeping one's hands visible when communicating.[5]

One of the best examples of a gesture with multiple meanings is the one where you touch the tip of your thumb to index finger to form a circle, leaving the three remaining fingers held up. In the United States, this gesture has traditionally meant that everything is okay. However, some extremist groups use this same gesture to identify and connect with people who agree with their ideology.[6] The same gesture can signify a sex act in some South American countries and a sexual insult in several European countries on the Mediterranean. To the French, however, the sign may indicate that someone is a "zero," and in Japan it is used to symbolize money.[7]

Clearly, the "okay" gesture is not always okay, and the same is true of many gestures. Bottom line: gestures can have different meanings for different audiences, so analyze your audience and check the appropriateness of any gestures you plan to use.

Posture and Movement

Posture and *movement* involve how you stand, sit, and change your position when speaking. Taken together, they can either enhance or detract from your presentation. Effective speakers use their bodies to take charge of a presentation, convey physical confidence, and move with comfort and conviction.

Canadian computer scientist Dr. Joy Buolamwini uses an open stance—relaxed shoulders, open arms, and upturned palms—to convey confidence and approachability as she invites her audience to consider the biases and benefits of AI.

POSTURE

Your **posture**—the way you hold your body—communicates: A comfortable posture can radiate **CONFIDENCE** ▶ **(212–13)** and stage presence. A disengaged or uncertain posture can communicate apprehension or lack of interest. Whether you're standing or sitting, not only does an alert posture add to your credibility, but it also aids proper **BREATHING FOR SPEECH** ▶ **(229–31)** and gives you a strong stance from which to gesture.

Speakers who look comfortable and confident in front of an audience use an **open posture**. Their shoulders are relaxed; their arms are not crossed or touching their bodies. To visualize the open position, imagine that you are about to hug someone or that you've opened your palms, turning them up, as if to say, "I have nothing to hide." An open posture

For an example of a speaker who maintains a strong and open posture throughout a complex presentation, see Notable Speaker: David Epstein, page 398.

puts nothing between you and your audience—it opens you up to others, making you appear accepting and confident, not self-protective and concealed. This posture also opens your airways and helps you **PROJECT YOUR VOICE** ▶ **(235–36)** without straining.

You may be able to choose whether to sit or stand during your presentation. Standing comes with certain advantages, allowing you to take charge and capture audience attention. As a practical matter, it's easier to see your audience and maintain eye contact if you stand, and it's also easier to gesture and practice breath control if you have your full body's length to use. If you're seated during your presentation, aim to sit as straight up as possible and make use of other nonverbal cues to connect with your audience. You'll still be able to do some gesturing, and you'll want to be sure your facial expressions are supporting your speech.

In situations where there are other speakers— for instance, in panel discussions—find a way to stand up or move front and center for a portion of your presentation (if it's appropriate and doesn't break any rules). Get up and use a flip chart or move to the head of a conference table—and make space for other speakers to do the same. Whether you are standing or sitting, movement can also help you convey confidence with your audience, and we'll cover that next.

Whether you're sitting or standing, practice speaking with an open posture to convey confidence to your audience.

MOVEMENT

Effective speakers move comfortably and purposefully as they speak. **Movement** that is natural and meaningful can attract attention, channel nervous energy, and emphasize a point. Lack of movement or, worse, aimless or repetitive movement can distract audience attention and dampen interest. There's almost nothing more boring than something that never moves and nothing more distracting than something that moves about erratically.[8]

Speakers often use movement to achieve **IMMEDIACY** ▶ **(213–14)**. They move around the room, occasionally moving closer to the audience.

If you're lingering in a corner or against the wall when speaking, you'll have a tough time engaging your audience. Even though a lectern provides a convenient place to put your notes, it may also seem like a barrier between you and your listeners, so try not to spend all your time behind it. Move away from it and speak at its side. In this way, you'll be visible and will have freedom of movement while still having your notes nearby.

Getting closer to your audience—vocally, physically, and emotionally—can be challenging for some speakers. If you can't easily stand, walk, gesture, speak clearly, or maintain eye contact, remember that you can deliver a strong presentation as long as you are comfortable and speaking as you would in everyday life. If you use a wheelchair or will be seated, you may prefer to place your notes on a low table, rather than using a lectern or juggling notes with a microphone. If you cannot see or hold eye contact, you may adapt to your audience by speaking in a strong voice and positioning yourself to face where the audience is seated. As an audience member, it is equally important to **LISTEN RESPECTFULLY ● (35–37)** to all speakers who may be using similar strategies to speak comfortably and clearly.

Appearance

A speaker's **appearance** can affect the success or failure of a presentation. Audiences see you before they hear you. And what they see will make a strong first impression. Obviously, you cannot change physical characteristics such as your height, basic body shape, or facial structure—these are the result of genetics. Fortunately, you do not have to look like a movie star or wear the clothes of a supermodel to make a favorable impression on your audience.

Our students routinely ask, "What should I wear when I give a presentation?" Our first answer is always this: dress to create a positive impression. How do you know whether an outfit will create a good impression? By being aware of and responsive to the components of the **RHETORICAL SITUATION ● (6–11)**. What you wear should be appropriate for the **OCCASION ▲ (61–68)** and meet audience expectations. The last thing you want is an audience distracted or annoyed by what you're wearing. In one of our classes, a student delivered an emotional presentation about child abuse while wearing a T-shirt with a large yellow happy face on the front. How could she have ignored or been oblivious to the contradictory message her T-shirt was conveying? Effective speakers devote significant attention to what they wear and to the impression their appearance makes on the audience.

In online presentations, your appearance can include your attire, background, and camera framing. See Chapter 4.5 **ONLINE PRESENTATIONS** ▶ for advice specific to speaking online.

In addition to wearing clothing that is appropriate for the rhetorical situation, make sure you are *comfortable* in what you're wearing. If your shoes pinch, you'll be preoccupied with the pain and won't move naturally. An outfit that looks and feels good while trying it on at home may feel constricting when you are sitting on a stage or standing at a lectern for a longer period of time. If you perspire a great deal, wear cool fabrics and colors that mask wet stains. Presentations can be stressful enough, so don't wear anything that adds another source of discomfort. This doesn't mean you should show up in your joggers or favorite ripped jeans (unless it's appropriate for your rhetorical situation).

As a general rule, dress for the occasion—and maybe a bit more formally—on presentation days. But do you need to break the bank on a wardrobe to make a positive impression? No. Your clothes don't have to be expensive, and they don't have to make a fashion statement. Again, the speaking occasion and your audience's expectations should guide you. If you know in advance that everyone will be wearing cowboy boots, workout clothes, or fishing waders, use your best judgment and consider joining them, wearing something that complements what they're wearing, or dressing more professionally.

At the same time, and especially if you have a strong sense of style, don't abandon a signature piece of clothing or accessory just to fit in. Some of our most distinguished colleagues wouldn't look right without these unique items: Sam would not be Sam without his bow tie. Ellen needs her dark eyeglass frames to fully be Ellen. Being yourself means finding clothes and colors that fit *you* as a speaker.

Although it's perfectly fine to have a signature style, make sure that anything on your body supports—and doesn't distract from—your over-all message and speaking purpose. A bad hair day, an offensive tie, or poorly chosen accessories can devalue your credibility and cheapen your message. If your hair falls in your face and requires rearranging through-out your presentation, your audience will be both distracted and prob-ably annoyed, so find a way to keep it up and away from your face. If you've brought things with you that might become fidgets during your presentation—a pen, coins, keys, or even a handbag—set them aside, away from where you'll be speaking.

In short, your presentation should be the center of your audience's attention. If something about your appearance might distract your listen-ers, fix it or leave it behind. Find an appropriate and comfortable outfit that will also enhance your credibility and strengthen your message.

Conclusion

Your body is uniquely yours. If it's short or tall, big or small, it won't change for a presentation—you are who you are. But what *can* change is how comfortable you feel in your own skin as you speak.

The key is to become comfortable with all five components of physical delivery: eye contact, facial expressions, gestures, posture and movement, and appearance. Your attention and eye contact should be directed to indi-vidual members of your audience for most of your presentation. Your facial expressions should match the meaning of your message. Your gestures should emphasize important ideas and do so naturally. Your posture and movement should project confidence and conviction that lend support to your purpose. Your appearance should be appropriate for the occasion while also genuinely reflecting who you are. Physical delivery skills are a significant determinant of your ability to achieve expressiveness, confi-dence, stage presence, and immediacy.

4.4 Presentation Aids

Since the advent of presentation software like PowerPoint, Prezi, Google Slides, Keynote, and Canva, many audience members expect speakers to display slides of images and text during their presentations. And why not? It's become easy—even fun—to create memorable audiovisual slide shows.

But **presentation aids**—the audio, visual, and hands-on materials available for presenting and highlighting key ideas and supporting material in a presentation—are not limited to what you can project on a screen. From simple notes on a whiteboard to elaborate audiovisual productions, from homemade cookies to samples of perfume, appropriate presentation aids engage your audience's senses in a way that boosts their interest, enhances message comprehension, and stimulates critical thinking.

The Benefits of Presentation Aids

Presentation aids are common and expected in many rhetorical situations. Used poorly, presentation aids can be a distraction, but used wisely they offer many benefits. Presentation aids can

- Engage audience attention and interest
- Enhance clarity and comprehension
- Set an appropriate mood
- Convey meaning better than words alone
- Save you and your audience time, particularly when trying to explain **COMPLEX IDEAS** ✳ **(388–97)** or a set of **STATISTICS** ■ **(135)**

Consider what your listeners want and need to know, understand, and remember *before* creating presentation aids. Ask yourself, "How could presentation aids help me achieve my purpose?" Only after answering this question should you explore the types of aids that might be useful. Some presentations are almost impossible to give without aids. Try, for example, making a presentation about American Sign Language without demonstrating any signs or showing examples of letters in the American Manual Alphabet.

In some cases, you may decide that presentation aids aren't necessary. Your **VOCAL DELIVERY** ▶ **(229–45)** and **PHYSICAL DELIVERY** ▶ **(249–59)** may be enough to capture and hold audience interest and influence their attitudes. For example, demonstrating a yoga pose may be more effective than showing a photograph of it. At the same time, know the rules about using visuals in your classroom or organization. At some companies, PowerPoint slides are mandatory. At others, no one is allowed to use slides. Some teachers appreciate and even require slides; others forbid them for most presentations or strongly recommend that you judiciously limit the number.

For an example of a speaker who uses her physical delivery as a presentation aid, see Notable Speaker: Yassmin Abdel-Magied, page 225.

If you decide to use presentation aids, they should not define your presentation. Imagine you have a technology issue and can't display your presentation aids. Would you still be able to effectively deliver your presentation? If the answer is no, or if you're not sure, you're probably relying too much on your aids. Keep one basic principle in mind: presentation aids are only aids; they are *not* your presentation. Before deciding on using presentation aids, consider these questions to determine if there's a more effective option:

Will your presentation aids gain and maintain audience attention?	*or*	Will telling a story, describing an event, sharing memorable examples, or asking the audience questions achieve the same goal?
Will your presentation aids clarify and reinforce your ideas?	*or*	Will examples or analogies achieve the same goal?
Will your presentation aids enhance your audience's comprehension?	*or*	Will more rigorous audience analysis help you adapt your message and delivery to your audience more effectively than using presentation aids?

Types of Presentation Aids

Once you decide that presentation aids could enhance your presentation, the next task is deciding which type or types of aids you should use. Here we examine how the most common types of presentation aids can be used to explain and reinforce key points and achieve your purpose. We begin this section with an example of a table, which is only one of the many types of aids:

Type of Presentation Aids	General Purpose
Tables	Present detailed information in an easy-to-reference visual
Graphs	Compare data and show patterns
Pie charts	Show proportions in relation to a whole
Diagrams and models	Depict a process or show an object on a smaller scale

Type of Presentation Aids	General Purpose
Photographs and illustrations	Depict a concept or message with more immediacy and emotion
Maps	Help explain the scale of a place or phenomenon
Handouts	Provide a printed or digital document with information that audience members can reference during and after the presentation
Video clips, sound effects, and GIFs	Deliver supporting material in memorable and engaging ways
Props	Help you demonstrate or illustrate a point

TABLES

A **table**, like the one shown above, presents detailed information in an easy-to-reference visual. Tables can summarize and compare data or depict goals, functions, recommendations, and guidelines. Items listed in a table may be numbered, bulleted, or simply set apart on separate lines. Most word processing and slide programs have templates for making attractive tables in various colors and designs.

GRAPHS

Graphs, one the most common presentation aids, are primarily used to compare data and show patterns. They can be used to answer the question "How much?" If your presentation includes a lot of data as **SUPPORTING MATERIAL** ▇ **(134–51)**, it can be more effective to show that data in a compelling and clear visual rather than reciting a series of numbers or statistics. Graphs can illustrate trends that show increases or decreases, such as how the price of gas has gone up or down over a period of months. Or they can represent countable things, like the number of different responses to a survey question.

There are a variety of graphs that highlight different kinds of data, which can help you inform and persuade, engage or entertain audience members, and enhance your credibility as a competent speaker. The following are examples of some common types of graphs.

Bar graphs show differences in values or amounts.

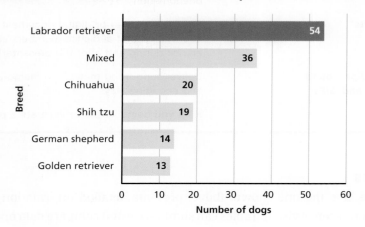

Labrador Retrievers Are the Most Popular Breed in Town

Line graphs compare changes over time for more than one group. They are more precise than bar graphs when tracking small changes.

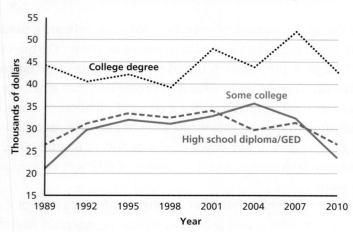

More Education Means More Income
Median wages over time based on education level, ages 22–29

Area graphs fill in the space below the points in a line graph with a color and are used to depict individual and competing trends.

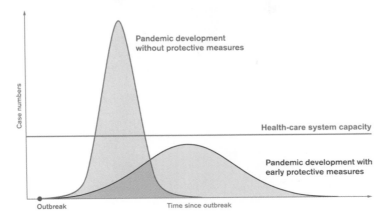

Pictographs use icons or symbols to visualize simple data in a more dramatic and interesting way.

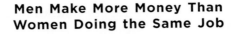

PIE CHARTS

Pie charts show proportions in relation to a whole—for example, of transfer students at a university who are enrolled in specific departments.

Pie charts should be easy to comprehend at a glance. They do not provide the detailed data found in graphs. Generally, you should arrange the wedges in a pie chart in a progressive order from small to large. Pie charts work best when they are simple in design, clearly labeled, and have no more than seven "slices" showing the relationships between the parts and the whole. If you have more than six categories, group the remainder into

The Engineering Program Has the Smallest Percentage of Transfer Students

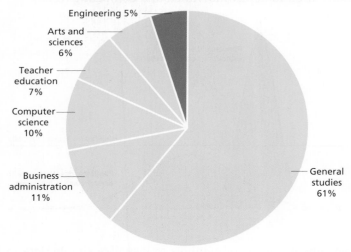

Engineering 5%

Arts and sciences 6%

Teacher education 7%

Computer science 10%

Business administration 11%

General studies 61%

The Anatomy of a Flower

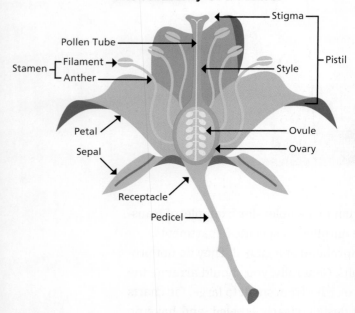

Stigma

Pollen Tube

Stamen — Filament
Anther

Style

Pistil

Petal

Ovule

Sepal

Ovary

Receptacle

Pedicel

Diagrams can be used to show the inside of something in two dimensions.

an "other" category. To add emphasis, use contrasting colors, intense shading, or thick border lines to make sure every slice of the pie is clearly separated.

DIAGRAMS AND MODELS

Diagrams include organizational charts (for example, showing who reports to whom in a business) and flowcharts that depict a process—the steps in assembling a piece of furniture, baking a cake, or even delivering a presentation. You can use diagrams to chart timelines, provide floor plans, or look inside a physical object like an engine, heart, or flower. Diagrams can be especially helpful when you need to explain a process or complex structure.

Models represent an object on a smaller scale than the original, usually three-dimensionally. They can range from a small physical model of a historic car to a larger see-through model of a car engine with visible and working components. Doctors often use models to show a patient the parts of a heart or the bones in a foot. Much like diagrams, models can be simple or elaborate, made at home or purchased, held in your hand or shown on a screen.

PHOTOGRAPHS AND ILLUSTRATIONS

Photographs and illustrations depict a concept or message with immediacy and emotion. They are especially effective at quickly portraying something visually unique or complex. Consider how difficult it would be to describe a piece of art or a style of architecture without a photograph or illustration. They can also depict abstract ideas. For example, Albert Einstein's image has become a symbol for genius, and the Statue of Liberty symbolizes freedom and liberty.[1]

Photos and illustrations can also help you tell a **STORY** ⁛**(323–32)** or convey emotion. For instance, when describing the destruction of rain forests in South America, you can use a series of aerial photos showing how drastically they've shrunk in the last few years. **POWERFUL WORDS** ⁛**(308–9)**, such as *heartbreaking*, *terrifying*, and *awesome*, register more memorably when reinforced by an appropriate photograph or illustration.

Cartoons are a type of illustration that comments on, pokes fun at, or ridicules a real situation or issue in a clever, succinct way. When thoughtfully used, cartoons can amuse your audience and help them understand a point almost immediately. If you decide to **USE HUMOR** ⁛**(340–42)**, make sure it is actually funny and appropriate for your audience and situation.

For an example of a speaker who uses photographs to tell a story about food insecurity in South Los Angeles, see Notable Speaker: Ron Finley, page 258.

THE PUBLIC SPEAKING PROCESS

Cartoons poke fun at real situations.

MAPS

Maps "translate data into spatial patterns"[2] and help explain the scale of a place or phenomenon. Maps can, for example, show the location and context of a troubled traffic intersection or a critical battle scene. Maps can also show a progression in space and time. Consider how hurricane forecasts show locations that may be affected by a storm at different points in time. Whereas a complex line graph or table can show that same data, maps provide an instant snapshot of data in context.

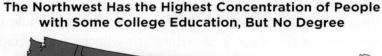

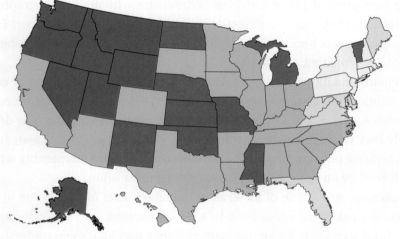

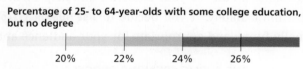

A map can help you show the spatial patterns of data.

HANDOUTS

If you have a complex message or will be referencing lots of supporting material, a printed **handout** allows listeners to focus on your presentation instead of taking notes. You might also provide additional information, references, or key points in a handout—but don't distribute a whole manuscript of your speech before you begin. And before making a handout, consider whether audience members need one. Will a handout help your audience understand your message—or will it be a distraction? And when should you share it with your audience?

- ***Before you speak.*** Research finds that distributing handouts prior to a lecture enhances learning.[3] Place a stack on a table near the entrance of the room or pass them out before your presentation.

- ***After you speak.*** Some handouts, like a copy of important data or a set of directions for a recipe, will be most helpful after your presentation. Tell your audience you'll distribute handouts when you finish speaking—and let them know what the handout contains so they can focus their attention on you and your message.

If you're tempted to distribute a handout in the middle of your presentation, don't. It is distracting and time consuming and unnecessarily interrupts listener focus and interest.

VIDEO CLIPS, SOUND EFFECTS, AND GIFs

In general, people are often more engaged by videos, sound effects, GIFs, and animated graphics than by bulleted lists. Video and animated visuals can be more memorable and explain concepts more efficiently than text.[4]

If you plan to use videos and sound clips, check their authenticity and accuracy. Today, **GENERATIVE AI** ● **(50–55)** can create realistic-seeming images, video, and audio to depict any imagined or purposefully misleading idea or situation. In fact, in October 2023, Wendy McMahon, the CEO of CBS, said that only 10 percent of the early videos of the Israel-Hamas war were usable, due in part to the influx of AI-generated deepfakes.[5] Deepfake videos can be shocking, compelling, and attention grabbing, but using them will hurt your credibility as an **ETHICAL** ● **(43–57)** speaker.

Here are some guidelines for using visuals, sound effects, GIFs, and animated graphics:

- ***Make sure they support your message, occasion, and purpose.*** A cute cat video might be fun to share with your friends, but you'll almost never need one in a presentation. On the other hand, a video or sound clip of expert testimony can be more impactful than reading the same quote yourself.

- *Keep them brief.* Audience members are there to watch and listen to *you*, not your video.

- *Care about your credibility.* Use high-quality video and provide ORAL CITATIONS ■ (150). Poor resolution, awkward angles, or unverified images can distract audience members and lead them to question your skills and credibility.

- *Don't project them for too long.* Reels, GIFs, and sound effects that repeat on a loop can be terribly distracting. Show them once or twice, then move to the next or a blank slide.

PROPS

Physical objects, or **props**, such as martial arts gear, a coin collection, or scuba diving equipment, can help you demonstrate or illustrate a point. Like handouts, make sure they are relevant to your purpose and will clarify or reinforce the content of your message. Follow these suggestions:

- *Pick one or two props.* When talking about how to scuba dive safely, don't fumble through showing the fins, mask, respirator, compass, and so on. Instead, focus on showing one element, like how a compass works to help scuba divers navigate.

- *Organize your props* before you start speaking. Lay them out, in the order you will be using them. When not using a prop, set it aside.

- *Don't use distracting props.* Your dog might be charismatic, but don't bring it to class.

- *Make sure they're visible.* Holding a coin up won't work, so you may need to pass it around—just remember that having listeners passing around an object during your presentation may be distracting.

- *Practice using your prop* until it's seamless.

MATCH THE TYPE OF PRESENTATION AID TO YOUR PURPOSE

No matter how attractive and engaging your presentation aids look or sound, they may fall short if they don't match and support the content of your presentation. Choosing the right type of presentation aid to use relies on matching the aids you choose to your **PURPOSE ▲ (109–18)**, as shown in the following table:

Purpose	Type of Presentation Aid
To explain the parts of an internal combustion engine	• Drawing of an engine • Physical pieces of an engine • Animated graphic of an operating engine
To compare rap music and talking blues	• Video or audio excerpts of each musical form • Live performance • Table comparing distinct musical characteristics
To learn the causes and treatment of sickle cell anemia	• Table listing symptoms • Diagram or illustration of a sickle cell anemia blood cell • Family tree diagram tracing inheritance of the disease
To persuade audience members to take action against climate change in the United States	• Graph of trends since 1950 • Map of recent weather disasters in the United States • Handout listing verified nonprofits that raise awareness about climate change

APPLYING ETHICAL STANDARDS TO PRESENTATION AIDS

No matter what type of presentation aids you plan to use, apply **ETHICAL STANDARDS ● (48–50)** to how you select, prepare, and use them. If you alter an image or use a portion of a video as a presentation aid, make sure the edited version accurately reflects the original context and meaning. When depicting data in a graph or table, ensure it's not presented in a way that deliberately misleads your audience.

As is the case in all presentations, you have an ethical and legal responsibility to **CITE ■ (149–51)** any presentation aids that are someone else's work or design. As a student, you may use copyrighted material without requiring permission or paying a fee to the rights holder under a set of "fair use" rules for educational purposes. But you must first use the **SIFT METHOD** ■ **(145–47)** to check whether the material is accurate and credible and then identify and acknowledge its source. And always include citations for materials drawn from books, articles, and websites.

Creating Digital Slides

The most frequently used presentation aids are **digital slides**, usually created using software such as PowerPoint, Prezi, Google Slides, Keynote, and Canva. Used effectively, they display **SUPPORTING MATERIALS** ■ **(135–39)** in the form of text, graphs, pictures, and/or multimedia when the audience expects or needs it the most.

There are lots of advantages to using slides. You can make and modify visuals quickly and easily. Bullet points reduce complex messages to simple, understandable statements. Well-designed images and text attract and focus audience attention, are easy to present, and can be seen by audiences large and small. And in **ONLINE PRESENTATIONS** ▶ **(282–301)**, it is often easier for your audience to see a slide than a prop or diagram. When deciding how and when to use slides, keep the following suggestions in mind:

- Make sure your presentation is clear and well **ORGANIZED** ■ **(152–70)** before creating your slides. As you revise your outline and notes, you may need to revise your slides.

- If a digital slide—no matter how beautiful, clever, or tragic—does not support your **CENTRAL IDEA** ■ **(156–57)** or **KEY POINTS** ■ **(153–56)**, delete it.

- Assess the number and sequence of your slides. Are they in the best order? Are there too many or too few?

BASIC STRATEGIES FOR CREATING SLIDES

Even with the best intentions, equipment, and cutting-edge software, slides won't have an impact if they're unattractive, distracting, or difficult to follow, or if there are so many that your presentation gets lost in a long march of slides. Regardless of the types of visuals you choose, use these strategies for creating your slides:

- Use clear and assertive titles.
- Preview and highlight.
- Build sequentially.

Use Clear and Assertive Titles A slide's **title** should capture your audience's attention and communicate a clear idea or conclusion, not a topic. Suppose you are speaking about how women often are paid less than men for the same job. "Wages for Men and Women" is vague; "Men Make More Money than Women Doing the Same Job" is specific and much stronger. Assertive titles also make images more accessible to people who may be listening to a presentation rather than viewing it.

Clear and assertive slide titles reduce the risk that audience members will misunderstand your message. Consider the following pie charts. Which chart directs your attention to the most significant information? Without a headline, most viewers would probably focus on the West, which accounts for almost half of profits. But perhaps the purpose of the chart was instead to highlight regions with the most growth potential. Putting a title on your visuals reinforces your message and ensures your audience focuses on the aspect of the data you want to emphasize.[6]

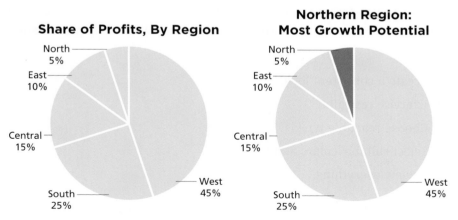

Without an effective headline, your visual aid may distract and confuse your audience.

Preview and Highlight Your slides don't need to include every fact, statistic, and quotation from your talk. Instead, your visuals should preview what you will say and highlight the most important facts and features. Your audience needs to see only what clarifies or enhances your message.

Including a brief outline of your presentation in your slides gives your audience an **INTERNAL PREVIEW** ■ **(167)** of your organization. It's your table of contents. When the outline first appears, it provides your listeners with a chance to see the scope of your message. You can then return to it at key moments to highlight your progress, perhaps with a marker or change in font color.

Build Sequentially Use what is called **progressive disclosure** to reveal each concept on a slide individually so listeners do not get ahead of you. This will focus their attention on you rather than the words or images on the screen. Progressive disclosure is useful when you want to build a chart or table by adding sections to it in sequence. By building your visuals sequentially, you raise audience anticipation, focus on the point you are talking about without visual distractions, and in some cases, save a punch line or conclusion until the end.

VISUAL DESIGN PRINCIPLES

For an example of a speaker who uses powerful images in a consistent design format to transform small facts into clear and captivating graphics, see Notable Speaker: David Epstein, page 398.

You could take an entire course on visual design for presentation slides! There are even specific recommendations for **DESIGNING SLIDES FOR ONLINE PRESENTATIONS ▶ (294–97)**. A few of these principles stand out as established guidelines for creating purposeful, effective, and memorable presentation slides:

- Create a consistent look.
- Exercise restraint.
- Choose readable type.
- Select suitable colors and templates.
- Review everything.

Create a Consistent Look Regardless of your message, make sure your slides have a uniform appearance throughout your presentation. Create a master design for your presentation to ensure consistency. No matter what sort of visual element you present within that design, it should complement that overall look and feel.

Exercise Restraint Presentation software makes it possible to use a dazzling array of graphics, fonts, colors, and other visual elements, as well as sound effects—especially with new AI-powered slide generators. Resist the temptation to use them all. Declutter! A fireworks background can overpower your message. An under-the-sea template can drown your words. More often than not, a simple slide or image is more effective and memorable than a complex one. Here are some recommendations:

- *Slides should be visual!* Replace words with graphics, images, and diagrams when you can. If you can easily explain something with words alone, you don't need a slide.

- *Use fewer words.* Your slides are not your presentation. Instead of complete sentences, use key words or phrases to highlight important information.

- *Limit the number of bullet points on a slide.* A popular rule for slides is the 6 × 6 rule: use no more than six lines of text (except for the title) with no more than six words per line.

- *Limit the number of slides.* Fifty slides don't convey information better than 10 carefully curated slides.

- *Avoid potential distractions.* Don't use the trite ornamentation that comes with presentation technology or overused audio such as drum rolls, chimes, and old cash register sounds. They do nothing but distract.

Choose Readable Type In general, don't use more than two different typefaces on a slide. Avoid ornate and difficult-to-read type. Instead, choose legible typefaces, such as Helvetica, Calibri, Arial, Aptos, and Times New Roman. Also avoid using all uppercase letters: CAPS take up more space, take more time to read, and can be interpreted as shouting instead of emphasis. Bold or italics can provide emphasis, but if overused, can be visually distracting.

Some designers recommend specific type sizes for slide presentations: 44-point type for titles, 32-point type for subtitles, and 28-point type for text. In general, we recommend a minimum type size of 24 points. When in doubt, go bigger. Here's a tip: Print your slides on 8½" × 11" paper, then set each page on the floor. Stand up straight and look down at the page. If you can read every word clearly, the type size is probably large enough.

Select Suitable Colors and Templates Choose colors that ensure your text is legible and engaging. If you use a light background, use dark text, and vice versa. Consider whether the color scheme is appropriate for your rhetorical situation and purpose. When in doubt, stick to proven color schemes. Many presentation programs recommend sets of colors that effectively contrast with each other, such as blue and orange. Avoid red and green, which contrast but can be indistinguishable for some people with color blindness. When creating graphs, use colors to highlight essential data. In a bar graph, for example, you might color one bar red and leave all of the other bars gray to emphasize one data point.[7]

Review Everything Review your slides for spelling, grammar, and design problems. Misspellings or format changes can decrease your credibility. If you have to say, "I know many of you won't be able to see this," you should redesign your slide so it's visible. And although **GENERATIVE AI** ● **(50–55)** can create slides for you, AI doesn't know your material, purpose,

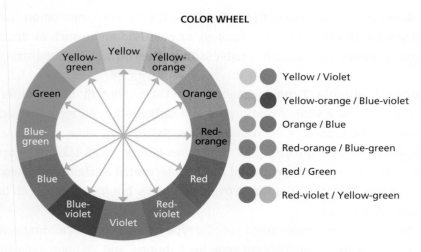

A color wheel can help you find a variety of complementary color options.

or audience. Assess all auto-generated slides and predesigned slide decks and make sure they meet these guidelines and support your purpose.

Delivering Presentation Aids

After preparing your presentation aids, use two delivery techniques to integrate them smoothly into your presentation. First, speak **EXTEMPORA-NEOUSLY ▶(215)**, or at least try to sound as though you're speaking that way. Unless the presentation is highly technical, use notes sparingly. Second, establish and maintain **EYE CONTACT ▶(249–51)**. Rather than reading from a slide or focusing on your prop, look at audience members as much as you can. This will help you adapt to audience **FEEDBACK ●(39–40)** and keep their attention on your presentation.

The following table provides additional recommendations for delivering presentation aids:

DELIVERING PRESENTATION AIDS	
Timing	• Generally, it's better to show the visual aid after you've started speaking.
	• Display the aid for as long as a person needs to read the text twice. This allows time for them to listen to you *and* process what's on your slide.
	• When you finish talking about an aid, put it aside. Don't continue to display it as you move to the next point.
	• Plan for verbal **TRANSITIONS ▪(168–69)** between visual aids. Avoid lengthy pauses as you set up a prop or move from one slide to another.
	• Use a blank slide when visual content isn't needed so you can refocus audience attention on *you*. (Many presentation programs have a shortcut that you can use to display a blank black or white screen.)
Pointing	• Avoid laser pointers. Their beam is small and can be difficult to hold steady. If necessary, rest your hand or a rigid pointer gently on a flip chart, board, or screen.
	• Put the pointer down when you are finished with it. Don't wave it around.
	• In many online presentations, you can use your computer's cursor as a pointer.

DELIVERING PRESENTATION AIDS	
Explaining	• Show and tell at the same time. Give verbal cues as you handle a prop or point to a slide component.
	• Explain what is relevant and important about the aid.
	• In most cases, don't read aloud all the written words on your slide (though sometimes you may want to read an important phrase in its entirety for emphasis).

PRACTICE ▶ (220–24) using your presentation aids as often and as rigorously as you would for any other presentation. Talking and handling a visual aid of any kind is, in fact, doing two things at once. Speaking well while glancing at a screen or handling an object requires focus and reliance on strong, competent delivery skills.

Conclusion

If you decide to use them, remember that presentation aids are only aids; they are *not* your presentation. Strategically chosen, well-crafted presentation aids can grab audience attention, engage their interest, and convey your message better than words alone. There are many different types of—and designs for—presentation aids. Your task is to decide which ones will be most useful and most effective in achieving your purpose.

Well-chosen and crafted presentation aids can increase the time you need to practice, as well as the length of your presentation. Just as you should practice your vocal and physical delivery, you should work on the timing and handling of your aids. They must be well rehearsed so you can share them as part of your message. In the end, *you* may be the presentation aid best remembered by the audience.

ShaoLan Hsueh

Chinese is one of the most difficult languages to learn. Recognizing this challenge, ShaoLan Hsueh used her creative talents as a tech entrepreneur to help people learn to read her native language. She founded Chineasy, an award-winning method for learning to recognize traditional and simplified forms of Chinese characters, which she developed while trying to teach her children Chinese. In her 2013 TED talk, Hsueh walks the audience through learning the language "with ease!"

Search Terms

To locate a video of this presentation online, enter the following key words into a search engine: ShaoLan Learn to read Chinese TED talk. The video is approximately 6:11 in length.

What to Watch For

[0:00–1:34] ShaoLan Hsueh grew up in Taiwan, where her mother, a calligrapher, taught her how to draw every stroke for each Chinese character. She describes how much she loves the beauty, shape, and form of Chinese characters, but acknowledges that, to non-native speakers, the language can be "as impenetrable as the Great Wall of China." Her first slide helps the audience visualize the metaphor of penetrating the great wall of Chinese language as she begins to explain how that might be done.

[1:42–2:05] Hseuh recommends learning Chinese characters by associating them with something you already know how to visualize. She demonstrates this method with eight building block characters, displaying an illustration to help her audience visualize each one. For example, the Chinese character for *person* looks like a person going for a walk. The Chinese character for *flame* looks like a person with their arms up yelling for help because they are on fire. Throughout her talk, she uses very simple language to describe each character, letting each slide do the "talking" for her.

[2:06–2:51] After presenting them individually, Hsueh displays the eight building block characters on one slide to reinforce their meaning before explaining how they can be used to learn more characters. The uniform appearance and design of her slides makes it easier for the audience to focus on the message.

[2:52–3:40] Hsueh often uses movement and physical delivery as a presentation aid, reinforcing the association between the shape of each Chinese character and its meaning. Explaining that the building block characters allow you to learn new characters, she demonstrates that the Chinese character for *big* looks like a person stretching their arms wide, "saying 'It was this big.'"

[4:48–5:05] As she moves into the presentation's final section about how characters can be used to learn phrases, there is a long pause between her previous slide about individual characters and the next slide. She uses a verbal transition to avoid an awkward pause: "So, after we know the characters, we start learning phrases."

[5:36–6:10] Her very brief conclusion uses the character for *exit*, illustrated on her final slide, to help her get off the stage. She describes the character for *exile* on the left: two mountains stacked, referring to the ancient Chinese practice of exiling enemies to the mountains. She notes that the character for *mouth*, on the right, tells you where to get out. Together the characters mean "exit," which she does promptly after thanking her audience.

EXERCISE

After reviewing Hsueh's speech, reflect on these questions:

1. Imagine if Hsueh had a technology issue and couldn't display her presentation aids. Do you think she would still be able to deliver her presentation effectively? Explain your answer.

2. What were the key points of Hsueh's presentation? How did her slides differ for the introduction, conclusion, and each key point?

3. How could she use progressive disclosure to prevent the audience from getting ahead on the slides that feature more than one illustration?

4. Were there any slides that were not needed because she could easily explain the point with words or physical movement alone?

5. How did she use humor verbally and on her slides? Did her use of humor help or hinder the success of her presentation?

6. How did her language match the nature and style of her slides?

4.5 Online Presentations

> ### 🔍 A BRIEF GUIDE TO THIS CHAPTER
>
> - **What's different about presenting online?** (p. 282)
> - **Preparing to present online** (p. 285)
> - **Delivering your presentation online** (p. 290)
> - **Adapting to a synchronous audience** (p. 297)
> - **Adapting to an asynchronous audience** (p. 299)

Have you ever needed to fix something and found yourself looking for a tutorial on YouTube? Are you one of the millions of people who watch a recorded TED talk every day? Perhaps you're one of the 150 million Americans who are on TikTok.[1] Maybe you've listened to some of the 48 million episodes on 2 million active podcasts.[2] Or maybe you've watched an online lecture by one of your professors or had a remote job interview using a platform such as Microsoft Teams or Zoom. If you've seen or done any of these things, you've experienced an **online presentation**—a recorded or live presentation that is hosted or uploaded onto an online platform.

In this chapter, we'll discuss online speaking as a form of delivery: one that requires you to adapt your vocal and physical delivery and your use of presentation aids for presentations that require you to speak directly to a camera.

What's Different about Presenting Online?

It's just as important to consider the rhetorical situation for speaking online as it is for in-person presentations. So, what makes presenting online different?

There are two additional—and important—factors to consider when preparing and delivering an online presentation. The first and most obvious difference is that an online presentation is *mediated*. Meaning: instead of sharing the same physical space as the audience, you use a device such as a laptop to communicate with them. And second, because online presentations are mediated, audiences are likely to experience them less intensely than if they were viewing or listening in person.[3] In online presentations, there's a greater chance that an audience member may feel disconnected from a speaker—even during a live (rather than recorded) online presentation. As communication scholars April Kedrowicz and Julie Taylor point out, online presentations always present the possibility that "if a speaker is not particularly engaging or informative or fails to foster a connection, the audience can tune out and choose to participate in a different presentation event."[4] In other words, the online medium impacts how you ENGAGE WITH YOUR AUDIENCE ∴ (303–61).

Knowing what's different about online presentations also means knowing the difference between an online presentation that's appropriate for a classroom or workplace and one you'd find on social media. While a social media influencer may deliver an inspirational monologue from the driver's seat of their car or while walking down the street, it's important to remember they have a very different audience, occasion, and purpose than you would have when speaking to classmates or colleagues.

There are many kinds of online presentations—whether for a class assignment, a Zoom meeting, an interview, or digital portfolio. The key to making them effective and memorable is knowing how your online setting will impact the elements of your rhetorical situation and to use that knowledge to adapt your presentation for online delivery. This chapter will help you do just that.

TYPES OF ONLINE FORMATS

Online presentations can occur live and in real time, or they can be recorded for viewing later. In other words, they can be either *synchronous* or *asynchronous*. **Synchronous communication** occurs when you present and/or interact with your audience in the same digital space and time, such as a live lecture or online meeting. Depending on the platform, you may or may not be able to see your audience during a synchronous presentation. For example, a speaker using the Zoom *webinar* format will not see their audience members, whereas a speaker using the Zoom *meeting* format will see every participant. During **asynchronous communication**—the sort of communication that YouTube, podcast platforms, and other recorded media enable—you and your audience are not communicating with one another at the same time. Unlike a synchronous presentation, you can re-record or edit an asynchronous presentation. Later in this chapter we'll provide detailed guidelines for adapting your presentation to synchronous and asynchronous situations.

Some online presentations are **hybrid**—they have both synchronous and asynchronous components. You may have taken a hybrid course that combines online learning with on-campus attendance. In this format, you may watch recorded lecture videos online as one part of the class and meet in person for the other part. Other hybrid formats include presentations where some audience members are in the same room as the speaker while others are participating online.

COMMON OCCASIONS FOR PRESENTING ONLINE

Online presentations—whether synchronous, asynchronous, or hybrid—take place in a wide variety of contexts and **OCCASIONS ▲ (61–68)**. These can range from classroom assignments to business presentations, from job interviews to press conferences.

Community groups—city councils, nonprofit organizations, and hobby enthusiasts—use online presentations to provide updates, connect with members, and share topics of interest. In 2022, escaped convict Danilo Cavalcante made national news while he was on the run for 14 days in Chester County, Pennsylvania. Local residents benefited from the daily press conferences streamed live by area government and law enforcement officials. They encouraged residents to attend hybrid town hall meetings (in person or online) to receive updates about efforts to improve prison security.[5]

When you think of interviewing for a job, do you imagine yourself sitting in a room with the interviewer, or do you see yourself sitting in front of a camera? A study conducted by a leading employment website found that 82 percent of employers reported using virtual interviews.[6] This means that how you use your web camera is just as important as what you wear and how you answer the questions you're asked.

Online delivery is also quite common for marketing presentations, sales updates, professional development seminars, and project management meetings. For example, an account manager might give an online presentation to clients about the progress of their advertising campaign. Not that long ago, this kind of presentation may have required an international flight and several days of travel. It can now be done online as part of a regular workday.

Online presentation technology has made it easier to connect with and present to people around the world. You may even feel less nervous when asked to speak online than if you had to travel great distances to give a presentation. But as you'll see in the rest of this chapter, you'll need to spend just as much time preparing and practicing for an effective online presentation as you would for any other.

Preparing to Present Online

When presenting online, you should begin, as always, with the six key elements of the **RHETORICAL SITUATION ● (6–11)**. Consider how your decisions will differ because you're speaking online rather than in person. For example, the criteria you apply when selecting your **CONTENT ■ (123–207)**—making sure it's up to date, accurate, relevant, and valid—becomes even more important in an online presentation, especially if it's recorded. Any incorrect statement, erroneous fact, biased source, or poorly explained concept can become part of a permanent audio or video record and may damage your immediate and even long-term **CREDIBILITY ▲ (74–81)**.

Particularly important is adapting to and preparing for the unique considerations of your **OCCASION ▲ (61–68)**—given that the setting, place, and time are all uniquely affected by the fact that you are not physically in the same location as your audience. In an online presentation, there are multiple ways to think about your setting, including the platform that's facilitating the presentation (like Zoom or Microsoft Teams) and the physical location where you're delivering your presentation, which can range from a fully equipped studio to a dorm room.

No matter where you deliver your online presentation, preparation is essential. Here we'll cover four major aspects of preparing for online delivery: *background, lighting, camera framing,* and *audio*.

MEETING VIEW ZONE   NON-MEETING ZONE

While you may not be able to control everything in your setting, make sure your background is decluttered and appropriate for your presentation.

BACKGROUND

What will viewers see behind you as you speak? Will a real or virtual background be more effective? Whichever you choose, remember that you want your audience to focus on you and your message, not your location. The following advice can work for any speaker presenting online on any budget.

- **Remove distractions.** Get rid of anything that could distract or disturb viewers. This can mean tidying up just the area that will be in view, turning off your overhead fan or television, and pushing the clutter, piles of clothes, and dirty coffee mugs out of view. Close your door to avoid interruptions from pets, family members, or friends.

- **Use an appropriate backdrop.** Once you've tidied up the background, make sure that whatever is left behind you is not distracting. You can use a bare wall or a wall with appropriate decoration. If you're speaking about something historical, for example, you could display a bookcase or a map behind you. You could even speak from a historic site (provided you could find a quiet space and uninterrupted time to do so).

- **Get creative!** If you're having trouble finding a background that isn't distracting, consider other locations, like an empty classroom or room in a library. You can also hang a solid color sheet to hide a distracting background or use a room divider.

- **Use a virtual background.** If you can't find or prepare an appropriate backdrop, most online presentation software includes virtual options. The most neutral option is to blur your background. If you choose something other than that, make sure the background matches your message and is not distracting. For example, you wouldn't use a background of a beach resort for a presentation about poverty. Some virtual background options include animation. While these may seem fun, moving images can distract your audience and can even harm viewers with conditions triggered by light and movement.

LIGHTING

Much like a distracting background, poor lighting can take the focus off your message. The most effective lighting setup reduces shadows and extreme contrasts, giving your face an evenly illuminated appearance.

The best way to accomplish effective lighting is to make use of two sources of light: a *key light* and a *fill light*. You don't need professional lighting equipment and can use desk lamps, clamp lights, or a window with natural light coming through it. The strongest light you have available is the key light and should be placed on one side of the camera and angled either up or down at you. The fill light should be placed on the other side of the camera, opposite the key light, so it can fill in the shadows from the brighter key light. Avoid backlighting, where the strongest light is behind you and casts your face in darkness, such as sitting in front of the window. It may take several adjustments to get the fill light positioned at just the right angle to achieve a pleasing effect.

If you have only one light available to you, set it up somewhat directly in front of you. There are many relatively inexpensive ring lights available for this purpose that provide a bright, diffused light. If you're in a room with only overhead lighting and no portable lighting available, try sitting slightly behind the overhead light so that it lights you from the front and not from behind.

For optimal lighting, place your brightest light in front of you, ideally right behind the camera. Place one or two other lights 45 degrees to either side, which will fill in the shadows and brighten your face.

On the left, the source of light comes from the window behind the presenter—leaving them in the dark. For more even lighting on the presenter's face, try using a key light and a fill light (right).

CAMERA FRAMING

Unlike in-person presentations where you are "framed" by the room you're speaking in and where your audience sees not only you but also one another, online presentations are narrowly framed in the rectangular "window" of a viewing screen. There are two important elements of framing to consider: *framing yourself* and *stabilizing the camera.* Use the following suggestions to *frame yourself* effectively:

- *Don't sit too close!* If you are presenting while sitting down, ensure that you are centered in the frame, you are viewable from the shoulders up, and the top of your head is not cut off. (If you decide to stand during your presentation, pay attention to how you are framed and how far you can move and still stay in the frame.)

- *Angle the camera at about eye level.* This will give viewers a straight-on view of your face—not your chin, the ceiling, or the top of your head. Too many speakers make the mistake of placing the camera below them—especially when using a laptop—forcing the audience to look up the speaker's nose! If you're using a laptop, place it on a stack of books or use a laptop stand. Many stand-alone web cameras are adjustable and can either sit on top of a screen or be placed on a tripod.

- *Use landscape orientation.* If you're using a smartphone to record your presentation, turn it horizontally to create a widescreen video, which is a more friendly viewing experience for your audience.

- ***Check recommended guidelines.*** If you're recording a video for a classroom assignment or for a specific social media platform, check their recommended guidelines for how to frame the video. In a classroom environment, for example, some instructors will specifically request that students include their entire body within the frame, much like you'd see in a recorded TED talk.

Stabilizing the camera is necessary to prevent your frame from being off-center, falling over during your presentation, or having your audience feel seasick from watching a shaky video. Avoid holding your device during your presentation—in this case, your laptop should not be on your lap! Set it on a stable surface. Smaller devices such as tablets and phones can be propped up against a stack of books or placed in stands made especially for them.

A laptop perched atop a stack of books allows you to maintain stability and eye-level perspective in online presentations.

AUDIO

Filmmakers have long known that audio quality is at least as important to a viewer's experience and engagement as the video quality. While many smartphones and computers have high-quality cameras, audio quality is not always as good. The built-in microphone of your recording device may also be too far away and can pick up distracting sounds. If you're in an environment with a lot of noise you can't control, consider using a separate microphone, such as a lapel microphone, a headset, or ear buds with a built-in microphone.

Whichever audio setup you choose, practice and listen to your recording to make sure your voice comes through clearly. And have a backup microphone in case your primary microphone isn't working well enough or at all.

Before you begin recording, turn off audible computer and phone notifications. Eliminate ambient noises—the fan from an air-conditioning unit, the television in another room. If you present or record indoors, use a room that is as soundproof as possible. Rooms with carpet are better than rooms with hardwood floors. If you're speaking outdoors or in public, avoid noisy areas and try to anticipate any interruptions that may appear. If possible, ask the people around you to stay quiet and/or hang up a sign indicating that you are recording a presentation.

See Chapter 4.2 **VOCAL DELIVERY** ▶ for advice on using external microphones.

Delivering Your Presentation Online

As we mentioned earlier, presenting in an online medium may seem less intimate and immediate to your audience. And because audience members have likely seen countless examples of slick online productions, they may expect your online presentation to be more professional and engaging than an in-person presentation. The key to getting it right is to record your practice sessions as they will be presented—with the same setting, lighting, camera framing, audio, same clothing, and so forth. You will quickly see if your presentation needs more work or is ready to go.

Let's now take a look at the elements of delivery that affect how your audience receives and understands your message when speaking online.

FORMS OF DELIVERY

Which **FORM OF DELIVERY** ▶ **(214–17)** works effectively for an online presentation? As with in-person presentations, you have several choices—or may be restricted to a particular style or script. If you can choose, **EXTEMPORANEOUS** ▶ **(215)** delivery generally works best. It allows you to appear spontaneous and engaging to audience members who are not in the same space as you are. And as with in-person presentations, **MANUSCRIPT** ▶ **(216)** delivery can make you appear dull and robotic. Although it may be tempting to read from a word-for-word manuscript, it takes a lot of skill and experience to do it effectively.

In short, your goal is to keep your online audience engaged by sounding and looking authentic, and the best way to achieve this is extemporaneous delivery.

VOCAL DELIVERY

The components of **VOCAL DELIVERY** ▶ **(229–45)** often need special consideration when speaking online. Your rate, pitch, inflection, and fluency, as well as the clarity and correctness of the words you use, may be amplified or muffled depending on the quality of your microphone and the technology used by audience members. They also become a permanent record of how well you delivered your message, so make sure you are pronouncing words clearly and appropriately. In general, try to use a warm and expressive voice, speaking as though you're having a personal conversation with each member of your audience.

PHYSICAL DELIVERY

Proper camera framing focuses the audience's attention on your face. That means **FACIAL EXPRESSIONS ▶ (251–52)** are especially noticeable when presenting online. As you speak, try to convey **IMMEDIACY ▶ (213–14)** with your face and upper body. Your expressions should reflect the feelings your words convey. But don't take this too far—avoid "acting out" facial expressions, particularly if they're not natural to you. More than anything, be yourself. Most audiences—even when listening to an audio-only program—can detect insincerity and playacting.

If you find it distracting to see yourself onscreen while you are speaking, many online platforms have a feature that enables you to turn off or hide the video of yourself. However, keep in mind that it may be useful to glance at yourself occasionally while speaking to make sure that you are appropriately energetic, engaging, and in frame.

Eye Contact The term "Zoom fatigue" was popularized during the COVID-19 pandemic when many people found themselves frequently giving and listening to online presentations—and found them to be exhausting. Media psychologist Jeremy Bailenson believes this is because "Zoom's interface design constantly beams faces to everyone, regardless of who is speaking. From a perceptual standpoint, Zoom effectively transforms listeners into speakers and smothers everyone with eye gaze."[7] You might think that this would make it easier for an online speaker to tell if their audience is looking at them. But it's actually the opposite: a speaker cannot simultaneously look into the camera and also see if their listeners are looking back at them.

So how should you manage your **EYE CONTACT ▶ (249–51)** when presenting online using a camera? While you should look at the camera frequently throughout your online presentation, you don't have to look directly at it for long periods of time—you can look around it.[8] This will help manage the fatigue and eye strain that accompanies looking at a screen for extended periods of time. It will also help facilitate a more natural eye contact that feels less intrusive to audience members. But don't spend a lot of time looking left and right or up and down—viewers will wonder what's going on offscreen!

In order to convey eye contact to your audience *and also* see them while you are speaking, alternate between looking directly into the camera and at your audience members onscreen. This can also combat the smothering effects of constant eye gaze.

Gestures and Movement Because most online presentations focus audience attention on your face and upper body regardless of whether you are standing or sitting, your freedom of movement and range of gestures are often restricted. As a result, online speakers must make more of an effort to convey nonverbal communication.[9]

You can use **GESTURES** ▶ **(252–55)** if they are in front of or close to the sides of your face. Rather than grand open gestures that include everyone in a large in-person audience, use gestures similar to those you'd use in a one-on-one conversation, like a slight nod or single raised finger to emphasize a point. For helpful examples, watch television commercials and talk-show hosts as well as podcasters who record video of their episodes for YouTube.

Appearance Your **APPEARANCE** ▶ **(257–59)** is of upmost importance when presenting in an online environment. Dress appropriately for the occasion from your shoulders down to your shoes. Even if you'll be sitting down to present, your full body may come into view if you need to move or stand up. If it's a business presentation, dress professionally. If it's an assignment for class, dress as you would if presenting in the classroom.

Test your presentation-day outfit on camera to see if there's anything that will distract your audience, including your hair, accessories, and clothing. Consider tying your hair back to avoid **FIDGETS** ▶ **(254)**, like pushing your hair behind your ears. Be mindful of the contrast between your clothing and the background. For example, a patterned background against patterned clothing can be distracting. Instead, consider a neutral background or one that won't clash with what you wear. If you have dark hair and are wearing dark clothing, a light background can provide helpful contrast. Likewise, a dark background works well if you are wearing light

A neutral background and well-chosen attire can help you stand out and look appropriate for the occasion, while a busy shirt and busy background can be distracting to your audience.

clothing and have light hair. Consider accommodating audience members with visual sensitivity by wearing solid and soft colors. Select any jewelry carefully: a watch may reflect light, and bracelets may make noise when you use your mouse or keyboard or flip through your notes.

Using Speaking Notes Since extemporaneous delivery is usually the best method for establishing a connection with an online audience, plan on using **SPEAKING NOTES** ▶ **(217–20)** to guide your thoughts while talking directly with the audience. There are two formats for using speaking notes for online presentations: *electronic notes* and *hard copy notes*. Even if you choose to use electronic notes, keep hard copy notes handy just in case you have technical problems with your electronic version.

It's easier to use electronic speaking notes if you have two screens available, like a phone and a computer or a computer with two monitors. You can place your notes on one screen and use the other for the online presentation platform. This prevents any confusion or difficulty with switching back and forth between windows on one screen or even trying to size windows to be side by side. And if you plan to display digital slides, consider copying your notes into the notes feature available with most slide presentation software. Using two devices allows you to display your slides on one screen for your audience to view while displaying your notes on another screen for your eyes only.

If you use a second device for your electronic notes, turn off the display lock so that you don't have to "wake up" the screen to see your notes. Use brief speaking notes and resist the temptation to display your entire manuscript. (Because your audience only sees your face, frequently

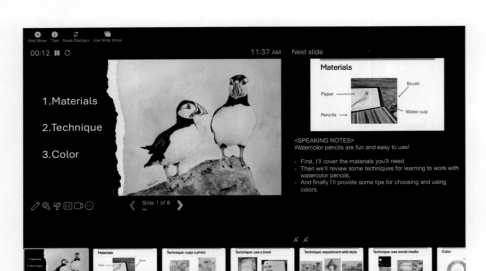

Digital slide programs like PowerPoint usually come with a handy presenter view, allowing you to see your notes alongside your current slide and the next slide.

looking up/down or left/right at your notes can be especially distracting in an online presentation.) Make sure you can easily read the notes on the device by leaning it on something sturdy like a stack of books or placing it in a cell phone stand, and silence all notifications so that you're not distracted by them while speaking.

If you have only one screen available, we recommend using a hard copy of your speaking notes. Hold your hard copy notes below the camera frame so they don't block the audience. Number multiple pages or cards so you don't get lost while speaking.

Whether you use electronic or hard copy notes, make sure you can still look at the camera. The audience will likely get distracted if you're looking down at hard copy notes or to the side at a second monitor.

PRESENTATION AIDS

Whether you use slide decks, documents, websites, props, or sounds, **PRESENTATION AIDS ▶ (260–78)** can be just as effective when speaking online, but you may need to adjust how you use them. No matter which presentation aids you choose, you should practice using them with your online presentation platform. Since not all software is the same, it's important to know exactly how you will bring your aids into view—and how you will return the focus back to your face so you can maintain your connection with your audience. Remember: you are your presentation's most important visual aid. And as with any presentation, you should always be prepared to speak without presentation aids in case a technical issue prevents you from using them.

Sharing Your Screen Sharing your screen is an effective method for displaying digital versions of presentation aids, including slide decks, websites, documents, and digital whiteboards. Before launching your online presentation platform, close all unnecessary windows and browser tabs, and use clear and simple file names for documents you plan to share. This will help you quickly locate your presentation aids when you share your screen.

No matter how much experience you have sharing your screen, practice doing it before your live or recorded presentation. For example, make sure you understand how slide decks are displayed using a single monitor. If you're using dual monitors, check which monitor your audience will see when you start sharing your screen.

Designing Slides for Online Presentations If your audience can view your slides clearly, you're more likely to accomplish your purpose. To help you achieve that, award-winning consultant Nancy Duarte's design firm recommends a critical best practice for creating slides for online presentations: "Start with a decision about the output of the presentation before starting any of the actual design."[10] In other words, think about what device your audience will likely use to view your presentation before CREATING DIGITAL SLIDES ▶ (272–77) and designing what they're going to see. If you're giving a webinar for work, it's reasonable to assume that people will view your presentation with a laptop. If you're posting a presentation on YouTube, it's more likely that people will use a mobile device. Duarte recommends following these guidelines when designing slides for online presentations:

- When the screen size goes down, the font size goes up.
- When font size goes down, add more space between lines of text.

- Use contrast with colors, gradients, textures, and images.
- When the screen size is small, use higher contrast.[11]

In many situations, you won't know how your audience will view your presentation. For such cases, follow two best practices for all online presentations. First, limit the amount of content on a slide. For example, a slide that describes three popular cat breeds using text and images would best be viewed online as three separate slides—one cat per slide. And second, remember to apply consistent design choices throughout the slide deck, including uses of typefaces, type sizes, and color. This will improve your audience's experience no matter the screen size used to view the presentation.

Using Sound Including audio in your presentation is an effective way to add multimedia to generate audience interest in your topic. Incorporating videos is the most common use of sound for online presentations, but sound alone can be effective as well. For example, audio of commercial planes flying overhead could enhance a presentation about noise pollution surrounding airports.

If you plan to play sound, check the settings for sharing sound on your computer through your online presentation platform, as it may not be a default setting.

Using Props Physical objects such as models, whiteboards, and drawings should be visible and legible in the frame—big enough to be seen but not so big they'll take your place in the presentation. You may find that you need to adapt your use of **PROPS ▶ (270)** given the constraints of your setting and camera placement. For example, you may not be able to use a life-size skeleton model to demonstrate the location of the tibia. In this case, a better option may be to use a slide with a diagram of where the bone is located.

When you hold up an object for the audience, allow time for your camera to focus on it clearly. You may need to adjust how close the object is to the camera, depending on the level of detail needed. A document camera can also be useful to project smaller objects for online viewing.

If you don't have access to a document camera, you can easily create one with a smartphone—and there are many tutorials online that explain how to do so.

If you would like your listeners to have their own copy of a document, you can upload it to a cloud service and provide a link to it either in the chat feature of the online presentation platform or by providing a QR code on a slide.

Adapting to a Synchronous Audience

Being an audience-centered online speaker involves the same decisions and principles that apply to any other speaking situation. Doing thorough **AUDIENCE ANALYSIS ▲ (90–96)** well ahead of your presentation is essential. Because your interaction with a synchronous audience may be limited—especially when you're not able to see them if you're using a webinar format—try to identify and keep your **TARGET AUDIENCE ▲ (90)** in mind as you prepare and deliver your presentation.

ENGAGING YOUR SYNCHRONOUS AUDIENCE

In a synchronous presentation, you are only visible to your audience in a small framing rectangle, and you may not be able to control or adapt to the distractions in each viewer's own setting. This makes it even more important to use effective strategies for generating and maintaining audience interest. Involving audience members—by asking questions, for instance— is an opportunity to test whether they understand, like, and accept your message. You can also set the tone for your presentation by playing appropriate music as audience members are logging onto the platform, along with displaying a slide with the title of the presentation, your name, and any other useful information.

Use Interactive Tools There are several ways to give your audience a reason to listen. Ask **WIIFT ▲ (93)**: "What's in it for them?" Once you've answered that question, consider using one or more of the following strategies to help keep your audience engaged:

- *Use a polling feature.* Most online presentation platforms have a polling feature, or you can use one of the many web-based polling apps. For example, during a presentation about law enforcement, you might administer an anonymous poll to find out how many audience members have been stopped by the police.

- *Organize breakout groups.* You can add variety to your presentation by using breakout rooms so that audience members can discuss a topic in small groups. Depending on the size of your audience, you can ask people to answer questions or share their experiences. Their responses can be gauged by using reaction emojis, such as a raised hand or clapping.

- *Ask questions.* You can ask your audience questions and instruct them to respond using the chat feature. You can also use the chat or Q&A feature to facilitate a **Q&A SESSION ∴ (350–61)** with your audience. If you decide to use the chat feature, consider establishing expectations about its use, noting any potential accessibility challenges. If possible, have someone monitor the chat for you, especially if there are a lot of audience members in attendance.[12]

- *Live closed captioning.* Captioning provides an accessible experience for all audience members and may help to foster more interaction by ensuring all audience members understand what's being said. Check with your platform provider or event host about the availability of this feature.

Use Audience Management Strategies What do you do if someone is talking during your online presentation? Do you make a general statement asking people to mute their audio? Fortunately, most online presentation platforms allow the presenter to mute all participants. If you are not a designated host of the online meeting, you can check with the host about options for managing the audio of audience members. You might find it useful to establish some expectations at the beginning of your presentation, such as:

- How the audience should use audio and mute themselves
- How to use the chat (and how chat will be used in the presentation)
- How to raise a virtual hand or use a Q&A feature to ask a question

You may also want to consider security options to protect your audience from disruptive guests. Requiring registration is an effective way of controlling access to the presentation. If registration is not an option and your event information is available to the general public, be aware of options for removing someone from the online presentation platform if they are disruptive.

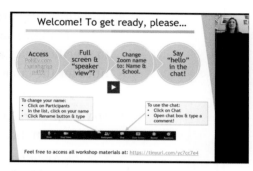

Consider using a slide at the start of your presentation to orient an audience to the platform and any engagement tools you plan to use.

Adapting to an Asynchronous Audience

Even though you will not have the benefit of a live audience when delivering an asynchronous presentation, you can still make decisions about how to adapt your presentation by conducting audience analysis beforehand. Keeping your **TARGET AUDIENCE ▲ (90)** in mind becomes even more important for an asynchronous presentation because you will not be able to adapt your presentation in the moment based on audience feedback, as you would during a synchronous presentation.

ENGAGING YOUR ASYNCHRONOUS AUDIENCE

Even though the audience is not "live," there are options for engaging with them asynchronously. Whether you are recording a presentation for a training webinar at work or for a product review on your YouTube channel, focusing on the purpose of your presentation will help you to do just that. A specific, achievable, and relevant **PURPOSE STATEMENT ▲ (115–17)** and a series of clear **KEY POINTS ■ (152–57)** can be useful in guiding the structure of an asynchronous presentation.

Keeping your purpose in mind, enlist one or more of the following strategies to keep your audience interested and engaged asynchronously:

- *Focus on the most important information.* Make sure the recorded presentation is not too long or that it can be broken into shorter segments that can more easily hold your audience's attention. Recommendations vary, but in general aim for segments that are less than 10 minutes.

- *Add navigation tools.* If you are posting your video on YouTube, consider creating a table of contents for the video that allows viewers to go to specific topics at specific moments. Use your key points as segment titles for the table of contents. Many video editing apps have a similar table of contents option as well.

- *Mix it up!* Vary your audience's viewing experience by using a mix of presentation aids throughout your recorded presentation.

- *Use engagement tools.* You can post a survey, allow comments, and provide a space for online discussion about your presentation. Depending on the editing software available for your use, you can include polls in the video itself for audience members to respond to or provide hotspots for webpages, documents, or other resources related to the presentation topic.

If you are recording multiple presentations for the same audience—on a YouTube or social media platform, for example—pay attention to metrics like the number of views and comments, the level of interaction, and how long people spend viewing the video. This information can help you determine if any modifications are needed for future recordings.

RECORDING AND EDITING YOUR ASYNCHRONOUS PRESENTATION

One of the major benefits of an asynchronous presentation is that you can practice the presentation multiple times, and you can edit the final recording before publishing it. Remember there is a difference between recording a video with your phone while at a friend's birthday party and recording a presentation such as an appeal for funding your start-up business. The former is candid, whereas the latter is more purposeful and focused on a goal. Don't wait until an hour before the deadline to begin working on the presentation! You need time to practice and also to take care of any potential technical problems.

The guidelines for online vocal and physical delivery apply to recorded presentations as well. You can use your laptop, desktop, phone, tablet, or stand-alone camera to record an asynchronous presentation. If you do not have access to editing software, the simplest way to record a video without worrying about editing is to use the record feature of an online presentation platform like Zoom. Essentially, you record your presentation in an online meeting where you are the only participant. There are dozens of options for free or low-cost editing applications that will allow you to delete unnecessary parts, balance audio levels, reduce background noise, correct color, and add captions.

Providing captions and/or a transcript for your viewers also makes your presentation accessible to people who have difficulty hearing, who don't speak your native language, and who are viewing from an environment that's not conducive to listening. Keep in mind that there may also be a legal requirement to provide captions—especially for videos that are published by agencies and organizations that serve the public, such as governments, public libraries, and nonprofit organizations.

Conclusion

Effective online presentation speakers pay special attention to how the medium they use impacts their audience. Synchronous presentations offer the chance to interact with their listeners, while asynchronous presentations offer the ability to re-record before posting. Remember that both synchronous and asynchronous online presentations require attention to the six key elements of the rhetorical situation: occasion, speaker, audience, purpose, content, and delivery. Specialized strategies—like preparing and adapting your background, lighting, audio, and presentation aids—will ensure that your online presentation looks and sounds professional. Speaking extemporaneously, rather than from a manuscript, can help you establish immediacy, and proper camera framing will make the most of your physical delivery. Applying these elements and our suggested strategies will help you prepare and deliver an effective online presentation.

PART 5
Engaging Your Audience

"How can I be more interesting?"

It's a question we often hear from students in communication courses. They want to know how they can gain and maintain their audience's attention throughout their presentation and how they can make their presentations more engaging, worthwhile, and memorable. This section offers some answers to these questions. By using expressive and vivid **LANGUAGE**, tapping the power of **STORIES**, generating **AUDIENCE INTEREST AND PARTICIPATION**, and preparing for and conducting **QUESTION-AND-ANSWER SESSIONS**, you can capture and keep your audience's interest from start to finish.

Engaging
Your Audience

5.1 Language and Style

The great American writer Mark Twain once declared, "The difference between the *almost right* word and the *right* word is really a large matter—'tis the difference between the lightning-bug and the lightning."[1] Well-chosen words lie at the heart of memorable presentations. The right words teach, influence, motivate, and delight listeners. While a well-researched and thoughtfully organized presentation can be convincing and easy to follow, carefully chosen **language** can get your audience to sit up, listen, and remember what you say. The words you choose matter.

Choosing the Right Words

Without words, we cannot create and share complex stories, follow and give detailed directions, or express and explain a full range of emotions. Well-chosen words do more than this: they can transform a dull speech into a captivating and memorable presentation. So how do you choose the right words for your presentation? Like any other decision, the key is in your rhetorical situation.

OCCASION ▲ (61–68)	Match your words to your occasion. Just as you wouldn't wear a ball gown to a barbecue, you wouldn't use grandiose words for an informal speaking occasion.
SPEAKER ▲ (72–85)	The words you choose reflect who you are. Don't try to sound like someone else. If you're not comfortable with the words in your presentation, your audience may sense your uneasiness and question your credibility.
AUDIENCE ▲ (88–105)	Use words that will resonate with your audience—who they are, what they know, and how they think. What vocabulary do they know? Technical terminology can be helpful—but only if your audience knows what it means. If your presentation requires the use of an uncommon word, or if you're using a familiar word in an unusual way, stop and explain it.
PURPOSE ▲ (109–18)	If your purpose is to inform, use words that clarify, explain, and/or demonstrate. If your purpose is to persuade, choose words that are vivid and powerful. And have fun with language if your goal is to entertain.
CONTENT ■ (123–207)	Use words that are specific and accurate. Consider using consistent terms or phrases for key points in your introduction, body, and conclusion to help your audience follow along and remember what you say.
DELIVERY ▶ (209–301)	With practice, you'll become more comfortable with your language, and as a result, your delivery will convey competence and confidence. Make sure your vocal and nonverbal delivery matches the meaning of your message.

Once you've addressed the elements of a specific rhetorical situation, you can consider how different kinds of words will help you convey your presentation's message.

CONNOTATIVE AND DENOTATIVE MEANING

Most words have many meanings and many definitions. The dictionary definition of a word usually focuses on one type of meaning—denotation. Personal thoughts and emotional reactions to a word evoke a second kind of meaning—connotation.

Denotation refers to the objective, literal meaning or meanings of a word. When you choose words, make sure you understand the possible definitions of the words in your presentation. Consider the word *snake*. It's a reptile, a movement with twists and turns (like a line that snakes around the block), or a plumber's tool used to clear out a drain. There's nothing emotional about these definitions. They have clear, common meanings.

Connotation, however, refers to the feelings that words arouse in a person who reads, hears, or speaks them.[2] Connotation is more likely than denotation to influence the way an audience responds to words. Let's take another look at the word *snake*. For some, a snake may have creepy or negative connotations, but to a naturalist a snake may be delightful or fascinating.

How would you describe an *assertive* person: *confident, direct, forceful, fierce,* or *hostile*? A word with negative connotations, such as *hostile*, will convey a different meaning than a word with positive connotations, like *confident*. Consider how your audience might perceive the positive and negative connotations of important words in your presentation.

ABSTRACT AND CONCRETE WORDS

Words range from abstract to concrete. An **abstract word** refers to an idea or concept that cannot be observed or touched, such as *love, patriotism, friendship, crime,* and *transportation*. They may not have the same meaning for everyone. A **concrete word** refers to specific items that can be perceived by our senses, such as *diamond engagement ring, American flag, friendship bracelet, pickpocketing,* and *electric bicycle*. They are clear and specific.

Concrete words are less likely to be misunderstood. Although abstract words can rally people around a shared value or goal, they can also lead to confusion. For example, many audience members may support the abstract idea of *national security*. But without a concrete definition, some listeners may think it means building a wall and restricting immigration, while others may think it refers to cybersecurity and gun control.

LANGUAGE AND TONE

The words you choose tell an audience not just what your presentation is about but also how you *feel* about your topic. The same way you might raise your voice or make dramatic gestures when you're passionate, or speak calmly and remain still when you're solemn, you should also consider modifying the tone of your language during key moments of your presentation. Here are three ways to achieve this:

- **Intense language** can make your point more interesting by dialing up the emotions of its implications. Instead of using a dull or neutral word like *friendly*, try a more intense word like *delightful* or *enchanting*. A *disgusting* meal sounds worse than a *bad* one.

- **Vivid language** can elicit strong, memorable images in the minds of your listeners by describing them with a higher level of detail. Compare *The glass broke* with *The champagne flute fell with a delicate crash, shattering into sharp confetti across the marble floor.*

- **Powerful words** are direct, concrete, and expressive. They communicate confidence and commitment to your purpose. Sunsets are more than *nice*; they can be *beautiful, glorious,* or *a glimpse of heaven.* Collecting signatures on a petition to remove an incompetent county commissioner is more than *important*; it's *urgent, critical,* or *our topmost priority.*

Consider the following example of intense, vivid, and powerful words from a student's persuasive presentation. Try reading her introduction out loud, paying attention to how her language created an unforgettable image:

> Picture two-year-old Joey. A hole in his throat so he can breathe. A tube jutting out of his stomach where a surgeon implanted a new esophagus. It all began when Joey found an open can of drain cleaner and swallowed some of its contents. But this isn't a speech about poisoning and how to prevent it. Joey's tragedy occurred because Joey's mother followed an old set of first-aid instructions. She gave him vinegar. Instead of neutralizing the poison, the vinegar set off a chemical reaction that generated heat and turned Joey's tiny digestive tract into an inferno of excruciating pain.

Be strategic with your use of intense, vivid, and powerful language. Speakers who are consistently too intense may jeopardize their credibility or even frighten their audience. Think of a favorite song. Is it all the same volume, or does it ebb and flow with the lyrics? In your presentation, you might deploy powerful words to address a key point, followed by more neutral language as you transition to the next big idea or dramatic example.

PERSONAL PRONOUNS

Personal pronouns—words such as *I, you, she, he, we,* or *they*—are substitutes for nouns or noun phrases. Personal pronouns can intensify the connection between you and your audience. "We shall overcome," for example, has significantly more power than "The nation shall overcome."

Use the pronoun *you* to get the attention of your audience and speak to them directly. Recall these words from President John F. Kennedy's famous 1963 inaugural address: "Ask not what your country can do for you. Ask what you can do for your country." Imagine if Kennedy had said, "People should not ask what the country can do for every citizen. People should ask what individuals can do for the country."

You can also use self-reference pronouns such as *I, me,* and *my* to take responsibility for your message and enhance your credibility in critical moments. "I have attended every city council meeting and advocated for more affordable rental units, but now I need your help." Here, too, take care not to go overboard. Look for moments when your personal experience will enhance—not distract—from your purpose.

ACTIVE VOICE

In grammatical terms, *voice* refers to whether the subject of a sentence performs or receives the action of the verb. If the subject performs the action, you are using an **active voice**. For example, "The student read the *Iliad*" is active. If the subject receives the action, you are using a **passive voice,** as in "The *Iliad* was read by the student."

The active voice can help you build momentum by keeping your sentences short and direct. The passive voice, on the other hand, can slow you down with extra words that take the focus away from the subject and place it on the object. Both active and passive voice have merit, depending on the context. For example, the winner at awards ceremonies is often announced in a passive voice, creating suspense by announcing the recipient last: "And the Oscar for best actress goes to Emma Stone." An active voice proclaiming "*Oppenheimer* is the winner" can be joyful, just without the anticipation. Notice the difference between the following passages in a passive voice and active voice.

Passive Voice	Active Voice
The petition should be signed by all of you.	Sign this petition.
I was raised with the help of my grandfather.	My grandfather helped raise me.
Mistakes were made by the coach.	The coach made mistakes.

POWERLESS WORDS AND CLICHÉS

Throughout your presentation, try to avoid **powerless words**, which can be bland and unconvincing:[3]

- *Hesitations and fillers.* Occasional hesitations like "um," "uh," "well," and "you know" are common and acceptable, but when used repetitively throughout a presentation, they can reduce the force of your language. **PRACTICING ▶ (220–24)** your speech can help you cut down on such fillers.

- *Qualifiers and hedges.* Words such as "sort of," "maybe," "kind of," and "I guess" communicate a lack of confidence and weaken your message.

- *Disclaimers.* Statements such as "I'm not an expert, but . . ." and "I'm in the minority, but . . ." imply that the audience should understand or make allowances for your lack of competence. If you thoroughly **RESEARCH ■ (134–51)** and prepare for your presentation, you can make your point without excuses.

- *Feeble intensifiers.* When speakers use feeble intensifiers such as "very," "really," "actually," "awfully," or "pretty" to modify a word, they may rob the phrase of its power. For example, "The research method is appropriate" is stronger than "The research method is really appropriate."

In addition to the aforementioned words, the overuse of clichés can rob a presentation of its power. A **cliché** is a trite expression that has lost its originality or impact through overuse, such as *crystal clear*, *a loose cannon*, or *hit the nail on the head*. In most cases, clichés should be avoided, because they limit the impact of your words. That said, there are creative ways to use a cliché in your presentation. For example, "as blind as a bat" could be a memorable way to begin a presentation on common misunderstandings about bats.

Figures of Speech

Figures of speech—also called rhetorical devices, stylistic devices, and language tropes—include a wide variety of word strategies that can make your message more vivid, memorable, and effective. **Figures of speech** are words or phrases used in an unconventional way to heighten the effect of a message and stir emotions.[4] They can reiterate ideas, highlight comparisons and contrasts, make associations, and create mental pictures. The following figures of speech are especially effective and useful for many speaking occasions.

REPETITION AND ALLITERATION

In oral poetry and storytelling traditions, speakers have long used **repetition** to help listeners remember cultural, historical, and religious information. Because listeners cannot go back and immediately rehear what a speaker has said, repetition helps reinforce important ideas, words, and phrases.

Can you recall any lines from—or the title of—Martin Luther King Jr.'s famous speech during the 1963 March on Washington?[5] In what became known as the "I Have a Dream" speech, he repeated "I have a dream" eight times. He said "let freedom ring" 10 times. These phrases are still repeated and remembered more than 60 years later.

You don't have to be a world leader to use repetition effectively. When activist Naomi Wadler was 11 years old, she spoke at the 2018 March for Our Lives rally, a student-led demonstration after the high school mass shooting in Parkland, Florida. She used repetition to call attention to victims of gun violence:[6]

> *I am here today* to represent Courtlin Arrington. *I am here today* to represent Hadiya Pendleton. *I am here today* to represent Taiyania Thompson, who at just 16 was shot dead in her home here in Washington, DC. *I am here today* to acknowledge and represent the African American girls *whose stories* don't make the front page of every national newspaper. *Whose stories* don't lead on the evening news.

Alliteration is a form of repetition using words and phrases that begin with the same sound. Although subtle, it's often found in memorable speeches. Ellen Johnson Sirleaf, former president of Liberia, utilized alliteration in her 2006 address to the US Congress. Notice how many words begin with the letter *F*:[7]

> *F*arming *f*amilies who *f*led the peace—who *f*led the *f*ighting for shelter in neighboring countries or *f*ound themselves displaced *f*rom their communities want a *f*resh start.

Alliteration captures audience attention because it makes language easier to remember. But overuse can sound like a tongue twister—"she sells seashells by the seashore"—rather than an effective and memorable phrase.

METAPHORS, SIMILES, AND ANALOGIES

A **metaphor** compares two things or ideas without using connective words such as *like* and *as*. Shakespeare's famous line "All the world's a stage" is a classic metaphor. The world is not a theatrical stage, but we do play many parts during our lives. Metaphors leave it to the audience to get the point for themselves.[8]

Metaphors are so deeply embedded in our language that we often use them without realizing it. Some of the best ones appeal to sensory experiences—what audience members see, hear, smell, or taste. Here are some sources of common metaphors:[9]

- *Sensory experiences.* You've probably tried something new by "getting your feet wet" or heard a loved one's voice as "music to my ears."

- **Body parts.** We refer to the *teeth* of a comb, *mouth* of a river, *foot* of a mountain, *tongue* of a shoe, and *head* of a corporation.[10]

- **Brightness and darkness.** Brightness is usually linked to happiness, health, life, and virtue, whereas darkness characterizes sadness, sickness, death, and low status. Martin Luther King Jr. compared the "sunlit path of racial justice" to the "dark and desolate valley of segregation."

- **Natural phenomena.** Metaphors often use natural phenomena and weather to describe serious consequences. We talk about being overwhelmed as "a flood" moving with "lightning speed." Politicians know that effective metaphors can distill complex ideas into simple phrases, such as a politician's promise to "drain the swamp."

Like metaphors, **similes** make a direct comparison between two things or ideas, but they usually link these items with *like* or *as*. "Float like a butterfly, sting like a bee," boxing champion Muhammad Ali famously chanted. And when US Supreme Court Chief Justice John Roberts gave a rainy-day commencement address at his son's high school, he humorously noted, "Rain, somebody said, is like confetti from heaven."[11]

Analogies expand similes and metaphors to help explain or clarify a concept. For example, you can describe electricity as water flowing through pipes, the heart as a pump, and the liver as a filter.[12]

Metaphors, similes, and analogies can also make an important part of your presentation more memorable. Activist Ron Finley, for example, became known as "a gansta gardener" after he included that analogy—and others—in his 2013 TED talk:[13]

To see how Ron Finley extends this analogy across his entire speech, see page 458.

> I'm an artist. Gardening is my graffiti. I grow my art. Just like a graffiti artist, where they beautify walls, me, I beautify lawns, parkways. I use the garden, the soil, like it's a piece of cloth, and the plants and the trees, that's my embellishment for that cloth. You'd be surprised what the soil could do if you let it be your canvas.

As you prepare a presentation, avoid **mixed metaphors** where mismatched comparisons are combined in an illogical and often laughable statement, as in this real example: "What we are dealing with is the rubber meeting the road, and instead of biting the bullet on these issues, we just want to punt."[14] Also keep your audience in mind. Every culture has different metaphors, similes, and analogies. If you describe something as a "Hail Mary," football fans in the United States might understand it as a last-ditch attempt, while it might evoke a religious prayer for others.

ANTITHESIS

Antithesis contrasts an idea with its opposite, usually in the same sentence and using parallel structure.[15] This can be used to present a stark choice between two alternatives and to express strong emotions. For example, in 2012, Susan Rice, then US ambassador to the United Nations, spoke in the General Assembly about the conflict between Israel and Gaza, noting "The absence of *peace* risks the presence of *war*."[16] Neil Armstrong used antithesis when he said, "That's one *small step* for *man*, one *giant leap* for *mankind*."[17] Likewise, Michelle Obama used antithesis when she offered her supporters this guidance: "When they go *low*, we go *high*."[18]

LISTS OF THREE

Recall the **RULE OF THREE** ■ **(155–56)**: audience members often expect speakers to have three key points. The pattern is so common that some people will even prepare to applaud after listening to the third item in a series. The same is true of words and phrases. Consider the familiarity of "stop, look, and listen," "see no evil, hear no evil, speak no evil," and "turn on, tune in, drop out." You might even repeat the same thing three times, as in the old joke, "How do you get to Carnegie Hall? Practice, practice, practice."[19]

The CORE Speaking Styles

Champion athletes have unique styles of play. Rappers have recognizable vocal qualities and language. Authors have distinctive ways of expressing themselves. The same is true of speakers.

Speaking style refers to how you use vocabulary, sentence structure and length, grammar, and figures of speech to convey a message.[20] Your speaking style can add a distinctive flavor, emotion, and immediacy to your presentation. Would anyone confuse the speaking styles of Joe Biden and Donald Trump? Probably not. Your speaking style can be as much of a personal signature as the individual words you choose.

There are four CORE speaking styles: clear, oral, rhetorical, and eloquent. As you develop your content and practice your delivery, you'll want to consider which elements from each style are appropriate for your presentation. It's important to remember that the CORE speaking styles are not separate and distinct; you'll use a combination based on your analysis of the **RHETORICAL SITUATION** ● **(6–11)**. All four are often heard in a single presentation, and each one can contribute to your credibility as an effective speaker in different ways.

THE CLEAR STYLE

Say what you mean and say it clearly. If your speaking style isn't clear, your audience may not understand what you're saying. Don't let flowery words and long, complex sentences get in the way of your message. Instead, explain difficult concepts or drive an important point home by using elements of the **clear style**:

- Common and concise words
- Concrete words
- Plain language
- Active voice

Consider, for example, the following excerpt from a speech by Greta Thunberg, delivered in November 2018 to explain why she left school to become a climate activist:[21]

> When I was about eight years old, I first heard about something called climate change or global warming. . . . I remember thinking that it was very strange that humans, who are an animal species among others, could be capable of changing the Earth's climate. Because if we were, and if it was really happening, we wouldn't be talking about anything else. As soon as you'd turn on the TV, everything would be about that. Headlines, radio, newspapers, you would never read or hear about anything else, as if there was a world war going on. But no one ever talked about it.

THE ORAL STYLE

There is often a big difference between the words we use for written documents and the words we use when speaking. The **oral style** resembles the way you talk in an everyday conversation, compared to how you'd write a report or formal message. When you use the oral style, forget what you may think is expected in a speech—formal language, perfect grammar, impressive vocabulary—and remember your purpose. Say what you mean by speaking the way you talk, not the way you write. The oral style can help you connect with your audience and is characterized by these features:

- Short words and short sentences
- Contractions and sentence fragments
- Common expressions and sayings
- Personal pronouns

Audiences often perceive speakers who use an oral style as more trustworthy and likable. Consider how one student made use of the oral style in their introduction to an informative presentation on CliffsNotes:

> Eight o'clock Wednesday night. I have an English exam bright and early tomorrow morning. It's on Homer's *Iliad*. And I haven't read page one. I skip tonight's beer drinking and try to read. Eight forty-five. I'm only on page 12. Only 482 more to go. Nine thirty, it hits me. Like a rock. I'm not going to make it.

The clipped sentence fragments, personal pronouns, contractions, and casual expressions together paint a vivid picture of a somewhat desperate student who is facing an exam unprepared.

THE RHETORICAL STYLE

The **rhetorical style** characterizes language designed to **PERSUADE** ◆ **(403–61)**, motivate, and/or impress an audience. Drawing on elements of the clear and oral styles, the rhetorical style also uses:

- Concrete words
- Short words and sentences

- Intense and vivid words and phrases
- Powerful words

For example, in President Barack Obama's 2020 eulogy for John Lewis, he extolled the bravery of a civil rights leader who in 1965, at the age of 25, led 600 protesters over the Edmund Pettus Bridge in Selma, Alabama, on a day that has come to be known as Bloody Sunday:[22]

> And we know what happened to the marchers that day. Their bones were cracked by billy clubs. Their eyes and lungs choked with tear gas. They knelt to pray, which made their heads easier targets. And John was struck in the skull. And he thought he was going to die, surrounded by the sight of young Americans gagging and bleeding and trampled.

THE ELOQUENT STYLE

Great novelists, poets, and playwrights have the remarkable ability to capture profound ideas and emotions with words. So do eloquent speakers. The **eloquent style** uses poetic and expressive language that makes a speaker's thoughts and feelings clear, inspiring, and memorable. Whereas you might use the rhetorical style to influence and persuade an audience on a range of issues, the eloquent style can be used in heightened moments and occasions to inspire, captivate, and thrill an audience. The eloquent style is characterized by:

- Personal stories
- Expressive delivery
- Figures of speech

Read the following excerpt of a speech delivered by Jon Stewart to the US House of Representatives.[23] Notice his use of short, clear sentences, specific language, and the rule of three.

> I can't help but think what an incredible metaphor this room is for the entire process that getting health care and benefits for 9/11 first responders has come to. Behind me: a filled room of 9/11 first responders. And in front of me: a nearly empty Congress. Sick and

dying, they brought themselves down here to speak—to no one. It's shameful. It's an embarrassment to the country. And it is a stain on this institution. And you should be ashamed of yourselves for those that aren't here.

Respectful and Inclusive Language

As you work on the language and style of your presentation, consider the potential impact your words may have on your audience. We're not suggesting that you say only what you think your audience wants to hear. Rather, you should use language that is inclusive and respectful of your audience so that they are more willing to listen to what you have to say.

USING LANGUAGE RESPECTFULLY

Although there are numerous ways to treat audience members with respect—showing up on time, paying attention to feedback, sticking to your time limit—perhaps the most important is the language you use to address them. By choosing your words respectfully, you acknowledge the universal humanity of all your listeners. This can range from avoiding curse words and derogatory language to ensuring that you refer to groups of people according to their preferences. Doing so will not only enhance your credibility, but it also will encourage your audience to take your message to heart.

While preferences may differ among individuals, try to use generally accepted terms. For example, *Black* and *African American* are both acceptable, but they refer to specific groups and thus are not interchangeable. The same is true of the initialism LGBTQ+ and *the gay community*—though the terms overlap, it's important to use the one appropriate to the topic at hand. You might refer to the person next door as an "older adult" or a "75-year-old neighbor"—or you may leave out their age entirely if it's irrelevant to your presentation. And use the correct term for people based on their place of origin. For example, *America* includes North, Central, and South America, so be specific. If you mean the United States, say the United States.

It can be challenging to identify and navigate the accepted terms for any given group. After all, it depends on who you're talking to or who you're talking about. In general:

- *Do your research.* Use the terms that the person or group uses to describe themselves. If you're in doubt, ask a friend, colleague, or someone representing a group to help you identify the most appropriate terms.

- *Consider your message.* Is the descriptive term relevant to your message? If not, describe the person or group in other ways.

USING INCLUSIVE LANGUAGE

Inclusive language, as its name implies, promotes inclusivity, respect for, and a fair representation of all audience members regardless of race, ethnicity, gender, sexual orientation, age, ability, socio-economic status, and other unique characteristics.[24] Inclusive language recognizes that everyone deserves the right words to describe who they are. (**Exclusionary language**, by contrast, offends and alienates by reinforcing stereotypes, widening the gap between you and your audience.)

The goal of inclusive language is to consciously choose words that do not marginalize individuals or groups based on their distinct attributes, which in turn enhances your credibility as a **TRUSTWORTHY ▲ (77–78)** and **LIKABLE ▲ (78–79)** speaker. Two ways to achieve this are person-first language and identity-first language. **Person-first language** puts the person before their characteristics or condition, such as: a *person living in a shelter, Nang from Thailand,* or *the novelist with bipolar disorder.* **Identity-first language** emphasizes a particular characteristic when that person sees it as an intrinsic part of their identity, such as: a *Deaf speaker, autistic writer, Black man,* or *transgender woman.*

Although we can't cover all kinds of inclusive language here, we address some of the most common forms in the sections that follow. For more detail, consult reliable and credible sources that provide current information on how to use appropriate terms in various contexts, such as the *Language, Please* website and the American Psychological Association's Inclusive Language Guide.[25] And when in doubt, refer to your **RESEARCH ■ (134–51)** and **AUDIENCE ANALYSIS ▲ (90–96)** to guide your language decisions.

Considering Race and Culture Though often unintentional, language that reinforces racial, ethnic, and cultural stereotypes is especially important to avoid. Consider *Indian giver*, a commonly (and casually) used phrase to describe someone deceitful, originating from a misunderstanding of bartering in Native American communities. Using such a phrase likely will lead to some or a total loss of your credibility. Instead of using such racial stereotypes to describe how you were cheated, for example, try using a **LIST OF THREE** ■ **(155–56)**: "Phone scammers preyed on my grandmother's trust. They posed as IRS agents. They took her money." There are over 170,000 English words in use—plenty of options to make your language vivid and memorable without including words and phrases that reinforce stereotypes.

Taking care to avoid cultural bias will also help you connect with an audience who doesn't share your background. Idioms and common phrases that are well known to you may not make sense to someone with a different native language. When choosing language:

- *Avoid stereotypes.* Instead, use figures of speech and/or intense, vivid, and powerful language for emphasis.

- *Explain common expressions.* If there's a chance your listeners won't grasp an idiom or cliché, take a moment to make yourself clear.

- *Look it up.* It's important to be informed. If you're ever in doubt about the origins of or intentions behind a word or phrase, look it up. You may be surprised by what you learn.

Considering Gender Writers and speakers once used the pronoun *he* to refer to any unspecified individual. *He* was also once commonly used to refer to a student, scholar, or a professional, whereas *she* was used to refer to a nurse, schoolteacher, or secretary. This kind of language introduced gender bias to presentations, often creating distance between speakers and their audience. Now, use of the generic *he* (and the more cumbersome *he or she*) has since been rejected in favor of the gender-neutral *they*.

Using gender-neutral language strengthens your credibility while also demonstrating respect for your audience. For example, if you say that every employer should be required to offer *maternity* leave, you may be inadvertently communicating that only women are caregivers. Instead, describing the advantages of a *parental* leave policy avoids this assumption and includes all kinds of parents in your presentation.

There are several ways to avoid gender bias with your language choices, including:

- *Use gender-neutral terms for jobs and professions. Server, firefighter,* and *flight attendant* are all examples of occupational titles that are not linked to a particular gender.

- *Use gender-neutral terms for nouns and adjectives.* Instead of *man-made material,* say *synthetic material.* Instead of *forefathers,* use *ancestors.* Choose *employees* rather than *manpower.*

- *Identify a person's gender only if you need to.* In most cases, you don't need to specify that you met with a *male* nurse, for example.

- *Use the singular* **they.** It avoids the preference of *he* over *she* when the subject's gender is unknown or irrelevant. "A skilled speaker pays special attention to *their* choice of words."

- *Avoid using a pronoun entirely.* In some cases, you can rephrase a sentence and remove the pronoun altogether, as in "Experienced speakers pay careful attention to language."

- *Use a person's desired pronoun.* It takes very little effort to learn whether someone goes by "he," "she," "they," or a variation. Using their desired pronoun confers respect and enhances your credibility.

Considering Ability Many of us use ableist language without realizing that we do. As you might guess, the term *ableism* refers to someone's ability—often the ability to see, hear, walk, and talk. Ableist language excludes people with physical or mental disabilities by using inaccurate definitions, derogatory terms, inappropriate analogies, and insults. Many ingrained expressions—words or phrases we use without thinking—are rooted in ableism. Think of phrases like "fallen on deaf ears" or "turning a blind eye." Sara Nović, a features correspondent for the BBC, explains that these phrases may seem harmless, but they assume that being deaf or blind is a deficit.[26]

Consider the following strategies:

- *Review your speech for ableist language.* If you find any, replace it.
- *Use literal instead of figurative language.* Rather than "turn a blind eye," say "ignore."[27]
- *Avoid words or phrases that promote harmful stereotypes.* "Victim of" and "afflicted by a disability," for example, convey the belief that the person is somehow damaged or unworthy of respect. Use person-first and identify-first language instead.

Conclusion

Your words matter. Time spent planning and choosing words is time well spent. If you're not sure that your words will gain and maintain your audience's attention, record a practice session and listen to it carefully. If your message seems dull, difficult to grasp, and gets bogged down, reconsider your words and look for ways to match your language to your audience and rhetorical situation.

Language has the power to personalize, enliven, and enrich your message, but using the wrong words can diminish your credibility or connection to your audience. Use inclusive rather than exclusionary language. Avoid words that reinforce biases, stereotypes, prejudices, and mislabeling or prevents audience members from understanding your message. Well-chosen language can instead enhance your credibility and connection with your audience—and make for a presentation that is memorable, exciting, and clear.

5.2 Telling Stories

 A BRIEF GUIDE TO THIS CHAPTER

- **The power of stories** (p. 323)
- **Finding stories** (p. 324)
- **Storytelling strategies** (p. 327)
- **Shaping stories** (p. 328)

Stories are everywhere. You might hear about a friend's most recent bad date or about the experience of a refugee on an episode of the *This American Life* podcast. You might read a riveting true crime novel or watch an entertaining new play. In all their many forms, **stories** describe experiences in a way that triggers listeners to imagine them or believe them as real.[1]

A story can be short or long, comic or tragic, personal or anonymous. The clergy use parables—stories with a lesson or moral—to apply religious teachings to everyday life. Parents tell children fables and fairy tales to demonstrate life lessons, like "slow and steady wins the race" or "appearances can be deceiving." And telling a story is one of the most powerful ways a speaker can engage an audience. This chapter provides detailed advice to help you find and use stories to explain and amplify your message.

The Power of Stories

As you begin preparing a presentation, consider how and when you might incorporate a story, perhaps to support a claim or stir emotions. Stories of facing a challenge, for example, can inspire audiences. Well-told stories can capture your audience's attention and enhance your credibility when you draw meaningful lessons from them. Consider this story told by Steve

Jobs, cofounder of Apple, during his commencement address at Stanford University in 2005:

> About a year ago I was diagnosed with cancer. I had a scan at 7:30 in the morning, and it clearly showed a tumor on my pancreas. I didn't even know what a pancreas was. The doctors told me this was almost certainly a type of cancer that is incurable, and that I should expect to live no longer than three to six months. My doctor advised me to go home and get my affairs in order, which is doctor's code for prepare to die.[2]

Jobs could have simply said, "I was diagnosed with terminal cancer." But the story he tells does so much more than define a medical diagnosis. You can see yourself in his condition. You can imagine the anxiety he felt, the sense of hopelessness. As the speech continues, Jobs talks about the lessons he learned—the value of doing what you want, the importance of family, and the wisdom of using your limited time wisely. Jobs lived for another six years after his commencement address. It still inspires listeners today.

Storytelling can also reduce your **SPEAKING ANXIETY ● (18–26)** because they're easy to remember, particularly when they're drawn from personal experiences. Even a short anecdote about something that amazed you, embarrassed you, or made you stop and think can be used as **SUPPORTING MATERIAL ■ (135–39)** to clarify a key point, support a claim, or provide an engaging introduction or conclusion. The stories you tell can and should reinforce your **PURPOSE ▲ (109–18)**.

Finding Stories

If you have a presentation coming up, keep your eyes and ears open for a story you can use. When you encounter a useful story in a newspaper, magazine, book, movie, or online, save it for later. When someone tells you a story that dramatizes a concept you'll be addressing, write it down. The best stories are often your own.

Student speakers often worry that they don't know any stories or that they don't know how to tell one. But everyone can tell a story when it's the right one. So where should you look for the right story?

YOU

You are a living, breathing collection of stories. The following table offers eleven suggestions for priming your personal story pump.

Your name	What's the story of your name? Were you named for someone? If so, what was their story?
	Does your name have a special meaning in your own or another language? Does it reflect your ethnic background?
	Have you changed your name? Why?
Your past	Start by filling in the following blanks: *When I was a* _____, *I* _____. For example, "When I was a swimming pool lifeguard, I saved about a dozen people from drowning." What happened? Why do you remember it so vividly? What did you learn that may benefit an audience?
Your family	Where does your family come from? How far back can you trace your lineage?
	Are there unique customs in your family?
	What's your family's ethnic background?
	Is there someone famous, funny, notorious, or eccentric in your family?
Your special places	Is there a special place in your life? A venue where your family holds reunions? A view from a beloved mountaintop? The place where you were married?
Your mentors	Who has helped guide you through life's challenges? Your parents, a teacher, a coach, a relative, a best friend, a mentor? What did they do for you? What advice did they share? Can their counsel benefit others?
Your successes	What have you done that makes you proud? Have you earned an award, helped people in need, done the right thing in a crisis, or survived a tragedy? How can your story of success help other people take pride in what they do or have done?
Your failures	What have you learned from a particular failure? How did failing make you feel? How did you overcome it? What did you do to make sure it wouldn't happen again? How can your failed experiences help other people?
Your values	What are your deep-seated values? Do you value fairness, honesty, tradition, equality, and/or justice? Do you value your family and friends, your country, your environment, or profession?
	Is there a story about why you strongly value what you believe and do?

For an example of using a personal story as an introduction to an informative presentation, see Notable Speaker: Susan Cain, page 205.

(Continued)

Your pivotal moments	When did you know you were an adult?
	What did you learn from being laid off or fired from a job?
	When did you first truly understand love?
Your pet peeves	What bothers you a lot? Bad customer service, a grade you didn't deserve, name-calling? Why? What happened?
Your special knowledge	What do you know that others might not know or be interested in knowing?
	Do you know how _____ was discovered?
	Do you know why the town of _____ was founded?
	Do you know that _____ happened here 100 years ago today?

YOUR AUDIENCE

If you have spent sufficient time **ANALYZING YOUR AUDIENCE ▲ (90–96)**, you should be able to find stories related to their interests, beliefs, and values. If your audience is community minded, you may share a story about a time when your church came together to help a family in need. If your audience loves sports, you may share a story about how you tore your hamstring the week after you made the varsity soccer team. If your audience has conflicting viewpoints, you may recount a recent news story about civilians from warring countries who came together to advocate for peace.

OTHER PEOPLE

All of us know people with fascinating backgrounds and experiences. Think of someone you could interview whose story might illuminate the subject of your presentation: a parent or grandparent who, against all odds, immigrated to the United States and created a successful business; a combat war veteran who heroically saved a friend; a professional musician, writer, actor, or athlete who overcame adversity to achieve their goals. But remember: if you're going to tell someone else's story, never use it to embarrass or divulge private information, and, if it's someone you know, get their permission before you tell it.

THE OCCASION

What's the **OCCASION ▲ (61–68)**? When and where will you be speaking? Does the venue have a fascinating history? How will the situation and setting affect your delivery? What's happening in the news or in the neighborhood? Was someone famous born on the day you're speaking? If Mother's Day is coming up, could you talk about something your mother said or did that is relevant to why you are speaking? What happened the first (or previous) time you attended this event or spoke in a similar situation or setting?

Storytelling Strategies

Most of us tell stories in everyday conversations. We can easily recount something that happened to us or something we witnessed. Telling a story in a presentation, however, is not the same as describing your day. A story told in a presentation must be carefully developed and delivered. And it must relate to your purpose and the **RHETORICAL SITUATION ● (6–11)**. The following strategies will help guide you through this process:

- *Use a simple storyline.* Long stories with complex themes are hard to follow and difficult to tell. If you can't summarize your story in fewer than twenty-five words, don't tell it.

- *Limit the number of characters.* Good storytellers distinguish their characters by modifying their **DELIVERY ▶ (209–301)**. Using a combination of distinctive volumes, rates, pitches, tones, and body movements can be tough. Unless you're an accomplished actor, look for stories with no more than three characters.

- *Connect with your listeners.* Your audience will pay close attention if they can connect emotionally with the setting, characters, and plot of your story.

- *Make a point.* Imagine you concluded your story with "And so what this means for you is . . ." The best stories, however, aren't as explicit as that. Instead, the message is usually obvious by the end. Whatever the point you're trying to make, it must be clear and connect with your **PURPOSE ▲ (109–18)**.

- *Tell it efficiently.* According to Shakespeare, "Brevity is the soul of wit." Try to tell your story in less than two minutes, not by speaking quickly but by **PRACTICING YOUR DELIVERY** ▶ **(220-24)** and knowing what details are essential and which you can omit.

- *Create tension.* Effective stories create uncertainty about what will happen next. Will Beauty kiss the Beast? Will Wonder Woman help win the war? Will Dorothy get back to Kansas? Did you get the job after flubbing a question at the interview?

- *Make it personal.* The best stories are often about you, the **SPEAKER** ▲ **(72-85)**. Talking about how you handled a difficult situation can, if well told, be far more interesting than a story about some historical figure who faced the same challenge.

- *Exaggerate effectively.* Think about the ways you might alter your delivery when reading to a child. Exaggeration can make a story more vivid. The tone of your voice, the sweep of your gestures, and your facial expressions add a layer of meaning and emphasis to your message.

- *Remember the rule of three.* Stories make frequent use of the **RULE OF THREE** ■ **(155-56)**: Three main characters, such as: Papa Bear, Mama Bear, and Baby Bear; Harry, Ron, and Hermione; the Scarecrow, the Tin Man, and the Cowardly Lion; Violet, Klaus, and Sunny Baudelaire. Think of the many times a folktale character is given three wishes, three guesses, or three tries to overcome adversity. Experienced storytellers know there is magic in the rule of three.

- *Practice for sense and rhythm.* Once you can tell a story without notes, **PRACTICE** ▶ **(220-24)** telling it to someone else—a friend, neighbor, or family member. Tell the story twice. The first time, ask them whether the story makes sense. The second time, ask whether the story flows from event to event and has a rhythm of its own. A well-told story has meaningful pauses and appropriate variations in delivery.

Shaping Stories

Memorable stories, no matter how short or simple, share similar elements. The beginning introduces a situation where someone has to overcome an obstacle or solve a problem. The middle explains what the characters did or didn't do to resolve the situation. And the end shows the resolution and, in some cases, offers a meaningful lesson.

The following story-building strategies can help you make sure all the right pieces of your story are in the right place:[3]

1. ***Title.*** You don't have to share the title of a story with your audience, but it can help you focus on the purpose of your story. A title such as "The Big Bad Man in the Back of the Building" suggests a very different story from one titled "The Happy Haven behind Our House." Does your title capture the essence, mood, or spirit of the story?

2. ***Background information.*** Where and when does the story take place? What is going on? Did anything important happen before the story begins? Use **VIVID LANGUAGE ∴ (308)** to set the time, place, and occasion of the story.

3. ***Character development.*** Who is in the story? What are their backgrounds and relationships to one another? What do they look and sound like? How do you want the audience to feel about them? Bring the characters to life with vivid descriptions and adapt your **DELIVERY ▶ (209–301)** to make each character distinct.

4. ***Action or conflict.*** What is happening? What obstacles or challenges did the characters face? What did they see, hear, feel, smell, or taste? How did they react to what's happening? Let the action build as you tell this part of the story.

5. ***High point (climax).*** What is the culminating event or moment of greatest intensity? What is the turning point in the action? When does the tension that's been building reach its peak? What sentence makes the story funny? All action should lead to a discovery, decision, or outcome. Show the audience how the character has grown or has responded to a situation or problem. If you don't include a climax or punch line, the story won't make sense—so make sure it has one!

6. ***Conclusion and resolution.*** How is the situation resolved? How do the important characters respond to the climax? The conclusion pulls the strands of the story together. Make sure you don't leave the audience wondering about the fate of a character. In some cases, a story doesn't need a conclusion— the climax or punch line may conclude it for you.

7. ***Central point.*** Is there a lesson to be learned from the story? How does it relate to the rest of your presentation? You don't need to state the central point. Just make sure you know what it is and that the story reflects its message.

The following example uses *The Three Little Pigs* as a model. Although this children's story is longer than one you might use in a presentation, it demonstrates the universal structure of most good stories.

Title
The Three Little Pigs

Background information
Once upon a time, three little pigs set off to seek their fortune.

Character development
Each little pig built a home. The first pig to finish working built a house made of straw. The second built a house made of sticks, and the third pig took even more time and built a sturdy house made of bricks.

Action or conflict
Soon a wolf came along. He blew down the house made of straw, so the first pig ran to the house of sticks. The wolf blew down the house of sticks, so both pigs ran to the house of bricks. Then the wolf went to the house of bricks and said, "Little pig, little pig, let me come in." All three pigs responded: "Not by the hair of my chinny chin chin." So the wolf huffed and puffed but couldn't blow the house in.

High point (climax)
The wolf was very angry. "I'm going to climb down your chimney and eat all of you up," he declared, laughing, "including your chinny chin chins." The pigs heard the wolf on the roof and hung a pot of water over a blazing fire. When the wolf jumped down the chimney, he landed in the pot of boiling water. The pigs quickly put the cover on it, boiled up the wolf, and ate him for dinner.

Conclusion and resolution
And the three pigs lived happily ever after.

Central point
Thoughtful planning and hard work pay off in the end.

ADAPTING A STORY FOR YOUR PRESENTATION

Good stories aren't always true stories—but they should always be believable and logical. In other words, they should make sense. More importantly, a compelling story will create the impact that you want for your purpose. Both "The Three Bears" and "Cinderella" and many stories depicted in plays and movies are works of fiction; they are not *true* in the sense of depicting real events. But all good stories—fact or fiction—contain *truths* that can support your presentation. **Story truths** refer to accepted principles that underlie the meaning and values in a story.

Peter Guber, producer of such films as *Rain Man*, *Batman*, and *The Color Purple*, describes the four truths of storytelling.[4] We've modified these story truths to help you adapt any story to any **RHETORICAL SITUATION** ● **(6–11)** :

1. *Truth to occasion.* Stories are rarely told the same way twice. If your time is limited, you'll have to shorten your story. If the **OCCASION** ▲ **(61–68)** is somber, you may tell only part of a story, modify some elements, or tell a different story entirely. For an inspirational story, you might focus more on triumphs or moments when the characters overcame obstacles.

2. *Truth to speaker.* When you speak truthfully and share your genuine feelings in a story, you enhance your credibility. When relevant, storytellers reveal their beliefs and **VALUES** ▲ **(95–96)** openly and honestly. Even if the story is fictional, a skilled storyteller conveys the anger, embarrassment, sadness, fear, or joy experienced by their characters.

3. *Truth to audience.* When you raise **AUDIENCE** ▲ **(88–105)** expectations about a story, make sure you meet them. If you promise a thrilling story, you have to follow through. If you use **HUMOR** ∴ **(340–42)**, your audience should laugh. Use personal pronouns such as *we*, *you*, and *I* to invite the audience to share the experience and feelings you describe.

4. *Truth to purpose.* What is your overall objective? Does the story express the values you believe in and want others to adopt as their own? When a story is true to your **PURPOSE** ▲ **(109–18)**, you can invest more energy and emotion into telling it—and you'll be more successful at reaching your audience.

In 2018, Oprah Winfrey accepted the Cecil B. DeMille Award for lifetime achievement at the Golden Globe Awards ceremony. She began with a story. Can you identify the ways that Winfrey achieved each of the four story truths?

> In 1964, I was a little girl sitting on the linoleum floor of my mother's house in Milwaukee watching Anne Bancroft present the Oscar for best actor at the 36th Academy Awards. She opened the envelope and said five words that literally made history: "The winner is Sidney Poitier." Up to the stage came the most elegant man I had ever seen. I remember his tie was white, and of course his skin was black, and I had never seen a black man being celebrated like that. I tried many, many times to explain what a moment like that means to a little girl, a kid watching from the cheap seats as my mom came through the door bone tired from cleaning other people's houses. But all I can do is quote the explanation in Sidney's performance in *Lilies of the Field*: "Amen, amen, amen, amen."[5]

Conclusion

You don't have to publish a novel or produce a film script to be a great storyteller. Stories are everywhere. You can begin by looking for them close to home. Is there a story about your name, your location, or your family? About a special place or mentor, a success or failure?

Good stories are more than spur-of-the-moment recollections or retellings of classic tales. The beginning introduces a challenging situation faced by the characters. The middle explains what the characters did or didn't do to resolve the situation. The end describes how they overcame the challenge and, in some cases, offers a meaningful lesson. The best stories are meticulously crafted, truthful, and strategically adapted to all elements of the rhetorical situation—especially to your purpose.

In 1972, Dr. Rita Pierson followed in the footsteps of her grandparents and parents to become an educator. For more than forty years, Pierson spent her professional life being a champion for students, teaching elementary school and junior high school as well as special education. She led numerous professional development workshops on a variety of topics focused on under-resourced learners and early intervention strategies. Pierson was also an antipoverty advocate and served her community in various capacities, always working to help those in need. In May 2013, at a TED Talks Education event, Pierson called on educators to be champions for their students. Her inspirational talk has been viewed more than 10 million times. Her family announced her sudden death in June 2013—just weeks after her TED talk aired on PBS.

Search Terms

To locate a video of this presentation online, enter the following key words into a search engine: Rita Pierson every kid needs a champion. The video is approximately 7:49 in length.

What to Watch For

[0:00–1:30] Pierson begins her talk by saying "I have spent my entire life either at the schoolhouse, on the way to the schoolhouse, or talking about what happens in the schoolhouse." Not only does this statement build her credibility, but it also describes the source of the stories she'll use to achieve her purpose. Note her use of "we" statements as a way to involve her audience: "And we know why kids drop out. We know why kids don't learn." The "we" statements also convey her unspoken message: "I'm talking to you! So listen up!"

[1:30–5:57] Pierson uses one- to two-minute stories both to organize her talk and to provide supporting material. All but the final story about her mother includes dialogue. She also uses humor to capture and hold the audience's attention. In some cases, it is a simple statement, such as "Tell a kid you're sorry; they're in shock." In other cases, she uses self-effacing humor to show the audience that she is an ordinary, fallible human being—and to show that even education experts get it wrong sometimes.

[6:12–7:35] Throughout the presentation, Pierson's delivery personifies the talents of a skilled storyteller. She is expressive, confident, immediate, and a model of stage presence. She maintains consistent and direct eye contact while smiling at appropriate moments. Her body movements are fluid and natural, helping establish her credibility and making her appear confident and relaxed. She effectively varies her volume, rate, pitch, and inflection to emphasize different parts of her message. When she tells the story of teaching a difficult class, her tone changes, her volume drops a bit, and she slows down her rate of speaking. In the opening and ending of her talk, her delivery communicates the urgency and seriousness of her message.

[7:14–7:43] Although she continues to share both amusing and consequential stories about students, she wraps up her talk by returning to the need for strong relationships between teachers and students. She calls out to her audience: "Every child deserves a champion, an adult who will never give up on them." She then skillfully uses short, urgent questions and answers to conclude because she knows that her audience is now with her. "Is this job tough? You betcha. Oh God, you betcha. But it is not impossible. We can do this. We're educators. We're born to make a difference."

EXERCISE

After viewing Pierson's speech, reflect on these questions:

1. What is the purpose of Pierson's presentation? How did she make this purpose relevant to her audience?

2. What strategies and supporting material did Pierson use to gain the attention of and engage her audience?

3. What other strategies could Pierson have used to involve the audience in her presentation?

4. Explain why you do or don't believe that Pierson's sense of humor supported her purpose. How did it strengthen or diminish her credibility?

5. Describe how Pierson's delivery (expressiveness, confidence, stage presence, and immediacy) affected audience interest, motivation, and recall.

5.3 Generating Interest

🔍 A BRIEF GUIDE TO THIS CHAPTER

- **Limit the length of your presentation** (p. 336)
- **Enliven your content** (p. 338)
- **Use humor** (p. 340)
- **Employ audience participation** (p. 343)

When communication students and professional speakers were asked to rate the importance of over 20 speaking skills—such as organizing a presentation, using your voice effectively, and reducing stage fright—one skill topped the rest: keeping your audience interested.[1]

As a speaker, you're often competing with many distractions for your audience's attention, especially in online presentations. And research shows that our attention spans are getting shorter.[2] So how do you maintain your audience's interest once they start listening to you? **STORYTELLING ⸪ (323–32)** is one of the most effective ways. We explore four other useful methods in this chapter.

Limit the Length of Your Presentation

In the 1970s, the US Navy tried to determine how long people can listen to and retain information. The answer: 18 minutes.[3] Carmine Gallo, author of *The Presentation Secrets of Steve Jobs*, calls 20 minutes the "Goldilocks Zone" of public presentations: not too short, not too long, but just right.[4] It's about the length of a riveting bedtime story, President John F. Kennedy's famous inaugural speech, and the time limit for most TED talks.[5] A similar number applies to virtual learning on a medium such as Zoom. Students' attention tends to fade after watching between 15 and 20 minutes of video.[6]

Many presenters are given time limits—but that doesn't mean you speak for the full amount of time you're allowed. If you have one hour for a business report, for example, it can be more effective to present for 20 or 30 minutes and spend the rest of the time doing a **QUESTION-AND-ANSWER SESSION ⁝ (350–61)** or an interactive **DEMONSTRATION ✳ (381–82)** .

In some cases, it might be wise to prepare two versions of your presentation: one that matches the assigned speaking time and one that is half of that. For example, if you've prepared a 20-minute presentation for a particular occasion, know how you would quickly cut it by 10 minutes or more if needed. You may be surprised to find that in some cases the shorter version is stronger because it focuses on the essence of the message you want your audience to understand and remember.

The following questions can help you shorten your presentation:[7]

For an example of a speaker who connects with his audience and achieves his purpose in a short amount of time, see Notable Speaker: George W. Bush, page 69.

- Will audience members be able to reach the conclusion you want without your help? If so, don't burden them with irrelevant information, explanations, or visuals.

- Do you have too many examples or stories, potentially distracting listeners from your message? If yes, drop some of them.

- Have you said the same thing in too many different ways? Pick your most striking example, fact, or argument, and get rid of the rest.

- Is the audience already inclined to believe what you're saying? If so, don't spend a lot of time establishing **COMMON GROUND ▲ (89)** .

- Does the audience definitely need to know this? If not, delete or shorten any material that isn't directly relevant to your **PURPOSE ▲ (109–18)** .

Add time stamps to your **SPEAKING NOTES ▶ (217–20)** and practice what you intend to say out loud. You may discover that some sections are too long and vague while others are wonderfully brief and clear.

Enliven Your Content

Have you ever been half listening to someone speak when suddenly you hear something that grabs your attention? Here are some ways you can similarly get your audience to sit up and listen.

VARY SUPPORTING MATERIAL AND LANGUAGE STYLES

You are more likely to generate audience interest if you use multiple forms of **SUPPORTING MATERIAL ■ (135–39)**. For instance, after citing a startling statistic, share a dramatic example or tell a compelling, relevant story. Well-designed **PRESENTATION AIDS ▶ (260–78)** can visually reinforce your message—and they can capture audience attention when used sparingly and purposefully. A **FIGURE OF SPEECH ⋰ (311–14)** stands out from more neutral language and focuses attention on important ideas.

CONTRADICT AUDIENCE EXPECTATIONS

For an example of a speaker who contradicts audience expectations by correcting a commonly held misconception, see Notable Speaker: David Epstein, page 398.

If you say something that contradicts audience expectations, their interest may be aroused. For example, you could quote a Republican who argues for strong gun control, a songwriter who claims they don't listen to music, or a travel blogger who says their favorite place to go is home.

In a 2023 podcast interview, former Seattle Seahawks player Marshawn Lynch recounted a time early in his career when he was struggling to stay awake during a presentation from the team's financial adviser. Midway through the presentation, the adviser showed a slide with names of famous NFL players and their incomes. He then revealed that all those players went bankrupt, contradicting the expectation set up with the slide showing their incomes. Lynch said he suddenly started paying attention at that moment: "Now I'm up!"[8]

MAKE IT RELEVANT

If your audience sees no reason to listen to you, they won't. Why should they listen to or care about your topic if it's not relevant to their interests, wants, and needs? Ask **WIIFT ▲ (93)**: "What's in it for them?" Remember, it's all about audience analysis and adaptation.

Here's an example: Surveys report that almost half of drivers age 36 and older can change a tire while on the side of a road. Only 27 percent of 18- to 20-year-old drivers can do the same. If you are speaking to a group of college students about the importance of mastering this skill, you could make it more relevant by asking your audience questions like, "How many of you regularly drive a car? What would you do if you were driving to an important event and you had a flat tire?"

HIGHLIGHT CONSEQUENCES

Give your audience an important reason to listen to you. For example, an instructor in a chemistry classroom notices that the students aren't paying attention to safety procedures, so she tells the class, "This is an important warning. If you do this incorrectly, you can be seriously burned or blinded. Now let's review how to do this experiment safely."

USE NOVELTY

Most audience members enter the setting of a presentation without noticing much about it. Everything is familiar. There are seats, perhaps a lectern and some projection equipment. Then one day they walk into the same room and see something totally unexpected. You may begin a presentation by displaying an unexpected image of a train wreck or stand silently onstage, dressed as a tennis player. What is different is interesting. This is also why unexpected use of **VIVID LANGUAGE ⸫ (308)** can be so compelling.

For an example of using novel clothing, slides, and stories to gain attention, interest, and curiosity, see Notable Speaker: Yassmin Abdel-Magied, page 225.

PORTRAY EMOTIONS

In most presentations, audience members do not witness a full display of a speaker's emotions. If, however, a speaker pauses and chokes up, and a tear drops from one eye, the room may grow still. Everyone is paying attention.

We are not suggesting you cry while speaking. But if show your feelings honestly—whether it's fear, sadness, joy, anticipation, anger, surprise, or disgust—audience members are more likely to listen and remember your message. Showing your own feelings is one way to arouse audience interest and connect with *their* emotions.

Actress Hannah Waddingham uses expressive delivery to convey a somber message at the 2023 *Glamour* Women of the Year Awards.

USE EXPRESSIVE DELIVERY

One aspect of delivery that has a particularly strong impact on audience interest is **EXPRESSIVENESS ▶ (212)**—the vitality, variety, and sincerity you put into your presentation. An expressive voice and appropriate body movements can ensure that the audience hears you, sees you, and understands your message. Eye contact tells audience members, "I'm talking to you!" Establish verbal and nonverbal immediacy with physical closeness, a sense of humor, inclusive personal pronouns (like *us* and *we*).

Hannah Waddingham, an actress on the popular *Ted Lasso* series, is known for her bold speaking style and non-verbal expressiveness. But in her 2023 acceptance speech for *Glamour*'s Entertainer of the Year award, she used a more somber delivery: "I apologize if I am not as buoyant as I usually might be, but as a parent, as a single mother, the atrocities that are taking place around the world appall me to my core, and it would be remiss of me to not give my energy to that tonight." Though her tone is more subdued than usual, she still uses gestures to emphasize key points, a posture that conveys confidence, and eye contact that establishes rapport with the audience. Although she takes a bold position, she expresses herself sincerely as she highlights the key points and varies the delivery of her message.

Use Humor

Humor can defuse anger, ease tension, stimulate action, and encourage listeners to have a good time. Audience members tend to remember humorous speakers positively, even when they are not enthusiastic about the speaker's message. Humor takes many forms: stories, jokes, analogies, funny sayings, witty quotations, satire, puns, and visuals. Humor can also be a quick aside or a response to something that happens or is happening during your presentation. Once, while a friend was speaking in a large conference room, the presentation was disrupted by uniformed workmen who kept crossing the back of the room in both directions. Finally the speaker stopped and said, "What do these guys know that we should know about?" The audience laughed and then the speaker picked up where she was and continued.

Know your audience before deciding how and if to include humor. Some audiences respond well to one-liners, puns, funny stories, and goofy props. Others love funny quotations, cartoons, wacky definitions, laughable headlines, misspelled signs, and funny song lyrics. If used inappropriately, humor can distract from your message or create distance with your audience. The more thorough your **AUDIENCE ANALYSIS ▲ (90–96)**, the easier it will be to decide whether humor might heighten or hinder your ability to establish a positive connection with your listeners.

Explaining how to be humorous is something like explaining how to ice skate. You can read and watch videos about ice skating, but nothing will replace putting on a pair of skates and getting on the ice. The same is true with humor. Nothing replaces trying it—repeatedly—in front of real audiences. Try a few humorous lines first and test them out with a friend or classmate to get feedback.

SELF-EFFACING HUMOR

In many cases, *you* may be your own best source of humor. **Self-effacing humor**—your ability to direct humor at yourself—lowers the barrier between you and your audience by showing them you are an ordinary, fallible human being. You also don't have to worry about offending anyone if you are the butt of the joke. You could poke fun at your job, family, experiences, or failures.

Bono, the lead singer of U2 and cofounder of an AIDS relief organization, poked fun at his own failures during his 2004 commencement address at the University of Pennsylvania. Before speaking, he was given an honorary doctorate degree. He said: "Doctor of Laws, wow! I know it's an honor, and

For an example of humorous delivery, see Notable Speaker: Jordan Raskopoulos, page 246.

it really is an honor, but are you sure? Doctor of Law, I mean all I can think about are the laws I've broken!"

Self-effacing humor can also occur spontaneously. If you make a mistake—forgetting something, dropping a visual aid, using the wrong slide—smile and brush it off with a self-effacing comment. A sense of humor helps when there are equipment glitches too. For example, an educational consultant recently gave a Zoom presentation called "Tips for Teaching Online" to a group of teachers. As he began his introduction, his listeners chuckled, and one said, "You're muted!" Quickly, he turned on the sound, smiled, and said, "In the immortal words of George Bernard Shaw, 'Those who can, do. Those who can't, teach!'" Everyone laughed.

Although a little self-effacing humor can enhance your **LIKABILITY ▲ (78–81)**, it should be used sparingly. Too much self-effacing humor can undermine an audience's impression of your **COMPETENCE ▲ (75–77)** and weaken the power of your message.[9] In short, if you make too much fun of yourself, listeners may not take you or your message seriously.

APPROPRIATE HUMOR

Use what you've learned from your audience analysis to make sure your humor won't offend anyone. This is not about political correctness but about common courtesy and respecting audience sensibilities. In general, it's safe to apply the following guidelines for nearly any rhetorical situation:

- Use **INCLUSIVE LANGUAGE ⁙ (318–22)**.
- Don't tease your audience (unless the occasion is a roast).
- Avoid jokes about ethnicity, race, religion, gender identity, sex, politics, or other sensitive issues. Offensive humor will insult your audience and damage your credibility.
- Stay focused on your **PURPOSE ▲ (109–18)**. Don't mistake your presentation for a stand-up routine. If a joke or funny story doesn't have a meaningful connection to you and your message, don't use it, even if you think it's hilarious.

Employ Audience Participation

One of the best ways to generate audience interest is to get the audience involved early and often. Audiences pay more attention if they know that at some point they may be asked to participate. Although there are occasions where audience involvement is impossible or discouraged, many presentations offer opportunities for well-planned participation.

ASK QUESTIONS

Get audience members involved by asking for their reactions to what you've said. Even if audience members do little more than nod their heads in response, they will have become part of a transaction with the speaker.

A quick poll is an easy way to involve listeners. If you're presenting in person, pose a question and ask for a show of hands. If you are speaking online, many online presentation programs, like Zoom, have a **POLLING FEATURE ▶ (298)**. Here are simple questions to ask in a poll, either in person or online:

- How many of you know someone who . . . ?
- How many of you have visited . . . ?
- Have any of you heard about . . . ?
- Who here has attended a . . . ?

The responses may help you **ADAPT TO YOUR AUDIENCE ▲ (102–5)** while also letting audience members know whether they share common experiences, opinions, or beliefs. You can also be creative in the way you poll your audience. For example, a speaker on Zoom was talking about travel safety during the COVID-19 pandemic and asked her audience to briefly turn off their video if they felt uncomfortable about travel. Many screens went from live video to an image of initials. The effect was immediate: everyone now knew that a lot of people were worried.

You might also ask an open-ended question and invite your audience to chime in. At a Virginia Press Association's minority job fair, Marvin Leon Lake, public editor of the *Virginian-Pilot*, began his presentation with a true story about a journalism student who, at a previous job fair, had volunteered to be interviewed by a panel of strangers in front of an audience. The student went on to become a successful journalist. Lake then asked the audience: "What is the moral of this story?" Several audience members raised their hands to respond, and Lake responded positively to each of their answers. In doing so, he engaged his audience with a relevant story and a discussion about what it meant, and the students attending the job fair walked away remembering Lake's important lesson about being prepared to meet a challenge.

ENCOURAGE INTERACTION

Asking listeners to interact with one another can enhance interest, recall, and learning. At the start of your presentation, you can ask audience members to introduce themselves to the people sitting around them. Depending on the **PURPOSE ▲ (109–18)** of your message, you could invite them to briefly discuss a relevant topic. For example, in a talk about childcare, you could ask the audience to share the number, ages, and genders of their children with one another. If you're talking to young college students, ask them to identify where they live, their majors, or their career aspirations.

One of the real advantages of **ONLINE PRESENTATIONS ▶ (298)** is the opportunity to use chat features and breakout rooms to facilitate interaction. To effectively use them, you might:

- Suggest specific topics that you want audience members to discuss in the chat or activities you want them to perform in the breakout room.

- Assign a time limit and be ready to move on. A brief interaction is far better than dead air.

- Ask someone to lead each breakout room or monitor the chat for interesting responses that you can share with the larger group.

CONDUCT AN ACTIVITY OR DEMONSTRATION

You might use simple games or training exercises to involve audience members with your presentation and with one another. In a business pitch, you could ask your audience to brainstorm a name for a new product or suggest solutions to hypothetical or real problems.

Brief **DEMONSTRATIONS** ✳ **(381–82)** can also engage your audience's senses while reinforcing your message. For example, if you are speaking about a certain kind of textile, ask your audience to feel it. If your presentation is about a favorite food, encourage your audience to taste or smell it. Ask them follow-up questions to reinforce this connection. Does your chocolate chip cookie recipe produce a chewier, sweeter, and thicker cookie than another recipe?

Interrupting your presentation with an activity gives the audience a break, during which they can interact in different but meaningful ways. In some speaking situations, it might work best to ask for a volunteer. If so, make sure your volunteers aren't going to be embarrassed, and if possible, find a way to reward them afterward—with a small prize or special thanks. Once audience members see that volunteering is risk-free, they may be more willing to participate.

Conclusion

Remember that both professional and student speakers rank generating and maintaining audience interest as the *most* important speaking skill. Regardless of whether an audience arrives uninterested and indifferent or ready and eager to listen, you can enhance their interest and make your presentation memorable with engaging language, storytelling, and interactive strategies that adapt to what you know about them. Choose the strategies and skills that will work best for your speaking situation: shorten your presentation, enliven your content, use appropriate humor, and employ audience participation. If you choose strategies that take into account all six elements of the **RHETORICAL SITUATION** ● **(6–11)**, you are more likely to capture and maintain your audience's attention throughout and well after your presentation.

Kyle Martin

After dedicating his junior year of high school to diligent study and hard work, Kyle Martin was named valedictorian of his class and found himself delivering the commencement address at his 2019 high school graduation ceremony. In his speech titled "The 16th Second," Martin offered a surprising perspective on the value of working and sacrificing to accomplish a goal. His speech immediately went viral and has been viewed more than 23 million times. After high school, Martin attended Palm Beach Atlantic University on a full four-year scholarship based on academic merit, and he graduated in 2023 with a degree in history. He went on to attend the University of Virginia Law School.

Search Terms

To locate a video of this presentation online, enter the following key words into a search engine: Kyle Martin brutally honest valedictorian. The video is approximately 8:04 in length.

What to Watch For

[0:00–1:28] Martin begins his presentation with an introduction that might be expected in a commencement address—with an expression of gratitude for the parents, staff, teachers, and others at his school. From the start, he speaks with an energy and expressiveness that immediately captures the audience's attention. As valedictorian, Martin's credibility as a qualified and knowledgeable speaker had already been established ahead of time. He builds on this competence by speaking with dynamism—using a high level of energy, vigor, and commitment to transfer enthusiasm and passion from him to his audience.

[1:29–1:58] Martin tells the audience about the moment he learned he was in the running for the title of valedictorian, using humor to say "It was then that I decided I wanted it," causing the audience to laugh. He emphasizes that he worked hard to earn the title by pausing and making eye contact with the audience. With applause, they demonstrate their enthusiasm and support for him. He responds with a visible display of emotion—a sigh of relief after so much stress and sacrifice. By establishing his likability, Martin has given his audience a reason to want to continue to listen to him.

[1:59–2:25] Martin uses vivid descriptions—"my heart racing and my adrenaline pumping"—to invite his audience to experience the same excitement he did when he learned he was chosen as valedictorian. He raises his hand in a cheer as he shouts, "Yeah, I won!" He felt like he was "at the top of the pile of all [his] accomplishments." As exciting as the experience was for him, he repeatedly reminds the audience that all this euphoria lasted for only fifteen seconds. Each time he mentions fifteen seconds, he pauses to emphasize just how short-lived the feeling was then and now. The vividness of the "euphoric" moment is replaced by Martin's realization that "there must come a sixteenth second."

[2:28–3:09] The audience's laughter fades away as Martin describes his reaction to the moment he realized "that's it?" in the sixteenth second. With a drop in volume and continued intensity in his voice, Martin begins to contradict audience expectations of a valedictorian speech. After all his hard work, instead of celebrating his achievement, he concedes that he "felt nothing."

[3:11–3:40] Martin sets out to share what he figured out about the sixteenth second: working hard to achieve a goal "should not be done . . . at the expense of relationships with others." In a few short sentences, he describes the consequences he experienced: the time spent earning the privilege of delivering "a five-minute speech" as valedictorian "was paid for with a lack of attending to relationships in my life."

[3:43–5:06] Martin makes it relevant to his audience by inviting a segment of them—his classmates—to participate in a reflective exercise about the sixteenth second. He uses a range of examples they can relate to, in which they might choose prioritizing sports, academics, social media, or video games over investing in important relationships in their lives. He then uses humor to emphasize how they have the benefit of time on their side: "We are about to launch into life . . . and we haven't messed anything up yet!" He makes this advantage more clear by asking them to imagine "if it was [their] career [they] chose over [their] spouse, making money over spending time with their children, or being famous at the expense of their friendships.

[5:07–7:12] Martin spends the remainder of his speech encouraging the audience to invest in their relationships, including repairing any broken ones. In a counterintuitive move, he uses his valedictorian speech to explain why becoming valedictorian was not all that he thought it would be. Through using vivid descriptions, expressiveness, and a display of emotion, Martin concludes his speech by answering the WIIFT ("What's in it for them?") question: "Have no regrets in the sixteenth second."

EXERCISE

After viewing Martin's speech, reflect on these questions:

1. How did Martin establish common ground with his audience? Do you think he needed to spend more or less time doing so?

2. Did Martin vary his energy and expressiveness enough throughout the speech? Where, and to what effect?

3. What is one way Martin could have made the setting of his presentation more novel?

4. How would you describe his use of humor? Did you find it effective?

5. Do you think his audience would have been as eager to listen to him if he was not the valedictorian? Would they have seen his message as relevant to them if someone else had delivered it? Why or why not?

6. Considering the ways to generate interest, why do you think Martin's speech went viral in 2019 and has been viewed more than 23 million times?

5.4 Question-and-Answer Sessions

 A BRIEF GUIDE TO THIS CHAPTER

Today, audience members often expect that asking questions will be part of a presentation experience. Many business presentations conclude with a "Questions?" slide. Lectures and readings usually include time at the end for attendees to interact with the speaker. Online platforms use chat features that allow the audience to ask questions during and after a presentation. As an audience member, you might even be asked to come to a work meeting or a classroom discussion with questions prepared.

In a **question-and-answer (Q&A) session**, speakers give brief, impromptu responses to audience questions and comments. It is one of the most direct ways to engage an audience. In fact, some audience members like a useful Q&A session *better* than the presentation that preceded it! How you respond to questions and objections can affect audience members' perceptions of you as much as your delivery. Imagine a salesperson who delivers a polished, confident presentation about a product but struggles to answer a basic question about how it works. Imagine another speaker who speaks haltingly or avoids eye contact during their presentation but when asked for more details lights up and demonstrates their passion for and deep knowledge about the subject.

Participating in a productive Q&A session can make you and your presentation more interesting, believable, engaging, and memorable. On the other hand, poorly answered questions can diminish your credibility. Q&As focus on "you" in every sense—just *you* speaking spontaneously with few or no prepared notes and little or no practice. Although this informality might make Q&A sessions seem like casual add-ons to a presentation, they require careful preparation and consideration. How you handle audience questions and objections can be as important as what you say in the rest of your presentation.

When and Why to Use Q&A Sessions

In addition to adding an engaging element to a presentation, Q&A sessions directly benefit both the audience and the speaker. For an audience, a Q&A session provides an opportunity to interact directly with the speaker, to hear what others in the audience are thinking, and to evaluate the speaker's **CREDIBILITY ▲ (74–81)** based on how well they respond to audience questions and concerns. For a speaker, a Q&A session offers a way to clear up misunderstandings, clarify your opinions, provide more examples, and overcome doubt and opposition using a more conversational and natural style of speaking.[1] A productive Q&A can help you shine! You can talk and move more naturally and with more confidence while answering questions than when giving a meticulously practiced presentation. You may even become less self-conscious as you focus on a specific listener with a specific question.

Q&A sessions are held at all kinds of **OCCASIONS ▲ (61–68)** and in all sorts of locations and settings—from classrooms to presidential press conferences. A Q&A might be held after a presentation, or it might be the entire presentation itself. You might invite questions at key points during your presentation or address relevant questions that you see in a chat box during an **ONLINE PRESENTATION ▶ (282–301)**. Generally, you can address questions *after* your presentation, *during* your presentation, or in a *standalone* Q&A presentation.

Q&As FOLLOWING A PRESENTATION

Most Q&A sessions occur at the end of a presentation. For example, a building developer might propose a new apartment building at a city council meeting—after which the developer's team takes questions from council members and the public. In this kind of Q&A session, your purpose is the same as the **PURPOSE ▲ (109–18)** of your presentation. This is your opportunity to share more information, overcome objections, clarify misunderstandings, define difficult terms, provide better explanations of **COMPLEX IDEAS ✳ (388–97)**, extend **PERSUASIVE ARGUMENTS ◆ (403–61)**, inspire an audience to action, and further enhance your credibility.

In these cases, make sure you allocate enough time for the Q&A. Depending on the reason, time, place, and urgency of an issue, a Q&A session can be as long as or longer than a presentation. Other occasions will dictate the length of the Q&A session. In either case, make sure to let your audience know that you'll be answering questions so they have time to prepare. During your introduction, you might say, "We'll have 15 minutes for Q&A, so please save your questions for the end." This allows your audience to jot down their questions—and will also deter them from interrupting your presentation.

Q&As DURING A PRESENTATION

Sometimes a speaker or organization will encourage audience members to ask questions *during* a presentation. For example, at the US Supreme Court, attorneys spend months prepping for a hearing, then get two minutes to speak about their legal arguments before being interrupted by a justice with questions. More commonly, an audience member may ask for clarification about an unfamiliar concept, claim, or source during your presentation.

Answering questions during a presentation has the potential to disrupt the flow of your arguments, distract your audience from your key points, or cause you to run out of time. But in some cases, especially if your presentation is very long or complex, inviting questions at key moments or after each key point can help you adapt to audience feedback, keep your listeners engaged, set a friendlier tone, or clarify a point. And in an **ONLINE PRESENTATION ▶ (282–301)** that uses a chat or Q&A feature, it's not uncommon to see questions as they arise while you're speaking. Whether face-to-face or online, answering questions during a presentation is particularly useful if you sense uncertainty or confusion—especially if other attendees chime in with similar or related questions.

When responding to questions during your presentation, it's important to keep your answers short so you can move on to your next point without losing too much momentum. If a question is running on too long or is off topic, you can always say, "Great question! I'll answer in more detail if we have time after the presentation."

STAND-ALONE Q&As

A stand-alone Q&A session can also be the focus of an entire presentation, for example, during legislative or legal testimony, at a crisis briefing, or when an athlete takes questions from the media after a sporting event. These kinds of Q&A sessions may be planned well in advance or occur on the spur of the moment to address an emergency or urgent issue.

If a Q&A session stands on its own, your purpose is to answer your audience's questions and address their concerns as directly, thoroughly, and concisely as possible and to enhance your credibility. As with any presentation, you should have several **KEY POINTS** ▌ **(153–56)** you'd like to cover, but instead of following an organizational pattern, try to anticipate the kinds of questions you will be asked and think about how you'll link them to the key points of the message you want to convey.

Q&A Strategies and Skills

Once you've decided to include a Q&A session, there is a great deal you can do to make it a substantive experience for both you and your audience. Facilitating a Q&A session that will engage an audience and generate a positive, lasting impression of your message involves several key strategies: *predicting questions, encouraging thoughtful questions, giving strategic answers, adapting your delivery, listening actively and respectfully,* and *concluding impressively.*

PREDICTING QUESTIONS

Create a list of possible questions that might arise during or after your presentation. If you've spoken or answered questions about your topic several times already, what were some of the common questions? If you initially find it difficult to predict questions, and if allowed for your speaking situaiton, you can try prompting **GENERATIVE AI** ● **(50–55)** to help. As with any time you use generative AI to brainstorm, be specific and include details about your occasion, audience, topic, and purpose. You can even include your key points in your prompt. Here's just one example of a prompt you might use:

> I'm delivering an [informative/persuasive/celebratory] presentation on [topic] to an audience that [audience values, beliefs, and atti-tudes]. My purpose is to [purpose statement]. I'm going to give you a list of the key points and supporting material for my presentation. Please provide a list of questions from audience members who may agree with my claims and a list of questions from audience members who may disagree with my claims.

In addition to helping you prepare for possible questions from your audience, this kind of activity can reveal an important issue you haven't planned to address in your presentation, allowing you to adjust your key points accordingly.

ENCOURAGING THOUGHTFUL QUESTIONS

Just as a speaker is responsible for answering audience questions competently and honestly, audience members are responsible for the quality and relevance of the questions they ask. But what do you do if no one asks a question? Should you say, "Great!" and then sprint off the stage? No! You can use a variety of techniques to prompt audience members to ask worthwhile questions:

- *Avoid "Are there any questions?"* Those who don't have a question in mind may just sit there. Instead, ask "What are your questions?" or "Who has the first question?"

- *Take a breath.* If no one poses a question right away, pause and wait. It may feel uncomfortable—even a five-second pause can seem like five minutes—but think about this challenge from the audience's perspective. Just as you may need a moment to organize your thoughts for an answer, audience members will need time to frame their questions.

- *Pose a reverse question.* Instead of waiting for questions, ask the audience to share their views about what you've said. For example, you might ask an engaged audience member, "For you, what was the key takeaway from this session?"[2] When you ask these kinds of questions, you're seeking valuable feedback that can help you clarify, defend, repeat, or amplify what you've said.

- *Offer your own questions.* If after a significant amount of time has passed you still don't get any questions, offer some of your own: "One of the questions I often hear after my presentation is . . ." or "If I were in the audience, I'd want to know . . ."

- *Thank commendable questioners.* If an audience member asks an insightful question or something that effectively supports your purpose, you can thank them and then demonstrate their question's value in your response. This can encourage similar questions from other audience members. But don't say "good question" to everyone who asks a question—savvy audience members will know that your compliments are not sincere.

GIVING STRATEGIC ANSWERS

If we were to offer only one piece of advice about Q&A sessions it would be this: Answer the questions.

Although this advice may seem obvious, many of us have witnessed speakers avoid answering a question or change the subject in their answer. Your audience will notice if you evade the question, give a fake answer, or change the subject. It helps to anticipate and prepare for a variety of questions with the same care as the rest of your presentation. Here are some strategies to guide you:

- *Prepare likely answers.* Once you predict some likely questions, be prepared to answer them strategically. Use your central idea and key points as the basis for responses that will resonate most with your audience. **PRACTICE ▶ (220-24)** these answers alone or to a friend.

- *Prepare and share additional supporting material.* When you get a question and don't want to repeat what you've said in your presentation, you can share new information and **SUPPORTING MATERIALS ■ (135-39)** with ease if you have prepared for it in advance.[3] Develop a back-up list of facts, statistics, testimony, definitions, analogies, examples, and stories. Some presenters even create an index of **SLIDES ▶ (272-77)** with more detailed data to reference during Q&A.

- *Think before you speak.* In some cases you may want to respond immediately to a question, particularly if it is urgent or easy to answer. But unless you believe an instant response is appropriate, pause and reflect before answering. Audience members respect speakers who give visible, thoughtful consideration to their questions. Pausing also gives you time to think and develop a response—much as you would in an **IMPROMPTU SPEECH ★ (465–71)**.

- *Keep it short.* Unless the question is highly technical and demands a long response, your answers should be clear, brief, accurate, and truthful.

ADAPTING YOUR DELIVERY

The four qualities of **DELIVERY ▶ (209–301)**—expressiveness, confidence, stage presence, and immediacy—are just as important in a Q&A session. Your audience may even expect you to be *more* relaxed, authentic, and accessible during the Q&A. Generally, we've noticed when students answer questions immediately after a graded presentation, the speaking style they use to answer questions is more like that of their audience, and less like that of a formal speaker. This more conversational delivery can enhance your credibility and can leave audience members with an even more positive impression of you and your message.

On the other hand, looking bored, annoyed, or impatient or responding with condescension during a Q&A session sends a negative message. If the questioner or audience senses your negativity, your credibility may decrease. Remember, you are continuously making an impression as you listen. Establish and maintain full eye contact, smile, and lean or look toward the questioner.

LISTENING ACTIVELY AND RESPECTFULLY

Speakers and audience members should use their **LISTENING SKILLS ● (32–33)** to make sure they fully understand the meaning, purpose, and context of each question and answer. Both parties should consider whether questions and answers are clear or confusing, supportive or antagonistic, personal or impersonal. They also should "listen" to the questioner's and speaker's **NONVERBAL MESSAGES ● (35)** to accurately interpret the intended meaning of questions and answers.

Most questioners are well-meanng people seeking answers to genuine questions. Even if they don't phrase their questions well, you will sense what they want to know and can delicately answer their underlying concern. As you facilitate Q&A, listen actively and respectfully to questions posed by the audience:

- **Don't embarrass a questioner.** Most people don't ask questions they know to be stupid, even if they preface it with a statement like "This may be dumb, but . . ." Always begin by assuming their question is sincere, and do your best to answer it with the same seriousness as any other question, even if you think the answer is obvious. Your audience will appreciate your generosity.

- **Assist a nervous questioner.** Like speakers, audience members can experience **SPEECH ANXIETY ● (18–26)** when they ask questions. Help them through their nerve-wracking moment in the spotlight. Give them time to formulate their question. Encourage, praise, and thank them.

- **Help a questioner stay focused.** An overexcited questioner may end up giving a speech rather than asking a question. If this happens, try to interrupt politely and ask, "What's your question?" If they keep going, you may run out of time in your Q&A. Let the well-meaning but long-winded questioner know that your time is limited and that, in fairness, you want to give everyone in the room a chance to raise questions.

- **Clarify the ambiguous question.** Sometimes you may not be sure what exactly the questioner is asking. Rather than guessing and perhaps offering a nonresponsive answer, ask the questioner to clarify: "Help me understand . . ." "Tell me more . . ." or "Can you give me an example of . . ." After answering, you may want to check to ensure you answered the question.

- **Repeat or rephrase the question.** This helps all audience members hear the questions before you answer it, and it can make the question easier to answer if you put it in your own words. You may also be able to replace negative phrases with positive or neutral ones. For example, instead of repeating "Why does our PR office do such a lousy job of publicizing our achievements?" you could paraphrase the question as "What can our PR office do to better publicize our achievements?"

- *Anticipate follow-up questions.* In some cases, an audience member will ask you a follow-up question based on your answer to another question ("If what you say is true, then why . . ."). If you listen actively, you can anticipate and answer follow-up questions well. But don't let follow-ups become a conversation between you and one questioner. After or instead of answering the follow-up, you can invite the questioner to talk to you later and indicate that you want to give time for other audience members to ask questions.

CONCLUDING IMPRESSIVELY

Once an audience member asks the first question, you may find yourself with an overwhelming number of questions and not enough time to answer them. As you near the end of your allotted time or want to bring the questioning to an end, say, "I have time for two more questions." Then do just that. Answer two more questions and thank the audience for their participation.

Prepare a memorized or well-practiced conclusion to use when it's time to bring the Q&A to a close. Saying "thank you" is polite, but it's not a very memorable ending. Instead, return to your **CENTRAL IDEA** ▉ **(156–57)**, make references to the **CONCLUSION** ▉ **(198–203)** of your presentation, or talk about the future. Be prepared to share a memorable quotation or **STORY** ⸫ **(323–32)**. You could also refer to some of the audience's questions and how they helped emphasize the importance of your message. Even with a short concluding statement you can neatly and professionally wrap things up. If necessary or convenient, you may want to ask audience members to continue the conversation in another location or share your contact information to continue the conversation online. In this way, other audience members can ask their questions after you've cleared the stage or room for other speakers and activities.

Handling Hostile Questions

Because Q&A sessions open up the floor to any audience member with a question, you may encounter someone who does not represent the attitudes, knowledge, traits, or values of the audience as a whole.

Some questioners may be grandstanding or "trolling"—asking questions to attract attention, show off the expertise or power to the speaker, or impress other audience members.

Most audience members have little patience with such self-centered questioners. If you have **ANALYZED YOUR AUDIENCE ▲ (90–96)** and have a clear sense of the characteristics, attitudes, values, and needs of the majority of your listeners, you can get your Q&A back on track by briefly responding and then appealing to your audience for support. After answering the question, for example, you might shift the spotlight by pivoting to the rest of the audience with a question that begins, "How many of you agree . . . ?" This allows you to politely maintain control of the conversation while welcoming new questions—and possible disagreement—from other listeners.

Depending on your topic and the people in your audience, you may also be faced with one or more openly hostile questions. If this happens, don't panic. Even when an audience doesn't agree with what you've said, they will usually be sympathetic—and may become your best allies—if another audience member starts to harass you.

Here are some ways to deal with a hostile question from an antagonistic audience member:

- *Listen carefully, and don't strike back.* The last thing you want is to get drawn into an argument with one person. Taking a few seconds to think can help you stay calm and avoid an embarrassing response. Hostile questioners are trying to provoke you. Don't let them. Be diplomatic and keep your cool. Audience members may become just as tired of listening to a combative harangue as you are. When a questioner is being abusive, offensive, or threatening, don't allow them time for a follow-up but instead suggest they talk to you after the presentation. Then quickly move on to the next person who has a question.

- *Start with agreement.* Look for **COMMON GROUND ▲ (89)** and build your answer from there. For example: "Then we both agree customers are waiting much too long in line with their purchases. We just differ on how to speed up the checkout process." In addition, use fair and respected **EVIDENCE ◆ (425–26)** to support your answer.

It's important to accept differences of opinion while remaining true to your purpose. Work to build personal credibility and treat your audience with respect and by answering their questions as specifically as you can.

Asking Appropriate Q&A Questions

Thus far we've mostly discussed Q&A sessions from the speaker's perspective. But what about when you're in the audience? Just as a speaker is responsible for answering audience questions respectfully, honestly, and competently, audience members are responsible for the quality and relevance of the questions they ask. Before you ask a question or raise an objection, stop and ask yourself, "Why do I want to know this?" And "What will my question accomplish?" Then consider the fundamental elements of the rhetorical situation:

- Is this an appropriate question for this occasion?
- Am I a credible speaker?
- Will the audience appreciate my question?
- What's my purpose for asking a question?
- How does my question relate to the content of this presentation?
- How should I deliver my question?

You might ask questions out of confusion, perhaps because the speaker did not convey a key point clearly. You might ask questions because you think the speaker left out something important that the rest of the audience might benefit from. You might even feel an **ETHICAL** ● **(43–57)** need to point out an error or to question the speaker's claims. Whatever your motivation, here are some prompts that can help you ask a useful question:[4]

- Could you expand or further explain what you mean by . . . ?
- Here's how I'd summarize what you said . . . Is that correct? Have I misunderstood the point you're trying to make?
- I understand your views, but also know most scientific studies disagree with your perspective. How would you respond to research that says . . . ?

- The study you quoted used only university students (or only men, or wealthy people, or a small number of people) as subjects. Do your findings apply beyond that group?

- What evidence did you rely on to make your claims about . . . ? What's the source of your evidence? How does your evidence prove your point?

- What's the big picture here? How do your conclusions apply to other situations, such as . . . ?

Once you've finished your question, listen to the speaker's answer respectfully. If you have a follow-up question, keep it brief. And if you notice a lot of other audience members raising their hands, you may choose instead to give them a chance to speak to avoid monopolizing everyone's attention.

Conclusion

Depending on the rhetorical situation, there are significant advantages to adding a question-and-answer session to your presentation. The vast majority of Q&As change the nature of your relationships with your audience. As speakers, we "sometimes forget that the point of the presentation isn't to let us talk. It is to create an exchange of views and information. Q&A sessions transform the presentation from an empty exercise in lecturing to a real and fruitful learning experience."[5]

With the right preparation and practice, a Q&A session can be an invaluable addition to any presentation. Given enough notice, your audience may surprise you with how thoughtful and attentive they are with questions that enhance your message. If you're gracious, respectful, and organized as the speaker, the Q&A might even be the most effective part of your presentation! And if you're a member of the audience, keep your questions purposeful, fair, and clear so that the answer can serve the needs and interests of the audience as a whole.

PART 6
Speaking to Inform

Informative presentations come in many different forms: a corporate briefing, a convention presentation, a campus tour, a how-to video, an oral report, or a college lecture, to name a few. Over the course of your life, informative speaking will be the most common type of presentation speaking you will be asked to do. The chapters that follow provide helpful guidance about how you can enhance audience comprehension and skills when **REPORTING NEW INFORMATION** and **EXPLAINING COMPLEX IDEAS**.

Speaking to Inform

6.1 Understanding Informative Speaking

The volume of human knowledge is doubling every year.[1] As speakers, we have more access to more information than ever before—and that trend will continue throughout our lives. As a result, many of us experience information overload, which occurs when we're faced with so much information that it becomes challenging to process and use all of it to make decisions.[2] How do we sort through so much information, let alone decide what's important and how to report or explain what we've learned to other people? Welcome to the increasingly complex challenge of informative speaking! In this and the following chapters, we'll help you understand and apply the strategies and skills needed to create and deliver effective and memorable informative presentations.

An informative presentation is both efficient and effective when it gains and maintains audience attention, is well organized and well rehearsed, uses a variety of supporting material, is delivered expressively and confidently, and encourages audience involvement. But what exactly *is* an informative presentation?

What Is an Informative Presentation?

Informative presentations provide new information, explain complex concepts and processes, and/or clarify and correct misunderstood information. They do so by instructing, defining, enlightening, describing, reminding, and demonstrating. You will prepare and deliver many informative presentations throughout your life, so learning how to do them well will give you a competitive edge. Consider the following examples that identify the **SPEAKER** ▲ **(61–68)**, **OCCASION** ▲ **(72–85)**, **AUDIENCE** ▲ **(88–105)**, and **TOPIC** ■ **(125–33)** of four different informative presentations:

- A college student orally summarizes the purpose, methodology, and results of a research project to their instructor and peers in a science class.

- A charge nurse explains the policies and procedures for tracking patient medications to a group of newly hired nursing assistants.

- An experienced landscaper talks at a homeowners' association meeting about the various native plants that grow best in the local climate.

- The assistant vice president of a bank gives a tour to a group of elementary-school children.

As you can see, informative presentations can address a wide range of topics. But regardless of whether you're speaking to third graders in a classroom or CEOs attending a seminar, effective informative presentations help audience members understand and remember something of value.

At first, it may be difficult to determine where an informative presentation ends, and a **PERSUASIVE PRESENTATION** ◆ **(437–56)** begins. Most informative presentations contain an element of persuasion. Explaining the scientific causes of climate change might convince an audience that we need stricter laws regulating fossil fuel production and use. Demonstrating the proper way to change a tire could persuade listeners not to call the nearest garage because the task may not be as difficult as they once thought. Conversely, persuasive presentations have informative content. If you are trying to persuade people to eat healthier food, you will need to include factual information. There is, however, a clear dividing line between informative and persuasive presentations: your **PURPOSE** ▲ **(109–18)**. When you ask listeners to change their opinions or behavior, your speech becomes persuasive.

Informative Speaking Guidelines

Informative presentations often require a concerted effort to **ENGAGE YOUR AUDIENCE ∴ (303–61)**. In a communication class, students may have the opportunity to choose exciting topics, but most informative speakers don't have this advantage. Imagine, for example, the challenge facing a social psychology researcher who must explain how to analyze statistical methods or a human resources administrator who must compare the features of the health insurance policies offered by a company to new employees.

Given the pervasiveness of informative presentations, you've certainly encountered them in a variety of contexts. You may have vivid and long-lasting memories of some of them and absolutely no recollection of others. What made the memorable speeches exceptional? Generally, the most impressive informative presentations

- Include a value step
- Avoid information overload
- Employ sensory images

INCLUDE A VALUE STEP

Just because *you* love bluegrass music, photography, or bicycling doesn't mean listeners will share your enthusiasm. In most informative presentations, you *know* more and *care* more about your topic than your audience does. But if there's a good reason for you to make a presentation, there should be a good reason for your audience to listen. Don't rely on the audience to figure it out, though. Tell them by including a value step.

A **value step** explains why your message should matter to your audience and how it can affect their well-being and success. Incorporating a value step in the **INTRODUCTION ■ (191–98)** of your informative presentation gives them a reason to look forward to what comes next. Though not necessary for every speaking occasion, the inclusion of a value step at the beginning of a presentation can motivate disinterested audience members to listen. You might refer to the setting or emphasize the reason your audience is assembled. You could mention how a recent event has affected them in the past or will affect them in the future. Or you could involve them by asking questions or telling a **STORY ∴ (323–32)** about people who are like them.

Note how the following speaker uses a value step to motivate her audience to listen to a presentation about new rules in a staff evaluation plan, a potentially dull topic:

> Last year one of your coworkers was denied a promotion. She was well qualified—better than most applicants. She received the highest recommendations. But she wasn't promoted. She didn't get her well-deserved raise. Why? Because she didn't read the new rules in the staff evaluation plan and missed the revised deadlines. When it was time to give out promotions, her application wasn't in the pool of candidates. Today I'll explain key sections of that plan so that this doesn't happen to you.

Effective speakers ask themselves, "How will audience members benefit from listening to this presentation?" In other words, "What's in it for them?" or **WIIFT ▲ (93)**. Make a list of the ways the information you plan to share will be useful to your listeners. Ask yourself whether your presentation provides any of the following benefits:

- **Social benefits.** Will you describe strategies and skills for interacting with others more effectively in order to develop strong relationships, become more popular, resolve interpersonal problems, or even throw a great party?

- **Communal benefits.** Will your presentation serve your community, colleagues, friends, and family in a way that will improve the quality of their lives, work, or play?

- **Physical benefits.** Will you offer advice about improving the audience's physical health, tips on treating common ailments, or expert recommendations on diet and exercise?

- **Psychological benefits.** Will you explain common and interesting psychological topics, such as the causes and treatment of stress, depression, and anxiety, or will you provide descriptions of interesting—even seemingly bizarre—psychological disabilities? Will your presentation help audience members feel better about themselves?

- **Intellectual benefits.** Will you help your audience learn difficult concepts or explain intriguing and novel discoveries in science? Will you demonstrate the value of intellectual curiosity and creativity?

- *Economic benefits.* Will you show your audience how to make or save money? Will you explain or clarify monetary and economic concepts? Does your presentation offer advice about employment opportunities?

- *Professional benefits.* Will you demonstrate ways that audience members can succeed and prosper in a career field or profession? Will you provide expert instruction on mastering professional strategies and skills?

This list is not comprehensive, nor is it meant to prevent you from choosing more than one benefit. For example, an informative presentation on designing **DIGITAL SLIDES ▶ (272–77)** could have social, communal, and professional benefits for your audience.

Note how the following two examples identify several reasons that audience members may be motivated to listen to and remember what you say about the selected topic area:

Topic	Possible value steps
Combating fire ants	• Prevents painful, dangerous stings (*physical*)
	• Preserves gardens (*economic*)
	• Protects pets and local wildlife (*communal*)
Reading music	• Helps you become a better musician or more appreciative audience member (*professional and psychological*)
	• Helps you understand the complexity of musical compositions (*intellectual*)
	• Helps you talk about music with other music lovers (*social*)

By offering value steps early in your presentation and employing a variety of methods to **ENGAGE YOUR AUDIENCE ⁖(303–61)** throughout, you can turn a simple informative talk into a thought-provoking and memorable presentation.

AVOID INFORMATION OVERLOAD

As we mentioned at the beginning of this chapter, it's easy to feel overwhelmed by the quantity of information we receive, even if the information itself is clear and understandable. **Information overload**—the stress that occurs when you try to process, understand, and remember everything you hear and see—makes it difficult to sort what's useful from what's useless and to distinguish **VALID SOURCES** ■ **(143–47)** from misinformation.

As much as you may want to share everything you know about a subject, remember that information overload is also a major reason why audiences stop listening. *Less* information can mean *more* comprehension. If you carefully choose and edit the information you share, listeners are more likely to remember your message. Regardless of whether you deliver a 50-minute lecture or a 3-minute briefing, be courageous—offer your audience less so they will remember and get more out of your presentation. How do you do this? Narrow the scope of your purpose and topic.

Make sure your **PURPOSE STATEMENT** ▲ **(115–17)** is specific, achievable, and relevant. A tightly focused purpose statement can help you avoid the mistake of trying to cover too much material or asking too much of your audience. Consider the following exchange between a speaker and a listener:

> **LISTENER:** I heard your presentation on the new employee evaluation plan.
>
> **SPEAKER:** What do you remember about what I said?
>
> **LISTENER:** Well, you went through the plan page by page, explaining how the new provisions would apply.
>
> **SPEAKER:** What was one of the new provisions?
>
> **LISTENER:** Well . . . there was something about new forms to be filed with human resources, I think. I don't know—I'll look it up when I have to use it.

Exactly. The listener will look it up. The speaker's purpose—explaining the whole plan—was much too ambitious for a single presentation. Audience members are intelligent, but they won't remember everything you say.

How could this speaker simplify her presentation? First, she should make sure that all employees already have a copy of the evaluation plan.

She could then choose the essential elements to focus on during the presentation, knowing that the audience will be able to **ASK QUESTIONS ⸫ (350–61)** or look up the information later, if necessary. She might explain the differences between the new and old plans, or she could display the new forms employees must submit, along with their respective deadlines.

Perhaps the easiest way to avoid information overload is to remember two phrases: "Keep it simple, speaker" (KISS) and the **RULE OF THREE ▪ (155–56)**. Ask yourself if everything you plan to say is vital. If not, throw it out. Concentrate on no more than 3 (not 10!) important details. As tempting as it may be to tell a funny but irrelevant story or include a beautiful but distracting presentation aid, don't do it. Keep asking yourself whether your **KEY POINTS ▪ (153–56)** and **SUPPORTING MATERIAL ▪ (135–39)** directly support and advance a specific, achievable, and relevant purpose. KISS!

USE SENSORY IMAGES TO NARROW YOUR TOPIC

What does the topic "ice hockey" make you think of? Fights, penalty boxes, screaming fans, chaos on ice, and body checks? Could one informative presentation incorporate all these images? It's possible, but multiple subtopics may not get the time and attention they deserve. Similarly, a topic like "the wonders of herbal medicines" can conjure up an apothecary full of ingredients. "Chamomile," on the other hand, is easier to imagine—a strongly scented herb with tiny yellow blossoms.

Effective speakers make informative presentations more memorable by **USING LANGUAGE ⸫ (305–22)** and incorporating supporting material that evokes a sensory experience based on sight, sound, taste, smell, and/or touch. You can also use sensory images to **NARROW YOUR TOPIC ▪ (130–31)** and focus on an angle that will be specific and interesting. When one of our students chose garlic as the subject of his informative presentation, he was overwhelmed with information after completing his initial research, so he narrowed his topic to garlic's powerful odor and ways to get rid of it.

Looking for sensory images takes some creative thinking. If you plan to make a presentation about chocolate chip cookies, for example, you could begin by thinking about how to apply each of the five senses to your topic, then consider an informative presentation related to just one or—if you have the time—two senses:

Sense	Sense + Topic	Possible presentation topic
Sight	A tan cookie with visible dark chips	The science behind sugar caramelization
Sound	A cookie that snaps when broken	What makes store-bought cookies so crunchy
Taste	A sweet cookie with bitter chocolate	The tastes of different chocolates
Smell	The smell of cookies during and after baking	The history of using vanilla in baking
Touch	A cookie that can be chewy or crispy	How different sugars affect the texture of cookies

No matter your topic—whether it's advice for buying a new car, demonstrating how soap cleans, or explaining the Confederate loss at the Battle of Gettysburg—consider using sensory images to create a vivid, specific, and memorable informative presentation. You might be surprised by what you come up with.

Two Types of Informative Presentations

Many speakers believe that effective informative presentations require only a clear **PURPOSE ▲ (109–18)**, interesting information, and a logical **ORGANIZATIONAL PATTERN ■ (157–66)**. Certainly, these elements are essential. Even so, informative speaking also requires a sound strategy that matches your informative purpose and content to **AUDIENCE CHARACTERISTICS ▲ (90–96)**, interests, attitudes, and needs. In other words, you must look for, carefully analyze, and then choose the most appropriate methods for achieving your informative purpose in a particular rhetorical situation.

In her **theory of informative communication**, communication scholar Katherine Rowan explains how to make strategic decisions about the content and structure of an informative presentation. Her two-part theory focuses on the differences between informative presentations that report new information and those that explain complex ideas.[3]

When you **report new information**, your purpose is to create or increase audience awareness about an object, person, event, or procedure. Much like responsible news reporting, you are presenting accurate, interesting, and up-to-date information about a topic. Informative presentations that report new information answer the question "What did I learn?" or "What do I know now that I didn't before the speech?"

When you **explain complex ideas**, your purpose is to enhance or deepen audience understanding about a difficult term, a complex phenomenon, or a frequently misunderstood idea or concept. In addition to explaining *how* and *why*, good explanatory presentations also address the question "What does that mean?"[4]

For example, telling a group of new 10-speed bicycle owners how to shift gears more efficiently and effectively reports new information. Describing how the gears are constructed or why bicycles stay upright when a rider pedals at a particular speed requires a speaker to explain a complex idea. A presentation describing the origins of the Rosh Hashanah holiday to a non-Jewish audience is an example of reporting new information. But a talk clarifying *why* Rosh Hashanah is considered a High Holy Day is an example of explaining a more complex set of ideas. The following table provides additional examples of these two types of informative goals:

TYPES OF INFORMATIVE PRESENTATIONS

REPORTING NEW INFORMATION AND EXPLAINING COMPLEX IDEAS	
Goal: To report new information	**Goal: To explain complex ideas**
• How to make a chocolate cake	• The principles of baking
• A brief history of the Denver International Airport	• The architectural requirements of modern airports
• A report about a city council meeting	• An in-depth analysis of a proposed bill
• Local baseball trivia	• The role of baseball statistics on game-day strategy
• A short biography of Charles Darwin	• A description of natural selection

Effective informative speakers understand when they need to report new information and when they need to explain more complicated or misunderstood concepts and processes. Not surprisingly, different types of informative messages have different purposes and require different communication strategies. In the next two chapters, we examine Rowan's strategies and advice for developing each type of informative presentation.

Conclusion

The foundational elements of the rhetorical situation—occasion, speaker, audience, purpose, content, and delivery—are essential for every informative speech. First and foremost, effective informative speakers must know *why* they are speaking. They focus on their purpose as they research, prepare, and deliver their presentation.

Three important guidelines can improve the quality of your informative presentation and merit a positive response from your audience. Put a value step near the beginning of your presentation that identifies the ways that listeners can benefit from your talk; minimize information overload; and use sensory images to both narrow your topic and make your presentation more memorable.

As you think critically about the purpose of your informative presentation, make sure you know whether you will be reporting new information or explaining a complex idea. That determination will help you select effective informative strategies, strong supporting material, an appropriate organizational pattern, and, if needed, presentation aids to ensure that your presentation is as effective and engaging as possible.

6.2 Reporting New Information

A BRIEF GUIDE TO THIS CHAPTER

- **Strategies for reporting new information** (p. 375)
- **Informing about objects** (p. 376)
- **Informing about people** (p. 377)
- **Informing about events** (p. 378)
- **Informing about procedures** (p. 379)

Reporting new information is what journalists do when they answer the questions *who, what, where, when, why*, and *how*. They write about *who* is doing *what* to *whom*, as well as *where* and *when* an event occurred. They also report *how* or *why* something happened without explaining complex or difficult-to-understand details. New information is shared through newspapers, magazines, television networks, social media, books, and other sources.

Presentations that report new information have a similar focus. Speakers try to increase audience awareness about a topic by reporting accurate and up-to-date facts. They also report new information when giving instructions or demonstrating how to perform a task. At first, this kind of informative presentation may seem easy to prepare and deliver. Yet depending on the rhetorical situation—occasion, speaker, audience, purpose, content, and delivery—reporting new information can be as demanding as any other type of presentation.

Strategies for Reporting New Information

You face two major challenges when reporting new information. First, if your information is *very* new, an audience may have trouble grasping your key points. Second, they may need a reason to listen, learn, and remember.

Fortunately, we can turn to Katherine Rowan's theory of informative communication, in which she recommends four strategies for sharing new information with an audience:[1]

- *Include a value step in the introduction.* Tell audience members why this new information is important and beneficial to them.

- *Use a clear organizational pattern.* Provide an organizational structure that helps audience members understand and remember what you say.

- *Use multiple types of supporting material.* Use facts, statistics, testimonies, definitions, analogies, descriptions, examples, and/or stories.

- *Relate the information to audience interests and needs throughout the presentation.* If audience members see no reason to learn the information, they are likely to stop listening.

Presentations reporting new information differ from one another based on the choices you make when applying these four strategies. Two speakers can give very different informative presentations about the same subject, depending on the **VALUE STEP** ❋ **(367–69)**, how the content is **ORGANIZED** ■ **(152–70)**, the types of **SUPPORTING MATERIAL** ■ **(135–39)** used, and the prior knowledge and needs of the audience. To get a better understanding of this process, let's examine how to develop a presentation that reports new information about *objects*, *people*, *events*, and/or *procedures*. Notice how each outline—regardless of the topic area—includes a purpose, central idea, value step, organizational pattern, and related key points.

Informing about Objects

Students in communication classes often choose objects, such as a valuable coin or a reliable bicycle model, as the topic area of their informative presentations. After all, an object is tangible—it can be described, perceived by one or more of our **FIVE SENSES** ❋ **(371–72)**, and even brought to class and used as a **PRESENTATION AID** ▶ **(260–78)**. Objects can also include living things, such as fire ants or the invasive kudzu plant.

Informing about objects, however, can be challenging because an object is not by itself a purpose statement or central idea. Valuable coins or kudzu may spark your interest, but neither is enough to generate an informative presentation on its own. When developing an informative presentation about objects, focus on your **PURPOSE ▲ (109–18)** and **AUDIENCE ANALYSIS ▲ (90–96)**. Consider the following sample outline:

TOPIC AREA:	Fire ants
PURPOSE:	To familiarize audience members with the external anatomy of a fire ant
CENTRAL IDEA:	A tour of the fire ant's external anatomy will help the audience understand why these ants are so invasive and hard to exterminate.
VALUE STEP:	In addition to inflicting painful, sometimes deadly stings, fire ants can eat up gardens, damage homes, and harm pets and local wildlife.
ORGANIZATION:	**SPACE ARRANGEMENT ■ (159)** —a visual tour of the fire ant's external anatomy
KEY POINTS:	A. Integument (exoskeleton)
	B. Head and its components
	C. Thorax
	D. Abdomen

The above outline is just one of many possible ways to report new information about fire ants. If you had a different purpose—for example, familiarizing audience members with various methods for exterminating fire ants—you would need a different central idea, value step, organization, and set of key points.

Informing about People

Reporting new information about people is similar in many ways to giving presentations about objects. Like an object, people are tangible—in this case, flesh-and-blood personalities. You can focus on a historical or literary figure, a famous living individual, or someone you know. Regardless of whom you select, describe that person's life and accomplishments to tap audience interests and emotions, making sure that your purpose, central idea, value step, organizational pattern, and key points are a good match. If the person is well known, look for new, intriguing information to keep your audience engaged. If they aren't well known, think about how to describe them in such a way that will be most relevant to your audience. Consider how a presentation about Beyoncé or Thomas Edison, for example, would differ from a presentation about a noteworthy friend, a family member, or a little-known hero, writer, or artist.

The following outline includes a value step and key points that make the topic of early female blues singers relevant and interesting to audience members:

TOPIC AREA: Early female blues singers

PURPOSE: To demonstrate how three female blues singers of the 1920s have influenced popular musicians in later eras

CENTRAL IDEA: In the 1920s, Sippie Wallace, Bessie Smith, and Gertrude "Ma" Rainey paved the way for other female blues singers.

VALUE STEP: If you call yourself an honest-to-goodness blues and rock-and-roll fan, you should know more about the major contributions made by early female blues singers.

ORGANIZATION: **STORIES AND EXAMPLES ARRANGEMENT** ■ **(162–63)** —brief, interesting biographies of each blues singer supported with audio examples

KEY POINTS: A. Sippie Wallace

                    B. Bessie Smith

                    C. Gertrude "Ma" Rainey

Informing about Events

As you do with objects and people, you can report new information about historical or current events. History professors often center their lectures on important moments from the past. Politicians often speak to commemorate an event, such as the opening of a new museum. Business executives may review the company's founding to trace its evolving mission.

An event can be a single incident, such as an athlete winning an Olympic gold medal or the dedication of a new high school. An event can also be a series of incidents (for example, the events leading to the end of the Cold War), an annual holiday celebrated over the course of several days or weeks (for example, Kwanzaa, Ramadan), or milestones that became historic (for example, the race to the moon, the evolution of Title IX). Regardless of the event's date, size, or significance, the purpose of your presentation determines how you will talk about it.

The following example outlines a way of reporting new information to a non-Indian audience in an informative presentation about Diwali, an important holiday in India:

TOPIC AREA: Diwali

PURPOSE: To familiarize audience members with a significant holiday in India

CENTRAL IDEA: Most Hindus, Jains, Buddhists, and Sikhs in India observe Diwali as a family-centered national festival that celebrates universal values.

VALUE STEP: Learning more about one of India's major national holidays can help listeners understand that country's rich culture, its focus on family values, and how those fundamental factors affect US-Indian relations.

ORGANIZATION: **CATEGORICAL ARRANGEMENT** ■ **(157–58)** —the features of an unfamiliar holiday supported with visual images

KEY POINTS: A. Origins of Diwali

B. Meaning of Diwali

C. The five days of Diwali

Informing about Procedures

A procedure is a method or series of actions for doing something, usually in a specific order or manner. You can describe how to throw a curve ball, adjust a digital camera to maximize clarity and color, make a paper airplane, bake bread, ride a unicycle, play a bagpipe, or do CPR. In many rhetorical situations, audience members will not be able to throw a curve ball or play a bagpipe when you've finished, but they will better understand how it's done.

Informing an audience about a procedure focuses on *how* to do something rather than *why*. Changing a tire, assuming a basic yoga pose, and sewing on a button may not be difficult, but there are accepted steps for doing each of them well. For this reason, it often works well to use a time arrangement to organize such a presentation. Consider the following example about cooking hard-boiled eggs.

TOPIC AREA: Cooking hard-boiled eggs

PURPOSE: To teach listeners how to make foolproof hard-boiled eggs

CENTRAL IDEA: There are four steps to cooking perfect hard-boiled eggs.

VALUE STEP: To avoid wasting eggs that have cracked while cooking, follow the proper procedure for perfect hard-boiled eggs.

ORGANIZATION: **TIME ARRANGEMENT** ■ **(158)** —step-by-step instructions

KEY POINTS: A. Place eggs in cold water and bring to a boil.

B. Remove from the heat.

C. Let stand for 20 minutes.

D. Rinse in cold water.

Many athletic coaches, physicians, and business trainers share a seemingly simple method for teaching a procedure, the **tell-show-do** technique:

1. *Tell:* Verbally describe how to do a procedure.

2. *Show:* Physically demonstrate how to do a procedure.

3. *Do:* Ask audience members to do the procedure on their own with supervision.

Depending on the rhetorical situation, you may use one or more of these three approaches to achieve your purpose. For example, if you want to increase audience awareness about the viola, you *tell* listeners how it is played and how it differs from other string instruments. Then, if appropriate, you can *show* them by playing a short piece of music so they can hear what it sounds like. Or you could do the reverse (show-tell), first playing the viola and then sharing facts about its history, characteristics, and techniques. However, unless you are training a group of viola players, you would not let them *do* it because they would probably produce a horrible, screechy sound and might even damage your instrument.

TELL: DESCRIBE THE PROCEDURE

Every informative presentation about a procedure requires telling. Regardless of the topic, you may start by identifying the key steps of the process in their correct order. For example, anyone who has tried to cook a hard-boiled egg knows that following the right steps makes the difference between a perfect, uncracked hard-boiled egg and a mess of white albumen floating around in a pot of hot water.

Describing how to make foolproof hard-boiled eggs does not require a physical demonstration. It's a fairly simple procedure that can be described and, if needed, illustrated with a **DIGITAL SLIDE ▶ (272–77)** that shows each step in the process.

SHOW: DEMONSTRATE THE PROCEDURE

Telling audience members about a procedure may not cover—or even need to cover—every step in a process. *Showing* them how to do something requires a display of the details. This common type of presentation is called a demonstration speech. In a **demonstration speech**, your goal is to teach the audience how to do a procedure by physically presenting a series of essential steps with verbal instruction. Many people turn to YouTube when learning a skill—all these videos are demonstration speeches.

Demonstration speeches have two interdependent components: verbal instructions and a physical performance. In some cases, you may use presentation aids to illustrate the demonstration as you speak. Regardless of whether you are showing audience members how to use a new GPS system or how to assume a half-cobra yoga pose, you can accompany your demonstration with descriptions of how each step leads to a desired outcome.

When preparing a demonstration, make sure you can answer the following questions:[2]

- *Purpose.* Do you want your audience to understand how the procedure is done or be able to actually do it after viewing your presentation? Is the goal achievable?
- *Prerequisites.* What knowledge, skills, and materials do you need? What does the audience already know, and how can you build on that knowledge?
- *Action.* What steps or actions are needed to demonstrate the procedure?
- *Cautions and warnings.* What should you avoid, and what can go wrong? How can you fix it or solve any problems during the presentation?

Because demonstrations combine verbal instructions and a physical presentation, it's important to focus your audience's attention. The following guidelines can help:

- *Start with* why. Share your purpose and a **VALUE STEP ❋ (367–69)** during your introduction. State exactly *what* you want your audience to learn, as well as *why* and *how* this knowledge can benefit them.
- *Speak without notes.* Unless the demonstration is highly technical, try to speak **EXTEMPORANEOUSLY ▶ (215)**. This will allow you and your audience to stay focused on the demonstration.
- *Encourage questions.* Encourage audience members to **ASK QUESTIONS ∴ (350–61)** during and/or after the demonstration.

As with all kinds of presentations, it's helpful to learn from successful demonstrations. Observe common demonstrations like YouTube videos, infomercials, cooking programs, and athletic coaches to understand what works and what doesn't. For example, notice how the host of a cooking show often has all the ingredients and tools ready and available. In some cases, an interim procedure, such as peeling onions or chopping carrots, is completed in advance. Ask yourself, "What does my audience need to see and hear *now*, and what can I physically prepare ahead of time?"

DO: AUDIENCE PERFORMS THE PROCEDURE

Unlike reporting new information about objects, people, and events, informative presentations about procedures often include a section where audience members are asked to *do* (or at least try to do) the procedure. Clearly, you can't ask an audience to ride a unicycle or play a bagpipe unless you're teaching a unicycle or bagpipe class. You can, however, ask audience members to create an aerodynamic paper airplane, try a yoga pose, or communicate a simple sentence with American Sign Language. **AUDIENCE PARTICIPATION** ∴ **(343–45)** can enhance interest, learning, and recall, especially when teaching a procedure.

Here's an example of how Starbucks managers teach new employees how to make a latte:[3]

1. *Tell.* The manager provides a written recipe and describes the procedure for making the latte.
2. *Show.* The manager demonstrates how to make a latte, one step at a time.
3. *Do.* The manager asks each employee to make a latte in accordance with the recipe.
4. *Respond.* The manager assesses how well employees are making the lattes and provides feedback.

Notice the addition of a fourth step, *respond.* When training people to perform a task they will be required to do well, it is essential to provide feedback. Coach them individually or as a group, ask and answer questions as they practice, and offer praise and suggestions for improvement.

Conclusion

Informative presentations that report new information can be demanding for both speakers and audience members alike. They often compete with the cascade of information—including facts, data, opinions, quotations, definitions, examples, stories, and visual or oral depictions—that bombard us every day. Whether you're giving a tour of the external anatomy of a fire ant or showing classmates how to sew on a button, your most important goal is to develop a compelling value step based on your purpose and thorough audience analysis. This strategy will help you choose relevant supporting material and organize your key points to increase audience attention and comprehension.

Reporting new information becomes even more challenging when demonstrating a procedure. The tell-show-do technique can help you navigate this difficult process. Make sure you *tell* and *show* at the same time, speak extemporaneously, and encourage questions during and after a demonstration. When you include the *do* step, your presentation becomes a collaborative undertaking that requires the full attention of everyone involved. As you watch audience members practice a procedure, seek and answer their questions and offer constructive criticism and praise. The way you respond to their attempts can turn a humdrum presentation into one your audience will remember for a long time.

Mileha Soneji

From an early age, Mileha Soneji thought about how products might be redesigned to better suit the needs of the people using them. This led her to complete a bachelor's degree in product design and to pursue graduate studies in strategic product design. In 2015, she delivered a public speech about her uncle's experience with Parkinson's disease and her efforts to use human-centered design to improve his quality of life. The spill-proof cup she invented for him is available to the public and has been featured on National Public Radio and *HuffPost*. In her current position as a senior user-experience researcher, Soneji focuses on applying market analysis to user needs in order to guide product design.

Search Terms

To locate a video of this presentation online, enter the following key words into a search engine: simple hacks for life with Parkinson's. The video is approximately 6:57 in length.

What to Watch For

Soneji uses the categorical organizational pattern to touch on four key points: (1) defining Parkinson's disease and its effects on thousands of people and families, (2) creating a spill-proof cup, (3) making walking easier and more comfortable on flat surfaces, and (4) making "a smarter world" with simple solutions. She also uses several informative speaking strategies for reporting new information. In addition to a clear organizational pattern, she uses her own family as a backdrop to emphasize why her message is important and beneficial to all families.

[0:04–2:02] Soneji begins her presentation by telling a story about a favorite uncle who would play with the kids at family get-togethers. When he was diagnosed with Parkinson's disease, he went from being an energetic person to hiding from people because of his tremors. Using her uncle's story as a backdrop, she explains what Parkinson's is and notes that 60,000 people are diagnosed with the disease each year. She introduces her central idea: creative thinking can solve simple problems, which leads to a better quality of life for many Parkinson's patients and their families, and audience members.

[2:03–2:49] Soneji describes her quest to make everyday tasks easier for her uncle with Parkinson's disease by designing a no-spill cup. She displays the cup and illustrates how she solved the problem of liquid spilling out during a tremor with a diagram that explains why it works. The cup, she says, is not just for Parkinson's patients. The cup could also "be used by you, me, any clumsy person"— something the audience can value and use in other contexts.

[2:50–5:49] Soneji describes her second challenge: understanding why her uncle could descend and climb a staircase with ease but not walk on a flat surface. She shows a video of her uncle easily walking down steps. She follows with another photo and video of the "staircase illusion" floor, which tricks her uncle's brain into seeing a flat surface as a staircase. The audience responds with enthusiastic applause as they watch her uncle walking across the floor with the same relative ease he displayed on the stairs. She asks the audience to see how the staircase illusion can be used in homes and hospitals to help patients feel comfortable and "much more welcome."

[5:50–6:44] Her final key point emphasizes her central idea in a clear oral style: smart solutions can be simple and effective. She tells her audience to not be afraid of complex problems: "Break them, boil them down into much smaller problems, and then find simple solutions for them." Her conclusion gives audience members a reason to remember her presentation: "Imagine what we all could do if we all came up with simple solutions." Her concluding line is "Let's make a smarter world, but with simplicity." This summary reinforces her central idea in a warm and sincere speaking style.

EXERCISE

After viewing Soneji's speech, reflect on these questions:

1. What informative strategies for reporting new information did Soneji use most effectively to help her audience listen, learn, remember, and value her presentation?

2. How would Soneji's presentation have been different if she had not used videos of her uncle?

3. Does Soneji use a value step in her presentation? If so, explain whether or not you think she did so effectively.

4. Identify the purpose of Soneji's presentation. Did she achieve her purpose? Why or why not?

5. How does Soneji's credibility influence the audience's willingness to listen to her presentation?

6. In what ways, if any, could Soneji have improved the content and/or delivery of her presentation?

6.3 Explaining Complex Ideas

Unlike reporting new information, informative presentations that **explain complex ideas** assume that audience members are aware of a given subject but lack a deep understanding of it. These presentations answer questions such as "Why is this happening?," "What does that mean?," and "How does this work?" Consider the following questions and the extent to which you could explain the intricacies of each topic:

- Why do people yawn?
- What's the difference between stocks and bonds?
- What is the scientific basis for claims about climate change?
- Why do so many people misunderstand the nature of gluten?

To be an excellent explanatory speaker, you need to understand why questions like these are difficult to answer—and how to overcome those difficulties. In her research, Katherine Rowan suggests several strategies to deepen audience understanding when explaining complex ideas: *clarify difficult terms, describe scientific phenomena,* and *overcome audience confusion and misunderstanding.*[1] Although these strategies may overlap—for example, you may need to clarify a difficult term while describing a scientific phenomenon—we'll examine them separately to highlight the way they are used to achieve a specific informative purpose.

Clarifying Difficult Terms

Unlike an object, person, event, or procedure, a difficult term is often **ABSTRACT** ∴ **(307)**—rarely can you touch it, demonstrate it, or explain it with a simple definition. Try to explain *genome*, *quantum mechanics*, or the *electoral college* and you'll see what we mean.

For an example of clarifying a term (*introverts*) by explaining its features, see Notable Speaker: Susan Cain, page 205.

Presentations that **clarify difficult terms** explain what a difficult term means and, in some cases, what it does not mean. What, for example, is *rhetoric*? Many people think rhetoric refers to a speech that purposely deceives or misleads an audience rather than how it's used as a means of legitimate persuasion. Clarifying the meaning of a term can explain the differences between commonly confused words, such as *validity* and *reliability*, or *ethos* and *ethics*. It can also explain the functions of biotechnology or the scope of Islamic Sharia law.

Clarifying a difficult term is just that—difficult. It is a challenge for both speakers and listeners. Rowan suggests the following strategies:[2]

- *Define the term's essential features.* What are the consistent qualities in every example of the term? For instance, what is a defining feature of a mammal? Only mammals have three middle ear bones.

- *Use a variety of examples.* What are different, yet typical, examples of the term? For instance, humans, gorillas, whales, and bats are all mammals.

- *Contrast examples and nonexamples.* Can you think of common misconceptions about the term or how it's incorrectly used? For example, whales live their lives in the sea but are not fish; bats can fly but are not birds.

- *Quiz the audience.* Pose and answer questions, such as: "True or false? Only mammals have backbones." (False: Birds, fish, reptiles, and amphibians also have backbones.) You may also want to include a **QUESTION-AND-ANSWER SESSION** ∴ **(350–61)** to give audience members an opportunity request more information and clarification.

The following sample outline clarifies the meaning of the term *mammals* and explains, using the four recommended strategies, where and why humans are included in this class of animals:

TOPIC AREA: Humans as mammals

PURPOSE: To explain the essential features of animals identified as mammals

CENTRAL IDEA: Understanding the characteristics of mammals explains why humans are included in the classification.

VALUE STEP: Under the classification of mammals, humans share common characteristics and ancestors with 5,500 related animal species.

ORGANIZATION: **CATEGORICAL ARRANGEMENT** ■ **(157–58)** with Q&A session

KEY POINTS:
A. Essential features: All mammals have mammary glands for nursing young, hair on their skin, and three middle ear bones.

B. Varied examples: Mammals are divided into three subclasses based on reproductive characteristics.
1. Egg-laying monotremes: duck-billed platypus and spiny anteater
2. External-pouch marsupials: kangaroos, koalas, opossums, and wombats
3. Placentals: humans, whales, bats, cats, rats, and elephants

C. Nonexamples
1. Birds, fish, and reptiles have backbones but are not mammals.
2. Chickens, penguins, and platypuses lay eggs, but only platypuses are mammals.

3. Bats and birds fly, but only bats are mammals.

D. Quiz the audience

1. True or false? All mammals have some form of hair. (True: Young whales and porpoises have hair—and dolphins are born with small mustaches.)

2. True or false? Some mammals lay eggs. (True: The spiny anteater and duck-billed platypus lay eggs.)

In this outline, each key point applies a different strategy in a specific order. Why provide nonexamples or quiz the audience at the end? Both help ensure audience members understand the term you're defining. You could, however, integrate some of the strategies into a single key point by, for example, encouraging listeners to ask questions throughout the presentation: "I've listed three identifying features of mammals. Does anyone know of others?" Since many people have mistaken ideas about what makes a mammal a mammal, addressing the issue in your first key point would make the rest of your presentation go more smoothly.

Describing a Scientific Phenomenon

In some presentations, you may have to describe a complex scientific phenomenon to an audience unfamiliar with the underlying concepts. It's how a physicist might explain string theory without requiring an audience to understand its underlying theories. You may be familiar with this strategy if, for example, you've ever heard a scientist explaining the implications of their research on a podcast meant for general audiences.

When **describing a scientific phenomenon**, you're asking audience members to grasp something that may require specialized knowledge to understand. Here, you are looking for ways to enhance that understanding without using unfamiliar scientific terms, sophisticated statistical methods, or the complicated graphs and charts printed in research journals. Instead, you're describing what something is *like* rather than what it *is*.

Consider, for example, an explanation of supply-and-demand economics from a scientific paper: "System dynamicists believe that the availability of a product, rather than its rate of production, affects the market price and demand. This means that the inventory of a product is a major determinant in setting price and regulating demand."[3] Would you use this language in a presentation to an audience unfamiliar with the topic? Most certainly not. What you need is a simpler and more listener-friendly explanation. For example, you could begin by noting that *supply* refers to the quantity of a product that's available, and *demand* refers to how many people want the product. Then you could describe what happens when supply and demand interact.

Perhaps the biggest challenge when giving this kind of presentation is identifying the "big picture" for the audience—that is, the most crucial components from a multitude of potentially confusing ideas. Here are four recommendations that can help you describe the big picture to your audience:[4]

1. ***Provide clear, well-organized key points and various types of supporting material.*** Explaining a scientific process often uses a chronological, categorical, or compare/contrast **ORGANIZATIONAL PATTERN** ▇ **(157–66)**.

2. ***Use metaphors, similes, and analogies.*** Such **FIGURATIVE LANGUAGE** ⁖ **(311–14)** can help you compare an unfamiliar concept to something the audience already understands. For example, the term *blueprint* has been used to explain genetics. However, because a blueprint implies something that doesn't change, a better and easier-to-understand explanatory metaphor would be *baking bread*. Not only does it describe something that grows (yeast), but it also describes a process that can result in a different product depending on the circumstances—such as baking on dry or humid days or using different ovens.[5] Thus, despite the same "recipe" of genes, no

two people are genetically the same (with the exception of some identical twins).

3. ***Use presentation aids.*** A diagram of our solar system, an enlarged illustration of a COVID-19 virus, or an animation of plant growth are only a few examples of **PRESENTATION AIDS** ▶ **(260–78)** that may enhance your audience's interest in and ability to understand a challenging idea, theory, or process.

4. ***Use transitions, previews, summaries, and signposts.*** The complexity of a scientific phenomenon often requires the skilled use of **CONNECTIVE PHRASES** ■ **(167–69)** that separate the discrete principles of a complex idea into digestible parts (for example, "First, . . . Second, . . . Third, . . .").

In the following outline, a presentation about the complex weather patterns known as El Niño and La Niña[6] uses these strategies to help audience members understand these two scientific phenomena. Unlike explanatory presentations that clarify terms or overcome confusion and misunderstanding, the key points do not correspond to separate strategies. Rather, all the strategies can be used to explain each key point.

TOPIC AREA:	El Niño and La Niña
PURPOSE:	To explain how El Niño and La Niña affect the earth's weather
CENTRAL IDEA:	El Niño and La Niña are two related weather patterns that raise and lower the temperature of water in the equatorial Pacific Ocean, thereby affecting weather and climate conditions in the United States and around the world.
VALUE STEP:	El Niño and La Niña can affect the weather wherever you live, sometimes in dangerous ways.
ORGANIZATION:	**COMPARE/CONTRAST** ■ **(163–64)** with presentation aids (for example, maps, animations, and photos of severe weather)

KEY POINTS: A. What are El Niño and La Niña?

         1. El Niño (Spanish for "little boy," or "the Christ child" in Peru) warms the sea surface temperature in the Pacific Ocean near the equator.

         2. La Niña (Spanish for "little girl") cools the sea surface temperature in the Pacific Ocean near the equator.

         3. El Niño and La Niña are often "partners in a dance" in which subsequent weather and climate conditions vary depending on who is "leading."

     B. When do they occur?

         1. El Niño is a regularly occurring climate feature.

         2. La Niña is less predictable and causes extremely cold water temperatures and frequently serious weather conditions.

         3. As "brother-sister" events, El Niño and La Niña can interact or act independently.

     C. How do they impact the United States?

         1. El Niño's effects in North America

         2. La Niña's effects in the United States

         3. El Niño's and La Niña's lack of impact on climate change

Notice how all four strategies are integrated into each of the clear, well-organized key points. The metaphors of a little boy and little girl, dancing partners, and a brother-sister relationship are used throughout the presentation. Certainly, presentation aids would further enhance audience understanding of these phenomena. And although we haven't specified them in the outline, the presentation itself would include clear transitional phrases to separate the two characteristics, behavior, and impact of each weather phenomenon.

Overcoming Confusion and Misunderstanding

The third type of explanatory presentation seeks to **overcome confusion and misunderstanding**, a task that has grown increasingly important with the prevalence of false claims and misinformation. Why, for example, do people believe vaccines cause autism or that MSG is inherently harmful? Because people cling to strongly held beliefs that reinforce a particular viewpoint, even when those beliefs are proven false. As a result, informative speakers often face an uphill battle to replace erroneous beliefs with ones based on legitimate facts.

At first, an informative presentation may not seem the best way to explain what is and is not a fact. Wouldn't a persuasive presentation be more appropriate? It all depends on your **PURPOSE ▲ (109–18)**. Whereas a **PERSUASIVE PRESENTATION ◆ (437–57)** tries to change people's opinions and/or behaviors, an informative presentation tries to set the record straight with facts based on the work of reputable researchers and objective experts.

To overcome confusion and misunderstanding, we recommend four strategies used in the following order:[7]

1. ***State the misconception.*** Phrase the misunderstood claim in neutral terms to make sure its goal is to inform, not persuade—and to avoid a negative reaction from your audience. "Some people believe the earth is flat" is an unbiased statement that is less inflammatory than "The Flat Earth Society is totally wrong."

2. ***Acknowledge the misconception's believability and the reason(s) it is believed.*** Explain why audience members may be confused or misinformed about their beliefs. Scientific and historic claims often change with new research. Advertisers often stretch or misrepresent a product's power. Social media allows falsehoods to spread unchecked.

3. ***Provide contrary evidence.*** Make sure you choose legitimate, well-recognized experts whose conclusions have been tested as **VALID ■ (143–47)**. Cite the experts' credentials in your presentation. Use a range of **SUPPORTING MATERIAL ■ (135–39)**,

including facts, statistics, testimony, and stories. If appropriate, use **PRESENTATION AIDS** ▶ **(260–78)** to clarify the issue.

4. ***State and explain the more acceptable or accurate belief or theory.*** Phrase the corrected claim as accurately as you can. Instead of "The earth is round," say, "The earth is an irregularly shaped ellipsoid."

The following outline incorporates these four steps to help a speaker develop and deliver a presentation that overcomes misconceptions about a particular vaccine:

TOPIC AREA:	Vaccinating children for measles, mumps, and rubella (MMR)
PURPOSE:	To explain common misconceptions about the risks of this vaccine
CENTRAL IDEA:	Claims that the MMR vaccine is harmful and can cause autism have been disproven.
VALUE STEP:	Confusion and misunderstanding about the MMR vaccine have put the health and lives of many children in jeopardy.
ORGANIZATION:	**PROBLEM-SOLUTION ARRANGEMENT** ■ **(159–60)**
KEY POINTS:	A. Some parents refuse to vaccinate their children because they believe the MMR vaccine causes autism.
	B. This belief is understandable given a published study by Dr. Andrew Wakefield in 1998 and subsequent media hype about the MMR vaccine causing autism in British children.
	C. The study's link between the MMR vaccine and autism has been completely discredited by well-respected researchers and medical

organizations. Dr. Wakefield lost his medical licenses, and the paper was withdrawn by the journal that published it.

D. Vaccinated children are healthier and less likely to contract serious diseases and/or make other children sick.

Unlike a persuasive presentation that entreats parents to vaccinate their children against MMR, this example clearly fits the purpose of informative presentations: to instruct, define, enlighten, describe, remind, and demonstrate by reporting new information and/or explaining a complex idea. If it's successful, this presentation will encourage misinformed audience members to rethink what they believe about an issue.

Conclusion

Informative presentations can take many forms. If you're a news anchor or tour guide, most of what you do is report new information. But what if instead of sharing a recipe for making bread, you want to explain how yeast works? Or if instead of providing a short biography of Mozart, you explain the reasons his works are significant today and unmatched by his contemporaries? The difference between these examples is your purpose. Your purpose determines whether you're clarifying a difficult term, describing a scientific phenomenon, or overcoming confusion or misunderstanding. (Your purpose will also determine if you're speaking to persuade rather than to inform.) In this chapter, we have provided strategies for developing each type of explanatory presentation. But keep in mind that in some rhetorical situations you may need to apply more than one set of explanatory strategies at different points in your presentation.

A former senior writer at *Sports Illustrated*, David Epstein is a journalist whose work often focuses on the intersection of sports, medicine, and science. In 2014, he delivered a compelling TED talk based on his book *The Sports Gene: Inside the Science of Extraordinary Athletic Performance*. Epstein addresses the question of why contemporary athletes seem faster, better, and stronger than their historical counterparts. The large number and high production value of his presentation aids help him explain several complex ideas and misunderstood concepts about a variety of sports.

Search Terms

To locate a video of this presentation online, enter the following key words into a search engine: David Epstein athletes. The video is approximately 14:54 in length.

What to Watch For

Epstein uses numerous explanatory speaking strategies to achieve his goal of explaining why contemporary athletes are faster, better, and stronger than their historic counterparts:

- He clarifies an initially difficult concept by using multiple comparative examples, both obscure and well known (tall basketball players, small gymnasts, swimmers with long torsos, marathon runner with thin shins) accompanied by superb visuals, and by posing questions to the audience.

- He describes scientific phenomena using three key points, a clear organizational format, and effective transitions.

- He addresses and corrects misconceptions audience members may have about athletic ability by acknowledging what many people believe—that humans beings have evolved into better athletes over the last century—and then providing a more complicated explanation (but with clarity): that the improvements are largely due to technological innovations, specialized body types for different sports, and a more productive mindset in athletic training and competition.

[0:00–0:45] Epstein begins his talk with the Olympics motto: *"Citius, altius, fortius.* Faster, higher, stronger."* He then displays his first slide showing that the 2012 Olympic marathon winner beat the 1904 winner by almost one and a half hours. "So what's going on here?" he asks. Epstein's challenge is to explain complex phenomena that require a scientific understanding and a connection to frequently misunderstood beliefs about athletic abilities. He starts to meet this challenge by clearly identifying his central idea: "I want to take a look at what's really behind this march of athletic progress."

[1:12–2:53] Epstein's first extended example is a slide explaining that if Jesse Owens, winner of the 100-meter sprint at the 1936 Olympics, had propelled himself out of a block and run on a modern track, he would have been within a stride of beating Usain Bolt, considered the greatest sprinter of all time. Epstein uses this first example to preview his organizational structure and makes the first of his three key points: improved technology has improved athletic performance.

Every example he uses has its own recognizable structure, almost always accompanied by a slide. He introduces the examples and the differences between the pictured athletes—some famous, some not. Then he links the example to one of his key points— technology advancements, genetic differences, or athlete mindset—to explain differences in performance.

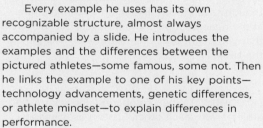

[4:21–4:52] Epstein examines the 100-meter freestyle world record in swimming. He uses a slide to explain that although "the record is always trending downward . . . it's punctuated by these steep cliffs," all of which reflect technological advancements: the flip turn, pool gutters that reduce water turbulence, and low-friction swimsuits. He zooms in on each of the "cliffs," getting four slides out of one.

[7:05–7:56] Throughout his presentation, Epstein demonstrates the value of multiple presentation aids to support key points. When discussing how the height and weight of athletes has changed over time, he uses a scatter graph to illustrate what researchers call the Big Bang of Body Types—the splintering of athletes' body types into specialized shapes and sizes, depending on which sport they compete in.

[7:57–8:55] Epstein uses four slides to explain why the number of basketball players who are seven feet tall doubled in a short period of time. He begins by showing an image of a basketball player. He then switches to an image of ten dots, one of which is yellow. The yellow dot represents the one player in ten in the NBA today who is at least seven feet tall. Next, he adds several more rows of gray dots to illustrate how rare it is to find a man who is seven feet tall in the general population. Finally, he makes a slightly different but related point by showing six dots—one of which is a basketball. Even though seven-foot-tall men are extremely rare in the general population, for every six such men that you might find, one of those six will play in the NBA!

[10:00–10:30] When comparing and contrasting athletes with each other, Epstein uses images that show them side by side. Parts of his presentation generate audience laughter, as when he compares the bodies of six-foot-four swimmer Michael Phelps and five-foot-nine runner Hicham El Guerrouj.

[11:35–14:00] By the time he reaches his third key point—changing mindsets change athletic performance—his explanation is not as clear as the first two (changing technology and changing gene pool). The presentation becomes more abstract and the slides less instructive.

EXERCISE

After viewing Epstein's speech, reflect on these questions:

1. To what extent do you better understand why modern athletes are faster, higher, and stronger?

2. How did Epstein use the strategies recommended for explanatory presentations? Was it easy or difficult to identify the strategies? Were they obvious or subtle? Does it matter if the audience can identify them?

3. How many key points were there? How many subpoints/examples were under each key point? What were the transitions?

4. In your opinion, which presentation aids were the most and least effective? Explain.

5. Epstein used more than two dozen presentation aids. Should he have used more words and fewer visuals? Or did he get it just right? Explain.

6. In what ways, if any, could Epstein have improved the content and/or delivery of his presentation?

PART 7

Speaking to Persuade

Persuasion—the process of convincing people to change their opinions or behavior of their own free will—is a fact of our daily lives. Contemporary rhetorician Andrea Lunsford has gone so far as to claim that "everything's an argument"[1]—that even sharing a straightforward piece of information is an attempt to persuade your listeners that what you're saying is truthful, accurate, and worth knowing. The three chapters that follow are all about persuasive speaking. They provide you with essential **PERSUASIVE STRATEGIES** for making your presentations more believable, influential, and memorable, and they will also help you sharpen your critical thinking skills when considering your own and others' **ARGUMENTS**.

Speaking to Persuade

7.1 Understanding Persuasion

When we've asked students to identify the speaking skills they believe are the most important in becoming an effective speaker, persuading others isn't usually high on their list. Keeping the audience interested? Yes! Organizing a presentation? Absolutely! Why not persuading others?

Persuasive messages bombard us from the time we wake up until the moment we end each day. Sometimes persuasion is obvious—a sermon, an advertisement interrupting a podcast, a plea for donations, a campaign speech. At other times, it's more subtle—a product endorsement on social media, an investment newsletter, a hint about a desired birthday present. Businesses use persuasion to sell products. Colleges use persuasion to recruit students and faculty. Even children use persuasive speaking to convince parents to let them stay up late or to buy them the newest toy. So what, exactly, is persuasion and why is it so important for speakers to learn how to use it wisely and well?

The Purpose of Persuasion

Persuasion strives to change people's opinions (what they believe, think, or feel) and/or their behavior (what they do). Persuasion can do more than change someone's opinion to its opposite. It can also change an opinion or behavior to something milder or stronger and even produce a new opinion or behavior where there was none.

Persuasive speaking is distinct from but is often dependent on informative speaking to achieve its goal. Experienced speakers know that in order to persuade an audience, they must present information. For instance, if you are asking audience members to reduce the amount of meat they consume, you will probably include information about the negative health and environmental consequences of consuming meat products. In most rhetorical situations, applying the basic principles of effective **INFORMATIVE SPEAKING** ✳ **(365–74)** is critical to your success as a persuasive speaker. So how do these two types of speaking differ? The dividing line between informing and persuading is your **PURPOSE** ▲ **(109–18)**.

Think of it this way: The primary goal of an informative presentation is *to tell your audience something important* by reporting new information, clarifying difficult terms, explaining complex ideas, and/or correcting misunderstood information. In a persuasive presentation, your primary goal is *to ask for something from your audience*—their agreement or a change in their opinions and/or behavior.

The following table shows how a persuasive presentation on a particular topic might ask the audience to change either their opinion or their behavior. Note the differences between the two goals.

Opinion	Behavior
Springy Shoes makes the best high-quality athletic shoes.	Buy Springy Shoes.
Your family is more important than your job.	Eat dinner with your family at least five times a week.
We need stricter drunk driving laws and punishments.	Write a letter to your state legislator supporting stricter drunk driving laws.
Chris has extreme views on almost every issue.	Vote for Fran, Chris's opponent.

In general, it is easier to persuade audience members to change their opinions than it is to convince them to do something they would *not* otherwise do. It can also be easier to convince an audience of something low risk rather than something deeply connected to their core values. Convincing an audience to try a new potato chip brand, for example, is usually easier than persuading them to change their opinion about political candidates, abortion rights, or religious beliefs. Bear in mind that persuading people to change their opinions or beliefs is not necessarily going to lead to a change in their behavior—and you may not be able to persuade everyone in your audience.

If your goal is to change behavior, you'll first need to persuade your listeners that your goal is reasonable, and then you'll need to motivate them to take some action as a result. It's a tall order, and in the rest of this chapter and the chapters that follow we discuss some of the strategies you can use to make this happen. But first, let's consider the ethical implications of persuasive speaking.

The Ethics of Persuasion

Successful persuasive speakers demonstrate an impressive mastery of the art of speaking—they have learned how to bring people around to their way of thinking. Changing other people's attitudes, opinions, beliefs, and/ or behaviors is, at its heart, an act of rhetorical power. But like most forms of power, persuasive power can be misused. Take a moment to consider some of advertisers, politicians, false conspiracy promoters, and con artists who try to persuade us in daily life. Their messages serve only their own interests and often do so by deceiving and misleading those who may be harmed by those interests.

You might wonder, "Can I learn the skills and techniques needed to become a more persuasive speaker and still be an **ETHICAL SPEAKER** ● **(44–48)**?" Yes, *but only if your purpose is ethical.* Abraham Lincoln, Mahatma Gandhi, and Martin Luther King Jr. wielded enormous rhetorical power with an ethical purpose. Unfortunately, some of the most evil people in history—including Adolf Hitler—have also been highly effective persuasive speakers. Persuasive skills can also be used as **propaganda**— in which a group of people try to manipulate public opinion for private goals by spreading a mixture of false and factual information.

So what's the difference between ethical persuasion and propaganda? The answer is that as an ethical persuasive speaker, you have two important commitments. First, you must establish genuine relationship with your audience and be committed to serving their needs, not just yours. The relationship between an ethical speaker and their audience should be mutually beneficial and transparent, whereas the aim of propaganda is to serve the needs of a particular organization or government. Second, ethical speakers are committed to honorable **VALUES** ▲ **(95–96)**—truthfulness, respect for people's rights, and concern for the audience's well-being. In other words, you must follow the principles in the **CREDO FOR ETHICAL COMMUNICATION** ● **(45)**.

In short, the act of persuading is not, in and of itself, unethical. In fact, we strongly believe that "very little of the good that we see in the world could be accomplished without persuasion."[2] It is certainly ethical to persuade others to donate money to a legitimate charity (if they can afford it) or to urge listeners to stop engaging in dangerous behavior (if they can avoid it). But persuasion becomes unethical if you distort the truth in order to persuade your audience to bully, intimidate, or even harm people who hold different opinions than yours, or if your purpose hurts your audience, misrepresents the truth, serves your own or an organization's self-centered interests, or violates the rights and freedom of others.

Persuasive Claims

All persuasive speakers make **claims**, statements that identify what they want their audience to believe and/or do. Rhetoricians have classified persuasive claims into four basic types: *claims of fact*, *claims of conjecture*, *claims of value*, and *claims of policy*. Each type serves a different function that, depending on your purpose, improves your ability to persuade.

CLAIMS OF FACT

A **claim of fact** contends that a statement about people, objects, or events is true and verifiable, such as:

- Viruses, not bacteria, cause the common cold.
- From 1990 to 2023, global carbon dioxide emissions have increased by more than 60 percent.
- There is no scientific connection between vaccines and autism.

When developing a legitimate claim of fact, use objective, verifiable **SUPPORTING MATERIAL** ■ (135–39) to substantiate your claim. Keep in mind there are often competing claims of fact. If you claim that there is no scientific connection between vaccines and autism, for example, you must be prepared to address audience members who disagree.

Chapter 3.2 **RESEARCH AND SUPPORTING MATERIAL** ■ provides strategies for evaluating the accuracy of facts and supporting material.

CLAIMS OF CONJECTURE

A **claim of conjecture** makes well-informed assumptions about the future based on strong, valid research and observable trends. Here are some examples:

- By 2045, non-Hispanic whites will become a minority group in the United States.
- The proposed spending bill will result in lower taxes for all middle-class citizens.
- Stricter enforcement of drunk driving will reduce the number of motor vehicle accidents.

Like claims of fact, claims of conjecture require supporting material based on expert opinions and valid data. They also require that you clearly describe the thought process you or a source use to support the claim. Much like claims of fact, there can be competing claims of conjecture, such as the following two public assertions about mail-in voting: *Mail-in voting will promote democracy by providing a convenient method for people to cast their ballots* and *Mail-in voting will threaten democracy by providing an insecure method for people to cast their ballots.*

CLAIMS OF VALUE

A **claim of value** identifies what is right or wrong in a particular situation, as these examples show:

- Forcing transgender people to use the bathroom of their birth sex is wrong.
- Banning immigrants from certain countries is fair and justifiable.
- It is unethical to knowingly share falsified images via social media.

To make such a claim, you should cite the most reliable and respected opinions and data you can find and connect those sources to your point of view and your **AUDIENCE'S VALUES ▲ (95–96)**. Claims of value can be challenging because audience members hold a variety of attitudes and beliefs. More so than claims of fact or conjecture, claims of value require you to be in tune with your audience's beliefs and attitudes—to be an especially **AUDIENCE-CENTERED SPEAKER ▲ (88–89)**. Keep in mind that what you see as immoral or wrong may seem appropriate and right by some of your listeners.

CLAIMS OF POLICY

A **claim of policy** proposes a particular course of action. Unlike a claim of conjecture that makes predictions about what may happen, a claim of policy promotes a solution to an immediate problem. The word *should* is often used in a claim of policy, as in the following examples:

- We should ban hate speech on campus.
- The government should cancel college student loan debts.
- Social media platforms should have stricter regulations to combat cyberbullying.

As is the case with all claims, audience members may not support your proposed actions. Think of the wide range of opinions on issues such as gun control, abortion, immigration, free speech, animal rights, and global climate change. Rarely can speakers advocate a position on any of these issues without considering and adapting to the multiple and often conflicting opinions of audience members.

Claims of policy usually require that you establish claims of fact, conjecture, and/or value as a basis for advocating a course of action. It is difficult to imagine a claim of policy that doesn't share facts, predictions, and value-based implications. Once you've done that, you can recommend the best or most practical action or solution—the means by which you propose to change things.

Consider how using each type of claim can support a presentation about bicycle safety on a college campus:

Type of claim	Function	Example
Fact	States that something is true, that an event occurred, that a cause can be identified, or that a theory correctly explains a phenomenon	A significant number of students ride bikes on campus.
Conjecture	Suggests that something will or will not happen in the future	Increasing enrollment and the popularity of bicycles will increase bike traffic accidents.
Value	Asserts the worth of something—good or bad; right or wrong; best, average, or worst	Irresponsible bike riders who defy and/or disregard traffic rules are endangering the safety of others.
Policy	Recommends a specific or new course of action or solution to a problem	We should develop and enforce traffic and campus rules to improve bike safety.

Persuading an audience to support the enforcement of stricter bicycle traffic rules, a claim of policy, is all but impossible unless you explain why. Claims of fact, conjecture, and value address the "why."

Persuasive Appeals

If you make a claim in daily life or to an audience, the response may be: "Prove it!" Like lawyers before a jury, persuasive speakers must prove their case. Many persuasive speakers rely on established strategies that go back 2,500 years to the Greek philosopher Aristotle. During the early fourth century BCE, Aristotle watched and listened to speakers in the courts and in the marketplaces of Athens. Based on his observations, he developed a multidimensional theory of persuasion in his *Rhetoric*.

Aristotle's ideas about the nature and features of persuasive speaking are complex and well worth reading. Here we focus on Aristotle's three major types of *appeals* that can be used to persuade an audience: *ethos*, *pathos*, and *logos*.[3]

See Chapter 2.2
SPEAKER ▲
for strategies on
improving your
speaker credibility,
or the extent to
which an audience
trusts you and
believes what
you say.

ETHOS: PERSONAL APPEALS

Aristotle and contemporary rhetoricians claim that a speaker's personal character—their **ethos**—is often the most fundamental and effective type of persuasive appeal. We also call this **SPEAKER CREDIBILITY** ▲ **(74–81)**. Audience members pay closer attention to and are more likely to agree with speakers they perceive as credible.

Consider how ethos operates in your everyday interactions. Do you believe what your favorite professors tell you? If you see them as honorable and reliable experts in their discipline, you probably do. Do you trust what a respected member of the clergy says? Again, if you have faith in the integrity and goodwill of that person, you probably do. Ethos is a powerful appeal—but you must *earn* it from your audience if you expect it to help you achieve your persuasive purpose.

Most speakers begin a presentation with some of their ethos already established in the audience's mind. This is called the speaker's **initial credibility**. A speaker's initial credibility may be quite low if the audience knows nothing about them (other than their physical appearance) before they speak; it may be high if the speaker's reputation for expertise and honesty precedes them; or it may be somewhere in between. Whether starting with low or high ethos, successful persuasive speakers work to *increase* or take advantage of their existing credibility during a presentation.

The effect you have on an audience's perception of your ethos *during* a presentation is called derived credibility. Your **derived credibility** may wax and wane during a presentation, based on many different factors: the quality and **ORGANIZATION** ■ **(152–70)** of your content, the nature and skill of your **DELIVERY** ▶ **(209–301)**, and the degree to which you convey the **DIMENSIONS OF CREDIBILITY** ▲ **(74–81)**—competence, trustworthiness, likability, and dynamism. Most of this book is devoted to helping you increase your derived credibility as you speak. In addition to the advice provided in other chapters, here are a few specific strategies you can use to enhance your speaker credibility in persuasive presentations.

Identify with Your Audience Rhetorical scholar Kenneth Burke describes successful persuasion as **identification**, a process by which the speaker and audience recognize their shared attitudes, ideas, feelings, values, and experiences. According to Burke, you can persuade another person if you talk their "language" through speech, gesture, tonality, order, image, and attitude, identifying your ways with theirs.[4] In other words, when you acknowledge the **COMMON GROUND ▲ (89)** you share with your audience, you are more likely to enhance your perceived credibility with that particular audience. For example, note how skillfully Donald Trump identified with his audience at a rally after his federal indictment:[5]

> In the end, they're not coming after me. They're coming after you—
> and I'm just standing in their way.

Personalize Your Message To enhance your credibility early in your presentation, you can provide personal information about yourself and/or the reason you are speaking. Here's an example:

> As I thought about the topics I might choose for this presentation, it occurred to me that because I am an economics major and my family owns its own business, I probably know more than most people about accounting. That's why I want to talk about the importance of budgeting.

Or you might display a photograph of your family's business and say, "Our family business has been open for more than 50 years and I've worked there for the last 5 years." Even if you are not pictured in the photograph, showing the business helps your audience imagine you in that setting.

Use Audience-Centered Supporting Material Right from the beginning of your presentation, introduce strong supporting material that the audience is likely to believe and that demonstrates respect for their beliefs and values. Here's an example:

> When schools were closed during the COVID pandemic, we were told that online and homeschooling would help your and my children learn. We watched dedicated teachers redesign their lessons and teach them online. I know that some of you stayed home with your children and took on the teaching. So what are the results now that the kids are back at school? We now know that about 35 percent of a normal school year's worth of learning was lost when in-person learning stopped.

Demonstrate Open Mindedness Show your audience that you have reviewed significant research and viewpoints about your topic and that you understand the basis for such opinions, as demonstrated in this example:

> For many years, I believed that there was no downside to using an electric vehicle. Only recently have I learned that there are hidden environmental costs of manufacturing batteries for them.

Borrow Other People's Ethos You can enhance your credibility by quoting an expert with high credibility whose knowledge, research, or public reputation is well known to the audience. And if that person is in some way connected to you, you can use their ethos as a support for your own. For example, you might say:

> If you ever find yourself needing to give your cat a bath, Dr. Parkman, a renowned veterinarian and expert about feline care, recommends placing a screen in the bottom of a sink so that your cat has something to grab on to instead of scratching you.

Not surprising, there is also **terminal credibility**—what audience members feel about you after you have finished your presentation. Although you may have earned credibility as you spoke, your presentation's CONCLUSION ■ (198–204) and the manner in which you respond during a QUESTION-AND-ANSWER SESSION ∴ (350–61) can determine whether your audience remembers you as a good person speaking well.

PATHOS: EMOTIONAL APPEALS

You may have seen the print and media ads by the American Society for the Prevention of Cruelty to Animals depicting a pitiful puppy or trembling chihuahua staring at you with big brown eyes. The copy may say, "Starved, abandoned, left to suffer" with information on how to donate or adopt a pet. During the height of the COVID-19 pandemic, images of exhausted health care workers with red, teary eyes evoked a wide range of emotions—from awe and admiration to sadness and fear. Appeals like these stir emotions—anger, desire, fear, pride, envy, joy, hate, jealousy, or pity. They can also target values such as justice, generosity, courage, forgiveness, and wisdom.

Aristotle referred to this form of persuasion—the use of **emotional appeals**—as **pathos**. An emotional appeal can strengthen a persuasive presentation by causing audience members to *feel something* while listening to you. As psychological studies have since confirmed, we are more likely to pay attention to, sympathize with, and remember arguments that (in addition to demonstrating truth) stir strong emotional responses in us. And in some cases, without being aware of it, we modify our beliefs to reflect the emotions we feel.

Emotional appeals—like this campaign for the American Society for the Prevention of Cruelty to Animals—often rely on images that evoke a strong emotional response.

Notice, for instance, how the following speaker uses emotional appeals to evoke audience sympathies and concerns about a scourge that kills almost 200 people in the United States every day.[6]

High school student Laurie Porter watched her mother cycle in and out of opioid addiction and rehab for years. Every time her mom promised to change and become part of Laurie's life again, Laurie knew it wouldn't happen. When she found a syringe in her mother's purse and two more in the dryer, she pleaded with her mother. "I cried, begged her to stop, but she was too out of it to care." What little money they had went to buying drugs. Sometimes Laurie would go without food so her sister could eat. Like thousands and thousands of other children, Laurie has become a member of Generation O: the children whose parents are opioid addicts.

Rather than relying only on evidence and statistics to demonstrate the significance of the opioid crisis, the speaker tells the story of one young person's personal and heartbreaking experience with it. **STORIES ∴ (323–32)** like this can evoke sympathy and fear. They can also help listeners understand that the same thing could happen to them or to someone they love. And, as a result, it becomes more likely that they will support a speaker's proposed action to address it.

Of all the emotions a speaker can appeal to, fear may be the most powerful, most frequently used, and most researched. Many public messages use **fear appeals**. Think about the extent to which fear appeals have affected your attitudes, opinions, and behavior about where to live, what to major in, who to vote for, and which cities to travel and avoid traveling to.

What explains the power of fear appeals? Many thinkers believe that fear is the most primal, basic emotion—one of the few that we share with the rest of the animal kingdom. Philosopher Martha Nussbaum describes fear as "the earliest emotion in human life. Whereas anger requires sophisticated thinking, fear only needs 'an awareness of danger.'"[7]

As powerful as fear appeals can be, however, they are not always successful. Persuasion scholar Richard Perloff notes that it isn't easy to frighten the people you're attempting to persuade. Even if you succeed in scaring most of your listeners, your fear appeal may not produce a change in their attitude other than making them anxious and unsettled. However, when a fear appeal is well crafted and well delivered, and when it is used for a good reason (for example, to prevent your listeners from putting themselves or their loved ones in harm's way), it can be very effective. So how do you make successful fear appeals? Here are a few suggestions:[8]

- *Be direct.* Don't beat around the bush or scare your audience. Dramatic, high-fear messages are more effective than those that soften the dangers or dire outcomes. Use **VIVID LANGUAGE ∴ (308)** to explain how your audience's current opinions or behavior can have dreadful consequences.

- *Make it personal.* Audience members must believe that what is being threatened could happen to them. Most people have never had a car accident after drinking alcohol. You might tell them about people who said the same thing before they killed a family in a head-on collision. Other audience members may be more concerned about what might happen to people they love. For this group, the best fear appeals tell listeners they ought to do something because if they don't, their loved ones may suffer horribly as a result.

- *Avoid overused threats.* The best fear appeals are novel. Just about every teenager ignores the overused threats parents make. The "Just say no" campaign didn't succeed in keeping youth away from drugs. A parent who repeatedly threatens "If you don't do well on this exam, you won't get into college" may be met with a teen's snarky reply: "Sure, I won't get into any school." Creative persuaders come up with fear appeals that listeners have not considered before.

- **_Discuss solutions._** This last piece of advice is key: Once you've scared audience members, tell them how to prevent the problem or minimize the danger. Drunk driving ads don't simply tell you not to drink. They tell you to "drink responsibly"—have a designated driver, leave your car at home, or call a cab. Think of it this way: you have made them sick with fear; now it's time to make them well.

Making an emotional appeal can be a justifiable and effective means of persuasion. But emotional appeals—and especially fear appeals—also have the potential to be used in malicious and unethvical ways. Critical thinkers in an audience can analyze whether the emotions aroused by a speaker are applicable and appropriate to the occasion and the purpose, but it shouldn't be up to them alone. As an **ETHICAL SPEAKER ● (43–57)**, you should make decisions that both achieve your persuasive purpose and serve your audience's best interests. Revving up fans at a pep rally or evoking sympathy by telling a sad story may be relevant and reasonable, but stirring up emotions based on fabricated facts and doubtful conclusions violates the values that every ethical speaker should uphold.

LOGOS: APPEALS TO REASON

The third form of persuasion, **logos** (also referred to as **appeals to reason**), relies on well-crafted claims that are reasonable and sensible. The success of logical appeals depends on your and your audience's ability to think rationally and critically in order to arrive at a justified conclusion. Unlike ethos and pathos, logos does not rely on who you are or how well you arouse audience emotions. Instead, it depends on building clear and compelling arguments, supporting your claims with relevant and valid **SUPPORTING MATERIAL ■ (134–51)** (facts, statistics, testimony, definitions, analogies, examples, stories, and audio/visual aids), and then tying all these elements together with good reasoning. An effective appeal to reason meets four criteria:

1. The claims in your presentation are true and verifiable.
2. The supporting material you use to justify your claims is valid and relevant.
3. There is a strong connection between your claims and the supporting material that justifies them.
4. The content and sequence of claims in your presentation support and strengthen your position.

As the most complex type of persuasion, appeals to reason require speakers to understand the nature and strategies for building strong arguments and to recognize and refute weak (or deliberately misleading) ones. The following chapter, **THINKING CRITICALLY ABOUT ARGUMENTS** ◆ **(420–36)**, will go into more detail about how to create strong arguments and recognize flaws in weak arguments.

For an example of a presentation using all three persuasive appeals (ethos, pathos, and logos), see Notable Speaker: Zach Wahls, page 106.

MATCHING APPEALS TO YOUR PURPOSE

All three types of appeals can be very persuasive depending on your analysis of the rhetorical situation. Although you may rely on one type of appeal more than another, using all three will make sure you reach audience members who may not be convinced or moved by one type of appeal. You may, for example, begin with an emotional story and then present logical appeal to describe the significance of a problem and ways to solve it. Or begin with reliable statistics to demonstrate the overall seriousness of a problem and then share emotional examples to show how it affects individual people, families, or communities.

No matter how you use emotional and logical appeals, remember that the most important type of appeal is *ethos*—whether the audience believes, trusts, and likes you. Gass and Seiter, two persuasion scholars claim: "There is only one overriding generalization about credibility that persuaders can 'take to the bank.'" High-credibility speakers are more influential than low-credibility speakers which "is as close as you can come to a universal 'law' of persuasion."[9]

Conclusion

When preparing a persuasive presentation, make sure you develop a series of strong claims and consider how (and in what combination) you will use the three main types of persuasive appeal: ethos (personal appeals), pathos (emotional appeals), and logos (appeals to reason).

Effective speakers do everything they can to enhance their ethos, from identifying with the audience, personalizing their message, and using supporting material. In the end, remember that your *ethos* is determined by your audience. Audiences are more likely to pay attention to and remember arguments that stir strong emotions, so *pathos* can be a highly effective type of persuasive appeal. Just be sure you use emotional appeals ethically to achieve your purpose, especially when using fear appeals. *Logos* is the basis for rational arguments—the justifiable ideas and content in your presentation and the words you use to express them, all tied together with sound reasoning.

Persuasion affects everyone. In daily encounters with family members, friends, colleagues, and acquaintances—whether face-to-face or via media—we cannot escape the constant stream of persuasive messages. We are asked to join, buy, salute, condemn, enjoy, participate, learn, and decide what is supposedly best for us and others. That is the goal of persuasion: to change people's opinions and/or behavior. To accomplish your persuasive goal, be an ethical speaker who establishes credibility, uses sound reasoning, and makes appropriate emotional appeals.

7.2 Thinking Critically about Arguments

🔍 A BRIEF GUIDE TO THIS CHAPTER

With the explosion of social media platforms, there's no limit to the number of arguments people produce and consume. You probably engage in several arguments daily. You might watch politicians and news pundits debate about political issues; you might disagree with a family member's social media post about gun control; you might argue about the best and worst movies of the Marvel Cinematic Universe on an online forum; and so on.

This chapter will help you think critically about a variety of arguments, providing a foundation that champions rational thinking rather than radicalism; listening rather than lashing out; mediation rather than "winning"; and debate rather than defamation. And as a persuasive speaker, thinking critically about arguments can help you persuade an audience in a way that respects differences of opinion while also seeking a reasonable outcome. Persuasive speaking is, after all, most effective when speakers use reasonable and ethical persuasive strategies to change audience opinions and behavior.

The Good Argument

First and most importantly, we need to clarify what we mean by *argument*. In some contexts, an argument might refer to a heated disagreement or a fight between people, concluding with one party feeling distressed and defeated and the other feeling dominant and victorious (and perhaps a little guilty). But that sort of argument is not the focus of this chapter.

A persuasive argument—the kind we're discussing in this chapter—is an *alternative* to a fight. In persuasive speaking, an **argument** is a persuasive **CLAIM ◆ (408–11)** supported by **EVIDENCE ◆ (425–26)** and reasons for accepting it. Good arguments are the means of persuading audience members to change their opinion or take an action of their own free will. Arguments advocate a position, examine competing ideas, and influence others.

A *good* persuasive argument is more than a recitation of facts and statistics or a series of anecdotes and expert testimony assembled in a haphazard way. Many persuasive presentations initially sound compelling and have what seem to be well-constructed arguments, but they are just the opposite. By the time you finish reading this chapter and the next one, you should be able to identify a good persuasive argument—one that is reasonable, ethical, and civil.

There are entire courses of study devoted to the process of thinking critically about arguments. For the purposes of persuasive speaking, there are established principles and strategies to help you evaluate and analyze the arguments you wish to make as well as those you read and hear. Let's start by looking at the concept of reasoning.

Reasoning

The process of constructing and analyzing an argument is called **reasoning**. Put another way, to reason is to draw conclusions from new or existing information with the aim of seeking the truth. When your reasoning produces an argument that is worth believing (or confirms that someone else's argument is worth believing), it becomes a *well-reasoned argument*. Every well-reasoned argument offers statements (sometimes called **premises**) that support and lead us to accept its *claim* (sometimes called its **conclusion**).

Both speakers and audience members need to know how to use valid reasoning to assess the strengths and weaknesses of a persuasive presentation. Here we present several common types of reasoning and an example of how they might have been used in a presentation to persuade an audience to take precautions to stop the spread of COVID-19. They are not in any particular order because one type of reasoning is not necessarily stronger than the others given differences in a speaker's **PURPOSE ▲ (109–18)** and **RHETORICAL SITUATION ● (6–11)**.

Type of Reasoning	Definition	Example
Cause	Actions or inactions that consistently give rise to a predictable effect—another action, phenomenon, or condition. *A causes B.*	In 2019, a mysterious new respiratory and vascular disease appeared in Wuhan, China. All the patients with this disease were found to have a new coronavirus in their system. This coronavirus—soon named COVID-19—was identified as the cause of the disease.
Sign	Observations about a phenomenon that are linked so frequently that a particular effect is predictable. The sign does not cause the effect but is evidence of the effect. *A and B occur at the same time.*	Most confirmed COVID-19 patients experience some combination of the following symptoms: fever, dry cough, breathing difficulty, muscle aches, chills, tiredness, and loss of taste and smell.
Generalization	A series of examples that share characteristics or outcomes considered reliable as descriptions or predictions that are true in most situations. *A, B, C, D, and E are examples of this claim.*	Contact tracers and public researchers report that many COVID-19 patients attended large indoor gatherings with people who weren't wearing masks or social distancing. Conversely, fewer people contracted COVID-19 if they were consistently isolated and masked.
Classification	Grouping various objects on the basis of their commonly known properties; taking what is known to be true about a group of people, objects, events, and phenomena as true about an individual member of the group. *If you did A, you are similar to others who did A.*	Countries that instituted universal mask wearing, social distancing, business shutdowns, quarantines, and strict border control had the lowest COVID rates and deaths. New Zealand had one of the lowest rates of infection in the world, probably because it instituted all these actions.

Type of Reasoning	Definition	Example
Analogy	A comparison of two otherwise different things based on similar qualities, functions, and/or characteristics in order to conclude that what is true about one is likely to be true about the other. *If it works or is similar to A, it should work for B.*	Wearing a mask to protect yourself and others from COVID-19 is like wearing a seat belt or not driving when drunk.

THINKING CRITICALLY ABOUT REASONING

When you create and analyze an argument, keep in mind that they are almost never 100 percent true. There may be exceptions. It is therefore necessary to apply critical thinking skills each time you encounter them. Begin this process by asking analytical questions: Is there a better conclusion based on your reasoning in the argument? Is a comparison between one thing and another (as in the case of an analogy or classification) both *real* and *relevant* to the conclusion? In short, if an alternative conclusion seems more likely than the one in an argument, or if comparisons don't seem real or relevant, the argument is weak. And if that is the case, modify or completely change your argument and reject someone else's argument accordingly.

Persuading an audience to accept your claims and conclusions can be supported by **PERSONAL APPEALS** ◆ **(412–14)** and **EMOTIONAL APPEALS** ◆ **(414–17)** (ethos and pathos) as much as by **APPEALS TO REASON** ◆ **(417–18)** (logos). Even Aristotle noted that ethos and pathos can be more effective and powerful than logical arguments—and that they are not necessarily invalid or unethical means of persuasion. As an audience member, consider the degree to which an argument is based on one of these other forms of proof. Knowing the difference between the speaker's use of ethos, pathos, and logos in a persuasive presentation will sharpen your critical thinking about your own arguments and help you identify flawed arguments you read or hear.

THINKING CRITICALLY ABOUT FACTS, INFERENCES, AND OPINIONS

As you think critically about arguments and reasoning, you need to understand how facts, inferences, and opinions differ.

	Definition	Example
Fact	A statement about a person, object, or event that can be proven true or false	Maia always turns in her work on time.
Inference	A statement that extends beyond facts to reach a conclusion that may not be provable, often adding unproven information to an observation	I'm sure Maia will continue to turn in her work on time.
Opinion	A statement that evaluates or judges the facts and inferences in a situation	Maia is a responsible and reliable person.

As you listen to—and make—arguments, keep these differences in mind. If you can identify the claims you hear as facts, inferences, or opinions, you can more easily identify the strength and validity of the argument being made.

The Toulmin Model of Argument

There are many different models that help us analyze and build strong, clear, well-reasoned arguments, but one in particular is especially useful for students of persuasive speaking. Developed in the 1950s by Stephen Toulmin, a philosopher and the author of *The Uses of Argument*, the Toulmin model of argument has become a mainstay in communication studies.[1]

The **Toulmin model of argument** explains that a complete argument requires three fundamental components: a *claim*, *evidence*, and a *warrant*. In many speaking situations, one or more of three additional components—*backing* for the warrant, *reservations*, and *qualifiers*—are also necessary.[2] Regardless of whether you are putting together an argument for a presentation or you are an audience member listening to a speaker make an argument, you should think critically about all of Toulmin's components to determine whether the message is worthy of belief.

CLAIM

In Toulmin's model, a claim answers the question "What is the argument trying to prove?" As you now know, a **CLAIM** ◆ **(408–11)** states the conclusion or position that a speaker advocates in a presentation. It is the idea or opinion you want the audience to believe or the action you want them to take. For example, a speaker could claim that "communication skills are the most important characteristics to look for when recruiting new employees" or that "capital punishment does not deter violent crimes." When developing or analyzing the validity of an argument, your first critical thinking task is to identify the claim.

EVIDENCE

Evidence answers the question "How do you know that?" In a complete argument, you must support and justify a claim by providing evidence for its acceptance. Evidence consists of relevant, verified, and valid **PERSUASIVE APPEALS** ◆ **(411–18)** and **SUPPORTING MATERIAL** ■ **(135–39)**.

Evidence strengthens and secures belief in an argument—and can enhance your credibility as an ethical speaker. If you claim that millions of Americans cannot afford adequate health insurance, **STATISTICS** ■ **(147–49)** from a reputable source can help justify your claim. If you are trying to demonstrate the benefits of an early diagnosis of diabetes, you may tell two contrasting **STORIES** ■ **(137–38)**—one about a person with an early diagnosis and one who wasn't diagnosed until the disease had ravaged their body.

Both speakers and audience members should think critically about the quality of the evidence used to support a claim. Use the **SIFT METHOD** ■ **(145–47)**—"stop, investigate, find, and trace"—and think critically about the validity of the evidence.

In addition, make sure your persuasive evidence is *compelling* by making it novel, believable, and dramatic.

- *Novel evidence.* Evidence that is new or not widely known is more compelling and engaging than evidence that is well known to an audience. This lesson is not lost on advertisers who change their ads once a particular version becomes too familiar. Effective persuaders look for fresh new supporting material to engage their audience.

- *Believable evidence.* If you suspect that audience members will doubt the truth of your evidence, address the reasons for their possible skepticism and take care to explain the accuracy and authority of the evidence you've presented. Establish the credibility of your **PRIMARY SOURCE** ■ **(146–47)** by identifying other respected sources that reach the same conclusion. If the source of your evidence has high credibility, mention the source *before* presenting your evidence in your presentation.

- *Dramatic evidence.* When using evidence for a persuasive presentation, find ways to dramatize its importance. **STATISTICS** ■ **(135)**, for example, are often more dramatic when they are used in attention-getting comparisons and examples like this one: "Motorists pay twice as much to repair cars damaged by potholes than our government spends to fix the same holes. Why not save motorists money by investing in better road repair?"

WARRANT

A **warrant** provides the reasoning needed to answer the question "What gives you the right to make that claim based on that evidence?" The warrant links the evidence to the claim by explaining why the evidence is relevant and how it supports the claim.

The nature of warrants differs in every argument, depending on the rhetorical situation. In some cases, your warrant will establish the credibility of the source of your evidence. In another case, it can explain how a study was conducted. Warrants can identify cause-and-effect relationships, connect signs or symptoms to a phenomenon, draw a connection between one example and other examples in the same class, establish the credibility of a source or speaker, and appeal to the motives, values, and emotions of the audience.

The illustration on page 427 shows how the basic "T" of the Toulmin model represents the three fundamental components—claim, evidence, and warrant—of an argument.

The words you put in each box of the Toulmin model are not an argument. They are the strategic building blocks you need to create a valid claim. Thus, an argument advocating the need for affordable swimming lessons for children might sound something like this:

According to the Centers for Disease Control and Prevention, drowning is a leading cause of death among children. Research shows that safety precautions—such as lifeguards or parental supervision,

Evidence ───•

THE BASIC "T" OF THE TOULMIN MODEL

EXAMPLE OF THE TOULMIN MODEL

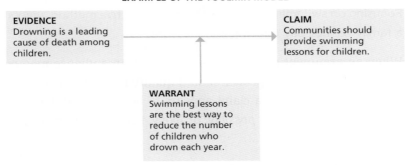

staying in shallow water, and using flotation devices—are not enough. Basic swimming lessons are the answer. Therefore, communities should increase accessibility of affordable swimming lessons for all children. Unlike other life hazards, the ability to swim at an early age can make the water a delightful experience rather than a tragedy.

●——— Warrant

●——— Claim

BACKING, RESERVATIONS, AND QUALIFIERS

In addition to the three primary elements of an argument, there are three supplementary components of the Toulmin model: *backing, reservations,* and *qualifiers*.

Backing, or what Toulmin called "support for the warrant," certifies the validity of the argument's warrant or provides more data and information justifying it. If audience members question why the warrant should be accepted as the link between the evidence and the claim, backing can be crucial. In the case of the preceding example, the backing could be in the form of more information about the credibility of the expert cited in the warrant—for example:

A number of organizations, such as the YMCA, the American Red Cross, and the National Water Safety Action Plan, recommend swimming lessons as the primary way to prevent fatal drownings.

Not all claims are true all the time. The **reservation** component of the Toulmin model recognizes exceptions to an argument's claim or indicates that a claim may not be true under certain circumstances. When you acknowledge a reservation, you have anticipated reasonable questions or objections from audience members. Generally, a reservation is expressed by the word *unless*, as in:

> Focusing on swimming lessons is the most effective method, *unless* a family cannot pay for swimming lessons.

When an argument contains reservations or an audience member is likely to have doubts, the speaker should qualify the claim. The **qualifier** states the degree to which a claim appears to be true. Qualifiers usually include the words *probably, possibly,* or *likely.* For example, consider this claim with a qualifier:

> Providing affordable swimming lessons for all children is *most likely* the best way to prevent drownings.

The following figure illustrates a six-part model of an argument:

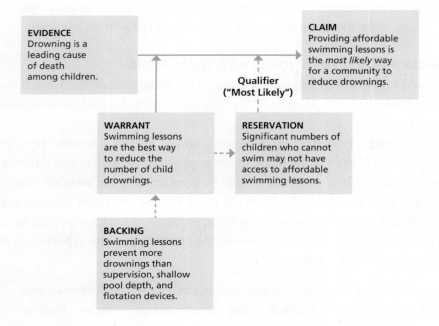

Avoiding Fallacies of Argument

If you **LISTEN EFFECTIVELY** ● **(30–34)** and think critically about presentations, you will encounter good and bad arguments. Skilled speakers and listeners recognize flawed arguments by identifying fallacies. A **fallacy** is an error in thinking that has the potential to mislead or deceive others. Fallacies can be intentional or unintentional. However, when an unethical communicator misuses evidence or reasoning, or when a well-meaning speaker misinterprets evidence or draws erroneous conclusions, the result is still the same—inaccuracy and deception.

For an example of arguments employing the components of Toulmin's model, see Notable Speaker: Yassmin Abdel-Magied, page 225.

After you've learned to identify a variety of fallacies, don't be surprised if you begin noticing them everywhere—in television commercials and political campaigns, on social media and talk radio, in podcasts and on YouTube, and in everyday conversations. (Most propaganda is built on a foundation of multiple fallacies.)

What, for example, is fallacious about an advertising claim that "no other aspirin is more effective for pain"? (All products labeled *aspirin* are the same; their active ingredient is acetylsalicylic acid.) Is it fallacious when a politician calls an opponent a radical socialist or a corrupt capitalist? (What is meant by "socialist" and "capitalist"? Calling an opponent insulting names is often used to avoid a discussion about real issues.)

What follows are some of the most common fallacies you'll encounter when reviewing your own arguments and listening to speakers support their claims. As an **ETHICAL SPEAKER** ● **(43–57)**, it is your responsibility to avoid using these fallacies in your own arguments and point them out in opposing arguments.

ATTACKING THE PERSON

The **attacking the person fallacy** has a Latin name—*ad hominem*—which means "against the man." An ad hominem argument makes irrelevant attacks against a person rather than against the content of a person's message. For example, responding to a claim about property taxes by saying "What would you know? You don't own a home!" attacks the person rather than the argument. Name-calling, malicious labeling, and attacking a person rather than the substance of an argument are ad hominem fallacies. Political campaign ads are notorious for attacking candidates in personal ways rather than addressing important public issues. In some cases, such attacks may be justified to expose an opponent's unethical, immoral, and dishonest statements and behavior. In these cases, such claims about a candidate's character are relevant to how they might conduct themselves in public office and so would not necessarily be considered a fallacy.

When a speaker talks about a person's character, intelligence, or credibility in a critical way, ask yourself these questions:

- Is the negative criticism of a person relevant to the claim the person is making?
- Is the personal attack a way of distracting the audience or avoiding a discussion of important issues, or is it a relevant critique of the person's credibility?
- How often does the speaker resort to attacking someone else rather than make a coherent argument?
- Are the attacks true and valid appraisals of the person?

APPEAL TO AUTHORITY

Expert opinion is often used to support arguments. However, when the supposed expert has no relevant experience on the issues being discussed, the **appeal to authority fallacy** occurs. You often see television and magazine advertisements in which celebrities praise the medicines they use, the companies that insure them, the financial institutions that manage their money, or the beauty products that make them look younger and more attractive. But their authority is only that they are well known, popular, and attractive—not that they bring any special expertise to their claims.

If a speaker is making an appeal to authority, ask yourself these questions:

- Does the speaker, or the person the speaker identifies as an authority, have the experience and qualifications to be an expert authority on the subject?
- Who benefits if you believe the authority—listeners or the so-called authority?
- Is the status of the authority a relevant criterion for accepting the argument's claims?

APPEALS TO POPULARITY AND TRADITION

The **appeal to popularity** and **appeal to tradition** fallacies, sometimes also called the *bandwagon appeal*, claim that an action is acceptable or excusable because it's popular and many people are doing it or because it's what we've always done. Just because a lot of people hold a particular belief or engage in an action does not make it right. Instead, it may mean that a lot of people are wrong. A speaker might state or imply that audience members are "out of it," or "behind the times" if they fail to join the majority and support a particular issue. This bandwagon appeal is also frequently used to justify and recruit people to join hate groups, unscrupulous financial schemes, and illegal actions.

When faced with an appeal based on what many people believe or do, ask yourself these questions:

- Is popularity or tradition a relevant criterion for making a decision?
- Is the appeal justified because it's popular or traditional?
- What are the disadvantages of following the crowd or holding on to a tradition in this case?

APPEAL TO EMOTIONS

The **appeal to emotions fallacy** happens when a speaker uses **PATHOS ◆ (414–17)** inappropriately, arousing audience feelings in order to manipulate their attitudes and behaviors or to distract listeners from a bad or non-existent argument. When appeals to emotions aren't consistent with facts and reasoning, but are a replacement for them, the speaker has unethically chosen to engage in the appeal to emotions fallacy. Obviously, an **ETHICAL SPEAKER ● (43–57)** may arouse justifiable fear when alerting audience members to alarming developments, pity when recounting a tragedy, or joy when revealing good news. However, when speakers appeal to emotions in order to conceal faulty reasoning, deceive an audience, or provoke unwarranted hatred or violence, their claims should be rejected and condemned.

When a speaker makes an appeal to emotions, ask yourself the following questions:

- Are the facts, situations, or stories that arouse emotions true?
- Are the speaker's emotional examples unusual or rare?

- Are the speaker's emotional examples a way of distracting listeners from considering the real issues?
- Beyond the emotional appeal, does the speaker include valid arguments with logical supporting evidence, warrants, and claims?
- Can the aroused emotions lead to attitudes, beliefs, and/or actions that harm innocent or trusting people?
- Do the emotional appeals serve only the speaker's self-interests?

BEGGING THE QUESTION

The **begging the question fallacy** is a type of circular reasoning in which the evidence meant to support an argument assumes the claim is true, as in:

> *Fortnite* (by Epic Games) is the best video game because Epic Games makes the best games and *Fortnite* is their best game.

Notice that there is no warrant in this argument because the evidence and claim are the same and assumed true. This type of fallacy often shows up when a speaker merely restates a claim by rearranging the ideas—providing a mirror image of the claim itself. Here's another example:

> Freedom of speech is one of the central values of open, democratic societies because open, democratic societies value freedom of speech.

In his book, *Begging the Question*, Douglas Walton writes that this fallacy uses "deceptive tactics to try to get a respondent to accept something as a legitimate premise that is really not, to slur over the omission, and to disguise the failure of any genuine proof."[3]

When a speaker is making an argument that seems circular, ask these questions:

- Does the argument assume that something unproven is true?
- Does the evidence (and warrant, if there is one) sound like the claim itself?

EITHER-OR

The **either-or fallacy** occurs when a speaker asks listeners to choose one of two answers or options. In most cases, the speaker has purposely or unintentionally overlooked other possible choices. Given that the either-or fallacy makes things seem simpler than they really are, it allows for memorable slogans, such as "You are either part of the solution or you are part of the problem" and "You are either with us or against us."

Challenging the either-or fallacy can be difficult if the person making the statement truly believes there are only two choices or if the two choices seem reasonable to most people. Here are some questions you can ask yourself, the person who makes the statement, and/or an audience:

- Are the two choices accurate and fair, or limited and unfair?
- Are there other possible options?
- Is there another option that the speaker may not want the audience to consider?

For example, if someone says "America: love it or leave it," you may point out that the choices are too limited and unfair—perhaps you don't love America but can't leave it. Or you could respond: "I love the United States, but throughout its proud history, there have been serious problems and crises—slavery, women's voting rights, civil rights—that required changes to the country's constitution." Or maybe: "I left America for a year, and I came back. I loved my time away, but I knew that America was the best place for me and my family."

FAULTY CAUSE

The **faulty cause fallacy** occurs when you claim that a particular situation or event is the cause of another event before ruling out other possible causes. For example, a statement like "We are losing sales because our sales team is not working hard enough" may overlook other causes for low sales, such as a competitor's superior product or a price increase that made the product less affordable. Often this fallacy involves confusing a merely *chronological* sequence of events with a *cause* preceding an *effect*.

Just because you catch a cold each year during cold-weather months doesn't mean that the cold weather caused your illness. (A virus is the cause of the common cold, and you are more likely to catch one when spending more time indoors.)

Faulty cause fallacies can be difficult to detect, in part because they're so common. When a speaker attempts to argue a cause-and-effect relationship, you should ask these questions:

- Has the speaker or sources of information identified the *real* cause?
- What else could explain why this happened?
- Are there multiple causes instead of just one?

HASTY GENERALIZATIONS AND SELECTED INSTANCES

All it takes to commit a **hasty generalization fallacy** is to jump to a conclusion based on too little evidence or too few experiences. This fallacy argues that if it is true for some, then it must be true for all. "Don't go to that restaurant—I went once, and the service was awful" is a hasty generalization. One negative experience does not mean that other visits to the restaurant would not be enjoyable.

When a speaker is making an argument and generalizing from a set of specific instances, you should ask these questions:

- Is the conclusion based on enough data and/or typical examples?
- Is there a significant number of exceptions to this conclusion?

The related **selected instances fallacy** is more sinister than the hasty generalization fallacy. It occurs when a speaker purposely picks atypical examples to prove an argument. Let's say that you are trying to convince a pro-environmental group that they should help elect a candidate to Congress. You know that the candidate whom you support has a record of voting against environment-friendly initiatives in the state legislature, yet you choose to tell the audience only about the one time their representative voted yes on a pro-environmental bill. In this case, you are using the fallacy of selected instances. Not only is your argument fallacious; it's also unethical.

When a speaker bases their arguments on a limited number of examples, ask yourself these questions:

- Are these rare or infrequent examples?
- How many times has the opposite occurred?
- Why did the speaker choose these particular stories or examples?

COMMON FALLACIES OF ARGUMENT	
Fallacy	**Definition**
Attacking the person (ad hominem)	Irrelevant attacks against a person rather than against the content of a person's message
Appeal to authority	An appeal to the authority of a supposed expert who has no relevant experience on the issues being discussed
Appeals to popularity and tradition (bandwagon appeal)	Claims that an action is acceptable or excusable because it's popular or because it's what has always been dovne
Appeal to emotions	Arousing audience emotions to manipulate them or to distract them from a bad or nonexistent argument
Begging the question	Circular reasoning in which the evidence meant to support an argument assumes the claim is true
Either-Or	Asking listeners to choose one of two answers or options.
Faulty cause	Claiming that a particular situation or event is the cause of another event before ruling out other possible causes.
Hasty generalizations and selected instances	Using too little evidence or atypical examples to prove an argument.

As you think critically about possible fallacies in the arguments you hear or present, keep in mind that there is something known as the **fallacy fallacy**, which is the incorrect assumption that just because an argument is fallacious, its conclusion must be wrong. Even if a speaker has used flawed reasoning to reach a conclusion, there is always a possibility that the conclusion is true. Suppose a speaker claims you should reduce the amount of gluten in your diet because so many people are now buying gluten-free products. The basis for the conclusion is an appeal to popularity fallacy. The number of people "now buying gluten-free products" doesn't prove anything about health benefits. In fact, it may prove that they've been misled and misinformed by advertisers. The conclusion, however—that one should consider reducing the amount of gluten in our diets—is nonetheless a good one for people with celiac disease or health issues related to food sensitivities.

Conclusion

A good persuasive argument is reasonable, ethical, and civil. Developing and analyzing arguments is not an easy task. It requires critical thinking and can be time consuming. It also requires an open mind and a willingness to question both seemingly innocent and controversial claims. What really matters is that both speakers and listeners have the knowledge, skills, and desire to test and, when appropriate, challenge what others say.

The process of reasoning is indispensable in making and thinking critically about an argument, and valid reasoning makes an argument believable. The Toulmin model of argument is one common way for speakers and audience members to understand the components of a sound argument and identify arguments that fall short of being believable. And identifying fallacious arguments is an invaluable skill for assessing the reasoning in an argument—and can make the difference achieving or failing to achieve the purpose of the argument.

Most speakers and audience members are not unreasonable, even if they disagree. They do, however, owe one another a thoughtful response. Ultimately, your credibility and ability to change audience attitudes and behavior depends on your ability to think critically as you create, use, and analyze arguments.

7.3 Rhetorical Strategies for Persuasive Presentations

> ## 🔍 A BRIEF GUIDE TO THIS CHAPTER
>
> • Use audience-centered strategies (p. 437)
> • Adapt your message to audience attitudes (p. 443)
> • Use persuasive organizational patterns (p. 449)

At this point, you should know a great deal about speaking to persuade. You know the types of claims and appeals needed to support your message, how reasoning justifies an argument, and the several common fallacies you should avoid. As important as it is to think critically and strategically about arguments, however, a rock-solid argument won't by itself persuade audience members to change their opinions or behavior. Successful persuasive speakers do more than present a series of **WELL-REASONED ARGUMENTS** ◆ **(421–24)**. They succeed by strategically developing and organizing their arguments into a coherent persuasive message. This chapter focuses on how to think about and strategically address the **RHETORICAL SITUATION** ● **(6–11)** for a persuasive presentation. We begin with the most important element: your audience.

Use Audience-Centered Strategies

Speakers who primarily dwell on what *they* want to accomplish in a persuasive presentation have it all wrong. It's not about you, the speaker. It's about what your **AUDIENCE** ▲ **(88–105)** wants, needs, and expects from you. Ultimately, audience members decide whether they believe you and whether they will change their opinions and behavior.

If you want to persuade audience members, you need to understand a fundamental property of human psychology: *inertia*, the unwillingness to change or take action. Most of the time, most of us believe and do what we've always or recently believed and done. The best way to overcome inertia is through *desire*: audience members rarely alter their opinions or behavior just because a speaker says they should; they must want or be willing to change. As a speaker, your job is to explain why the opinions and/or behaviors you advocate are more beneficial and attractive than the ones the audience currently hold or the actions they currently favor. Here we present several useful persuasive strategies that focus on your audience.

FOCUS ON YOUR AUDIENCE

Set reasonable goals	Aim for incremental changes in audience opinions and behavior, which may be wiser than asking for major changes.
Present both sides of an argument	Compare your own and opposing arguments to show your audience why yours are stronger.
Focus on audience benefits	Explain how your proposal will benefit audience members.
Avoid strong "do and don't" messages (psychological reactance theory)	To prevent negative reactions, avoid telling an audience what to do and what not to do.
Take the best route (elaboration likelihood model of persuasion)	Take a central or peripheral route to persuasion depending on audience members' interest, motivation, and ability to think critically.
Test your thinking on others	Ask people you know to read or listen to your presentation and provide honest feedback that can improve your presentation.

SET REASONABLE GOALS

Effective persuasive speakers seek incremental, achievable changes in audience attitudes and behavior. They rarely ask or expect people to make radical changes after hearing one presentation.

Think about who you were 10 or even 5 years ago. You probably held different attitudes than you do now. When did you change your viewpoints? Most likely not overnight. In fact, it probably took a while. Don't expect to significantly change an audience's opinion or behavior with one good presentation. Change often requires a campaign or a series of speeches. Thus, when you develop your arguments, look for ways to help your audience become less adamant about what they believe and more open to agreeing with you.

PRESENT BOTH SIDES OF AN ARGUMENT

As you plan a persuasive presentation, you may be tempted to tell your audience only your side of the story. After all, what if some listeners are distracted—or even persuaded—by opposing ideas and objections? It's a strong temptation, but you should resist it—both for ethical and strategic reasons.

Misleading an audience by presenting only one side of a controversial argument can be unethical. There may be good reasons for some listeners to believe they cannot or should not change their opinions or behavior. The wisest and fairest move—and part of the job of being an **ETHICAL SPEAKER** ● **(43–57)**—is to respectfully acknowledge opposing sides of an issue.[1]

Bringing up other points of view has the added benefit of strengthening your credibility and the persuasiveness of your appeal. You might say, for instance:

> Here is my position: _____. Others may tell you the opposite,
> so I'll explain why the other argument is weaker and even unwise.

Assume that your listeners know there is or must be another side. And yes, explicitly acknowledging that point of view and then arguing against it can be challenging. Effective persuaders meet that challenge head-on, using valid **CLAIMS, EVIDENCE, AND WARRANTS** ◆ **(424–28)** to address dissenting points of view. They explain what opponents want you to believe and do and why their arguments are flawed. Not only will you be more persuasive by taking this approach, the process of addressing what the other side might say will make *your* arguments stronger.

FOCUS ON AUDIENCE BENEFITS

Marketers and salespeople draw distinctions among the terms *features*, *functions*, and *benefits*. For these sales professionals, *features* perform *functions* that generate *benefits*, and *benefits* are what they try to sell.

Think about the image of a car you'd like to own. Like any car, it has four tires, doors, an engine, and other parts—these are its features. Together, these features get you where you want to go—this is their function. But few people buy a particular car because it has those features and functions. Every car has them. Instead, what sells a car are its benefits. For one person, safety, affordability, and reliability might matter the most. For another, prestige, status, and performance might be most important. Smart marketers and salespeople emphasize how the features and function produce unique benefits for the buyer.

Likewise, skilled persuasive speakers answer their listeners' most basic question—**WHAT'S IN IT FOR THEM (WIIFT)?** ▲ **(93)**—with a **benefits step**, an explicit explanation of how they will gain something important by accepting the argument or proposal. In contrast, inexperienced speakers (and unsuccessful salespeople) often spend too much time describing features and not enough time focusing audience attention on how their proposal will benefit them.

AVOID STRONG "DO AND DON'T" MESSAGES

How would you feel if a speaker got up and declared, "Listen up! I'm here to tell you that what you believe and do is wrong." This kind of statement can trigger a defensive, protective response—"Oh yeah, go ahead and try!"—which makes it much more difficult for a speaker to persuade you to change your beliefs or behavior.

Psychological reactance theory explains why telling an audience what they absolutely must do or must not do can produce the exact opposite reaction. When you perceive a threat to your freedom to believe and behave as you wish, you may go out of your way to try the forbidden behavior or rebel against the prohibiting authority.[2] During the COVID-19 pandemic, this dynamic was one reason some people refused to wear a face mask in public despite public health officials and respected medical experts telling them to do so.

Likewise, after years of telling young people to "just say no," we have learned that preaching abstinence (from alcohol, drugs, premarital and unprotected sex, or junk food) doesn't work very well. Instead, we're better off recommending behaviors that reduce the harms. Organizations devoted to addressing various social problems understand this principle very well. For example, some messages to reduce the harms of opioid use avoid saying "Don't use drugs." Instead, they suggest measures to reduce the harms of overdosing, like "Don't use alone" and "Be prepared to recognize an opioid emergency."

Consider the following approaches to reduce the likelihood that your audience will react negatively to your arguments:

- *Avoid strong, direct commands* such as "Don't," "Stop," and "You must."

- *Avoid extreme statements* that describe terrible and unrealistic consequences such as "You will die," "You will fail," or "You will be punished."

- *Avoid finger-pointing*—literally and figuratively. Don't single out specific audience members for condemnation or harsh criticism.

- *Advocate a middle ground* that preserves the audience's freedom and dignity while moving them toward attitudinal and/or behavioral change.

- *Invite audience members to share their viewpoints and suggestions* about a recognized problem so that both you and your listeners gain a better understanding of a complex issue.[3]

Keep in mind that the level of a threat and resulting negative reaction to a message will differ among audience members. These strategies are likely to produce a positive reaction from most audiences.

TAKE THE BEST ROUTE

Which **PERSUASIVE APPEALS** ◆ **(411–18)** are the most effective? The answer is . . . it depends on your audience. The **elaboration likelihood model of persuasion** claims that there are two distinct routes—*central* or *peripheral*—that listeners take when processing a persuasive message. As a speaker, you must decide which persuasive route to take based on an analysis of how willing and able audience members are to process your message.

When audience members are very interested and highly motivated to listen to your presentation and are likely to **THINK CRITICALLY ABOUT YOUR ARGUMENT** ◆ **(420–36)**, you will be more persuasive if you take a **central route to persuasion**. When taking the central route, use **APPEALS TO REASON** ◆ **(417–18)** to support your claims, including strong, valid, and believable **EVIDENCE** ◆ **(425–26)**. Acknowledge and argue against opposing points of view. Highly motivated, critical thinkers tend to counterargue when listening to a persuader. For example, they may think, "I just read an article that proves the opposite" or "That may be fine in Arkansas, but it won't work in New Jersey." These listeners expect direct, reasonable responses to their internal objections.

When audience members are less interested, less motivated, and less likely to think critically, you're better off taking an indirect, **peripheral route to persuasion**. Use evidence and rhetorical strategies that are more personal and less dependent on critical thinking. Exemplify **COMPETENCE** ▲ **(75–77)** and **LIKABILITY** ▲ **(78–81)** to build your credibility; these listeners are highly influenced by whether they like and believe you. Use vivid **EXAMPLES** ■ **(137–38)** and dramatic **STORIES** ⁂ **(323–32)** to support your arguments and rely on **EMOTIONAL APPEALS** ◆ **(414–17)** that motivate them to care. You may even take an "everything but the kitchen sink" approach because they often interpret the *quantity* of a speaker's arguments as more persuasive than the *quality* of the reasoning.

Of course, many audiences are composed of listeners with varying levels of interest, motivation, and critical thinking ability. In such cases, use a balance of appropriate central *and* peripheral strategies that appeal to a diverse audience. Highly involved critical thinkers may become impatient with your peripheral strategies while less involved audience members may become lost, bored, or annoyed when you present a detailed argument. If possible, you may need to identify one or the other type of listener as your **TARGET AUDIENCE** ▲ **(90)** and appeal primarily to them.

TEST YOUR THINKING ON OTHERS

As much as we may not want to admit it, all of us have deluded ourselves about something we strongly believe. As speakers, we also make flawed decisions about presentations. We may believe that everyone in the audience will follow a persuasive argument or be glued to every word we say. Experienced speakers avoid such self-deception by testing and retesting their messages on others.

Deliver your presentation to a "test" audience, even if only one or two people, and ask for **FEEDBACK ● (39–40)**—observations and questions that can help improve your presentation. They may be confused by a complex or abstract idea or unwilling to accept a claim or argument you think is fool-proof. They may feel manipulated by an argument or proposal or may be upset by an inappropriate example or word. If your test audience doesn't have an immediate reaction, ask these questions:

- What was the presentation's **CENTRAL IDEA ■ (156–57)**?
- What was interesting, boring, persuasive, supportive?
- Was the language **RESPECTFUL AND INCLUSIVE ⁙ (318–22)**? Were there any words they didn't understand?
- How effective was my **DELIVERY ▶ (209–301)**?

You don't have to adopt every suggestion or respond to every objection, but you should consider their reactions seriously. You may even discover that you've made excellent strategic decisions and your presentation is ready to go!

Adapt Your Message to Audience Attitudes

Among the many things that **AUDIENCE ANALYSIS ▲ (90–96)** can tell you about your listeners, one of the most important for persuasive presentations is determining the extent to which the majority of audience members are likely to agree or disagree with you. Think about this aspect of your audience's opinions as an attitude along a continuum from "strongly agree with me" to "strongly disagree with me."

CONTINUUM OF AUDIENCE ATTITUDES

Strongly agree with me — Agree — Undecided — Disagree — Strongly disagree with me

When you understand where audience members stand on an issue, you can begin the process of adapting your message to the people you want to persuade.

PERSUADING AUDIENCE MEMBERS WHO AGREE WITH YOU

People use the expression "preaching to the choir" to suggest that there is no reason to persuade a friendly, supportive audience. If they already agree, why try to change their minds? Yet members of the clergy preach to the choir all the time in sermons that rely on shared beliefs. The reason is that the strength and survival of a religious institution and its values lie with faithful members—those who already believe. A good sermon or member's testimony can strengthen that bond by reassuring loyal members that their faith is well founded and encouraging them to stand by their religious beliefs. In much the same way, a persuasive presentation to an audience of "true believers" can build even stronger agreement with the speaker.

You can strengthen your agreeable audience's attitudes and encourage behavioral change by adopting the following strategies:

- *Present new information.* New information and evidence are more persuasive and memorable than old information and familiar evidence. A new piece of confirming data or a new study gives your audience even more confidence in their favorable opinion of your argument. Avoid, as much as you can, repeating what listeners have heard many times before. At best, the old stuff may simply bore them; at worst, you may undermine the strength of their support.

- *Excite your audience's emotions.* Use **EXAMPLES** ■ (137–38) related to your central idea that stimulate your audience's feelings of attachment to you and your position. Use **VIVID LANGUAGE** ∴ (308) and **EXPRESSIVE DELIVERY** ▶ (212) to demonstrate that the opinions you share are not only justified but compelling and inspiring too.

- *Provide a personal role model.* Strengthen your credibility by telling your listeners **STORIES** ∴ (323–32) about what you have seen or done. Talk about the volunteer work you did for a nonprofit organization that landed you a permanent job or how you've successfully saved and invested your earnings. Explain how you overcame a serious problem or personal hardship to become who you are today. Tell them how supporting a particular cause has made a positive difference in your life and the lives of others.

- *Advocate a course of action.* If your listeners agree with you in principle but haven't yet changed their behavior, explain why and how they should pursue a specific course of action (sign a petition, vote for a particular candidate, change their eating habits, volunteer at a food bank).

Finally, when speaking to listeners who already agree with you, consider giving them an **inoculation**. According to social psychologist William McGuire, protecting audience attitudes from counterpersuasion by the other side is like inoculating the body against disease.[4] You can build up audience resistance by exposing flaws in the arguments of the opposition and showing listeners how to refute those arguments. Researchers have documented the power of inoculation in many contexts—from opposing political attack messages to preventing youths from joining gangs to combating fake news.[5] Inoculation works best when audience members care about an issue, because it makes them aware that their attitudes are vulnerable to attack and then provides them with ammunition against or resistance to the attack.[6] It also creates a more enduring change in attitudes or behavior.

PERSUADING AUDIENCE MEMBERS WHO DISAGREE WITH YOU

Audience members who are likely to disagree with you won't necessarily be hostile or rude, but persuading them is still a challenge. When listeners disagree with you, they have—at least in their own minds—good reasons for doing so. Understanding what those reasons are and how those listeners have come by those opinions is the first step in persuading them to consider a different point of view. Thorough **AUDIENCE ANALYSIS ▲ (90–96)** will help you get there.

Generally, it's a good idea to start with points of agreement with your audience. Standing with your listeners on **COMMON GROUND ▲ (89)**—a place where both you and your audience can agree—is often the key to persuading

audience members who don't share your opinions, values, or beliefs. If you can get listeners to nod their heads early in your presentation, they will be predisposed to listen to your arguments when you get to points of disagreement. Savvy speakers often start their presentations by raising ideas and issues that get people saying yes. In persuasion research, this strategy is called the "foot-in-the-door method." Persuaders get listeners to agree to something minor, and then they get them to agree to something just a bit bigger, and so on until listeners are agreeing with a speaker's major claims. Charities are famous for using this strategy. Send a charity $5, and next time you'll be asked to give $10 or $15. Give $10 to a political candidate, and they may ask you for $50 more.

Here are four additional tactics that are particularly effective for persuading audience members who may disagree with you:

- *Set achievable goals.* Do not expect listeners to change their opinions or behavior radically. Even a small step taken in your direction can eventually add up to a big change. Sometimes just getting an audience to listen to you is a victory.

- *Accept and adapt to differences of opinion.* Acknowledge the legitimacy of your audience's opinions and give them credit for defending their principles. **LISTEN WITH CIVILITY ● (35–37)** to their viewpoints before asking them to listen to and respect yours. Use a two-sided message in which you explain or compare two viewpoints and also show the superiority of your position.

- *Use fair and respected evidence.* Make sure your **SUPPORTING MATERIAL ■ (134–51)** is solid—true, verifiable, and unambiguous. Choose evidence from respected, unbiased sources.

- *Build your personal credibility.* Do everything you can to establish and build your **CREDIBILITY ▲ (74–81)** over the course of your presentation. Positive feelings about you can transfer to positive feelings about your message.

PERSUADING INDECISIVE AUDIENCE MEMBERS

Some indecisive audience members may not have an opinion about your topic because they are *uninformed*, *undecided*, or *unconcerned*. Whereas an **uninformed audience** is fairly easy to persuade because all they lack is strong, relevant information about an issue, an **undecided audience** has often given the issue a great deal of thought. They understand both sides of the issues and want to stay right where they are—in the middle. When speaking to an **unconcerned audience** whose members, for whatever reason, aren't particularly interested in or don't appreciate the importance of an issue, you need to give them a reason to listen and care. Knowing which type of persuasive strategy to apply in each case depends on the reasons for indecision.

STRATEGIES FOR PERSUADING INDECISIVE AUDIENCE MEMBERS		
For the uninformed	**For the undecided**	**For the unconcerned**
• Gain their attention and interest. • Present valid, relevant, and compelling information and evidence.	• Acknowledge the legitimacy of different viewpoints. • Provide new information or a different interpretation of familiar information. • Emphasize or reinforce the strength of arguments on one side of the issue.	• Gain their attention and interest. • Give them a personal reason to listen and care. • Touch their emotions. • Present novel, believable, and dramatic information and evidence.

In the following example, a college student began her presentation on the importance of voting by getting the attention of unconcerned students and giving them a reason to pay attention:

> How many of you applied for some form of financial aid for college? [*More than half the class raised their hands.*] How many of you got the full amount you applied for or needed? [*Less than one-fourth of the class raised their hands.*] I have some bad news for you. Financial aid may be even more difficult to get in the future. But the good news is that there's something you can do about it.

In the real world of persuasive speaking, you will face audiences with some members who agree with your message, others who don't, and still others who are indecisive. In such cases, you can focus your persuasive efforts on just one group, your target audience—the largest, most influential, or easiest to persuade—or you can seek common ground among all three types of audience members.

ADAPT TO CULTURALLY DIVERSE ATTITUDES

As you prepare to persuade an audience, do your best to understand, respect, and adapt to the various ways your audience may respond. You can improve the likelihood of persuading your audience if you adapt the content and structure of your message to your audience's **CULTURAL VALUES** ▲ **(95–96)** and how they process information.

Knowing whether your audience comes from an individualistic or collectivist culture will help you determine if audience members are more likely to be persuaded by appeals that value group identity, selflessness, and collective action[7] or by appeals that value personal wealth, health, and success.

There is also a difference in how cultures interpret verbal and nonverbal messages. In the United States, the United Kingdom, Germany, Scandinavian countries, and Switzerland, for example, audiences generally expect and comprehend messages that are clear, factual, and objective. Words are valued and believed. For example, persuasive appeals in a highly verbal culture are often direct—do this, buy that, drink this, avoid that, just do it! In advertising, this would be called a hard-sell approach to persuasion. The **PROBLEM-SOLUTION ORGANIZATIONAL PATTERN** ▇ **(159–60)** characterizes this kind of thinking.

In contrast, audiences in or from China, Korea, Japan, other Asian countries, and most Latin American countries expect messages that are implied and situation specific. Nonverbal behavior is often valued and believed more than words. Here, a soft-sell approach is a more appropriate persuasive strategy, allowing listeners to draw their own conclusions. Demonstrate benefits and advantages rather than advocating or demanding action. Make sure that your verbal and nonverbal messages are consistent with each other. When addressing this kind of audience, a **COMPARATIVE ADVANTAGES** ◆ **(450–51)** or **PERSUASIVE STORIES** ◆ **(452–53)** organizational approach may be more persuasive.

See Chapter 2.3 **AUDIENCE** ▲ to learn more about individualistic and collectivist cultural values.

Differences among cultures are very real. At the same time, be cautious about how you interpret and use this information. Are all Japanese listeners "we" focused and highly sensitive to nonverbal behavior? Of course not. Are all Americans aggressive "me" speakers? No. Effective persuasive speakers devote extra time and effort analyzing possible differences in their audience's cultural attitudes and behaviors.

Use Persuasive Organizational Patterns

No matter what sort of persuasive presentation you deliver, a clear and easy-to-follow **ORGANIZATIONAL PATTERN** ■ **(157–66)** is of paramount importance if you hope to achieve your **PURPOSE** ▲ **(109–18)**. Here we suggest five organizational patterns that are particularly effective in persuasive presentations.

PERSUASIVE ORGANIZATIONAL PATTERNS	
Problem-cause-solution	Justifies why the solution addresses the cause or causes of a problem
Comparative advantages	Offers a plan and shows how it will do a better job solving a problem or achieving a goal than other plans
Refuting objections	Addresses audience objections by refuting beliefs and attitudes that stand in opposition to your purpose
Persuasive stories	Share a series of well-constructed persuasive stories that engage and motivate audiences
Monroe's motivated sequence	Motivates audiences to do something that will benefit them and others by following five sequential steps

PROBLEM-CAUSE-SOLUTION

A speaker organizes a persuasive presentation in the **problem-cause-solution** pattern—which is similar to the **PROBLEM-SOLUTION ARRANGEMENT** ■ **(159–60)**—by first identifying a significant *problem*, then explaining why the problem exists or continues (the *cause*), and finally recommending a *solution*. This organizational pattern works best when you are proposing a specific course of action and need to justify why the solution you propose addresses the cause or causes of the problem. In the following outline, the speaker uses a problem-cause-solution organizational pattern to focus on the need for improving public education in the United States:[8]

Problem —→   A. American public school scores are falling behind those in other countries.
       1. The United States ranks 11th out of 79 countries in science and 30th in math.[9]
       2. China, Hong Kong, Singapore, Poland, Canada, Estonia, Finland, Slovenia, and other European countries consistently outperform the United States.

Causes —→   B. The United States lags behind for several reasons.
       1. American students spend fewer days and hours in school than students in most other countries.
       2. US teacher training programs are inadequate, and teacher evaluation systems are ineffective.
       3. Inequality in US public schools stems from state variations in property tax bases and teacher salaries.

Solution —→   C. Rigorous, national education standards for students, teachers, and instructional resource levels can significantly improve public education.
       1. Similar plans work well in other modern countries.
       2. National education standards can improve the quality and equity of public schools.

COMPARATIVE ADVANTAGES

The **comparative advantage** pattern is useful when your audience already agrees there is a significant problem or unmet goal (for example, to improve health care, minimize computer hacking, reduce racism and religious prejudices). This type of organizational pattern first describes your plan and then shows that your proposal will do a better job solving the problem or achieving a goal than other plans. It also shows that when compared to other plans, there are more advantages than disadvantages to your plan.

In the following outline, a speaker contends that an extended hunting season is a more advantageous way of reducing the serious problems caused by the growing deer population. After presenting a plan to reduce the deer population, each subpoint in the second key point explains how the plan will achieve the goal of reducing the deer population better than the regulations and laws that are currently in place.

> A. There is a plan that will help reduce the deer population.   ●——— Plan
> 1. The deer-hunting season should be extended.
> 2. States should allow hunters to kill more female deer.
> B. This plan will reduce the severity of the problem.   ●——— Comparative Advantages
> 1. It will save millions of dollars now lost from crops, gardens, and forest seedling damage.
> 2. It will reduce the number of deer ticks carrying Lyme disease.
> 3. It will reduce the number of automobile deaths and injuries caused by deer crossing highways.

REFUTING OBJECTIONS

Sometimes audience members agree there is a problem or difficult-to-make decision but are reluctant to do anything about it because they view your proposal as objectionable, risky, expensive, or difficult to do. Other audience members may come prepared to reject your persuasive message before hearing it because they are adamantly opposed, uninformed, or misinformed about the situation. The **refuting objections** organizational pattern addresses these concerns and doubts by structuring a presentation that explicitly refutes or overcomes beliefs and attitudes that stand in opposition to your purpose.

This organizational pattern begins by framing the problem: *Why don't (or won't) many people . . . wear a protective face mask during an epidemic*

/ visit a foreign country / vote for a particular candidate? Then it identifies the most common objections that prevent people from taking the desired action. The final section refutes the objections with strong, vivid evidence. In the following example, the speaker uses the refuting objections organizational pattern to encourage listeners to donate blood:

Problem ——●

    A. People should give blood but often don't.

        1. Most people think that giving blood is a good idea.

        2. Most people don't give blood.

Objections ——●

    B. There are several reasons people don't give blood.

        1. They're afraid of pain and needles.

        2. They're afraid that they could get a disease from giving blood.

        3. They claim that they don't have time or know where to give blood.

Refutation ——●

    C. These reasons should not deter you from giving blood.

        1. There is little or no pain in giving blood.

        2. You can't *get* a disease by *giving* blood.

        3. The Red Cross makes it easy and convenient to give the gift of life by scheduling blood donation clinics in many locations.

PERSUASIVE STORIES

See Chapter 5.2 **TELLING STORIES** ⸪ for advice on using relevant stories to connect with audience members.

STORIES ⸪ **(323–32)** capture and hold an audience's interest and can serve as a form of persuasive proof. Stories can also be used as the **KEY POINTS** ▪ **(153–56)** in a persuasive presentation. When using the **persuasive stories** organizational pattern, you rely on **EMOTIONAL APPEALS** ◆ **(414–17)** to show how people, events, and objects are affected by the change you are seeking. Or you may use **LOGICAL APPEALS** ◆ **(417–18)** to show why and how three relief agencies worked together to help pets displaced by the wildfires in Maui. This organizational pattern can be an effective way to present a persuasive speech to neutral audience members who are uninformed or are unable or unwilling to listen critically.

The following speaker uses a series of stories as the key points to convince an audience to support programs designed to help political refugees:

A. The stories of three refugee families demonstrate the need   ———— Stories
   for and the value of migration ministries.
   1. Story of Letai Teku and her family (Cambodia)
   2. Story of Peter Musooli and his sister (Ethiopia)
   3. Story of Naser Rugova and his family (Kosovo)
B. More support for migration ministries can save even more   ———— Outcome
   families who are fleeing foreign tyranny and persecution.

MONROE'S MOTIVATED SEQUENCE

In the mid-1930s, communication professor Alan Monroe at Purdue University took the basic steps of a sales pitch and transformed them into a method for organizing persuasive presentations. His five-step pattern soon became known as **Monroe's motivated sequence**.[10] Although Monroe's model incorporates aspects of the previously described organizational patterns, it specifically emphasizes the importance of motivating an audience to do something that will benefit them—and perhaps others. This organizational pattern has five sequential steps: *attention, need, satisfaction, visualization,* and *action.*

1. *Attention.* Gain audience attention and interest by using one or more of the methods recommended for creating effective **INTRODUCTIONS** ■ **(190–98)** to a presentation and for **ENGAGING YOUR AUDIENCE** ⸪ **(303–61)**. This step is also an opportunity to build your **CREDIBILITY** ▲ **(74–81)**.

2. *Need.* Describe a serious problem that needs to be solved or minimized, particularly in terms of how it affects your audience. This is also an excellent place to put a **VALUE STEP** ✸ **(367–69)** to explain why the audience should care about the problem and how solving it can lead to greater well-being

and success. Use the words *you* and *your* throughout this section, and emphasize the negative consequences of what will happen if the problem isn't solved.

3. **Satisfaction.** Propose a plan that will solve or minimize the problem you described in the need step. Explain why your plan is realistic, relevant, and workable, as well as why it is better than alternative plans. In some cases, you may need to address objections the audience has to your proposal.

4. **Visualization.** Help listeners envision the positive outcome of accepting the plan or recommendations described in the satisfaction step. Visualization is unique to Monroe's motivated sequence. Ask the audience to picture what their future will be like with—and without—your proposed solution. Use **VIVID LANGUAGE** ∴ **(308)** and powerful **EMOTIONAL APPEALS** ◆ **(414–17)** and **PERSONAL PRONOUNS** ∴ **(309)** (*you, your, we,* and *us*) to help listeners see themselves enjoying the benefits of your proposal in the future. The visualization step makes this organizational pattern particularly useful when audience members who are unconcerned and unmotivated or who are skeptical of or opposed to the proposed course of action.

5. **Action.** Always end with a **call for action**. Tell the audience what to do. Remind them why this action is necessary and how it will affect them in positive ways. A call to action should be concrete, achievable, and memorable, not wishy-washy or theoretical. For example, ask listeners to donate money, raise their hands in agreement, register to vote, eat less salt, or tell someone else what they've just heard. A poor call to action dilutes the power of a persuasive presentation; a great call to action stirs your audience to act enthusiastically and to remember you and your message. End your call for action with an inspiring and compelling **CONCLUSION** ■ **(198–204)**.

In the following example, a speaker uses Monroe's motivated sequence to organize the key points of a presentation about the devastating effects of worldwide pollution and climate change by beginning with a description of the slow destruction of the Great Barrier Reef in Australia, expanding it to similar problems closer to home, and concluding with a concrete and specific call to action.

A. Stories, examples, statistics, and testimony about Australia's ————— Attention
Great Barrier Reef
  1. My amazing trip to the Great Barrier Reef
  2. Descriptions of corals, marine life, and water quality
  3. Examples of similar sites near where the audience members live

B. Pollution and climate change are destroying beautiful and ————— Need
precious natural wonders.
  1. The Great Barrier Reef is being destroyed at a rapid pace.
  2. Other natural wonders are being destroyed.
  3. Our cities and towns, homes, national and state parks, lakes and seashores, farmland, and natural wildlife are in imminent danger.

C. What can you do to reduce pollution and climate change? ————— Satisfaction
  1. Reduce your carbon footprint and reliance on fossil fuels.
  2. Ride a bike or walk rather than driving short distances.
  3. Donate money or your time to organizations dedicated to saving the planet from pollution and climate change.
  4. Support candidates and elected officials who promise to protect the environment from pollution and climate change.

D. Imagine a world with less pollution and decreasing climate ————— Visualization
change.
  1. Envision the Great Barrier Reef as well as forests, public parks, productive farmland, and clean rivers and lakes in all their beauty.

2. Picture clean beaches, reduced forest fires, new national and state parks, fewer droughts and floods, and secure, and healthy food supplies.

3. Foresee generations of children swimming with Nemo and the turtles on a preserved reef.

Action ——•   E. Act now to make our world less polluted and less devastated by climate change.

1. Do at least one small thing every day to reduce environmental damage, such as: use public transportation instead of a car, consume less beef, reuse items instead of throwing them away. Tell your family, friends, and coworkers to do the same.

2. Join and support organizations dedicated to the cause. Write letters to the editors of news agencies and informational websites.

3. Contact candidates and elected officials and urge them to enact laws and regulations that will significantly decrease the negative effects of pollution and climate change.

Conclusion

Persuasive speaking is a challenging and consequential task. Great speeches have changed people's minds and behaviors in significant ways. They have motivated people to support a worthy political candidate, deepen their faith in a religion or cause, and rally citizens and troops in times of war and public emergencies. Most persuasive presentations do not seek or achieve such lofty goals. But they *can* modify thinking and make significant, beneficial changes in the daily lives of many people.

Because your success as a persuasive speaker depends on whether or not you convince members of your audience to change their opinions or behavior, begin with a careful analysis of your audience and their attitudes. Creating a persuasive presentation begins with knowing what they currently believe and then adapting to what you've learned in order to achieve a realistic persuasive goal. Then consider using the organizational patterns that are particularly well suited for persuasive presentations: problem-cause-solution, comparative advantages, refuting objections, persuasive stories, and Monroe's motivated sequence. Regardless of how you organize your persuasive presentation, practice and deliver your presentation in a manner that demonstrates expressiveness, confidence, stage presence, and immediacy in order to have the greatest persuasive impact on your audience.

In 2010, Ron Finley decided to do something about the "food desert" (a neighborhood with insufficient access to nutritious food) in his South Central Los Angeles community. He began by planting a garden in an unused patch of dirt, the parkway between the sidewalk of his house and the road. When the city of Los Angeles fined him for improper use of the parkway, which is owned by the city and not Finley, he fought back and began his journey toward activism on a grander scale. In 2013, he shared his urban gardening experience on the TED stage. Shortly thereafter, he launched the Ron Finley Project with a focus on community gardening and rejuvenation. With the support of several natural food companies, the project's goal is to create communities "where gardening is gangsta," and "where all ages embrace the act of growing, knowing and sharing the best of the earth's fresh-grown food."[11]

Search Terms

To locate a video of this presentation online, enter the following key words into a search engine: Ron Finley TED talk. The video is approximately 10:45 in length.

What to Watch For

Finley uses several persuasive speaking strategies to address his audience. Initially, most audience members know very little about him or the project he champions. He also knows that his audience isn't going to rise up and join his movement with seeds and shovels in hand. But they and the millions of people who watch his TED talk might become supporters of his cause—which is his primary purpose.

Finley's success depends in large part on his ethos. He exhibits competence, trustworthiness, likability, and dynamism—the hallmarks of credibility. He uses many kinds of evidence—enhanced by powerful presentation aids—that are novel, believable, and dramatic. His language makes his talk memorable: "food desert"; "gangsta gardener"; "growing your own food is like printing money."

Finley's presentation is also an example of how Monroe's motivated sequence can stimulate, inspire, and persuade an audience. His final call to action combines clear, oral, rhetorical, and eloquent language that brings the audience to its feet in an ovation.

[0:00–0:50] Finley begins his talk with a powerful introduction, a model of persuasion in itself, that puts him right in the middle of the story: "I live in South Central," he says, and then shows and describes three slides: "liquor stores, fast food, vacant lots." He explains that an attempt to change the name of South Central to South Los Angeles will look the same: "liquor stores, fast food, vacant lots." Then he cites a statistic also shown on a large slide: "Just like 26.5 million other Americans, I live in a food desert. South Central Los Angeles, home of the drive-through and the drive-by." His short sentences, ironic use of slides, and standout statistics gain attention, set the mood, connect to his audience, and announce his topic.

[0:51–1:10] Finley highlights the gravity of the situation by explaining that "the drive-throughs are killing more people than the drive-bys": the food options available to his neighbors have led to an obesity rate (which correlates with public health issues such as diabetes and heart disease) in South Central that is five times higher than it is in wealthy Beverly Hills. His claims rely on dramatic evidence that shows how different life can be for people who live no more than 10 miles apart from one another.

[1:11–1:55] Finley expresses his frustration at seeing the health effects of poor nutrition on his community. He evokes audience emotions by expressing his dismay about how wheelchairs are "bought and sold like used cars." Rather than relying solely on statistics, he describes the situation using pathos and powerful examples. He then says, "This has to stop. So I figured that the problem is the solution." [A slide appears: "Food is the problem and the solution."] Then he repeats: "Food is the problem and food is the solution." There is no mistaking his claim.

[1:56–3:39] Finley's ethos is rooted in his personal experience with urban farming. "So what I did," he says, "I planted a food forest in the front of my house. It was on a strip of land that we call a parkway." He shows two before-and-after slides to clarify what he means. He then tells the story of fighting city government, which first issued a citation and then a warrant for gardening on city-owned land. He won the fight, received media recognition, and garnered the support of a councilman in the process.

[3:40–7:28] Within his story about fighting the city government, he explains that the city owns the equivalent of "20 Central Parks" in vacant lots, which is "enough space to plant 725 million tomato plants." "Why the hell would they not okay this?" he asks. Finley skillfully uses facts, stories, examples, definitions, statistics, presentation aids, and in particular, analogies, and metaphors to support his arguments: "I'm an artist. Gardening is my graffiti. I grow my art."

[7:28–8:37] Turning his attention to the benefits of what he calls "gangsta gardening," he says, "Growing your own food is like printing your own money." Finley notes that "if kids grow kale, kids eat kale," and eating food that they grow helps them to understand the impact that food has on the mind and body. Beyond being able to eat what they grow, Finley explains that gardening gives kids an "opportunity . . . to take over their communities, to have a sustainable life." The ultimate benefit might just be that the next George Washington Carver will be produced out of kids who are gangsta gardeners—a benefit that would reach beyond Finley's immediate community.

EXERCISE

After viewing Finley's speech, reflect on these questions:

1. What does Finley do to enhance his credibility? Does he succeed? To what extent does his credibility function as a persuasive appeal?

2. Identify examples of how and where Finley uses emotional appeals in his presentation.

3. In what ways does Finley focus on the benefits of his project for people in South Central and/or benefits for the audience?

4. Which elaboration likelihood model route to persuasion does Finley use? Is it the "best route"?

5. How successfully does Finley use the sequential steps of Monroe's motivated sequence? Identify where they occur in his presentation.

6. Do you think Finley's audience will modify their opinions and/or behavior as a result of his presentation? Why or why not?

7. In what ways, if any, could Finley have improved the content and delivery of his presentation?

PART 8
Special Speaking Occasions

Every presentation occurs at a specific *time* and *place*, using a particular *medium*, and there is always one or more reasons why an audience assembles to hear it. These four factors constitute the presentation's *occasion*. The audience on certain occasions will have specific expectations about what you will say and how you should say it. Being aware of and adapting to these expectations is essential to your success as a speaker. The chapters that follow describe the key features of several special speaking occasions and suggest helpful guidelines and tips that are specific to each one.

Special Speaking Occasions

8.1 Impromptu Speeches

🔍 A BRIEF GUIDE TO THIS CHAPTER

- **Key features** (p. 466)
- **A brief guide to impromptu speaking** (p. 466)

Impromptu speeches—presentations for which a speaker has little or no preparation or practice time—are common. In some cases, they are so informal and casual you may not recognize them as presentations. When you've just returned from a vacation and your friend says, "Tell me about your trip!," you're being asked to speak impromptu. Same thing if you're asked to describe your career accomplishments to a panel of interviewers. How will you answer? By focusing on three highlights? By describing the trip day by day or your career achievements in chronological order? Or maybe by explaining *why* you wanted to take the trip or work in a particular field?

Now imagine yourself at a public meeting or rally. You disagree with one of the speakers, and the floor is opened for audience comments. How will you explain and express your disagreement? What's your purpose and central idea?

However you approach your answer, you have only a few moments to decide what you will say and how you will say it. In each of these situations and many others, the response you make will be an impromptu speech.

See Chapter 4.1 **DELIVERY DECISIONS** ▶ to review the difference between impromptu speaking and extemporaneous speaking.

Key Features

IMPROMPTU SPEECHES REQUIRE QUICK THINKING

The major difference between impromptu speeches and other kinds of presentations is that you have little or no time to prepare and practice. You must quickly determine what you will say. More than anything else, you should establish your **PURPOSE ▲ (109–18)** and **CENTRAL IDEA ■ (156–57)**—what do you want your audience to know, believe, or do as a result of listening to you speak? This kind of quick critical thinking continues throughout your impromptu speech until you've said your final word.

IMPROMPTU SPEECHES CAN SIGNIFICANTLY ENHANCE YOUR CREDIBILITY

Because impromptu presentations demonstrate what you already know and believe rather than information you've had time to practice and prepare, they also provide opportunities to build your **CREDIBILITY ▲ (74–81)**. If your impromptu speech demonstrates you are competent, trustworthy, likable, and dynamic, your listeners will be impressed and persuaded in the moment and more willing to accept and remember your message if you speak to them in the future.

See Chapter 1.2 **SPEAKING ANXIETY ●** to review methods for managing your speaking anxiety in impromptu situations, where the lack of preparation time can make you more nervous.

IMPROMPTU SPEECHES DON'T NEED TO BE POLISHED OR PERFECT, BUT THEY SHOULD BE PERSONAL

Impromptu speaking works best when a speaker's delivery is **IMMEDIATE ▶ (213–14)**, friendly, and genuine. Your audience won't expect a polished or professional delivery (in fact, they might distrust an impromptu speaker who seems too well rehearsed), but they will appreciate (and you will benefit) if your delivery is focused on making a genuine personal connection with them.

A Brief Guide to Impromptu Speaking

CONSIDER THE RHETORICAL SITUATION

OCCASION ▲ (61–68) Impromptu speaking occurs in response to an on-the-spot prompt or question from someone: a teacher may ask you to explain your answer to a discussion question, your boss may request a quick summary of your department's work on a project, or your friends may ask you to tell a story about an adventure you had. You are being asked to speak *right now*.

SPEAKER ▲ (72–85) Consider your speaking strengths. Are you most comfortable and confident when presenting **FACTS AND INFORMATION ✳ (375–83)** or telling **STORIES ∴ (323–32)**? Are any of your **VALUES ▲ (95–96)** relevant to this particular situation? Whatever your particular strengths and interests might be, lean on them. An effective impromptu speech rests on a foundation of confidence. Sticking to what you know and what you do well is the best way to build that foundation.

AUDIENCE ▲ (88–105) Because you will have no time to prepare and practice, adapting an impromptu speech to your audience happens in real time, right before and as you are speaking. If your listeners are colleagues, classmates, or friends whom you already know, remind yourself of what you already know about their characteristics, attitudes, beliefs, and values. But mostly, you will need to use your senses and your judgment to gauge how your listeners are responding while you speak. Observe and listen to them carefully before and while you are speaking and try to adapt to their **FEEDBACK ● (39–40)**.

PURPOSE ▲ (109–18) Determining the purpose of an impromptu speech must happen immediately. It all boils down to answering this question: "What do I want my audience to learn, believe, or do as a result of this speech?" It might help to frame your purpose as a phrase or slogan you can say and repeat with ease. For example, if you oppose a proposed increase to the sales tax, your purpose may be to persuade audience members that the proposed sales tax rate is too darn high. The phrase "too darn high" could then be used throughout your presentation: as a warning that the cost of living is already too darn high, that the economy will suffer if the tax rate is too darn high, and that the impact on the working class would be too darn high.

CONTENT ■ (123–207) Once you have decided on your purpose, spend the few seconds (or minutes, if you're lucky!) you have before speaking to identify the key points and supporting material that will bolster your purpose. Use a simple organizational pattern (suggested below) to arrange your ideas. Consider beginning with a **STORY** ∴ **(323–32)** you know well that will engage audience interest and/or emotions.

DELIVERY ▶ **(209–301)** The qualities of effective delivery apply to impromptu speaking just as much as they do to any other type of presentation. But don't worry—most audiences do not expect you to be polished when speaking impromptu. Most important is to maintain frequent **EYE CONTACT** ▶ **(249–51)** with your listeners, speak loud enough to be heard, and adopt a relaxed, **OPEN POSTURE** ▶ **(255–56)** while speaking so you connect with them and are sensitive to their responses as you speak.

ANTICIPATE IMPROMPTU SPEAKING SITUATIONS

In some rhetorical situations, you might know in advance that you may be called on to speak impromptu , like at a staff meeting, class discussion, or public hearing. If you foresee that happening, take time to think about what you might say in advance. Be ready to talk about ideas and information you already know about the topic. Share what you've learned in life or from a book, the news, social media, or a friend. A couple of examples, facts, or a good story may be all you need to support your central idea in an impromptu speech.

APPLY A READY-TO-USE ORGANIZATIONAL PATTERN

A clear, easy-to-follow **ORGANIZATION** ■ **(152–70)** is indispensable to an effective impromptu speech. Although you don't have much time to think about how to organize your presentation, you might consider one of the following simple organizational patterns.

Past, Present, Future This pattern uses **TIME ARRANGEMENT** ■ **(158)** as its organizing principle. A *past, present, future* time arrangement can be as focused as yesterday, today, and tomorrow or as far reaching as from the Stone Age to the post-AI era.

For example, if someone were to ask you to speak impromptu about the value of a college education, you might begin by explaining that in the early twentieth century, a college education was not necessary for most jobs and was something only the rich and gifted could afford to pursue. However, by the end of the last century, jobs that once required only a high-school diploma required at least a college degree. Today and in the future, as new technology changes the way we work, a college education is valuable for equipping individuals with the skills and adaptability to succeed in a more competitive and complex world.

Me, My Friend, and You In this pattern, you begin by explaining how the topic affects or has affected you, tell how it affects or has affected another person, and conclude with how it can affect your audience. For example, if you're advocating the importance of a college education, you can start with your own story—why you went to college, what you have gained from your experience, and why you like or liked it. Then, you can tell a story about someone else who did or didn't go to college. Finally, you can draw general conclusions about the importance of a college education for the members of this audience. The key to this pattern is moving from your personal experiences to establishing **COMMON GROUND ▲ (89)** with your audience.

State It, Prove It, Relate It, Conclude It In this pattern, you follow four steps: (1) here's my **CLAIM ◆ (408–11)**, (2) here's evidence that justifies the claim, (3) here are examples demonstrating the relevance of this claim to the audience, and (4) here's a summary of why listeners should believe this claim. You may state that, in your opinion, a college education is valuable. Next, offer reasons supported by examples that relate to the audience: a college education can prepare you for a career (examples of various careers), inspire you to become a lifelong learner (examples of respected and learned people), and help you meet interesting people who will be your good friends for the rest of your life (examples of your best friends). Finally, summarize why the members of this audience should pursue a college education.

See Chapter 7.1
UNDERSTANDING PERSUASION ◆ to review the main types of claims you might make and how to develop the one you choose into a coherent message.

USE YOUR THOUGHT SPEED

Time is precious to an impromptu speaker. If you're lucky, you may have a minute to jot down a few ideas before speaking. In most cases, you will have only a few seconds to prepare. The key to managing this time is to take advantage of your **THOUGHT SPEED** ● **(38)**—your brain's ability to think faster than you speak. Think about times when you've had a fast-paced, low-stakes conversation with friends. Was your mind filled with a lot of things you could say? Probably. Were you concerned about how you looked or sounded? Probably not. Instead, you were focused on contributing to the conversation.

Thought speed isn't a special skill you need to learn, but you do need to practice using it if you expect it to work when you're speaking. Used efficiently and effectively, thought speed gives you time—whether you're aware of it or not—to think about what you want to say.

KEEP IN MIND . . .

There Is No Time for Anxiety With so much going on just before and while delivering an impromptu speech, there is almost no time for **SPEAKING ANXIETY** ● **(18–26)** to creep into the process. Consider this: After students conclude a major presentation assignment in class, a classmate or the instructor may ask a question. Usually without more than a second's hesitation, most students answer the question with ease. They're not thinking about stage fright; they're thinking about their answer.

Buy Extra Time In the few seconds between the time you're asked to make impromptu remarks and the moment you start speaking, you have to come up with a plan for your presentation. You can stretch those seconds by following a few suggestions:

- *Pause thoughtfully.* Give yourself a few seconds to think before you speak. Your audience may appreciate that you are carefully considering what you want to say rather than scrambling for ideas.

- *Rephrase the question or prompt.* Repeat the meaning of the question in your own words. In addition to ensuring you heard and understood the question or topic for comment, it also gives you more time.

Use All-Purpose Quotations and Stories Most of us know a few quotations by heart—from a treasured book, a favorite writer or poet, song lyrics, or tag lines in famous commercials. Try memorizing a few all-purpose quotations you can apply to almost any speaking situation. Quoting some-one can make you sound knowledgeable and also gives you extra time to think about what you want to say. The same is true of stories. Build a store of engaging personal stories or stories you've heard or read that relate to your purpose or the topic.

Practice Impromptu Speaking When you are alone, with no pressure from an audience, practice impromptu speaking. Pick a news headline and create an impromptu speech in which you describe its importance and implications. Do an internet search for famous quotations and ran-domly choose one as the basis for impromptu remarks. As you practice, tap into your thought speed: one part of your thinking should focus on what you are saying and another part should focus on what you will say next. Make sure to practice aloud—you won't become comfortable using this technique any other way.

8.2 Introducing a Speaker

🔍 **A BRIEF GUIDE TO THIS CHAPTER**

- **Key features** (p. 473)
- **A brief guide to introducing a speaker** (p. 474)

When **introducing a speaker**, you are the warm-up act for the presenter you introduce. Your purpose is to motivate audience members to listen to and value the speaker and the speaker's message. You may have heard a speaker introduction before a guest lecture, at the beginning of a podcast episode, or at the start of a poetry reading. Done well, a good introduction of a speaker will give your listeners reasons to pay attention and admire and respect the presenter before they step up to speak.

Consider the following presentation to introduce a speaker at a national meeting of humanities scholars and educators. In this case, most audience members at this event knew Dr. Alicia Juarrero through the National Endowment for the Humanities, but they knew very little about her as an educator and advocate. Here's how one of the authors of this book introduced her:

> I am delighted to introduce Dr. Alicia Juarrero, our distinguished keynote speaker. You can read about her impressive background, honors, publications, and service to higher education in your program. But your program does not do justice to her work as an educator and advocate.
>
> If Alicia had lived during the Golden Age of Greece and had been a male citizen of Athens, I have no doubt that she would have founded the Academy—well before it was barely a gleam in Plato's eye. Because, first and foremost, Dr. Juarrero is a teacher. When

her college created its Faculty Excellence Award, no one doubted that Alicia would be the first recipient. Her distinguished résumé cannot capture the dedicated hours and effort she's spent helping educators and supporting working women in Cuba.

At the beginning of each semester, Dr. Juarrero shares a statement by Plato with her students: "Thinking is the talking of the soul with itself." To that Alicia adds, "I welcome only thinkers to my classes." And rest assured, if they don't come into her class as thinkers, they have plenty to think about by the time they leave.

Key Features

SPEAKER INTRODUCTIONS ARE NOT ABOUT YOU

Successful speaker introductions focus an audience's attention on the next speaker, not the present one (you). It's not necessary or even desirable to spend any speaking time building your credibility or enhancing your immediacy—your listeners only want to learn about the person you're introducing. At concerts, warm-up bands don't overshadow the main act. In introductions, the introducer should not compete for attention with the person they're introducing.

SPEAKER INTRODUCTIONS ARE HIGHLY FOCUSED

Effective speaker introductions are information-rich and focused. They don't stray from the point. Audience members should be too busy learning relevant and interesting information about the speaker to wonder, "Where is this going?" or "When will this end?"

SPEAKER INTRODUCTIONS MOTIVATE AUDIENCE INTEREST

At their best, speaker introductions not only inform the audience about the speaker's qualifications and characteristics but also persuade them that the speaker is admirable and trustworthy—someone well worth listening to.

See Chapter 2.3 **AUDIENCE** ▲ for advice on determining what will appeal to and motivate an audience.

SPEAKER INTRODUCTIONS FIND THE RIGHT BALANCE

A good speaker introduction avoids overly exaggerated praise while still complimenting the speaker's legitimate achievements. It shouldn't go on longer than necessary or pile on more information than is required to achieve its purpose. It interests audience members without giving away what the speaker will say. In short, it walks the ideal line between too little and too much.

A Brief Guide to Introducing a Speaker

CONSIDER THE RHETORICAL SITUATION

OCCASION ▲ **(61–68)** The reason for a speech of introduction is clear: a particular speaker needs to be introduced to a particular audience by someone who is already familiar (or at least more familiar) to the audience. Generally, speaker introductions are (and should be) brief and always precede the speaker's presentation. Although they occur in many different locations, the introducer is usually familiar with the place—an office, an organization's headquarters, a school—and is often a member of the community.

SPEAKER ▲ **(72–85)** Why are *you* introducing this speaker? Is there something about your relationship with the speaker that makes you the ideal person to introduce them? Or is the **CREDIBILITY** ▲ **(74–81)** you've already built with the audience the reason you were asked to introduce the speaker? Remember your introduction is not about you—it should focus audience attention on the speaker and should bolster their credibility, not yours.

AUDIENCE ▲ **(88–105)** What do your listeners *already* know about the speaker? What do they *need to* know? Given what you know about the audience, what do you think will convince them to pay attention to and care about this speaker? Look for at least one thing that will make the speaker especially interesting to this particular audience. What **COMMON GROUND** ▲ **(89)** do they share?

PURPOSE ▲ **(109–18)** Your general purpose is to introduce a distinctive *speaker* to a particular *audience* on a specific *occasion*. Your more specific purpose may vary depending on how well your audience knows the speaker. If, for example, the speaker is unknown to the audience, your purpose may be establishing the speaker's credibility. If the speaker's topic or reputation is controversial, your purpose may be to acknowledge that fact and encourage the audience to listen with an open mind. Ask yourself, "What can I say that will impress *this particular* audience about *this particular* presenter?"

CONTENT ■ **(123–207)** Determine the key points that will help you build a well-organized introduction. Look for and include the most relevant and interesting information about the person you're introducing—without overdoing it. Ask yourself, "What do I know or what have I learned about the speaker that will help achieve the purpose of this introduction?" Avoid sharing a random collection of unrelated comments. Include a **VALUE STEP** ✳ **(367–69)** that explains why the speaker's message is applicable to audience members and how it can affect their well-being and success.

DELIVERY ▶ **(209–301)** It may seem a small matter, but the most important aspect of delivery when introducing a speaker is this: Are you certain about how to pronounce the speaker's name? If you aren't sure, ask! As with many other presentations, **EXTEMPORANEOUS DELIVERY** ▶ **(215)** works well for a speaker introduction if you can keep the information about the speaker clear in your mind with minimal notes. If you decide to use a **MANUSCRIPT** ▶ **(219)**, practice your delivery instead of reading it word for word. Some speakers memorize the first few lines of an introduction and are skilled enough to modify what they say if needed. Although it's fine to turn and address the speaker when telling a story or emphasizing an achievement, you should spend most of the introduction looking at the audience, not at the speaker.

INTERVIEW THE SPEAKER BEFOREHAND

Introducing a speaker requires that you know more about them than the audience can learn by reading about them in a program or a flyer. The best way to do so is by talking with the speaker beforehand. But before you do, make sure to do research about the speaker on your own; this will enable you to ask better questions. Here are some questions to get your conversation started:

- What do you hope to achieve by addressing this audience? Is there some way my introduction can help you do that?

- Here's a summary of what I know about you. . . . What else should I know or consider sharing with the audience?

- How and why did you first become involved in this subject? Why is it personally important to you?

- What are the most important things you want this audience to know about you and/or your topic before you begin your presentation?

- Are there some people I should contact to learn more about you and your work or achievements? Is there an article you'd recommend or something you've written that I should read?

In some cases, a professional speaker or someone who frequently speaks to various groups will have a sample introduction you can use. It will cover what, in the speaker's opinion, the most important ideas and information are to emphasize in your introduction. You can use this information, but make the presentation your own—if all you do is read a prepared introduction, it won't sound like you and may not relate to your specific audience.

INTRODUCING YOURSELF

In some rhetorical situations, the audience may not know who you are. In fact, you may be introduced by someone else as the person who will be introducing the speaker. If you and the audience are not acquainted and you are not introduced by someone else, begin by introducing yourself and establishing quickly and directly your connection to the speaker:

> My name is _____ and I have taken—and passed—three philosophy classes taught by Dr. Alicia Juarrero. She is my favorite professor. I believe you will understand why I feel this way during and after her presentation.

KEEP IN MIND . . .

Repeat the Presenter's Name Mention the speaker's name several times during the introduction unless the audience knows the speaker well.

Avoid Clichés Trite, overused, and unoriginal CLICHÉS ∴ (310–11) undermine the unique impression of the speaker you're attempting to create.

Instead of an overused phrase such as "Tonight's speaker needs no intro-duction," simply tell your audience something they don't already know about this otherwise well-known person. If you're at a loss about how to end, don't resort to a tired phrase such as "without further ado." Instead, simply say, "Please join me in welcoming _____" or "I am honored to introduce _____," and then step aside.

Adapt to the Setting If you are responsible for introducing a speaker, you may also be the only person in charge of making sure the facilities and equipment are prepared and ready for use by the speaker. You'll be the first person speaking, so make sure you are familiar with the setting, both for your own and for the speaker's sake.

Begin the Applause At the end of your introduction, begin applauding until the speaker reaches the lectern or podium. This prompts your audi-ence to applaud. If appropriate, shake hands with the speaker. Then, when the speaker begins the presentation, **LISTEN ● (30–42)** closely. You might have to respond to a thank-you for a great introduction.

Dr. Ronald A. Crutcher and Courtney Britt

Search Terms

To locate a video of this presentation online, enter the following key words into a search engine: University of Richmond 2016 commencement Courtney Britt. The video is approximately 4:56 in length.

Introducing a Speaker: Commencement Address

[0:00–1:12] At the 2016 commencement at the University of Richmond, the university president, Dr. Ronald A. Crutcher, introduced Courtney Britt, a graduating student who would then introduce the commencement speaker. Crutcher lists many of Britt's accomplishments as well as her service to the university. Crutcher's speaking style is relaxed and very likable even as he reads prepared remarks. His less-than-a-minute introduction is just enough to establish her credibility without taking time from Britt's introduction or the commencement speaker's address.

[1:20–4:53] Within 30 seconds of beginning a three-and-a-half-minute introduction, Britt names Charlyne Hunter-Gault—a person known and described in the commencement program. She uses a chronological organizational pattern moving from Hunter-Gault's childhood and racial integration experience in college to her prestigious journalism career. Britt then lists many of the speaker's awards and honors. The conclusion is more personal: both Britt and Hunter-Gault are members of the same sorority, Delta Sigma Theta, which is committed to sisterhood, social justice, and public service. Britt reads her introduction from a manuscript that—if you look carefully—is typed in large, readable letters. For this formal commencement speaker introduction, the script is carefully written and read.

Do you think Britt did a good job inspiring audience interest in Hunter-Gault? How might she have improved her introduction?

8.3 Welcome Remarks

> ## 🔍 A BRIEF GUIDE TO THIS CHAPTER
>
> - **Key features** (p. 480)
> - **A brief guide to welcome remarks** (p. 481)

A common but underappreciated type of presentation, **welcome remarks** are often delivered when a group of people visit or join a school, company, or organization or to kick off special events or occasions. Here are some examples:

- An admissions officer welcomes high-school students and their parents to a campus visit.
- A youth group leader welcomes teenagers to a religious retreat.
- A corporate executive welcomes new employees to the firm's orientation week.
- The director of a living-history site welcomes daily visitors.

Welcome remarks require careful attention to your audience and to the upcoming occasion, which should be the focus of your greeting. In addition to helping an audience look forward to whatever will follow, the best welcome remarks make an audience feel the speaker knows who they are and why they are there.

The following excerpt is the beginning of a welcome speech delivered by Kristen Bub, an advanced doctoral student, to the incoming 2007 class at Harvard University's Graduate School of Education. Bub addressed the students about what to expect at the school and what she has learned along the way. Notice how her remarks connect the speaker, the university, and the audience.

> Good morning and welcome to the Harvard Graduate School of Education. It is both an honor and a privilege to stand before you today and welcome you to this amazing community. If you are anything like I was when I started, you are sitting there feeling a million different emotions and asking yourself a million different questions. "Did I make the right choice?" (*without a doubt*); "Is this worth the sacrifices I have made to get here?" (*absolutely*); and perhaps as you have already heard, you are not the admissions mistake. In fact, I can assure each and every one of you that you are here because you deserve to be, and because you can bring something new and exciting to this diverse learning community. So welcome![1]

Key Features

WELCOME REMARKS CONNECT YOUR AUDIENCE TO THE ORGANIZATION OR EVENT

The very name of this type of speaking occasion depicts its purpose: your job is to make your audience feel welcome. You should help your listeners understand how they fit in and how they can benefit from the session, tour, or experience they're about to have.

WELCOME REMARKS ARE NOT ABOUT YOU

Although you may be the chosen representative of an organization and the first person audience members encounter, you are not what the occasion is all about. Unlike someone making a **TOAST** ★ **(499–504)** or **PRESENTING AN AWARD** ★ **(485–90)**, your listeners don't need to feel a personal connection to you. Other than your title or relationship to the organization, there isn't much more your audience needs to know about you.

WELCOME REMARKS HIGHLIGHT YOUR ORGANIZATION

Your presentation should make a positive impression on the audience about the organization you represent (for example, "When I give campus tours, I am always amazed by this campus—the college's history, buildings, and faculty"). If your listeners feel comfortable, eager, and interested in the event or organization as a result of your remarks, you will enhance your organization's credibility, and you will have created a positive communication climate that benefits everyone.

WELCOME REMARKS ARE BRIEF (BUT NOT TOO BRIEF)

Welcome remarks should be more than a simple "Hello, here's what will happen; enjoy!" But they shouldn't be much longer than Kristen Bub's example at the beginning of this chapter. In most situations, you should give only enough detail to make it clear you know something specific about the audience and to make them comfortable in their new environment, but once you've done that, your job is done.

See Chapter 5.3 **GENERATING INTEREST ∴** to transform a humdrum welcome into one that overcomes audience disinterest, uses humor and stories, and cultivates audience participation in a brief amount of time.

A Brief Guide to Welcome Remarks

CONSIDER THE RHETORICAL SITUATION

OCCASION ▲ (61–68) A group of visitors or guests have arrived at a school, a company, or an organization and need someone to make them feel welcome and to familiarize them with the reasons and agenda for their visit. Welcome remarks are very brief and occur on or near the site where the visit or tour is happening.

SPEAKER ▲ (72–85) Audience members simply need to know who you are and why you are welcoming them—your job title or position in the organization may be all that's needed to make this clear to them. If, like Kristen Bub, you were once in the same position as your listeners, you might say something to make this clear, but remember to keep this aspect of your remarks brief.

AUDIENCE ▲ (88–105) Do you know anything about your audience's personal goals and history? What interests, attitudes, and values do they share with the organization? Connecting your audience to your organization in some way will increase their interest and sense of connection to it. If you don't know anything about your audience until they show up, you might **ASK A QUESTION ∴ (343–44)** or two by show of hands before you begin.

See Chapter 2.3 **AUDIENCE ▲** to help you understand, respect, and adapt to the audience.

PURPOSE ▲ (109–18) Your overarching purpose is to make your audience feel appreciated and welcome. If this is the beginning of a long-term relationship (for instance, an orientation for new students or employees), you should link your audience's goals and aspirations to the organization and help your listeners feel they belong. If this is a onetime event (a guided tour of a factory or museum, for example), your purpose is to generate interest and enthusiasm for the event by making it clear how they will benefit from it.

CONTENT ■ (123–207) Welcome remarks should be brief, friendly, inclusive, and positive. Ask yourself, "What can I say in a short amount of time that will engage the audience and highlight the reason for or the importance of the event?" Use a simple **ORGANIZATIONAL PATTERN ■ (157–66)** that features an engaging **INTRODUCTION ■ (190–98)** and memorable **CONCLUSION ■ (198–204)** .

DELIVERY ▶ (209–301) Welcome remarks should be natural and friendly and should establish **IMMEDIACY ▶ (213–14)** with your listeners. **EXTEMPORANEOUS DELIVERY ▶ (215)** is best, but if you've written down your remarks, practice them enough so you don't (or rarely) need to consult your notes.

LINK YOUR AUDIENCE AND YOUR ORGANIZATION

With welcome remarks, the **COMMON GROUND ▲ (89)** you're looking for isn't something you share with your audience; it's something that's shared by your audience and the organization you represent. You're the link between them! Answering the following questions can help you connect the group you represent to members of the visiting audience:

- How much does the audience know about your organization?
- Why is the audience attending this event, and why is your organization hosting it?
- What are the visiting group's mission, goals, and reputation? How are they similar to or different from your organization's mission, goals, and reputation?

- Are audience members' characteristics, attitudes, beliefs, values, and goals similar to those in your organization? Is there a meaningful organizational slogan, motto, or mission statement you can share?
- What are the expectations of your guests for the event and your organization?

ORGANIZING WELCOME REMARKS

As with any presentation, there are numerous ways to organize the content of a welcome. The following **OUTLINE ■ (176-89)** depicts a typical bare-bones template for a welcome:[2]

I. Introduction
   A. Introduce yourself (and your title or function) to the audience.
   B. Welcome the audience (and, if applicable, their organization) to the occasion or name of the event and to the host/sponsor, and thank the audience for coming.
   C. Briefly describe the host/sponsor (the business, organization, agency) and the occasion/event.

II. Body
   A. Preview highlights of the event or occasion.
   B. Explain how audience members can benefit by attending and/or participating.
   C. Welcome and answer questions.

III. Conclusion
   A. Briefly review the agenda/schedule and make any announcements, if needed.
   B. Introduce the next speaker, if appropriate.
   C. Conclude by generating enthusiasm and appreciation for what's to come.

KEEP IN MIND . . .

Adapt Your Speaking Style to Your Audience If you and the audience are already acquainted and share common characteristics and attitudes, you can use a casual, conversational speaking style. If you and the audience are new to each other, you might want to use a more formal style to demonstrate professionalism and respect for your listeners.

Highlight Benefits Emphasize important ("you won't want to miss") features that will occur during the event or during your listeners' time as members of the organization and how audience members can benefit from them.

Acknowledge Important Individuals Recognize the visiting group's leader or other important audience members by name somewhere in your welcoming remarks. Make sure you correctly pronounce their names (and the name of the group you are welcoming).

Stick Around after You Finish Speaking Don't rush out the door. Someone may have a question or need your help. Even if you do nothing more than stand at the back of the room for a few minutes, you will be further extending the goodwill created by your welcome.

8.4 Presenting and Accepting an Award

> ## 🔍 A BRIEF GUIDE TO THIS CHAPTER
>
> • Key features of presenting an award (p. 486)
> • A brief guide to presenting an award (p. 487)
> • Key features of accepting an award (p. 490)
> • A brief guide to accepting an award (p. 492)

Organizations of all sorts—from a small-town high school to the international Nobel Prize committee—hold awards ceremonies for similar reasons: to recognize individual or group excellence, to motivate others to strive for higher goals, and to publicly call attention to a person or organization and its good work.

The logistics of awards ceremonies vary. Some, such as the Academy Awards or the Nobel Prize ceremony, are carefully choreographed. The majority of awards ceremonies, however, are smaller events occurring in less formal settings, such as schools, offices, community organizations, corporations, city halls, houses of worship, and summer camps. These different settings—and occasions—carry specific expectations with them (level of formality and type of dress, time limits, traditions concerning what is said and how it is said).

There are two central figures in every awards ceremony: the person who presents the award and the person who accepts the award. Obviously, presenting an award and accepting an award are connected. They literally go hand to hand—the speaker hands an award to a recipient who accepts it. But they are *not* the same kind of presentation. The rhetorical situation for the presenter is quite different from that of the recipient—even though they occur one right after another. In this chapter, we will cover each type of presentation separately.

Key Features of Presenting an Award

Presenting an award involves introducing and praising the contributions of the person receiving the award. The presenter describes the award and its importance and also identifies the recipient and explains why the recipient is being honored.

Here's an excerpt from a famous award presentation by Egil Aarvik, chairman of the Norwegian Nobel Committee, presenting the Nobel Peace Prize to Elie Wiesel in 1986:[1]

> I doubt whether any other individual, through the use of such quiet speech, has achieved more or been more widely heard. The words are not big, and the voice which speaks them is low. It is a voice of peace we hear. But the power is intense. Truly, the little spark will not be put out, but will become a burning torch for our common belief in the future. Truly, prisoner number A 7713 has become a human being once again—a human being dedicated to humanity. . . .
>
> It is in recognition of this particular human spirit's victory over the powers of death and degradation, and as a support to the rebellion of good against the evil in the world, that the Norwegian Nobel Committee today presents the Nobel Peace Prize to Elie Wiesel. We do this on behalf of millions—from all peoples and races. We do it in deep reverence for the memory of the dead, but also with the deep-felt hope that the prize will be a small contribution which will forward the cause which is the greatest of all humanity's concerns—the cause of peace.

PRESENTING AN AWARD IS NOT ABOUT YOU

It is, of course, an honor to be chosen to represent an organization giving an award, but you should remember that you are not what the occasion is all about. Successful award presentations focus an audience's attention on the award and the recipient. It's not necessary or even desirable to spend any speaking time building your credibility or enhancing your immediacy—the audience wants only to join you in celebrating an achievement. If most audience members don't know who you are and you are not introduced by someone else, begin with a simple introduction, as in: "My name is _____, and I chaired this year's selection committee."

YOUR REMARKS DEPEND ON WHAT THE AUDIENCE KNOWS

During some award presentations, the audience knows who the winner is but may not know very much about the significance of the award or how the winner was chosen. (An example might be a popular celebrity receiving an award from a small nonprofit organization.) During other award ceremonies, the audience knows a great deal about the significance of the award but not much about the recipient (for example, an up-and-coming musician, writer, or artist receiving a MacArthur Foundation "Genius" Award). In either case, a successful award presenter will make sure that by the presentation's conclusion, the audience better understands the award and why the recipient deserves it. How much time the presenter spends discussing the background and significance of the award or the background and contributions of the recipient depends on what the audience knows.

A Brief Guide to Presenting an Award

CONSIDER THE RHETORICAL SITUATION

OCCASION ▲ (61–68) The reason for an award presentation is reflected in its name: someone is being honored with a gift or award in recognition of a specific achievement or overall excellence. The timing of an award presentation is determined by the organization hosting the award ceremony and can range from a few minutes to a longer, formal presentation. Award presentations often occur at celebratory events, and the logistical details about the timing are usually choreographed and planned with great care. If other members of the organization will be assisting in the award presentation (for instance, coming onstage with a trophy or other object to be presented to the recipient), talk to them beforehand to coordinate what will happen. Make sure the facilities and equipment are prepared and ready for use.

See Chapter 4.1
DELIVERY
DECISIONS ▶
for advice on
delivering your
presentation
sincerely and
naturally.

SPEAKER ▲ (72–85) You may want or need to clarify why *you* are presenting the award—your position in or relationship to the organization giving the award, for instance—but beyond that, keep the focus on the award (and its sponsor) and the winner. One way to do this is to ensure you are comfortable and **CONFIDENT ▶ (212–13)** delivering the presentation. A nervous, scattered presenter will distract attention from the award and its recipient. So play to your strengths as a speaker, stay in your comfort zone, and use your skills to honor the recipient.

AUDIENCE ▲ (88–105) Ask yourself, "What do the listeners already know about the award recipient? What do they *need* to know? Why should they pay attention and/or care about this award? How can I demonstrate the importance and benefits of the award and its significance to the audience?" Answering these questions requires **AUDIENCE ANALYSIS ▲ (90–96)** to determine what your audience knows, believes, wants, and expects.

PURPOSE ▲ (109–18) Your general purpose is clear: to present an award to a worthy recipient. Your specific purpose can vary depending on what the audience knows about the recipient and the award. If the audience doesn't know much about the winner, your purpose is to highlight the person's background, achievements, and **CREDIBILITY ▲ (74–81)**. If the audience knows the recipient but not much about the award, you'll want to make sure to explain its significance.

CONTENT ■ (123–207) Learn as much as you can about the award recipient (including, and most importantly, the pronunciation of their full name if you are unsure of it!) and the significance of the award. Research the person's background, achievements, personal characteristics, and opinions. Begin with an attention-getting **INTRODUCTION ■ (190–98)**. Use **STORIES ∴ (323–32)** and examples to stimulate the audience's interest and feelings. Provide a clear and vivid description of the winner's accomplishments. Identify the values, virtues, and benefits of the award. If appropriate, mention past award winners. Pay particular attention to the **SPEAKING STYLES ∴ (314–18)** and strategies you use. Whereas eloquence may be appropriate and expected for conferring a prestigious, international prize, a clear conversational style may be better suited for a local club award presentation. Finish with a heartfelt **CONCLUSION** ■ **(198–204)**.

DELIVERY ▶ **(209–301)** An award presentation is not an occasion for impromptu speaking. If possible, use **EXTEMPORANEOUS DELIVERY** ▶ **(215)**—which allows you to maximize eye contact and seem spontaneous but also well prepared. When an award winner has a long list of accomplishments, or you want to read something the winner has said or written, a **MANUSCRIPT** ▶ **(216)** may be needed. Practice your delivery so you can maintain eye contact with your audience rather than reading most of it word for word. If you recognize the winner at the beginning of your presentation, look directly at the audience and occasionally at the winner (regardless of whether that person is seated on stage or still in the audience). If you reveal the winner at the end, look at the audience up until the moment you announce the winner.

REVEALING THE WINNER

In some situations, award recipients and audience members know who will be honored at the event. In other situations, the name of the winner is a secret known by only to a few people. Whereas Nobel Prize winners know in advance, major book award winners may not. Nor do most local recipients of "best athlete" or "best pizza" prizes.

When neither the award winner nor the audience knows who will win the award, you have an important decision to make: Should you surprise the award winner and audience at the end of your presentation, or should you identify the award winner at the beginning? Although it may be fun to keep the nominees and audience guessing, identifying the person at the beginning may be the better choice, particularly if audience members don't know the recipient very well or at all. (That is not the case for the Golden Globes or college football's Heisman Trophy.) If you name the winner at the beginning of your presentation, you can invite the person to join you at the front of the room or on the stage. If you reveal the winner at the end of your presentation, invite the person to come forward and join you. Some of these decisions may be determined by the traditions of the organization. Make sure to ask the organizers if they have a preference.

See Chapter 5.1
**LANGUAGE AND
STYLE** ⁂ to
understand how
your language
choices can
enhance the value
of an award and
the merits of the
winner.

KEEP IN MIND . . .

Enlist Language Strategies to Achieve Your Purpose Take another look at Egil Aarvik's eloquent Nobel Peace Prize presentation (p. 486). What lifts his presentation to a higher stature is his language. Aarvik's words are clear and brief—as are most of his sentences: "The words [referring to Wiesel] are not big, and the voice which speaks them is low. It is a voice of peace we hear. But the power is intense." He contrasts big and small, peace and power, and repeats the simple word "is" in three sentences. Writing this kind of presentation is not easy because every carefully chosen word and phrase contributes to achieving its purpose.

Perfect the Handoff If you are handing someone an object or envelope, present the award with your left hand and shake the person's right hand. Practice this gesture at home before the event—it's worth the effort. This is the moment for photographs, so you'll want to avoid an awkward handoff. Once you've handed the award to the recipient, step aside so the winner is the center of attention.

Make Sure They Don't Remember You Most audience members remember who receives an award, particularly if it's someone they know or the award is highly prestigious. If the presentation of the award is done well, they will rarely remember who presented the award. When audiences *do* remember who presented the award, it is almost always for the wrong reason—namely, because the presenter has done something to call attention to themselves, diminishing the specialness of the event and the honor for the recipient. If you achieve your purpose, motivating your listeners to appreciate the winner's achievement and the significance of the award, you will not be remembered. Strive to not be remembered!

Key Features of Accepting an Award

Presenting and accepting awards are not the same. **Accepting an award** involves expressing your gratitude for the honor you're receiving and acknowledging its significance. It is also an occasion to praise the organization or group that sponsors the award and hosts the event. It may even be an opportunity for you to raise awareness about a cause or principle you believe in. While every award ceremony has a different setting and set of expectations, there are some features all acceptance speeches share.

ACCEPTANCES OFTEN FOLLOW RULES AND TRADITIONS

Many awards ceremonies have become traditions with a rich history and established customs and conventions. Although famous recipients may flout or simply be unaware of the conventions of such ceremonies, it is generally expected that recipients will have some familiarity with the cultural norms of the event and will shape their acceptance to conform to them.

ACCEPTANCES EXPRESS GRATITUDE FIRST AND FOREMOST

An award or honor presentation bestows on a recipient the respect and acknowledgment of an entire community. It is a significant public gesture, even in small, intimate, and informal settings. As such, it merits a respectful and gracious response. The most successful acceptance speeches usually begin and end with a sincere expression of gratitude.

ACCEPTANCES OFTEN PRAISE THE AWARD GIVER

In addition to expressing personal thanks to individuals, acceptance speakers usually praise the organization or group granting the award—for the work they do, for the principles they profess, and/or for the causes they support. Successful acceptance speeches support the beliefs, values, and commitments of the organization giving the award and its members (who may represent the majority of audience members).

ACCEPTANCES MAY ADVOCATE A RELATED CAUSE

Some award winners use acceptance speeches to promote a public or personal cause. Generally, it is inappropriate and even offensive to advocate an unrelated or unpopular cause. However, in some rhetorical situations, doing so can raise the quality and impact of the honoree's remarks, especially if the cause is closely aligned with the values of the audience and the organization giving the award. For example, in his acceptance speech for the Academy Award for Best Actor in the film *The Revenant*, Leonardo DiCaprio said, "Climate change is real, it is happening right now. It is the most urgent threat facing our entire species, and we need to work collectively together and stop procrastinating."[2]

A Brief Guide to Accepting an Award

CONSIDER THE RHETORICAL SITUATION

OCCASION ▲ (61-68) The reason for an award acceptance is as straightforward as the act of presenting one: someone (you—congratulations!) is being honored with a gift or award in recognition of a specific achievement or overall excellence and is invited to say a few words in gratitude. The occasion, timing, and planning of an awards ceremony are determined and managed by the event organizers. Potential or preannounced award recipients are given directions about when to rise, where to go, what to wear, and how long to speak. Depending on the formality and significance of the award, accepting an award can be an informal, brief thank-you or a longer, scripted address at a public event.

SPEAKER ▲ (72-85) Your **INITIAL CREDIBILITY ◆ (412)** will be high because you are being honored, even more so if the person presenting the award to you does a good job of explaining who you are and why you are receiving the award. Even so, a poor acceptance speech can change how the audience feels about you. Don't squander your credibility. If you know you will be receiving an award, develop an appropriate and meaningful acceptance speech based on the advice in this chapter.

AUDIENCE ▲ (88-105) Audience members may know and will have heard many wonderful things about you. Your role is to **CONNECT ▲ (72-73)** with them. Justify their good feelings and the respect they've bestowed on you with their attendance, attention, and applause. Remember: most of your listeners are representatives of, or at least affiliated with, the organization or group that has honored you. Show them you are grateful, delighted, and honored by the award. Tell them you revere *their* work and their values.

PURPOSE ▲ (109–18) Accepting an award has two main purposes: first, to thank those who sponsor and give the award, and the people who helped you earn it. Second, and maybe more important, to explain the value of the organization and its mission. In some cases, as we've already indicated, you may advocate a related worthy cause that reflects their mission.

CONTENT ■ (123–207) The first and perhaps last words out of your mouth should be an expression of gratitude. Make a list of those you want to thank and bring it with you so you don't forget someone. Explain why the award means a great deal to you. You may also tell a brief personal **STORY ∴ (323–32)** related to the work you've done to earn the award and use a bit of **SELF-EFFACING HUMOR ∴ (341–42)**. Praise the other nominees if they are known. Use some of your time to emphasize the importance of the cause for which you are being honored. End with an inspirational **CONCLUSION ■ (198–204)**. If you're having difficulty finding the right words, use a quotation by someone who captures your feelings.

DELIVERY ▶ (209–301) If you know in advance that you will receive an award, prepare and **PRACTICE ▶ (220–24)** what you will say. **EXTEMPORANEOUS DELIVERY ▶ (215)** is best; the most memorable acceptance speakers use very few or no notes at all—other than having the names of people or organizations that must be thanked and perhaps a brief list of **KEY POINTS ■ (153–56)**. Unless the awards ceremony is formal, significant, and public, avoid reading from a manuscript because it can detract from your expressiveness, confidence, stage presence, and immediacy. Maintain as much eye contact as possible and zero in on some of the important people in your audience as you thank them or praise their work. And smile!

See Chapter 4.1 **DELIVERY DECISIONS ▶** for help developing expressiveness, confidence, stage presence, and immediacy.

KNOW WHAT'S EXPECTED, JUST IN CASE

If you know you will be receiving an award and have never attended the event, find out what is expected of recipients. Make sure you can answer the following questions: Should you acknowledge the presenter? Whom should you thank? If known, are you expected to acknowledge the other nominees by name or as a group? What is the time limit?

Many award ceremonies do not announce the winner(s) in advance. Some identify the finalists but wait for the event to crown the victor. So what should you do if you're a nominee? If you are one of a limited number of nominees or finalists, you should prepare and practice remarks—just in case. Some of the worst award ceremonies have been marred by winners who could have but didn't prepare in advance.

APPLY IMPROMPTU SPEAKING STRATEGIES IF YOU'RE CAUGHT OFF-GUARD

If you are totally surprised when you hear your name as the winner of an award or recipient of an honor, use **IMPROMPTU SPEAKING ★ (465–71)** strategies and skills to see you through. As you walk to the front of the room or onto a stage, think about what you want to say and the people you need to thank. Apply a ready-to-use impromptu speaking format, such as "past, present, future" or "me, my friend, and you" to organize your remarks. And make sure you emphasize the importance of the award and its purpose.

USE APPROPRIATE LANGUAGE STYLES

Consider which of the four **CORE SPEAKING STYLES ∴ (314–18)**—clear, oral, rhetorical, and eloquent—are most appropriate. The **LANGUAGE ∴ (305–22)** used in acceptance speeches ranges from casual and colloquial to eloquent and inspirational. Your analysis of the rhetorical situation should help you make informed choices about the language you use when accepting an award. Consider the following remarks made by two different speakers accepting prestigious prizes:[3]

> Hi guys. My name is on here [*points at the award plaque*]. I'm not gonna lie, I'm pretty shook right now. I'm just trying to think of something funny to say, but it's hard because I might vomit any time. If that happens, don't worry. I think someone in my group has Altoids. You got Altoids?

This is how Nana Kwame Adjei-Brenyah opened his 2019 acceptance speech when he won the PEN/Jean Stein Book Award for *Friday Black*, a book of short stories. The award recognizes works that break new ground, reshape boundaries, and have the potential for a lasting influence. Although Adjei-Brenyah's language style may seem inappropriate for a prestigious awards ceremony, his informal response was an impromptu beginning to an acceptance speech in which he went on to say he had wanted his stories to be out in the world:[4]

> I felt like maybe they could help somebody feel seen. Maybe they could push the conversation in a direction that mattered. I thought maybe if I imagined a world a little bit worse than ours, maybe collectively we could imagine a world that's much better.

Adjei-Brenyah varied his language style over the course of his acceptance speech. It resonated with a "voice" that readers who know his work would recognize and find familiar. His authentic use of language made the speech a memorable success.

Now read the opening sentences of Elie Wiesel's acceptance speech when he won the 1986 Nobel Peace Prize. He was a celebrated writer, revered international spokesperson, and a Jewish survivor of the Auschwitz and Buchenwald concentration camps.[5]

> It is with a profound sense of humility that I accept the honor you have chosen to bestow upon me. I know: your choice transcends me. This both frightens and pleases me. It frightens me because I wonder: do I have the right to represent the multitudes who have perished? Do I have the right to accept this great honor on their behalf? . . . I do not. That would be presumptuous. No one may speak for the dead, no one may interpret their mutilated dreams and visions. It pleases me because I may say that this honor belongs to all the survivors and their children, and through us, to the Jewish people with whose destiny I have always identified.

See Chapter 5.1 **LANGAUGE AND STYLE** ∴ to explore language styles and strategies that are appropriate for you, the audience, and your purpose.

Wiesel's award was not a surprise, and he was not limited to a few minutes. The profound significance of the Nobel Peace Prize called for a manuscript speech that was finely crafted and eloquent, and Wiesel achieved this by employing a model of language strategies that lifted his presentation to classic heights.

KEEP IN MIND . . .

Limit the Number of Thank-Yous Don't overwhelm the audience with a long thank-you list. Name the key people who were most influential in supporting you and the mission of your work as well as key sponsors. If appropriate, you may also thank the presenter of the award.

Honor the Time Limit If you are given a time limit, honor it. If you are not given a time limit, resist the temptation to talk for more than a few minutes unless you know for certain that your audience expects something longer. Prepare and practice your remarks in advance so you know you can say what's important in the time you have.

Speak from the Heart Go beyond the expected words of thanks. Share how you feel at this moment and why the award has value for both you and the audience. Speak authentically and with feeling.

Speak with Few or No Notes If you know in advance that you will be expected to speak when accepting an award and that you will have a limited amount of time, consider memorizing your presentation, but bring your notes or manuscript with you in case you need them. When the award is a complete surprise, you won't have any notes, but you can bring the program (if there is a written program) with you to the podium to make sure you thank the sponsors and, perhaps, other nominees.

Search Terms

To locate a video of this presentation online, enter the following key words into a search engine: Berta Cáceres Goldman Prize acceptance speech 2015. The video is approximately 3:00 minutes in length.

Acceptance Speech: 2015 Goldman Prize

In 2015, Berta Cáceres received the prestigious Goldman Environmental Prize, which honors the achievements and leadership of grassroots environmental activists from around the world. Cáceres cofounded COPINH (the National Council of Popular and Indigenous Organizations of Honduras). Among many other efforts, she led a grassroots campaign against Sinohydro, the world's largest dam developer, to terminate its contract for the construction of the Agua Zarca hydroelectric dams project in the Indigenous Lenca peoples' territory. Challenging such a powerful transnational corporation cost Cáceres her life. She was murdered in March 2016. In 2018, seven men who had been hired by the company constructing the dam were convicted of her murder and sentenced to 30–50 years.[6]

Other than beginning with "Gracias, buenos noches," Cáceres does not repeat the word "gracias" (thank you) until the very end of her speech. Nor does she explain the importance of the award. The audience knew why she'd won. They were there to thank *her*. Her final full sentence recognizes and dedicates the award to people "who gave their lives" to the struggle. And then she ends with "muchas gracias" (thank you very much).

Cáceres uses a manuscript—as do most speakers accepting highly prestigious and visible awards. Her vocal and physical delivery animates her message, emphasizes critical sentences, and reveals her uncompromising and emotional dedication to a cause.

Cáceres speaks in Spanish. Even if you don't understand Spanish, watch and listen to how she emphasizes what seem to be powerful phrases and the way her voice and movements highlight her devotion and fearlessness to a cause. If you know Spanish, you will appreciate the strength, resolve, and marvel of her message. For readers who do not know Spanish or need a translation to ensure better comprehension, the translation below captures her skillful use of stylistic devices (repetition, alliteration, metaphor, and the rule of three). Consider the power of "¡Despertemos! ¡Despertemos humanidad! Ya no hay tiempo." (Let us wake up! Let us wake up, humankind! We're out of time.) Her heroic call is similar to Greta Thunberg's entreaties about climate change.[7]

In our world-views, we are beings who come from the Earth, from the water, and from corn. The Lenca people are ancestral guardians of the rivers, in turn protected by the spirits of young girls, who teach us that giving our lives in various ways for the protection of the rivers is giving our lives for the well-being of humanity and of this planet.

COPINH, walking alongside people struggling for their emancipation, validates this commitment to continue protecting our waters, the rivers, our shared resources and nature in general, as well as our rights as a people. Let us wake up! Let us wake up, humankind! We're out of time.

We must shake our conscience free of the rapacious capitalism, racism and patriarchy that will only assure our own self-destruction. The Gualcarque River has called upon us, as have other gravely threatened rivers. We must answer their call.

Our Mother Earth—militarized, fenced in, poisoned, a place where basic rights are systematically violated—demands that we take action. Let us build societies that are able to coexist in a dignified way . . . in a way that protects life. Let us come together and remain hopeful as we defend and care for the blood of this earth and of its spirits.

I dedicate this award to all the rebels out there, to my mother, to the Lenca people, to Río Blanco and to the martyrs who gave their lives in the struggle to defend our natural resources. Thank you very much.

8.5 Toasts

A **toast** is a celebratory ritual where a group of people are invited to raise their glasses and drink together to honor a person, a couple, a group, an occasion, or an accomplishment. The term *toast* comes from an old English tradition of putting a spiced piece of toast in an alcoholic drink to add more flavor. Toasts bring attention to something special—they "spice up" and add flavor to a celebration.

Most of us, at some point in our lives, will give a toast. If you have attended a wedding, a special birthday party, or an athletic banquet, you've probably lifted your glass and toasted the newlyweds, guest of honor, or most valuable player. Toasts can also celebrate a shared milestone: Our tenth anniversary in business! The opening of our new fine arts building! Our soccer team's victory! Sometimes toasts are spontaneous and unplanned; for instance, you may be moved to make a spontaneous toast to good friends sharing a meal. Others are longer, well-planned tributes, spoken at a brother's wedding, for example, or at a retirement dinner for a respected company manager.

A toast can be as solemn as a prayer or as risqué as a wedding-night joke. It should remind an audience why they are attending a special celebration. Because toasts are supposed to make everyone feel good, they can be more emotional, inspiring, and joyful than other types of presentations.

Key Features

TOASTS ARE A PERSONAL GIFT

Toasts are a gift to the audience in need of some **ENTERTAINMENT ▲ (114)** and **ENGAGEMENT ∴ (303–61)**. Guests perk up and quiet down when they see someone pick up a microphone with a drink in their hand. A toast gives you a few privileged minutes to bestow a personal gift on people you love or a group you admire. It also honors your relationship with a person or group by demonstrating how pleased and proud you are to have them in your life. A well-thought-out toast can also create or reinforce a bond among the attendees who now have a basis for interacting with one another.

TOASTS OFTEN HAVE A "HOOK"

A hook (much like the shiny fishing hooks that attract and catch fish) is something that captures audience attention. It can be a famous birthday or historical event that occurs on the toast day or a little-known **STORY ∴ (323–32)** about the person being toasted. A hook can also be a related joke, an impressive fact, or an inspiring story. The best hooks make an audience want to hear more. Look at how the following statements can hook an audience depending on how you complete each sentence:

> "Tonight you will learn why [Spencer is called Hawk.]"
>
> "Do you know the story about [Lina and the runaway alligator?]"

See Chapter 5.3 **GENERATING INTEREST ∴** if you want to generate interest, use humor, and actively involve audience members.

TOASTS OFTEN HAVE A ONE-LINE SALUTE

Some toasts are brief, no more than a single line. This may be appropriate when several people are making toasts. The best toasts have more to say, demonstrating you've taken time to create a personal gift, tribute, or heartfelt thank-you to people you care about.

In either case, they often end with a one-line salute as you raise your glass. The salute can be fun to write on your own—or in collaboration with **GENERATIVE AI ● (50–55)**. You can also find examples online or in books devoted solely to toasts. Here are just a few:

- "May you always work like you don't need the money; may you always love like you've never been hurt; and may you always dance like there's nobody watching." (Jack Canfield, coauthor, *Chicken Soup for the Soul*)

- "As I toast this beautiful and blissfully happy couple, I know that 'wherever they go, there is Eden.'" (Adapted from Mark Twain, *Eve's Diary*)

- "Here's to friends and family who know us well but love us just the same." (Traditional)

- "To the man who has always been the architect of his own happiness, may your retirement be a masterpiece!" (ChatGPT)

TOASTS SHOULD BE PREPARED WELL IN ADVANCE

Although some so-called toasts are little more than spontaneous remarks made in the company of others—for example, a simple "Congratulations!" or a rambling set of stories ending with "Bottoms up!"—these toasts are rarely worth remembering. The best and most meaningful toasts, the ones everyone remembers and treasures, require considerable thought, days of preparation, and multiple **PRACTICE ▶ (220-24)** sessions to reach their potential and impress an audience.

A Brief Guide to Making a Toast

CONSIDER THE RHETORICAL SITUATION

OCCASION ▲ (61-68) The timing of a toast may be determined by the organizers of the event where the toast occurs (for example, a wedding coordinator may call you to the stage during cocktail hour or after a meal), or it may be a spontaneous event. Toasts can be very brief, but some are longer—a few minutes or more. They can be made in an array of locations, including bars and restaurants, workplaces and other institutional settings, and they may be formal or informal.

SPEAKER ▲ (72-85) Consider why *you* are making this toast on this occasion. Do you need to explain your relationship to the person, people, or event? If you are very close to the person or people you are toasting, think about what you know, feel, and are willing to share with others. Many toasts reveal as much about your feelings and experiences as they do about the object of the toast. But don't get carried away by making yourself the main character in the story.

AUDIENCE ▲ (88–105) How will you **ADAPT ▲ (102–5)** to what listeners already know and feel about the person(s) or occasion honored by the toast? In some cases, you will need to share background information or something they don't know. What do they expect to hear in the toast, and how can you meet those expectations? Although toasts are often humorous, they should not offend audience members who might consider the content inappropriate.

PURPOSE ▲ (109–18) The primary purpose of a toast is to celebrate a person, couple, group, or occasion and to draw in the audience to feel a bond with one another. Ask yourself, "How can I celebrate the person or group I'm toasting and help the audience join in the celebration?" Give audience members who don't know one another a reason to talk to other guests as well as the motivation to talk to the person(s) you toasted.

CONTENT ■ (123–207) Celebrate the person, couple, group, or occasion with special stories, accomplishments, personal experiences, and more. If you decide to use a quotation from another source (book, poem, song lyric, well-known story), make sure it is relevant and meaningful. Despite what you may have seen in comic TV shows and films, don't offend or embarrass the person you're toasting or the audience. Many toasts include humorous stories—usually in the first half—to engage audience attention and emotions. But if you wonder whether the **HUMOR ⸪ (340–42)** is appropriate or might not appeal to all, think twice about your choices. More sincere statements should be shared closer to the end.

DELIVERY ▶ (209–301) Whether the occasion is formal or informal, try to project a spontaneous and natural speaking style. Rehearse the toast until you can speak **CONFIDENTLY ▶ (212–13)**, **EXPRESSIVELY ▶ (212)**, and **FLUENTLY ▶ (240–41)** with limited or no notes. Do not read your toast word for word. When you read a toast, your **CREDIBILITY ▲ (74–81)** diminishes, the audience will lose interest, and your message may not seem genuine. The best toasts seem spontaneous and inspired because they are well prepared and skillfully rehearsed.

ORGANIZING A TOAST

Most toasts do not need a formal or complex organizational pattern, particularly if they are brief. But if your toast is longer than a few sentences, put your ideas in a strategic order. For example, consider a past, current, and future format, or expand on three words that describe the person(s) or occasion. Consider a simple organizational structure: begin with a hook, share brief background information, tell a good **STORY** ∴ **(323-32)**, and conclude with personal observations.

MAKING A TOAST MEMORABLE

Use an appropriate **SPEAKING STYLE** ∴ **(314-18)** that suits the rhetorical situation and generates audience interest and engagement. Avoid overused adjectives (*nice, funny, great, cool*) that can lose their power and importance in a toast. Instead, tell a brief story that demonstrates someone's kindness or how the person's sense of humor defused an uncomfortable situation. Also avoid clichés. Would this person literally give the shirt off his back to a stranger or bend over backward for a friend? A brief story is a better way to visualize someone's admirable characteristics, especially one that uses **INTENSE, VIVID, AND POWERFUL LANGUAGE** ∴ **(307-9)** to help audience members see, hear, and feel what's going on.

KEEP IN MIND . . .

Be Direct and Brief Your job is to say what everyone else is feeling. Try to capture those feelings in your toast without losing your focus or getting sidetracked. Keep the toast short and simple. Listeners are unlikely to want or remember a long-winded toast. Don't let audience members get tired of holding their glasses up in the air.

Adjust Your Delivery Make direct **EYE CONTACT** ▶ **(249-51)** with audience members and at the person(s) or group you are toasting. Stand up

See Chapter 4.1 **DELIVERY DECISIONS** ▶ for guidance on choosing a delivery mode and practice techniques.

in a place where everyone can see and hear you. If you are nervous, slow down. Remember, meaningful pauses create anticipation. If there is a **MICROPHONE ▶ (234–35)** available, use it. Without a microphone, you may need to **PROJECT ▶ (235–36)** your voice to command attention and reach everyone. Smile!

Drink First Conclude by raising your glass, smiling, and extending an invitation to everyone in attendance: "Now please join me in a toast to _____." You may want to clink the honored person's glass or "air clink." Then sip your drink, and everyone will sip with you.

NOTABLE SPEAKER
Bill Nighy

Search Terms

To locate a video of this presentation online, enter the following key words into a search engine: Bill Nighy About Time best man speech. The video is approximately 1:05 in length.

A Toast: From *About Time*

In the 2013 British film *About Time*, a father (played by Bill Nighy), offers a 127-word wedding toast that lasts 63 seconds. That is a very slow rate of speaking, but given the father's role, his message, and his evident feelings, this toast works. So much so that the clip is one of the most watched and favorite examples of a wedding toast.

Before watching the toast, read it. It's not many words. As a text, it's a bit odd. But the father hooks and involves his audience in his first sentence with a subtle and amusing statement about this son's "many failings as a man and as a table tennis player." When he playfully lists the only three men he has ever loved, his son is the final person named. Then he makes a transition to saying something meaningful and sincere about his son. The toast is delivered beautifully by a talented actor using words written by a screenwriter. Even so, it is a model of a fine meaningful, poignant toast.

> Later on, I may tell you about Tim's many failings as a man and as a table tennis player. But important first is to say the one—big thing. I've only loved three men in my life. My dad was a frosty bugger so that only leaves dear Uncle Desmond, um, B. B. King— obviously—and this young man here. I'd only give one piece of advice to anyone marrying. We're all quite similar in the end. We all get old and tell the same tales too many times. But try and marry someone—kind. And this is a kind man, with a good heart. I'm not particularly proud of many things in my life. But I am very proud to be the father of my son.

8.6 Eulogies

  A BRIEF GUIDE TO THIS CHAPTER

- **Key features** (p. 507)
- **A brief guide to giving a eulogy** (p. 508)

Eulogies are tributes that praise the dead and celebrate their lives. Most people think of a eulogy as a speech delivered shortly after a person's death. Some eulogies, however, are delivered years later to commemorate the anniversary of a death or to celebrate an important person's historical achievements.

A eulogy is one of the most challenging presentations to create and deliver. You are talking to an audience of bereaved people and are probably feeling the loss of someone who mattered to you. Despite the weight of this challenge, each eulogy is an opportunity to celebrate someone's life. It offers closure and comfort to the person's friends and loved ones. Despite their differences in content, note how the following excerpts from three eulogies honor the memory of the deceased:

> She had a luminous quality—a combination of wistfulness, radiance, yearning—to set her apart and yet make everyone wish to be a part of it, to share in the childish naiveté which was so shy and yet so vibrant. (Lee Strasberg, famous teacher of the "method" acting style, speaking about Marilyn Monroe)[1]

> The thing about John's life was the amazing sweep of it. From a tiny prison cell in Vietnam to the floor of the United States Senate. From troublemaking plebe to presidential candidate. Wherever

John passed throughout the world, people immediately knew there was a leader in their midst. In one epic life was written the courage and greatness of our country. (Former US president George W. Bush, speaking about Senator John McCain)[2]

I was so privileged . . . to witness the magnitude of talent of this singer's singer, this musician's musician. And let me add for you that behind her God-given, natural talent, was the drive of a total perfectionist. After we decided on the material for an ensuing album, she would go into Aretha mode and privately rehearse, practice, and prepare. By the time she came into the studio, she literally owned the song. Everyone in the studio would be in awe of her mastery when she stepped up to the microphone. (Clive Davis, founder of Arista Records, speaking about Aretha Franklin)[3]

Key Features

EULOGIES FOCUS ON THE DECEASED

As nervous as speakers may be before and while delivering a eulogy, they should always understand that the presentation isn't about them. Rather, it pays tribute, says farewell, and evokes cherished memories of the person who has passed away. Notable eulogies capture the essence of the person—what made the person special.

EULOGIES CREATE A COMFORTING, SHARED EXPERIENCE

Eulogies offer comfort and a sense of commonality that everyone in attendance can share. Rather than being mournful, a eulogy can be enriching and inspiring. Addressing audience members by name or by affiliations (family, friends, coworkers) creates a distinctive and memorable shared experience. Writing and presenting a eulogy can also be of great comfort to a speaker.

See Chapter 2.3 **AUDIENCE** ▲ to help you think carefully about the emotions and needs of your listeners.

AUTHENTICITY IS MORE IMPORTANT THAN PERFECT DELIVERY

Eulogies that are remembered and appreciated express ideas and emotions that are genuine and truthful: in other words, they are authentic. It's okay to look, sound, and feel nervous, emotional, and grief-stricken. Many

See Chapter 1.2
**SPEAKING
ANXIETY** ● if you
need advice about
managing your
nervousness.

speakers find it difficult to maintain their composure while delivering a eulogy. No one in the audience will think less of you if you cannot finish a eulogy or if you falter in its delivery.

A Brief Guide to Giving a Eulogy

CONSIDER THE RHETORICAL SITUATION

OCCASION ▲ (61–68) The reason for a eulogy is clear: a person has died, and that person's friends, associates, and loved ones want to honor their life and share in a comforting social ceremony to express their grief. The timing of a eulogy is determined, of course, by the deceased's passing and also by the family or loved ones who have planned the memorial service or ceremony. The setting may be a building or location that some attendees consider sacred or revered—a house of worship, for example, or the grounds of a cemetery—or it may be another space that has been set up for the occasion, such as a funeral home, a relative or friend's home, or a familiar and appropriate workplace room or auditorium. In some cases, a eulogy addresses a major tragedy, as in presidential eulogies for the victims of mass shootings, terrorism, insurgencies, and natural disasters.

SPEAKER ▲ (72–85) Make sure you know why *you* are doing this eulogy for this person. If some audience members do not know who you are or your relationship to the person you are eulogizing, briefly explain why you are speaking. Remember that a eulogy is not about you. It is all about the person you are honoring—a gift to those who knew and cared about the person.

AUDIENCE ▲ (88–105) You have two audiences when delivering a eulogy: the immediate loved ones of the deceased and the larger audience of friends and acquaintances. Make **EYE CONTACT ▶ (249–51)** with the immediate family at various points in the eulogy, offering them comfort for their loss. At other points, acknowledge the grief and shared memories of all others present. In some cases, you may need to provide biographical information about the person. In other cases, you can assume that everyone knew the person well. Also consider the audience's expectations and frame of mind. Is a humorous story appropriate or inappropriate? Does the audience expect a formal or informal presentation?

PURPOSE ▲ (109–18) A eulogy has two related goals: to comfort those who grieve and to honor the deceased person. How can you celebrate the values and accomplishments of the person and adapt to the emotional context? Consider using the language of traditional **VALUES ▲ (95–96)** to describe the deceased person, such as *courage, compassion, loyalty, honesty, humility, patience, generosity, empathy, kindness, tolerance, fairness, a sense of humor*, among others. These words are widely understood, and the qualities they identify are universally admired. Think carefully about which ones apply to the deceased, and use them sparingly, so these descriptors feel (and are) specifically appropriate to the person being honored. The most effective eulogies are simple and straightforward. Remember your goals, and craft your eulogy around them.

CONTENT ■ (123–207) Make the eulogy brief, typically no more than a few minutes. Your job is not to talk about everything the person has done. Instead, use your relationship with the deceased person to focus on a theme that, in your mind, defines the person—a great parent, a wonderfully funny neighbor, a gifted sailor, a brilliant teacher. Then reflect on a few vivid details or **STORIES ∴ (323–32)** that highlight the person's characteristics, achievements, or values. "He drove people crazy with those mismatched pairs of socks. But that was just who he was: a fantastical nonconformist with a fabulous sense of humor." If your own words seem inadequate, are there meaningful quotations you can use?

DELIVERY ▶ (209–301) Rehearse the eulogy and try to keep your voice steady and loud enough to be heard by your audience. Can you speak at an appropriate **RATE ▶ (236–38)** and pause to signal thoughtfulness and importance? Is your eulogy an appropriate length—brief rather than long-winded? Although notes allow more **EYE CONTACT ▶ (249–51)** and connections with the audience, a **MANUSCRIPT ▶ (216)** may be necessary to help you through a highly emotional tribute. Family members often ask speakers for copies of their eulogies, so make sure your words are the ones you want preserved for posterity.

ORGANIZING A EULOGY

Most eulogies use a simple **ORGANIZATIONAL PATTERN** ▪ **(157–66)**. Two common methods for organizing a eulogy are **CHRONOLOGICAL** ▪ **(158)** and **STORY-BASED PATTERNS** ▪ **(162–63)**. You may, for example, follow the person's development and achievements chronologically from an early age or from when you became acquainted. Or you may prefer to share a series of stories that personify someone's beliefs, values, and/or personality traits. Or do both. You may even consider using a creative organizational pattern: you could write a final letter to the deceased person or review the person's favorite TV shows or films and describe famous scenes that capture an emotional moment or personality trait.

The most important thing to do at the **BEGINNING** ▪ **(190–98)** of a eulogy is to make sure people know who you are and why you are speaking: "My name is Emma, and I was Sofia's college roommate for four years and her faithful friend since then," for example. The **ENDING** ▪ **(198–204)** of a eulogy can take different forms, but the most powerful endings connect the deceased person's life to the lives of the people assembled to honor that person. "Sofia will always be an inspiration to me. I am, and I believe everyone in this room is, a better person because of her. How blessed we are to have known her."

KEEP IN MIND . . .

Listen to the Eulogies That Precede Yours Frequently, more than one person will offer a eulogy. Family members and friends may stand up and share remembrances. **LISTEN** ● **(30–42)** carefully to what they say. You don't want to repeat the same story. When it's your turn, connect your eulogy to what has been said before if you can.

Avoid Presumptions or Trite Statements Don't tell audience members you know what they are going through, that they should be happy the suffering is finally over, or that they will be fine in a few weeks. Even if such statements are well meant, audience members want and need to go through their own grieving process.

Use Language That Inspires and Consoles Great eulogies often use **LANGUAGE ∴ (305–22)** that is eloquent, expressive, and even poetic. They rise above everyday language to make the occasion feel as special as the person being honored. Of course, if eloquence doesn't feel natural to you, don't force yourself to use language in this way. Above all, use language that authentically expresses your feelings.

Consider Laughter Most of today's memorial services are celebrations. It's okay to tell a funny story about the deceased. A little laughter takes the tension of sadness away. Obviously, your **HUMOR ∴ (305–22)** must be in good taste.

Search Terms

To locate a video of this presentation online, enter the following key words into a search engine: Oprah Winfrey Rosa Parks eulogy. The video is approximately 4:10 in length.

Eulogy for Rosa Parks

In October 2005, the activist Rosa Parks, whom the United States Congress in 1999 had honored as "the first lady of civil rights," died at the age of 92. A week after her death, a memorial service at the African Methodist Episcopal Church in Washington, DC, was held in her honor. Tributes were paid to her legacy by politicians, activists, personal acquaintances, and celebrities, including one of the most respected individuals in American media, Oprah Winfrey. Here's an excerpt from her moving eulogy, a video of which is widely available online:[4]

I grew up in the South, and Rosa Parks was a hero to me long before I recognized and understood the power and impact that her life embodied. I remember my father telling me about this colored woman who had refused to give up her seat. And in my child's mind, I thought, "She must be really big." I thought she must be at least a hundred feet tall. I imagined her being stalwart and strong and carrying a shield to hold back the white folks. And then I grew up and had the esteemed honor of meeting her. And wasn't that a surprise. Here was this petite, almost delicate lady who was the personification of grace and goodness. And I thanked her then. I said, "Thank you," for myself and for every colored girl, every colored boy, who didn't have heroes who were celebrated. I thanked her then. And after our first meeting I realized that God uses good people to do great things. And I'm here today to say a final thank you, Sister Rosa, for being a great woman who used your life to serve, to serve us all. That day that you refused to give up your seat on the bus, you, Sister Rosa, changed the trajectory of my life and the lives of so many other people in the world. I would not be standing here today nor standing where I stand every day had she not chosen to sit down. I know that. I know that. I know that. I know that, and I honor that. Had she not chosen to say we shall not—we shall not be moved.

8.7 Team Presentations and Public Group Discussions

🔍 A BRIEF GUIDE TO THIS CHAPTER

- **Key features of team presentations** (p. 514)
- **A brief guide to team presentations** (p. 515)
- **Key features of public group discussions** (p. 519)
- **A brief guide to public group discussions** (p. 522)

Previous chapters in this book have focused on your role as a solo speaker presenting to an audience. The ability to speak for and by yourself is an important life skill, but working and communicating with others is no less important. Success in today's complex world often depends on your ability to communicate in groups.

Everyone works and speaks in groups—at school and on the job; with family members, friends, and coworkers; and in such diverse locations as sports fields, battlefields, courtrooms, and classrooms. Much of this group communication is conducted without an audience present: every person who attends a closed-door work-team meeting, for example, is an active participant and may be asked to speak. Because this is a book on presentation speaking, this chapter focuses on the strategies and skills needed to communicate effectively in group-based situations. Specifically, we examine two types of presentational group communication: *team presentations* and *public group discussions*. Let's look at each one separately.

Key Features of Team Presentations

Team presentations occur when the members of a cohesive group work together to prepare and deliver a well-coordinated presentation to achieve a specific agreed-upon **group goal**.[1] Organizations as diverse as nonprofit agencies and global corporations rely on team presentations to make proposals, compete for major contracts, and request funding.

Team presentations can demonstrate whether a group or company is competent enough to perform a task or take on a major responsibility. For that reason, team presentations often have high stakes.[2] Here are some examples:[3]

- A software start-up makes the "short list" of businesses being considered for a contract to retool a Fortune 500 company's inventory and customer-service management systems. A team consisting of the CEO, the director of sales, and the director of product development deliver an hour-long presentation and demonstration to the relevant management group of a prospective company in a bid to win the contract.

- In an attempt to increase government funding of a public university, a college president asks a team consisting of an administrator, a professor, a staff member, and a student government representative to deliver a presentation to the state legislature's appropriations committee. The legislature gives the team 20 minutes to make its case.

- A professional football team seeks backing for a new stadium by bringing a well-rehearsed group of executives and star players to a public meeting where they explain how the stadium will enhance the economic development and prestige of the community without adversely affecting the surrounding neighborhoods.

See Chapter 7.3
RHETORICAL STRATEGIES FOR PERSUASIVE PRESENTATIONS ◆ if your team presentation requires a well-justified argument.

TEAM PRESENTATIONS HAVE AN AGREED-UPON GROUP GOAL

Having a common goal is the single most important factor that separates successful from unsuccessful team presentations.[4] Much like a solo speaker's **PURPOSE** ▲ **(109–18)**, a group's agreed-upon goal will determine the communication strategies and skills needed to achieve that goal.

TEAM PRESENTATIONS ARE A GROUP PRODUCT

A team presentation is not a random collection of individual, independent speeches; it is a team product. Team presentations are the ultimate group challenge because they require efficient and effective decision making as well as coordinated performances.

TEAM PRESENTATIONS BALANCE STRUCTURE AND SPONTANEITY

An effective team presentation needs a balanced approach: it should be carefully organized and rehearsed *but also* flexible and adaptable. Team members must be well prepared with their own presentations *and* prepared to adapt to listeners' questions. They must be able to tactfully correct a team member's misstep *and* support a needed adaptation during the presentation. Members should also be prepared to address **LOGISTICAL PROBLEMS ▲ (67–68)**, such as a technological issue with presentation aids, *and* adapt to an unexpected shortening or lengthening of their time limit.

A Brief Guide to Team Presentations

CONSIDER THE RHETORICAL SITUATION

OCCASION ▲ (61–68) Team presentations occur whenever the need arises to use a team's shared expertise and speaking skills to achieve a rhetorical purpose. Depending on the occasion, level of detail, and number of presenting team members, the resulting team presentation may be of moderate length (15–20 minutes) or may last as long as an hour—often followed up with a **QUESTION-AND-ANSWER SESSION ∴ (350–61)**. Sometimes team presentations are held in a place that may be unfamiliar to the team beforehand (for example, in another company's corporate offices). Go to the location early to make sure the setup and equipment meet the team's needs. Be prepared to make changes if you don't have the equipment you requested.

SPEAKER ▲ (72–85) The "speaker" in a team presentation is the team as a whole. The team must demonstrate its overall competence, trustworthiness, likability, and dynamism. Consider the composition of your team: What is each team member's greatest strength? What can they speak about most competently and confidently? Use team members strategically; capitalize on their strengths. One weak link can jeopardize an entire team's **CREDIBILITY ▲ (74–81)**.

AUDIENCE ▲ (88–105) Learn as much as you can about your listeners using **AUDIENCE ANALYSIS ▲ (90–96)**. Who will be there? What are their characteristics, interests, attitudes, and values? Do you have a clear sense of their respective status, responsibilities, and influence? If possible, the team should spend time with audience members before the presentation and adapt their presentation to what they've learned from these informal chats. If there is a primary decision maker in the audience, consider that person your **TARGET AUDIENCE ▲ (90)** and adapt to what you learn about the person's background and beliefs. Finally, if your audience is entirely made up of members of a specific organization (for example, a government entity or community association), make sure your message addresses the **VALUES ▲ (95–96)** and needs of that organization.

PURPOSE ▲ (109–18) Develop a shared goal that is specific, relevant, and achievable. Make sure every member understands, fully supports, and is well prepared to achieve that goal. Each team member should know the purpose of their particular portion of the presentation and make sure it supports the shared goal. It helps to think of the shared goal as similar to the purpose of a solo presentation and each team member's purpose is a key supporting point.

CONTENT ■ (123–207) Research and select ideas and **SUPPORTING MATERIALS ■ (134–51)** that are relevant, varied, and persuasive. Make sure that all **ARGUMENTS ◆ (420–36)** include at least a claim, evidence, and warrant and, if needed, backing for the warrant. Make sure the overall organization of the team presentation is clear and that the individual presentations logically flow from one to the other. Link each presentation to the next with effective **TRANSITIONS ■ (168–69)**.

DELIVERY ▶ (209–301) Practice the entire presentation several times. Because you're working as a team, offer feedback and adjust individual presentations and the group's presentation as a whole after every practice session. Use well-prepared, coordinated, professional-caliber **PRESENTATION AIDS ▶ (260–78)**, if needed. A last-minute request from a key audience member may require adjustments to the speaking order or a slight change in the focus of a team member's presentation.

COORDINATING A TEAM PRESENTATION

Every team presentation should have a leader who launches the presentation and serves as the link between the other presenters. The leader tells listeners how the team's presentation is organized, introduces the presenters, directs questions to appropriate members, and wraps up the entire presentation with a well-crafted, well-delivered **CONCLUSION ▓ (198–203)** .[5] Ideally, this responsibility should be given to your most **DYNAMIC▲ (81)** and **CONFIDENT ▶ (212–13)** speaker, but sometimes the team's most senior member assumes this mantle, regardless of their speaking skills. When this happens, it is the responsibility of every team member during practice sessions to provide feedback and advice that enhances the team leader's performance. If nothing improves, consider inviting two or three associates to offer a critique—which is not a bad idea for any team presentation. And, if possible, make sure one of them has more authority or rank than the team leader.

Team presentations require a great deal of preparation time, effort, and resources—so they need to be very carefully coordinated and choreographed. Marjorie Brody, the author of *Speaking Your Way to the Top*, puts it this way:[6]

> To be effective, team presentations must be meticulously planned and executed. They must be like a ballet, in which each dancer knows exactly where to stand, when to move, and when to exit from the stage. . . . If a team works like a smooth, well-oiled machine, if one member's presentation flows into the next presentation, and if all members present themselves professionally and intelligently, the impression left is one of confidence and competence.

KEEP IN MIND . . .

Focus on Every Detail Every team member should know *every* detail of the team's presentation. Don't just focus on your own part.

Emphasize a Theme In addition to the group goal, consider developing a theme, slogan, or metaphor for your team presentation that is repeated and woven into each member's presentation.

Use Your Time Wisely Get the most out of each minute. If you have been given 30 minutes for a team presentation, time your group and make sure it's no longer than 25 minutes. Despite your best efforts to plan every second of a team presentation, it usually will take more time in front of an audience, especially if team members make minor changes to adapt to audience feedback.

Assume Leadership Functions if You Don't Have a Team Leader In the absence of a designated leader, each team member can introduce the next team speaker, preview the importance of the topic, and bolster the speaker's credibility. In addition to giving the speaker's credentials, a brief relevant story about the person can give the audience another reason to listen.[7]

Don't Contradict Your Teammates Although you may at times need to tactfully correct a teammate's error, you should present a united front. Your audience will notice if one team member repeatedly disagrees with or contradicts what other members say.

Only One Person Answers Each Question Sometimes everyone on the team feels the need to chime in, but when an audience member asks a question, only the person with the most knowledge of the issue should answer. More than one response takes extra time and often adds little value.

See Chapter 5.4 **QUESTION-AND-ANSWER SESSIONS** ⁑ for help conducting a productive question-and-answer session.

Pay Attention to Your Teammates as They Speak When one person is speaking, it's not uncommon to see their teammates staring into space, reading or writing notes, or even whispering to other team members—behaviors that will distract listeners from the presentation. Be a model of **EFFECTIVE LISTENING ● (30–34)**. It's important to demonstrate the level of engagement you'd like to see from your audience. Every team member should look at and, where appropriate, nod as their teammate is speaking.

Key Features of Public Group Discussions

Public group discussions occur when a group of selected people speak in front of and for the benefit of an audience about a predetermined topic. Group discussions are less tightly coordinated than team presentations, and although the members of the group generally follow an agenda and stay focused on a particular topic, they may not coordinate their respective presentations with one another to achieve a common group goal. Although presenters in a public group discussion may share a general goal—for example, three student government association members might make individual presentations opposing a proposed tuition increase at the monthly public meeting of the college's board of trustees—they don't typically choreograph their efforts. The most common types of group discussions are *panel discussions*, *symposiums*, *forums*, and *governance groups*.

TYPES OF PUBLIC GROUP DISCUSSIONS

Panel Discussions A **panel discussion** occurs when several participants—who may or may not know one another in advance—discuss a common topic for the benefit of an audience. Panel discussions are common on television and radio, on podcasts, at professional organizations' conventions, and during special events hosted by colleges and universities, houses of worship, art and culture festivals, public libraries, and other public institutions. The participants in such discussions talk with one another in order to educate, influence, or entertain an audience. A moderator typically controls the flow of communication.

Symposiums In a **symposium**, group members—again, who may or may not know one another in advance—present short, uninterrupted presentations to an audience on different aspects of a topic. For example, a university may sponsor a symposium on the state of the US economy where an elected official, an economist, a union officer, and a small business owner each give uninterrupted talks about ways to protect and bolster the economy. Although symposium members may disagree with one another, their collective goal is to educate audience members by sharing their expertise and perspectives and perhaps to persuade listeners that their perspectives on the topic are valuable.

Forums A **forum** often follows a panel discussion or symposium and gives audience members the opportunity to comment or ask questions. Some forums invite open discussions, letting audience members share their concerns about a specific issue. Others give the public an opportunity to ask questions of and express concerns to elected officials and experts. In some cases, members of the group may ask questions of one another. A conscientious moderator tries to give audience members and group members the opportunity to interact.

Governance Groups A **governance group** makes public policy decisions, usually in public settings open to public audiences. State legislatures, city and county councils, and the governing boards of public agencies and educational institutions must conduct most of their meetings in public. At colleges and universities, student government and other student associations often invite the entire campus community to attend their meetings. In the United States, perhaps the most visible and most public governance group of all is the US Congress. With only a few exceptions (for example, national security briefings), Congress cannot deny the public access to its deliberations, many of which are broadcast on the C-SPAN network. The decisions made by a governance group are often partisan and sometimes controversial, and they are generally determined by a vote of its members. These votes, along with the comments each member makes during deliberations, become part of the public record.

GROUP DISCUSSIONS FOLLOW AN AGENDA

An **agenda** is an outline of the topics to be discussed in a group meeting. They are indispensable in, but not limited to, private staff and executive group meetings. Public governance groups use agendas to make sure they get through critical and legally required topics of public interest. Panel discussions use them for the same reason but may be more flexible if a particular topic engages the audience more than others. Even a symposium may give participants an agenda that designates how much time they have for their own presentations, the time the moderator needs to introduce the participants and topic, and the time being set aside for a public forum.

GROUP DISCUSSIONS REQUIRE THE COOPERATION AND RESPECT OF ALL MEMBERS

Although the individual participants of a public group discussion may not share the same goals or opinions, they do share a common interest in ensuring the discussion benefits the audience. Participants should respect the agenda and rules of the discussion, and show respect for other speakers, even if they don't agree with them. If individual members disrespect other presenters (for example, by showing visible irritation or boredom when they speak), the audience may question the credibility of the entire group and the legitimacy of the event overall.

GROUP DISCUSSIONS CAN MIX DIFFERENT FORMATS

A public group discussion may include many features of panel discussions, symposiums, forums, and governance groups. Near the end of a symposium, a moderator may conduct a panel discussion among participants to discuss the topic as a whole. That may be followed by an audience forum. A governance group may interrupt its deliberations to hear a short symposium from constituent group members with a particular point of view. And, particularly at local government and public board meetings, there may be open time for a **QUESTION-AND-ANSWER SESSION** ⁖ **(350–61)**.

A Brief Guide to Public Group Discussions

CONSIDER THE RHETORICAL SITUATION

OCCASION ▲ (61–68) Public group discussions occur for many different reasons. The main thing to determine or identify is the kind of group discussion—panel discussion, symposium, forum, or governance group—you are participating in, on which topic, and with what goal. These multiple factors define the "reason" for the group discussion and your contributions. The time, duration, and place of the discussion will be determined by the organizers of the discussion, which, of course, may include you, as a member of the organization or group that will be convening the discussion. In some of these groups—particularly the symposium—there will be rules about how much time is allotted to each speaker and to the discussion as a whole, but others will be more open ended.

SPEAKER ▲ (72–85) Establish both the group's and each participant's credibility by sharing members' credentials and relevant experiences with the audience. Accept your responsibilities to the public audience and to an outside group or organization you may be representing. Capitalize on your strengths and consider how you can best contribute to the presentation.

AUDIENCE ▲ (88–105) As with any presentation, research the audience's characteristics and attitudes using **AUDIENCE ANALYSIS ▲ (90–96)**. Consider and respect the audience's needs and expectations as well as their **FEEDBACK ● (39–40)** during or after the group presentation. In some cases, other group members may be an equally important audience you want to inform and/or influence.

PURPOSE ▲ (109–18) The common purpose of any public group discussion is to **BENEFIT THE AUDIENCE ▲ (93)** in some way—to educate them about a topic, to deliberate and make a decision that benefits them, to give them the opportunity to voice their concerns and ask questions. Acknowledge that the goals of individual members and the group may differ. Consider if those differences are compatible or conflicting. If there is disagreement among group members, strive to keep the presentations objective and civil.

CONTENT ■ **(123–207)** Include appropriate, interesting, and memorable content that is clear and well organized. Avoid repeating what other members have said unless it's to state that you agree or disagree with them or need to add more information. Use a clear, listener-friendly **ORGANIZATIONAL PATTERN** ■ **(157–66)** in your presentations with a limited number of **KEY POINTS** ■ **(152–70)**. Stick to time limits so every member has an equal say.

> See Chapter 5.3 **GENERATING INTEREST** ⁞ to capture audience attention and heighten audience involvement.

DELIVERY ▶ **(209–301)** Plan and **PRACTICE** ▶ **(220–24)** your delivery in the style you will give it: standing or sitting, with or without a microphone or notes, speaking formally or informally, using **PRESENTATION AIDS** ▶ **(260–78)** (if appropriate), and so on. Dress appropriately and be courteous. When participating in a public discussion, remember you are "onstage" all the time, even when you aren't speaking. Even if you disagree with what other members say, look at and respect other members when they speak—and hope they will do the same for you.[8]

MODERATING A PUBLIC DISCUSSION GROUP

Many public group discussions include a designated moderator who controls the flow of participation and, in the case of a forum or question-and-answer session, gives audience members an equal opportunity to participate. At the beginning of a group discussion, a moderator may **WELCOME** ★ **(479–84)** the audience and explain the event's purpose and topic. Depending on the type of group and the occasion, a moderator may also provide an overview of the event's agenda, introduce the speakers, and indicate whether there will be time for member interaction and audience questions. From then on, the moderator looks and listens to both the speakers and audience members to ensure the session achieves its purpose. As is also the case with controlling vehicle traffic, the moderator explains and enforces the "rules of the road" for the discussion. Here are some general guidelines to use if you are serving as the moderator:

- Keep track of the time, and enforce time limits. This task requires tact, **EFFECTIVE LISTENING** ● (30–34), and a respect for the needs of speakers *and* audience members.

- Be prepared to interrupt members who talk too much, drift from the topic, engage in inappropriate behavior, rudely interrupt others, and/or break agreed-upon rules.

- Protect the rights of group and audience members by guaranteeing their right to speak when appropriate.

- Guarantee the rights of group and audience members to speak on different sides of an issue by balancing participation between frequent and infrequent contributors as well as between members who support and those who oppose a proposal.

KEEP IN MIND . . .

Public Group Discussions Require Significant Planning Group discussions usually involve more time and preparation than simply scheduling a single speaker. The event must be well planned in terms of the choice of a place, the selection and preparation of participants, the logistics, and (in many cases) the publicity needed to attract an audience.

People Problems May Arise Some members may be well prepared and energized. Others may rarely contribute because they are unprepared or want to avoid conflict and extra work. Strong, dominating members can put pressure on others that stifles dissent. Although no one wants to work with difficult or unpleasant members, you may have no choice. A good moderator should intervene to resolve problems and control levels of participation. In some cases, if there is no moderator, another member can interrupt someone who is speaking longer than the time limit or is behaving inappropriately. Even the audience may react negatively to a problem member and call for fairness and civility.

Conclusion

In her book, *Keeping the Team Going*, Deborah Harrington-Mackin responds to a question frequently asked by her management team:[9]

> *Question*: I like the idea of having team members speak on panels and give presentations, but how can I trust that they will give the right answers under pressure?

> *Answer*: I'm always pleasantly surprised at how competent, composed, and prepared team members are when they sit on panels or give presentations. Remember, they're in the spotlight and want to look and act their best.

We agree with Harrington-Mackin, but we also know there is a lot more involved in effective group presentations than hoping and trusting they will turn out okay. In this chapter, we provided key strategies and skills that can help you and other group members deliver successful presentations adapted to your group and audience's needs.

We also trust that you will always consider the six elements of the rhetorical situation—occasion, speaker, audience, purpose, content, and delivery—regardless of where, when, and why you are engaged in the art and craft of presentation speaking.

Glossary / Index

A

Aarvik, Egil
    presenting an award, 486
    using language strategies, 490
Abdel-Magied, Yassmin
    Notable Speaker, 225–28, 339, 429

abstract word, 307 A word that refers to an idea or concept that cannot be observed or touched and therefore may not have the same meaning for everyone. *See also* CONCRETE WORD
    clarifying difficult terms, 389–91

accents, 242–45

accepting an award, 490–96 A speaking OCCA-SION where the recipient expresses gratitude for receiving an award and acknowledges the award's significance. *See also* PRESENTING AN AWARD
    guidelines, 492–96
    key features, 491–92

accessibility
    accommodation services, 66
    in adapting physical delivery, 257
    in selecting colors for digital slides, 276
    in using inclusive language, 321–22

active voice, 309–10 When the subject of a sentence performs the action of the verb: *The student read the* Iliad. *See also* PASSIVE VOICE

Adams, Eric
    on communicating ethically, 56
Adjei-Brenyah, Nana Kwame
    award acceptance speech, 494–95

agenda, 521 An outline of the topics to be discussed in PUBLIC GROUP DISCUSSIONS or in private group meetings.

AI (artificial intelligence). *See* GENERATIVE AI

alliteration, 311–12 A FIGURE OF SPEECH in which a SPEAKER uses a series of words or phrases that begin with the same sound: *The dictator is not disarming. To the contrary, he is deceiving.*

analogy, 313–14 A FIGURE OF SPEECH that compares two different things to highlight some point of similarity. Analogies expand SIMILES and METAPHORS and can serve as SUPPORTING MATERIAL.
    describing a scientific phenomenon, 392–94
    as a reasoning type, 423

Anderson, Marge
    concluding with a story, 200–201
answering questions. *See also* QUESTION-AND-ANSWER SESSION
    answering effectively, 355–56
    leaving time for, 66

Note: This glossary / index defines key terms and concepts and directs you to pages in the book where you can find specific information on these and other topics. The words set in SMALL CAPITAL LETTERS are themselves defined in the glossary / index.

call for action, 454 A strategy used near or in the conclusion of a PERSUASIVE PRESENTATION that asks the AUDIENCE to do something beyond LISTENING to the SPEAKER.

categorical arrangement, 157–58, 172, 379, 390 An ORGANIZATIONAL PATTERN that divides a large TOPIC into smaller categories within that topic.

cause-and-effect arrangement, 160–61 An ORGANIZATIONAL PATTERN that either presents a cause and its resulting effect (cause-to-effect) or describes the effect that results from a specific cause (effect-to-cause).

central idea, 156–57 A single-sentence summary of your overall MESSAGE and KEY POINTS. Also called a *thesis statement.*

central route to persuasion, 442 One of two routes to persuasion in the ELABORATION LIKELIHOOD MODEL OF PERSUASION, which works best when your AUDIENCE is very interested and likely to engage in EFFECTIVE LISTENING. Use strong, VALID EVIDENCE to support your CLAIMS, and respectfully acknowledge but also refute opposing points of view. *See also* PERIPHERAL ROUTE TO PERSUASION

channel, 10–11 The medium or media used by SPEAKERS and AUDIENCE members to transmit MESSAGES to one another.

chunking, 153 A method for identifying potential SUPPORTING MATERIAL by recording distinct ideas on separate note cards or sticky notes and sorting the best of them into separate KEY POINTS. *See also* MIND MAPPING

citation, 149–51 The practice of citing the sources of your SUPPORTING MATERIAL in a presentation. *See also* ORAL CITATION

D

defamation, 55   A false statement that damages a person's reputation, either through writing and pictures (libel) or through speech (slander).

defensive listening, 32   A poor LISTENING habit in which AUDIENCE members assume that a SPEAKER'S controversial or critical statements are personal or unjust attacks. Rather than trying to understand the speaker's MESSAGE, defensive listeners focus only on how to challenge the speaker's position.

definition, 136   A type of SUPPORTING MATERIAL that explains or clarifies the meaning or meanings of a word, phrase, or concept.

delivery, 10, 211–14   The ways in which SPEAKERS use their voice and body during a presentation.

The four qualities of effective delivery include CONFIDENCE, EXPRESSIVENESS, IMMEDIACY, and STAGE PRESENCE. *See* PHYSICAL DELIVERY and VOCAL DELIVERY

demographic information, 91–92   Information gathered through AUDIENCE ANALYSIS that includes, but is not limited to, race, age, gender, ethnicity, nationality, religion, citizen status, occupation, place and type of residence, income, educational level, political perspective, organizational affiliation, and social standing.

demonstration speech, 381–82   A type of INFORMATIVE PRESENTATION that shows AUDIENCE members how to do a procedure, accompanied by verbal instructions and, in some cases, responses to audience FEEDBACK. *See also* TELL-SHOW-DO

denotation, 306–7   The objective, literal meaning or meanings of words. *See also* CONNOTATION

derived credibility, 412–14   The varying effects a SPEAKER has on an AUDIENCE's perceptions of the

hybrid, 284 A type of presentation that occurs when the audience includes members who attend in-person and members who attend virtually. *See also* ASYNCHRONOUS COMMUNICATION and SYNCHRONOUS COMMUNICATION

hypothetical example, 137 A fictional example that can be used to explain a complicated concept in simpler terms or to illustrate a KEY POINT, often by asking an AUDIENCE to imagine themselves in an invented situation. *See also* STORIES

I

identification, 412–13 A persuasive strategy in which both the SPEAKER and AUDIENCE recognize that they share common attitudes, ideas, feelings, values, experiences, and personal qualities.

identity-first language, 319 LANGUAGE that emphasizes a particular characteristic that a person may see as part of their identity, such as *Deaf speaker* or *autistic writer*. *See also* PERSON-FIRST LANGUAGE

illustrations, and photographs, 267, 271 A category of PRESENTATION AIDS used to depict an action or skill, enliven interest in a MESSAGE, direct AUDIENCE attention, and/or evoke emotions.

immediacy 213–14, 256–57, 291 A quality of effective DELIVERY that refers to the ways in which a speaker's verbal and nonverbal behaviors convey warmth, involvement, psychological closeness, availability, and positivity.

impromptu delivery, 214–15 A form of DELIVERY that occurs when a presentation is delivered with few or no notes. *See also* EXTEMPORANEOUS DELIVERY; MANUSCRIPT DELIVERY; MEMORIZED DELIVERY

impromptu speech, 465–71 A common type of PRESENTATION in which the SPEAKER delivers a coherent MESSAGE with little or no preparation or practice time.
    guidelines, 466–71, 494
    key features, 466

inclusive language, 319–22   LANGUAGE that promotes respect for and a fair representation of all audience members regardless of race, ethnicity, gender, sexual orientation, age, ability, socioeconomic status, and other unique characteristics.
    as ethical choice, 46
    when using humor, 342–43

individualism-collectivism, 95–96 A continuum describing the degree to which a culture prefers independence, on one end, or interdependence, on the other.

inference, 424 A CLAIM that goes beyond established FACTS to reach a conclusion that may not be provable.

O

occasion, 7, 61–71 The reason, time, place, and medium for a presentation.

online presentation, 282–301 A presentation delivered online, either recorded or delivered live using an online platform. *See also* HYBRID PRESENTATION; ASYNCHRONOUS COMMUNICATION; SYNCHRONOUS COMMUNICATION

open posture, 255 A natural and confident speaking POSTURE in which your shoulders are relaxed and your arms are not crossed or touching your body.

open-ended questions, 98–99 A type of SURVEY question that asks AUDIENCE members to provide detailed answers by using probing words such as *what* and *why*. *See also* CLOSE-ENDED QUESTION

opinion, 135, 424 A personal attitude, belief, or judgment that is arguable but not necessarily settled: *I think the acting in* Black Panther: Wakanda Forever *was better than the acting in* Top Gun: Maverick. *See also* FACT

optimum pitch, 239 The natural PITCH at which you speak most easily and expressively.

oral citation, 150 A form of DOCUMENTATION where you state the source of your SUPPORTING MATERIAL aloud during your presentation.

pictographs, 265 A type of PRESENTATION AID that uses a series of repeated icons or symbols to visualize simple data.

pie charts, 265–66, 273 A type of PRESENTATION AID that shows proportions (slices) in relation to a whole (pie).

pitch, 238 A component of VOCAL DELIVERY that describes how high or low your voice sounds.

plagiarism, 49–50, 54–55, 132, 149–51 Failure to provide accurate DOCUMENTATION or give due credit to the sources of your information, and/or presenting another person's key ideas and statements as your own.

posture, 255–56 A component of PHYSICAL DELIVERY that describes the way you position your body when standing and sitting.

powerful words, 308 LANGUAGE that expresses CONFIDENCE, certainty, and commitment to your PURPOSE.

powerless words, 310 LANGUAGE that is bland and unconvincing, with frequent use of FILLER PHRASES.

preliminary outline, 179–81 A simple OUTLINE that helps you initially develop and arrange your KEY POINTS and SUPPORTING MATERIAL into a sketch of your presentation.

premises, 421–23 A statement within an ARGUMENT that leads to a conclusion (or CLAIM) when connected by sound REASONING.

presentation, 6 Any time a SPEAKER creates meaning with verbal and nonverbal MESSAGES and establishes a relationship with AUDIENCE members, also referred to as *presentation speaking*. *See also* PUBLIC SPEAKING

presentation aids, 260–81 The supplementary audio, visual, and hands-on resources available for presenting and highlighting KEY POINTS and SUPPORTING MATERIAL in a presentation.

behave as they wish, they go out of their way to do the forbidden behavior or rebel against the prohibiting authority.

public group discussions, 519–25 A speaking OCCASION where a group of selected people speak in front of and for the benefit of an AUDIENCE about a predetermined TOPIC. The most common types are FORUMS, GOVERNANCE GROUPS, PANEL DISCUSSIONS, and SYMPOSIUMS.

public speaking, 6 A specific kind of PRESENTATION in which a SPEAKER addresses a public AUDIENCE, like in community, government, educational, or organizational settings.

purpose, 109–21, 130 The outcome you are seeking as the result of making a presentation.

purpose statement, 115–18 A single sentence that states the specific, achievable, and relevant goal of your presentation.

Q

qualifiers, 424, 427–28 A supplementary component of the TOULMIN MODEL OF ARGUMENT that states the degree to which a CLAIM appears to be true, usually by using words such as *probably*, *possibly*, or *likely*.

question-and-answer (Q&A) session, 350–61 A segment of or specific kind of PRESENTATION where a SPEAKER gives brief impromptu responses to AUDIENCE questions and comments and, in some cases, may ask the audience to answer questions. Also referred to as *Q&A*.

ability to give appropriate and meaningful FEED-BACK that signals you have or have not heard and understood the SPEAKER.

rhetoric, 6   The art of influencing the thinking, feelings, and behavior of an AUDIENCE.

Rhetoric (Aristotle), 5–6

rhetorical situation, 5–13   The particular circumstance in which you speak to influence what your listeners know, believe, feel, and/or do. The six core elements of the rhetorical situation are AUDIENCE, CONTENT, DELIVERY, OCCASION, PURPOSE, and SPEAKER.

rhetorical speechmaking process, 5–17, 44–48

rhetorical style, 316–17   A fundamental SPEAKING STYLE in which a SPEAKER uses short words and sentences, VIVID LANGUAGE, and POWERFUL WORDS to persuade, motivate, and/or impress AUDIENCE members.

Rice, Susan
    using antithesis, 314
Rowan, Katherine
    theory of informative communication, 372–74, 376, 388

rule of three, 155–56   A general guideline stating that AUDIENCES are more likely to understand and remember three KEY POINTS (as well as three words, phrases, or items in a row) instead of two, four, or more.
    avoiding information overload, 371
    as figure of speech, 314
    in storytelling, 328

S

sample, 148   A representative group of people, objects, items, or phenomena selected from a population as a whole for a statistical study.

sampling bias, 148   In a statistical study, a bias that occurs when categories of individuals in the overall population are intentionally or inadvertently excluded from the SAMPLE.

scientific method arrangement, 161–62   An ORGANIZATIONAL PATTERN that follows the well-established steps prescribed for conducting RESEARCH and publishing results in journals.

secondary source, 147   A document or publication that describes, reports, repeats, or summarizes information from primary sources and other secondary sources. *See also* PRIMARY SOURCE

selected instances fallacy, 434–35   A FALLACY in which the SPEAKER purposely picks atypical EXAMPLES to support an ARGUMENT.

selective listening, 31–32   A poor LISTENING habit in which AUDIENCE members pay attention only to MESSAGES they like or agree with, or avoid complex, unfamiliar information that contradicts or challenges OPINIONS they already hold.

self-centered interests, 93   Subjects that interest AUDIENCE members because there is something they can gain or lose by not paying attention. *See also* TOPIC-CENTERED INTERESTS

self-effacing humor, 341–42   The ability to direct humor at yourself, often used to connect with

Y

Credits

Photos

Page xi (left column): Franz Perc/Alamy Stock Photo; Vicki Couchman/Camera Press/Redux; Brooks Kraft/CORBIS/Corbis via Getty Images; Shutterstock; Ray Tamarra/Contributor/Getty Images; Xinhua/Alamy Stock Photo; Courtesy of Sebastian Wernicke; **p. xi (middle column):** David Hartley/Shutterstock; dpa picture alliance/Alamy Stock Photo; Don Arnold/WireImage/Getty Images; Courtesy of Mileha Soneji; **p. xi (right column):** Dan Callister/Shutterstock; Walter McBride/WireImage/Getty Images; Courtesy of Goldman Environmental Prize; Collection Christophel/Alamy Stock Photo; AP Photo/Manuel Balce Ceneta.

Page 2: RvS.Media/Basile Barbey/Getty Images; **p. 14:** Franz Perc/Alamy Stock Photo; **p. 19:** Don Arnold/WireImage/Getty Images; **p. 27:** Vicki Couchman/Camera Press/Redux; **p. 44:** Franz Perc/Alamy Stock Photo.

Page 58: Kyodo News Stills via Getty Images; **p. 69:** Brooks Kraft/CORBIS/Corbis via Getty Images; **p. 79:** David Hartley/Shutterstock; **p. 81:** Walter McBride/WireImage/Getty Images; **p. 82:** Lisa Lake/Getty Images; **p. 86:** Shutterstock; **p. 104:** AFP via Getty Images; **p. 106:** Ray Tamarra/Contributor/Getty Images; **p. 119:** Xinhua/Alamy Stock Photo.

Page 122: Courtesy of the Wharton People Analytics Initiative, The Wharton School, University of Pennsylvania; **p. 128:** Courtesy of Mileha Soneji; **p. 138:** Shutterstock; **p. 144:** New Africa/Shutterstock and Nathan Weisser/Shutterstock; **p. 169:** Dan Callister/Shutterstock; **p. 171:** Courtesy of Sebastian Wernicke; **p. 205:** David Hartley/Shutterstock.

Page 208: Yassmin Abdel-Magied/The Bent Agency; Xinhua/Alamy Stock Photo; **p. 225:** dpa picture alliance/Alamy Stock Photo; **p. 235:** Araya Doheny/Getty Images; **p. 239:** Walter McBride/WireImage/Getty Images; **p. 241:** Vicki Couchman/Camera Press/Redux; **p. 246:** Don Arnold/WireImage/Getty Images; **p. 255 (top):** Michael Buckner/SXSW Conference & Festivals via Getty Images; **p. 255 (bottom):** Dan Callister/Shutterstock; **p. 256:** Derek Meijer/Alamy Stock Photo; **p. 261:** dpa picture alliance/Alamy Stock Photo; **p. 265:** CalypsoArt/Shutterstock; **p. 267 (top):** Walter McBride/WireImage/Getty Images; **p. 267 (bottom):** Dan Hayward/Naked Pastor; **p. 274:** Dan Callister/Shutterstock; **p. 286:** Shannon Wheeler/CartoonStock; **p. 288:** fizkes/Shutterstock; **p. 292:** SDI Productions/Getty Images; **p. 293:** JiaYing Grygiel; **p. 299:** Courtesy of Sarah Grison.

Page 302: Maskot/Getty Images; **p. 313:** Walter McBride/WireImage/Getty Images; **p. 325:** David Hartley/Shutterstock; **p. 337:** Brooks Kraft/CORBIS/Corbis via Getty Images; **p. 338:** Dan Callister/Shutterstock; **p. 339:** dpa picture alliance/Alamy Stock Photo; **p. 341:** Don Arnold/WireImage/Getty Images.

Page 362: Courtesy of Mileha Soneji; **p. 385:** Courtesy of Mileha Soneji; **p. 389:** David Hartley/Shutterstock; **p. 398:** Dan Callister/Shutterstock.

Page 402: Todd Williamson/Getty Images; **p. 418:** Ray Tamarra/Contributor/Getty Images; **p. 429:** dpa picture alliance/Alamy Stock Photo; **p. 458:** Walter McBride/WireImage/Getty Images.

Page 462: Leah Flores/Stocksy; **p. 497:** Courtesy of Goldman Environmental Prize; **p. 505:** Collection Christophel/Alamy Stock Photo; **p. 512:** AP Photo/Manuel Balce Ceneta.

Text

Anderson, Marge: Excerpts from "Looking Through Our Window: The Value of Indian Culture," *Vital Speeches of the Day*, Vol. 65, Issue 20, pp. 633–34, 1999. Reprinted courtesy of the Estate of Marge Anderson.

Cáceres, Berta: Speech accepting 2015 Goldman Environmental Prize. https://youtu.be/AR1kwx8b0ms. Reprinted by permission of Goldman Environmental Prize.

Line Art

Notes

1.2 Speaking Anxiety

1. Michael T. Motley, *Overcoming Your Fear of Public Speaking: A Proven Method* (Boston: Houghton Mifflin, 1997), 3.

2. Chapman University, "America's Top Fears 2018: Chapman University Survey of American Fears," *The Voice of Wilkinson* (blog), October 16, 2018, https://blogs.chapman.edu/wilkinson/2018/10/16/americas-top-fears-2018.

3. Jannik Linder, "Statistics Reveal Widespread Public Speaking Fear among Individuals Globally," *Gitnux Report 2024*, Gitnux, July 17, 2023, https://gitnux.org/public-speaking-fear-statistics.

4. "Quotes by Elvis," Graceland: The Home of Elvis Presley, accessed July 24, 2024, https://www.graceland.com/quotes-by-elvis.

5. Motley, *Overcoming Your Fear*, 27.

6. Virginia P. Richmond, Jason S. Wrench, and James C. McCroskey, *Communication Apprehension, Avoidance, and Effectiveness*, 6th ed. (Boston: Pearson, 2013).

7. Lori Darrell and S. Clay Willmington, "The Relationship between Self-Report Measures of Communication Apprehension and Trained Observers' Ratings of Communication Competence," *Communication Reports* 11, no. 1 (1998): 87–95.

8. Karen Kangas Dwyer, *Conquer Your Speech Anxiety: Learn How to Overcome Your Nervousness about Public Speaking* (Belmont, CA: Thomson, Wadsworth, 2005).

9. Thomas Gilovich and Kenneth Savitsky, "The Spotlight Effect and the Illusion of Transparency," *Current Directions in Psychological Science* 8, no. 6 (1999): 165–68.

10. John A. Daly, Anita L. Vangelisti, and David J. Weber, "Speech Anxiety Affects How People Prepare Speeches: A Protocol Analysis of the Preparation Process of Speaking," *Communication Monographs* 62, no. 1 (December 1995): 383–97.

1.3 Listening

1. Judi Brownell, *Listening: Attitudes, Principles, and Skills* (New York: Routledge/Taylor & Francis, 2018), 344.

2. This finding summarizes several research studies on communication and listening time. All these studies rank listening as the communication skill we use most of the time.

3. Brownell, *Listening*, 14–18.

4. P. M. Forni, *Choosing Civility: The Twenty-Five Rules of Considerate Conduct* (New York: St. Martin's Press, 2002), 9.

5. Christopher Borrelli, "Essayist Roxane Gay's Critical Voice Is Booming," *Chicago Tribune*, updated December 18, 2018, https://www.chicagotribune.com/2014/10/24/essayist-roxane-gays-critical-voice-is-booming/.

6. Victoria L. Spring, C. Daryl Cameron, and Mina Cikara, "The Upside of Outrage," *Trends in Cognitive Sciences* 22, no. 12 (2018): 1067–69, https://doi.org/10.1016/j.tics.2018.09.006.

7. Ralph G. Nichols, "Ten Bad Listening Habits," *Supervisor's Notebook* 22, no. 1 (New York: Scott Foresman, Spring 1960), https://www.millersville.edu/gened/files/pdfs-faculty-handbook/15-ten-bad-listening-habits.pdf.

8. Nichols, *Supervisor's Notebook*.

9. Pam A. Mueller and Daniel M. Oppenheimer, "The Pen Is Mightier than the Keyboard: Advantages of

Longhand over Laptop Note Taking," *Psychological Science* 25, no. 6 (April 23, 2014): 1159–68, https://doi.org/10.1177/0956797614524581; 2018 correction: "Corrigendum: The Pen Is Mightier than the Keyboard: Advantages of Longhand over Laptop Note Taking," *Psychological Science* 29, no. 9 (July 31, 2018): 1565–68, https://journals.sagepub.com/doi/10.1177/0956797618781773/.

10. Inspired by the Audience's Bill of Rights, in Gene Zalazny, *Say It with Presentations*, rev. and expanded ed. (New York: McGraw-Hill, 2006), 4–6.

1.4 Ethics and Free Speech

1. Quintilian, *Institutes of Oratory*, in *The Rhetorical Tradition: Readings from Classical Times to the Present*, ed. Patricia Bizzell and Bruce Herzberg (Boston: Bedford/St. Martin's, 2001), 418.

2. National Communication Association, Credo for Ethical Communication, rev. 2017, https://www.natcom.org/sites/default/files/Public_Statement_Credo_for_Ethical_Communication_2017.pdf.

3. Judi Brownell, *Listening: Attitudes, Principles, and Skills*, 6th ed. (New York: Routledge/Taylor & Francis, 2018), 408–9.

4. ChatGPT, response to "Describe the dangers of 100 degree plus ocean temperature on the Florida coast," OpenAI, August 3, 2023, https://chat.openai.com.

5. S. S. Sundar, and M. Liao, "Calling BS on ChatGPT: Reflections on AI as a Communication Source," *Journalism & Communication Monographs*, 25, no. 2 (2023): 165–80, https://doi.org/10.1177/15226379231167135.

6. Harvard University Information Technology, "Getting Started with Prompts for Text-Based Generative AI Tools," Harvard University, August 30, 2023, https://huit.harvard.edu/news/ai-prompts.

7. "GPT-4," OpenAI, March 14, 2023, https://openai.com/research/gpt-4.

8. Sara Merken, "New York Lawyers Sanctioned for Using Fake ChatGPT Cases in Legal Briefs," Reuters, June 26, 2023, https://www.reuters.com/legal/new-york-lawyers-sanctioned-using-fake-chatgpt-cases-legal-brief-2023-06-22.

9. Simon Friis and James Riley, "Eliminating Algorithmic Bias Is Just the Beginning of Equitable AI," *Harvard Business Review*, September 29, 2023, https://hbr.org/2023/09/eliminating-algorithmic-bias-is-just-the-beginning-of-equitable-ai.

10. Bronson Dant, "Using AI in Writing: Ethical Implications and Personal Responsibility," LinkedIn, September 20, 2023, https://www.linkedin.com/pulse/using-ai-writing-ethical-implications-personal-bronson-dant-pmp/?trackingId=%2F5DYISegTdqQKMMVGWBF0Q%3D%3D/.

11. E. A. Gjelten, "Does the First Amendment Protect Hate Speech?" Lawyers.com, updated November 2, 2020, https://legal-info.lawyers.com/criminal/does-the-first-amendment-protect-hate-speech.html.

12. Ronald C. Arnett, "The Practical Philosophy of Communication Ethics and Free Speech as the Foundation for Speech Communication," *Communication Quarterly* 38, no. 3 (Summer 1990): 208–17, 215.

2.1 Occasion

1. Carmine Gallo, "Why a 20-Minute Presentation Always Beats a 60-Minute One," *Forbes*, January 24, 2013, https://www.forbes.com/sites/carminegallo/2013/01/24/why-a-20-minute-presentation-always-beats-a-60-minute-one/?sh=1af2ae495177.

2. Granville N. Toogood, *The New Articulate Executive* (New York: McGraw-Hill, 2010), 84–85.

3. Dorothy Leeds, *Power Speak: Engage, Inspire, and Stimulate Your Audience* (Franklin Lakes, NJ: Career Press, 2003), 196.

2.2 Speaker

1. Robert H. Gass and John S. Seiter, *Persuasion: Social Influence and Compliance Gaining*, 7th ed. (New York: Routledge, 2022), 89.

2. John A. Daly and Madeleine H. Redlick, "Handling Questions and Objections Affects Audience Judgments

of Speakers," *Communication Education* 65, no. 2 (2016): 164–81.

3. Alison Wood Brooks and Leslie K. John, "The Surprising Power of Questions," *Harvard Business Review*, May–June 2016, 60–67, https://hbr.org/2018/05/the-surprising-power-of-questions.html.

4. Gass and Seiter, *Persuasion*, 101.

5. "Text: Obama's Re-election Victory Speech in Chicago," Reuters, November 7, 2012, https://www.reuters.com/article/usa-election-obama-speech-text/text-obamas-re-election-victory-speech-in-chicago-idINDEE8A60BA20121107.

6. Madison Medeiros, "Elizabeth Holmes' 2014 TED Talk Is Infuriating to Watch Now," Refinery 29, March 18, 2019, https://www.refinery29.com/en-us/2019/03/226701/elizabeth-holmes-ted-talk-healthcare-2014-quotes-transcript. See also John Brandon, "If You Watched This Elizabeth Holmes TED Talk from 2014, It Was Clear She Was a Fraud from Day One," *Inc.*, March 14, 2018, https://www.inc.com/john-brandon/the-truth-about-theranos-how-we-were-all-laundered-by-this-spin-machine.html.

7. Bobby Umar, Lida Citroën, and Tom Popomaronnis, "How Can You Recover Your Credibility as a Thought Leader?" LinkedIn, last modified August 21, 2023, https://www.linkedin.com/advice/1/how-can-you-recover-your-credibility-thought; and David Cox and Sharon Cox, "Restoring Your Credibility at Work Requires a Plan of Action," *Third Party Blogger*, accessed January 6, 2024, https://www.thirdpartyblogger.com/blog/restoring-credibility-work (blog discontinued).

8. Cox and Cox.

2.3 Audience

1. Some of the early research efforts in this area include Geert Hofstede, Gert Jan Hofstede, and Michael Minkov, *Culture and Organizations: Software of the Mind*, 3rd ed. (New York: McGraw-Hill, 2010); Geert Hofstede, *Culture's Consequences: Comparing Values, Behaviors, Institutions and Organizations across Nations*, 2nd ed. (Thousand Oaks, CA: Sage, 2001); Edward T. Hall, *The Silent Language* (Greenwich, CT: Fawcett, 1959); and Edward T. Hall, *Beyond Culture* (Garden City, NY: Anchor, 1997).

2. Emily Crockett, "The Woman Who Inspired Martin Luther King's 'I Have a Dream' Speech," Vox, January 16, 2017, https://www.vox.com/2016/1/18/10785882/martin-luther-king-dream-mahalia-jackson. See also "Mahalia Jackson, the Queen of Gospel, Puts Her Stamp on the March on Washington," *History*, November 13, 2009, updated March 16, 2021, https://www.history.com/this-day-in-history/mahalia-jackson-the-queen-of-gospel-puts-her-stamp-on-the-march-on-washington; and a *Wall Street Journal* video interview with King's adviser and speechwriter, Clarence B. Jones, in *How Martin Luther King Went Off Script in "I Have a Dream,"* YouTube, August 24, 2013, https://www.youtube.com/watch?v=KxlOlynG6FY.

3.1 Choosing a Topic

1. Ethan Mollick, Co-Intelligence: Living and Working with AI (New York: Portfolio/Penguin, 2024), 57.

3.2 Research and Supporting Material

1. National Academies of Sciences, Engineering, and Medicine, *Reckoning with the U.S. Role in Global Ocean Plastic Waste* (Washington, DC: National Academies Press, 2022), nap.nationalacademies.org/catalog/26132/reckoning-with-the-us-role-in-global-ocean-plastic-waste.

2. The information cited in this speech is adapted from Lonnie Hanauer, letter to the editor, *New York Times*, March 2, 2019, A20. It was updated March 15, 2024, to include contemporary pricing, using numbers from the following sources: Hilary Brueck, "US Patients Can Spend More than $3,000 per Pen for the Exact Same Life-Changing Arthritis Drugs that People in Some European Countries Get for Free," November 7, 2022, https://www.businessinsider.com/us-patients-spending-more-on-drugs-europe-patent-thickets-humira-2022-10; and Sydney Lupkin, "Blockbuster Drug Humira Finally Faces Lower-Cost Rivals," *Shots: Health News from NPR*, NPR, July 20, 2023, https://www.npr.org/sections/health-shots/2023/07/20/1188745297/humira-threatened-by-yusimry-low-cost-rival.

3. Adapted from Steven D. Levitt and Stephen J. Dubner, *Freakonomics: A Rogue Economist Explores the Hidden Side of Everything* (New York: William Morrow, 2005), 55–56.

4. Negar Maleki, Balaji Padmanabhan, and Kaushik Dutta, "AI Hallucinations: A Misnomer Worth Clarifying," arXiv, submitted January 9, 2024, https://arxiv.org/abs/2401.06796v1.

5. Andrea Baer and Dan Kipnis, "Evaluating Online Sources: Simple Strategies for Complex Thinking," Campbell Library, Rowan University, last updated September 7, 2023, https://libguides.rowan.edu/EvaluatingOnlineSources.

6. Mike Caulfield, "SIFT (The Four Moves)," *Hapgood* (blog), June 19, 2019, https://hapgood.us/?s=SIFT+%28The+Four+Moves%29.

7. "How Does the Gallup U.S. Poll Work?" Gallup, accessed March 7, 2024, https://www.gallup.com/224855/gallup-poll-work.aspx.

8. "Overweight & Obesity Statistics," National Institute of Diabetes and Digestive and Kidney Diseases, accessed July 24, 2024, https://www.niddk.nih.gov/health-information/health-statistics/overweight-obesity#prevalence. See especially the section titled "Prevalence of Overweight and Obesity."

9. Aubrey Gordon, *What We Don't Talk about When We Talk about Fat* (New York: Penguin Random House, 2020), 51.

3.3 Organizing Content

1. Michael J. Gelb, *Present Yourself! Capture Your Audience with Great Presentation* (Rolling Hills Estates, CA: Jalmar Press, 1988), 10–15.

2. See the chapters on reading and writing quantitative and qualitative research reports in Joann Keyton, *Communication Research: Asking Questions, Finding Answers* (Boston: McGraw-Hill, 2001), 314–45.

3. Richard Bullock, *The Norton Field Guide to Writing*, 6th ed. (New York: W. W. Norton, 2019), 439–40.

4. Dorothy Leeds, *Power Speak: Engage, Inspire, and Stimulate Your Audience* (Franklin Lakes, NJ: Career Press, 2003), 122–23.

5. Michael M. Klepper with Robert E. Gunther, *I'd Rather Die than Give a Speech* (Burr Ridge, IL: Irwin, 1994), 6.

3.4 Framing and Outlining

1. Thomas Leach, *How to Prepare, Stage, and Deliver Winning Presentations* (New York: AMACOM, 1993), 97.

2. The speech framer was developed by Isa Engleberg as an alternative and supplement to outlining. See Isa N. Engleberg and John A. Daly, *Presentations in Everyday Life*, 3rd ed. (Boston: Pearson, 2009), 217–18.

3.5 Introductions and Conclusions

1. Samantha Delouya, "Bob Iger Made $31.6 Million as Disney's CEO Last Year," CNN Business, January 16, 2024, https://www.cnn.com/2024/01/16/business/bob-iger-disney-pay/index.html.

2. Margaret Muller, "'I Have Down Syndrome': Student's Speech Proves Value of Hard Work," *Washington Post*, September 14, 1999, Health, 9.

3. Ronald Reagan, "Address to the Nation on the Explosion of the Space Shuttle *Challenger*" (speech, Oval Office, Washington, DC, January 28, 1986), Ronald Reagan Presidential Library & Museum, National Archives, accessed February 22, 2024, https://www.reaganlibrary.gov/archives/speech/address-nation-explosion-space-shuttle-challenger.

4. Marge Anderson, "Looking through Our Window: The Value of Indian Culture," *Vital Speeches of the Day* 65, no. 20 (1999): 633–34.

5. Muller, "I Have Down Syndrome," 9.

6. Robert M. Franklin, "The Soul of Morehouse and the Future of the Mystique" (speech, President's Town Meeting, Morehouse College, Atlanta, April 21, 2009), Internet Archive Wayback Machine, accessed March 15, 2024, https://web.archive.org/web/20130601050137/http://giving.morehouse.edu/Document.Doc?id=37.

4.1 Delivery Decisions

1. Nina-Jo Moore, Mark Hickson III, and Don W. Stacks, *Nonverbal Communication: Studies and Applications*, 6th ed. (New York: Oxford, 2014), 4.

2. Brian Cutler, Steven D. Penrod, and Thomas E. Stuve, "Juror Decision Making in Eyewitness Identification Cases," *Law and Human Behavior* 12, no. 1 (1988): 41–55; and Bonnie Erickson, Allan E. Lind, Bruce C. Johnson, and William M. O'Barr, "Speech Style and Impression Formation in a Court Setting: The Effects of 'Powerful' and 'Powerless' Speech," *Journal of Experimental Social Psychology* 14, no. 3 (1978): 266–79.

3. Kathy Tyner, "Stage Presence: What It Means, Why It Matters, and How to Improve It," KD Conservatory, accessed July 24, 2024, https://kdstudio.com/tag/stage-presence/.

4. Based on authors' observations as well as descriptions in Carmine Gallo, *The Presentation Secrets of Steve Jobs: How to Be Insanely Great in Front of Any Audience* (New York: McGraw-Hill, 2010).

5. Peter Andersen, "Immediacy," in *Encyclopedia of Communication Theory*, ed. Stephen W. Littlejohn and Karen A. Foss (Los Angeles: Sage, 2009), 501.

6. Judee K. Burgoon and Aaron E. Bacue, "Nonverbal Communication Skills," in *Handbook of Communication and Social Interaction Skills*, ed. John O. Greene and Brant R. Burleson (Mahwah, NJ: Lawrence Erlbaum, 2003), 195–96; James Kennedy, Paul Baxter, and Tony Belpaeme, "Nonverbal Immediacy as a Characterisation of Social Behaviour for Human–Robot Interaction," *International Journal of Social Robotics* 9, no. 1 (2017): 109–28; and "Immediacy in the Classroom: Research and Practical Implications," NAGT Workshop, accessed February 14, 2023, https://serc.carleton.edu/NAGTWorkshops/affective/immediacy.html#:~:-text=Immediacy%20Defined&text=Non%2Dverbal%20immediacy%20includes%20behaviors,encouraging%20student%20input%20and%20discussion.

7. In addition to cues the authors use, see the following sources for more: "Speech Delivery Manuscript Markings.doc," Studylib, accessed February 13, 2023, https://studylib.net/doc/6619623/speech-delivery-manuscript-markings.doc; and "The Best Trick for Natural Delivery? Marking Your Script," Oratium, September 22, 2015, https://www.oratium.com/the-best-trick-for-natural-delivery-marking-your-script.

4.2 Vocal Delivery

1. Nina-Jo Moore, Mark Hickson III, and Don W. Stacks, *Nonverbal Communication: Studies and Applications*, 6th ed. (New York: Oxford University Press, 2014), 265–67.

2. Lyle V. Mayer, *Fundamentals of Voice and Articulation*, 13th ed. (Boston: McGraw-Hill, 2004), 55.

3. Mayer, 66.

4. Richard L. Street Jr., Robert M. Brady, and William B. Putnam, "The Influence of Speech Rate Stereotypes and Rate Similarity on Listeners' Evaluations of Speakers," *Journal of Language and Social Psychology* 2, no. 1 (1993): 37–56; Roy F. Baumeister and Brad J. Bushman, *Social Psychology and Human Nature* (Boston: Cengage Learning, 2021), 275; and Jeremy Dean, "Talking Fast May Be a Sign of Intelligence and Has Other Advantages," *Psyblog*, November 21, 2022, https://www.spring.org.uk/2022/11/talking-fast.php.

5. Susan D. Miller, *Be Heard the First Time: A Woman's Guide to Powerful Speaking* (Herndon, VA: Capital Books, 2006), 100.

6. Hilda B. Fisher, *Improving Voice and Articulation* (Boston: Houghton Mifflin, 1966,) 168–74; and Matt Ramsey, "10 Secrets to a Remarkable Speaking Voice," Ramsey Voice Studio, March 6, 2021, https://ramseyvoice.com/speaking-voice/.

7. Michael Powell, "Deliberative in a Manic Game: Barack Obama," *New York Times*, June 4, 2008, A18.

8. Michael Erard, *Um: Slips, Stumbles, and Verbal Blunders, and What They Mean* (New York: Pantheon Books, 2007), 243–44.

9. National Geographic for AP Special Features, "The 'Um' Factor: What People Say between Thoughts," *Baltimore Sun*, September 28, 1992, 1D and 3D.

10. Erard, *Um*, 96.

11. John McWorter, *Word on the Street: Debunking the Myth of a "Pure" Standard English* (Cambridge, MA: Perseus, 1998), 143, 145–46.

12. "Barack Obama: Commencement Address at the U.S. Military Academy" (West Point, NY, May 22, 2010), American Rhetoric Online Speech Bank, accessed July 24, 2024, https://www.americanrhetoric.com/speeches/barackobama/barackobamawestpointcommencement.htm; and "President Obama at Hampton University" (commencement speech, Hampton University, Hampton, VA, May 9, 2010), YouTube, May 9, 2010, https://www.youtube.com/watch?v=Hwg636CQnrc.

13. Carol Stewart, "Should a Person Change Their Accent to Fit In or to Progress?," LinkedIn, September 17, 2021, https://www.linkedin.com/pulse/should-person-change-accent-fit-progress-carol-stewart-msc-finstlm#:~:text=Our%20accents%20are%20part%20of,have%20to%20change%20their%20accent.

14. Vershawn Ashanti Young, Rusty Barret, Y'Shanda Young-Rivera, and Kim Brian Lovejoy, *Code-Meshing, Code-Switching, and African American Literacy* (Anderson, SC: Parlor Press, 2018), 77.

15. ChatGPT, response to "How to copy if you have a strong accent or very different dialect when speaking," OpenAI, September 20, 2023, https://chat.openai.com; and ChatGPT, response to "How to adapt to and treat people with heavy accents," OpenAI, September 20, 2023, https://chat.openai.com.

4.3 Physical Delivery

1. Roxanne Bauer, "The Impact of Making Eye Contact around the World," *World Economic Forum*, February 26, 2015, https://www.weforum.org/agenda/2015/02/the-impact-of-making-eye-contact-around-the-world/.

2. Marjorie Brody, *Speaking Your Way to the Top* (Boston: Allyn & Bacon, 1997), 10.

3. Mark L. Knapp, Judith A. Hall, and Terrence G. Hogan, *Nonverbal Communication in Human Interaction*, 8th ed. (Boston: Cengage, 2014), 258.

4. Carl Zimmer, "More to a Smile than Lips and Teeth," *New York Times*, January 24, 2011, http://www.nytimes.com/2011/01/25/science/25smile.html.

5. Everett M. Rogers and Thomas M. Steinfatt, *Intercultural Communication* (Prospect Heights, IL: Waveland, 1999), 174.

6. David Neiwert, "Is That an OK Sign? A White Power Symbol? Or Just a Right-Wing Troll?" Hatewatch, *Southern Poverty Law Center*, September 18, 2018, https://www.splcenter.org/hatewatch/2018/09/18/ok-sign-white-power-symbol-or-just-right-wing-troll.

7. Rogers and Steinfatt, *Intercultural Communication*, 172; and Guo-Ming Chen and William J. Starosta, *Foundations of Intercultural Communication* (Boston: Allyn & Bacon, 1998), 81–92.

8. Ron Hoff, *I Can See You Naked* (Kansas City, MO: Andrews McMeel, 1992), 83.

4.4 Presentation Aids

1. Stephen M. Kosslyn, *Clear and to the Point: 8 Psychological Principles for Compelling PowerPoint® Presentations* (New York: Oxford University Press, 2007), 184.

2. Kosslyn, 210.

3. Elizabeth J. Marsh and Holli E. Sink, "Access to Handouts of Presentation Slides during Lecture: Consequences for Learning," *Applied Cognitive Psychology* 24, no. 5 (2010): 691–706.

4. Christian Tarchi, Sonia Zaccoletti, and Lucia Mason, "Learning from Text, Video, or Subtitles: A Comparative Analysis," *Computers & Education* 160 (January 2021): 104034.

5. Kate Marino, "Newsrooms Should Be Prepared for Deepfakes at a 'Staggering' Scale," *Axios*, October 12, 2023, https://www.axios.com/2023/10/12/mcmahon-misinformation-cbs-deep-fakes-bfd.

6. Gene Zelazny, *The Say It with Charts Complete Toolkit* (New York: McGraw-Hill, 2007), 18–19.

7. Kiran Ajani, Elsie Lee, Cindy Xiong, Cole Nussbaumer Knaflic, William Kemper, and Steven Franconeri, "Declutter and Focus: Empirically Evaluating Design Guidelines for Effective Data Communication," *IEEE Transactions on Visualization and Computer Graphics* 28, no. 10 (2022): 3351–64.

4.5 Online Presentations

1. "Celebrating Our Thriving Community of 150 Million Americans," TikTok, March 21, 2023, https://newsroom.tiktok.com/en-us/150-m-us-users.

2. Ying Lin, "10 Powerful Podcast Statistics You Need to Know in 2024," *Oberlo* (blog), December 21, 2023, https://www.oberlo.com/blog/podcast-statistics.

3. Erik Geelhoed, Kuldip Singh-Barmi, Ian Biscoe, et al., "Co-present and Remote Audience Experiences: Intensity and Cohesion," *Multimedia Tools and Applications* 76 (2016): 5573–606.

4. April A. Kedrowicz and Julie L. Taylor, "Shifting Rhetorical Norms and Electronic Eloquence: TED Talks as Formal Presentations," *Journal of Business and Technical Communication* 30, no. 30 (2016): 352–77.

5. "Chester County to Hold 2 Town Hall Sessions to Address Prisoner Escape, Residents' Concerns," WHYY, September 18, 2023, https://whyy.org/articles/chester-county-town-hall-sessions-prisoner-escape/.

6. Liz Lewis, "2021 Hiring Trends," Indeed Lead, October 14, 2021, https://www.indeed.com/lead/2021-hiring-trends-report.

7. Jeremy N. Bailenson, "Nonverbal Overload: A Theoretical Argument for the Causes of Zoom Fatigue," *Technology, Mind, and Behavior* 2, no. 1 (2021), https://doi.org/10.1037/tmb0000030.

8. Brenda K. Wiederhold, "Connecting through Technology during the Coronavirus Disease 2019 Pandemic: Avoiding 'Zoom Fatigue,'" *Cyberpsychology, Behavior, and Social Networking* 23, no. 7 (2020), https://doi.org/10.1089/cyber.2020.29188.bkw.

9. Bailenson, "Nonverbal Overload."

10. Chariti Canny, "Cut through the Noise: How to Design Slides for Virtual Presentations," Duarte, accessed March 12, 2024, https://www.duarte.com/design-slides-for-virtual-presentations/#:~:text=For%20the%20virtual%20presentation%20designer,key%20information%20on%20the%20slide.

11. Canny.

12. Advait Sarkar and Sean Rintel, "The Rise of Parallel Chat in Online Meetings: How Can We Make the Most of It?" *Microsoft Research Blog*, August 3, 2021, https://www.microsoft.com/en-us/research/blog/the-rise-of-parallel-chat-in-online-meetings-how-can-we-make-the-most-of-it/.

5.1 Language and Style

1. Letter from Mark Twain to George Bainton, October 15, 1888, quoted in George Bainton, comp. and ed., *The Art of Authorship: Literary Reminiscences, Methods of Work, and Advice to Young Beginners* (New York: Appleton, 1890), 87–88.

2. S. I. Hayakawa and Alan R. Hayakawa, *Language and Thought in Action*, 5th ed. (San Diego, CA: Harcourt Brace Jovanovich, 1990), 43.

3. Robert H. Gass and John S. Seiter, *Persuasion, Social Influence, and Compliance Gaining*, 6th ed. (New York: Routledge, 2018), 177; James Price Dillard and Linda J. Marshall, "Persuasion as a Social Skill," in *Handbook of Communication and Social Interaction Skills*, ed. John O. Greene and Brant R. Burleson (Mahwah, NJ: Lawrence Erlbaum, 2003), 505–6; and Richard M. Perloff, *The Dynamics of Persuasion*, 5th ed. (New York: Routledge, 2014), 281–83.

4. This definition is a conglomerate of explanations offered by the most current *Oxford Learner's Dictionary*, *The Cambridge Dictionary*, *Collins Dictionary*, and a variety of websites.

5. "Read Martin Luther King Jr.'s 'I Have a Dream' Speech in Its Entirety," *Talk of the Nation*, NPR, updated January 16, 2023, https://www.npr.org/2010/01/18/122701268/i-have-a-dream-speech-in-its-entirety.

6. "11-Year-Old Naomi Wadler's Speech at the March for Our Lives (Full)" (speech, March for Our Lives, Washington, DC, March 25, 2018), NBC News, YouTube, March 25, 2018, https://www.youtube.com/watch?v=C5ZUDImTIQ8; emphasis added.

7. Ellen Johnson Sirleaf, Address to a joint meeting of the US Congress (speech, US Congress, Washington, DC, March 15, 2006), American Rhetoric Online Speech Bank, accessed July 24, 2024, https://www.americanrhetoric.com/speeches/ellenjohnsonsirleafuscongress.htm.

8. Max Atkinson, *Lend Me Your Ears* (New York: Oxford University Press, 2005), 221.

9. Ronald H. Carpenter, *Choosing Powerful Words* (Boston: Allyn & Bacon, 1999), 109–11.

10. R. L. Trask, *Language: The Basics*, 2nd ed. (London: Routledge, 1995), 128.

11. John Roberts, "I Wish You Bad Luck" (commencement address, Cardigan Mountain School, Canaan, NH, June 3, 2017), JamesClear, accessed July 25, 2024, https://jamesclear.com/great-speeches/i-wish-you-bad-luck-by-john-roberts.

12. Atkinson, *Lend Me Your Ears*, 224.

13. Ron Finley, "A Guerilla Gardener in South Central LA," TED talk, YouTube, March 6, 2013, https://www.youtube.com/watch?v=EzZzZ_qpZ4w.

14. Statement quoted in Mickey Ciokajlo, "Hospital Layoffs Put on Hold," *Chicago Tribune*, June 6, 2007, https://www.chicagotribune.com/news/ct-xpm-2007-06-06-0706051099-story.html.

15. Jenny Maxwell and Jana Daley, "Rhetorical Device of the Month: Antithesis," Buckley School, February 20, 2019, https://www.buckleyschool.com/magazine/articles/rhetorical-device-of-the-month-antithesis/#:~:text=%22To%20him%2C%20your%20celebration%20is,lines%20from%20a%20recent%20speech.

16. Susan Rice, "Remarks Following UN Vote on Palestinian State Observer Status" (speech, UN General Assembly, New York, November 29, 2012), American Rhetoric Online Speech Bank, accessed July 25, 2024, https://www.americanrhetoric.com/speeches/susanricepalestinianobserverstate.htm; emphasis added.

17. Neil Armstrong, "'One Small Step for Man': Moment of Neil Armstrong's Famous Line" (remarks from Moon landing, July 20, 1969), YouTube, July 17, 2019, https://www.youtube.com/watch?v=J6jplPkbe8g; emphasis added.

18. Michelle Obama, "First Lady Michelle Obama at DNC 2016" (speech, Democratic National Convention, Philadelphia, July 25, 2016), Democratic National Convention, YouTube, July 26, 2016, https://www.youtube.com/watch?v=cBxTwFiF9QI; emphasis added.

19. Matt Carlson, "The Joke," Carnegie Hall, accessed July 25, 2024, https://www.carnegiehall.org/Explore/Articles/2020/04/10/The-Joke.

20. Lani Arredondo, *The McGraw-Hill 36-Hour Course: Business Presentations* (New York: McGraw-Hill, 1994), 147.

21. Greta Thunberg, "The Disarming Case to Act Right Now on Climate Change," TEDx Stockholm, November 2018, https://www.ted.com/talks/greta_thunberg_the_disarming_case_to_act_right_now_on_climate_change?subtitle_en/.

22. Barack Obama, "Barack Obama's Full Eulogy at John Lewis's Funeral" (eulogy, Atlanta, GA, July 30, 2020), *Washington Post*, YouTube, July 30, 2020, https://www.youtube.com/watch?v=V1pKoCq1bn0.

23. Brandon Carter, "Jon Stewart Blasts Lawmakers in Hearing for Sept. 11 Victim Compensation Fund," NPR, June 11, 2019, https://www.npr.org/2019/06/11/731706492/jon-stewart-blasts-lawmakers-in-hearing-for-sept-11-victim-compensation.

24. Karishma Manchanda, "Inclusive Language: What It Is and What It Is NOT?" LinkedIn, June 14, 2023, https://www.linkedin.com/pulse/inclusive-language-what-karishma-manchanda-cdp-cdt-.

25. For examples of preferred terms and advice, generally, see "Style Guidance," *Language, Please,*

accessed July 25, 2024, https://languageplease
.org/style-guide/; and Heather Farr and Syanne
Olson, *Inclusive Language Primer: Communicating
with Respect* (Research Park, NC: RTI International, 2022), http://www.rti.org/sites/default/files
/inclusivelanguageprimer.pdf. See also guidelines
offered by specific style manuals, including *MLA
Handbook*, 9th ed. (New York: Modern Language
Association of America, 2021), ch. 3; *The Chicago
Manual of Style*, 18th ed. (Chicago: University of
Chicago Press, 2017), ch. 5; and *The Publication
Manual of the American Psychological Association*,
7th ed. (Washington, DC: APA, 2020), ch. 5. Online,
the APA has also published a second edition of its
handy "Inclusive Language Guide," accessed July 25,
2024, https://www.apa.org/about/apa/equity-diversity
-inclusion/language-guidelines.pdf.

26. Sara Nović, "The Harmful Ableist Language You
Unknowingly Use," BBC, April 5, 2021, https://www
.bbc.com/worklife/article/20210330-the-harmful-ableist
-language-you-unknowingly-use.

27. Nović.

5.2 Telling Stories

1. Annette Simmons, *Whoever Tells the Best Story
Wins* (New York: AMACOM, 2007), 19.

2. See Steve Jobs's 2005 Stanford commencement
address embedded in "Steve Jobs to 2005 Graduates:
'Stay Hungry, Stay Foolish,'" Stanford Report, Stanford
University, June 12, 2005, https://news.stanford.edu
/stories/2005/06/steve-jobs-2005-graduates-stay-hungry
-stay-foolish.

3. Based on Joanna Slan, *Using Stories and Humor:
Grab Your Audience* (Boston: Allyn & Bacon, 1998),
89–95 and 116.

4. Peter Guber, "The Four Truths of the Storyteller,"
Harvard Business Review, December 2007, https://hbr
.org/2007/12/the-four-truths-of-the-storyteller.

5. "Read Oprah Winfrey's Rousing Golden Globes
Speech," CNN, January 10, 2018, https://www.cnn
.com/2018/01/08/entertainment/oprah-globes-speech
-transcript/index.html.

5.3 Generating Interest

1. John A. Daly and Isa N. Engleberg, *Presentations in
Everyday Life* (Boston: Houghton Mifflin, 2001), 3–4
and 21.

2. Gloria Mark, *Attention Span: A Groundbreaking
Way to Restore Balance, Happiness, and Productivity*
(New York: Hanover Square Press, 2023).

3. Granville N. Toogood, *The Articulate Executive:
Learn to Look, Act, and Sound Like a Leader*
(New York: McGraw-Hill, 2010), 83.

4. Carmine Gallo, "Why a 20-Minute Presentation
Always Beats a 60-Minute One," *Forbes*, January 24,
2013, https://www.forbes.com/sites/carminegallo
/2013/01/24/why-a-20-minute-presentation-always
-beats-a-60-minute-one/?sh=1af2ae495177.

5. Marla Tabaka, "How to Give the Speech of a
Lifetime," *Inc.*, March 3, 2014, https://www.inc.com
/marla-tabaka/how-to-give-the-speech-of-a-lifetime-in
-18-minutes-or-less.html.

6. Laura Lynch, "How Long Should Videos Be for
E-Learning," Learn Dash, January 17, 2019, https://
www.learndash.com/how-long-should-videos-be-for
-e-learning.

7. Alan M. Perlman, *Writing Great Speeches: Professional Techniques You Can Use* (Boston: Allyn & Bacon,
1998), 52.

8. "Marshawn Lynch," *SmartLess*, Apple Podcasts,
November 6, 2023, https://www.smartless.com
/episodes/episode/2386453c/marshawn-lynch.

9. Stephen M. Kromka, "Laughing at Oneself:
Outcomes of Instructor: Self-Disparaging Humor Use
in the Classroom" (paper presented at the Florida
Communication Association annual convention,
Tampa, FL, October 14, 2023).

5.4 Question-and-Answer Sessions

1. Gary Genard, "4 Reasons Why Q&A Is a Presentation
Tool You Need to Master," *Gary Genard's Speak for
Success!* (blog), Genard Method, January 6, 2013,
https://www.genardmethod.com/blog/bid/168862/4

-reasons-why-q-a-is-a-presentation-tool-you-need-to
-master#:~:text=The%20truth%20is%20that%20Q
,both%20you%20and%20your%20audience.

2. Thomas Wedell-Wedellsborg, "4 Ways to Fix the Q&A Session," *Harvard Business Review*, August 19, 2014, https://hbr.org/2014/08/four-ways-to-fix-the-qa-session.

3. Tim Calkins, "How to Nail the Q&A Portion of Your Presentation," Quartz, September 20, 2018, https://qz.com/work/1397156/how-to-manage-questions-after-a-presentation.

4. Based on Laura Sangha, "Asking Questions of Speakers: Top Tips," The Many Headed-Monster, February 23, 2017, https://manyheadedmonster.wordpress.com/2017/02/23/asking-questions-of-speakers-top-tips.

5. "1+0 Simple Ways to Get the Most out of Your Q&A Session," *SocialTables* (blog), accessed July 25, 2024, https://www.socialtables.com/blog/attendee-engagement/qa-session.

6.1 Understanding Informative Speaking

1. John W. Michell, "The Future of the Human Workforce," *Forbes*, June 30, 2023, https://www.forbes.com/sites/forbesbooksauthors/2023/06/30/the-future-of-the-human-workforce.

2. Erin E. Rupp, "Feeling Overwhelmed? How to Protect Yourself from Information Overload," *Able* (blog), September 30, 2023, https://able.ac/blog/information-overload/#:~:text=Today%2C%20the%20world%20has%20access,it%20can%20also%20be%20overwhelming.

3. Katherine E. Rowan, "A New Pedagogy for Explanatory Public Speaking: Why Arrangement Should Not Substitute for Invention," *Communication Education* 44 (1995): 236–50; and Katherine E. Rowan, "Informing and Explaining Skills: Theory and Research on Informative Communication," in *Handbook of Communication and Social Interaction Skills*, ed. John O. Greene and Brant R. Burleson (Mahwah, NJ: Lawrence Erlbaum, 2003), 403–38.

4. Rowan, "A New Pedagogy," 242–43; and Rowan, "Informing and Explaining Skills," 419–20.

6.2 Reporting New Information

1. Katherine E. Rowan, "Informing and Explaining Skills: Theory and Research on Informative Communication," in *Handbook of Communication and Social Interaction Skills*, ed. John O. Greene and Brant R. Burleson (Mahwah, NJ: Lawrence Erlbaum, 2003), 412–19.

2. David K. Farkas, "The Logical and Rhetorical Construction of Procedural Discourse," *Technical Communication* (February 1999): 42–43, http://www.jstor.org/stable/43088601; and Michael Steehouder and Hans van der Meij, "Designing and Evaluating Procedural Instructions with the Four Components Model," *2005 IEEE International Professional Communication Conference Proceedings*, 797–801, https://ieeexplore.ieee.org/document/1494254/.

3. Ashley Chiasson, "Terminology Tuesday: Tell, Show, Do," *Ashley Chiasson* (blog), April 5, 2016, http://ashleychiasson.com/blog/terminology-tuesday-tell-show-do/.

6.3 Explaining Complex Ideas

1. Katherine E. Rowan, "Informing and Explaining Skills: Theory and Research on Informative Communication," in *Handbook of Communication and Social Interaction Skills*, ed. John O. Greene and Brant R. Burleson (Mahwah, NJ: Lawrence Erlbaum, 2003), 403–38; and Katherine E. Rowan, "A New Pedagogy for Explanatory Public Speaking: Why Arrangement Should Not Substitute for Invention," *Communication Education* 44 (1995): 236–50.

2. Rowan, "Informing and Explaining Skills," 420–22; and Rowan, "New Pedagogy," 243.

3. Joseph Welan and Kamil Msefer, "Economic Supply and Demand," MIT System Dynamics in Education Project, January 14, 1996, https://ocw.mit.edu/courses/sloan-school-of-management/15-988-system-dynamics-self-study-fall-1998-spring-1999/readings/economics.pdf.

4. Rowan, "Informing and Explaining Skills," 422–24.

5. Barbara Katz Rothman, *The Book of Life: A Personal and Ethical Guide to Race, Normality and the Human Gene Study* (Boston: Beacon Press, 2001), 23. See also

Cynthia Taylor and Bryan M. Dewsbury, "On the Problem and Promise of Metaphor Use in Science and Science Communication," *Journal of Microbiology & Biology Education* 19, no. 1 (2018), https://www.ncbi.nlm.nih.gov/pmc/articles/PMC5969428.

6. Matt Rosenberg, "An Overview of El Nino and La Nina," ThoughtCo., August 27, 2020, thoughtco.com/el-nino-and-la-nina-overview-1434943; National Oceanic and Atmospheric Administration, "What Are El Niño and La Niña?" National Ocean Service, accessed February 19, 2021, https://oceanservice.noaa.gov/facts/ninonina.html; "What Are El Niño and La Niña?" American Geosciences Institute, accessed July 25, 2024, https://www.americangeosciences.org/critical-issues/faq/what-are-el-nino-and-la-nina; and David Funkhouser, "El Niño: The Basics," *State of the Planet* (blog), Earth Institute/Columbia University, July 2, 2014, https://blogs.ei.columbia.edu/2014/07/02/el-nino-the-basics.

7. Rowan, "Informing and Explaining Skills," 424–26.

7.1 Understanding Persuasion

1. Andrea Lunsford and John R. Ruszkiewicz, *Everything's an Argument*, 9th ed. (Boston: Bedford/St. Martin's, 2021).

2. Robert H. Gass and John S. Seiter, *Persuasion: Social Influence and Compliance Gaining*, 7th ed. (New York: Routledge, 2022), 4.

3. Aristotle, *The Complete Works of Aristotle: The Revised Oxford Translation*, ed. Jonathan Barnes, Bollingen Series (Princeton, NJ: Princeton University Press, 1983), 1:2155.

4. Kenneth Burke, *A Rhetoric of Motives* (Berkeley: University of California Press, 1969), 55.

5. Matt Dixon, "Trump Delivers Fiery Post Indictment Speech: 'They're Coming after You' " NBC News, June 10, 2023, https://www.nbcnews.com/politics/donald-trump/trump-deliver-fiery-post-indictment-speech-georgia-rcna88561.

6. "UTSW Q&A: Experts Talk about Opioid Abuse, Risks, Treatment," University of Texas Southwest Medical Center, August 16, 2023, https://www.utsouthwestern.edu/newsroom/articles/year-2023/aug-q-a-opioid-abuse-risks-treatment.html.

7. Martha C. Nussbaum, *The Monarch of Fear: A Philosopher Looks at Our Political Crisis* (New York: Simon & Schuster, 2018), 24.

8. Richard M. Perloff, *The Dynamics of Persuasion: Communication and Attitudes in the 21st Century*, 7th ed. (New York: Routledge, 2020), 353–54.

9. Gass and Seiter, *Persuasion*, 102.

7.2 Thinking Critically about Arguments

1. Jay Verlinden, *Critical Thinking and Everyday Argument* (Belmont, CA: Wadsworth Thomson Learning, 2005), 79.

2. Stephen E. Toulmin, *The Uses of Argument* (London: Cambridge University Press, 1958); and Stephen Toulmin, Richard Rieke, and Allan Janik, *An Introduction to Reasoning* (New York: Macmillan, 1979).

3. Douglas N. Walton, *Begging the Question: Circular Reasoning as a Tactic of Argumentation* (Westport, CT: Greenwood Press, 1991), 285.

7.3 Rhetorical Strategies for Persuasive Presentations

1. Robert H. Gass and John S. Seiter, *Persuasion: Social Influence and Compliance Gaining*, 7th ed. (New York: Routledge, 2022), 239.

2. Jack W. Brehm, *A Theory of Psychological Reactance* (New York: Academic Press, 1966).

3. Sonja K. Foss and Karen A. Foss, *Inviting Transformation: Presentational Speaking in a Changing World*, 4th ed. (Long Grove, IL: Waveland, 2019), 11.

4. William J. McGuire, "Inducing Resistance to Persuasion: Some Contemporary Approaches," in *Advances in Experimental Psychology*, ed. Leonard Berkowitz (New York: Academic Press, 1964), 192–229.

5. See, for example, Sander van der Linden, Jon Roozenbeek, and Josh Compton, "Inoculating against

Fake News about COVID-19," *Frontiers in Psychology* 11 (2020), https://doi.org/10.3389/fpsyg.2020.566790.

6. Gass and Seiter, *Persuasion*, 234–38.

7. Sharon Shavitt and Michelle R. Nelson, "The Role of Attitude Functions in Persuasion and Social Judgment," in *The Persuasion Handbook: Developments in Theory and Practice*, ed. James Price Dillard and Michael Pfau (Thousand Oaks, CA: Sage, 2002), 150.

8. Moriah Balingit and Andrew Van Dam, "U.S. Students Continue to Lag behind Peers in East Asia and Europe in Reading, Math and Science, Exams Show," *Washington Post*, December 3, 2019, https://www.washingtonpost.com/local/education /us-students-continue-to-lag-behind-peers-in-ea st-asia-and-europe-in-reading-math-and-science -exams-show/2019/12/02/e9e3b37c-153d-11ea-9110 -3b34ce1d92b1_story.html.

9. OECD (2023), *PISA 2022 Results (Volume I): The State of Learning and Equity in Education*, PISA, OECD Publishing, Paris, https://doi.org/10.1787/53f23881-en; and John Williams, "US Ranking in Math," Let's Go Learn, November 7, 2022, https://www.letsgolearn.com /math-assessment/us-ranking-in-math.

10. Alan H. Monroe, *Principles and Types of Speech* (Chicago: Scott, Foresman, 1935).

11. Ron Finley Project, accessed May 6, 2024, https:// ronfinley.com.

8.3 Welcome Remarks

1. Kristen Bub, "Welcome Speech to 2007's Incoming Class" (speech, Harvard Graduate School of Education, Cambridge, MA, September 11, 2007), Harvard Graduate School of Education, accessed July 25, 2024, https://www.gse.harvard.edu/news/07/09/welcome -speech-2007s-incoming-class.

2. Susan Dugdale, "How to Give a Great Welcome Speech," write-out-loud, September 10, 2019, https:// www.write-out-loud.com/welcome-speech.html.

8.4 Presenting and Accepting an Award

1. Egil Aarvik, "Award Ceremony Speech" (transcript of Nobel Peace Prize presentation speech to Elie Wiesel, 1986), Nobel Prize, accessed May 6, 2024, https://www.nobelprize.org/prizes/peace/1986 /ceremony-speech.

2. Deirdre Durkan, "Oscars: 10 Winners and Presenters Who Dedicated Their Speeches to a Cause," *Hollywood Reporter*, February 13, 2018, https://www .hollywoodreporter.com/lists/oscars-10-winners -presenters-who-dedicated-speeches-a-cause-1083819/.

3. Nana Kwame Adjei-Brenyah, "Nana Kwame Adjei-Brenyah Wins the 2019 PEN/Jean Stein Book Award" (acceptance speech, New York, February 27, 2019), "Winners' Speeches from the 2019 Literary Awards Ceremony," PEN America, accessed May 5, 2024, https://pen.org/2019-literary-awards-transcripts. A transcript accompanies the video on this site.

4. Adjei-Brenyah.

5. Elie Wiesel, "Elie Wiesel—Acceptance Speech" (Nobel Peace Prize acceptance speech, Oslo, Norway, 1986), Nobel Prize, accessed May 6, 2024, https://www .nobelprize.org/prizes/peace/1986/wiesel/acceptance -speech/. A transcript accompanies the video on this site.

6. Kelle Louaillier, "The Women Who Blazed the Trail for Social Justice," *Corporate Accountability*, March 31, 2017, https://corporateaccountability.org/blog/women -blazed-trail-social-justice/; and "Case History: Berta Cáceres," Front Line Defenders, accessed April 16, 2021, https://www.frontlinedefenders.org/en/case /case-history-berta-c%C3%A1ceres.

7. Amazon Web Services, accessed May 6, 2024, https://course-building.s3-us-west-2.amazonaws .com/Public_Speaking/transcripts/BertaCaceres AcceptanceSpeech2015_transcript.txt.

8.6 Eulogies

1. Lee Strasberg, "Marilyn Monroe's Eulogy," Funeralwise, accessed May 6, 2024, funeralwise.com /celebration-of-life/eulogy/monroe/.

2. "Read George W. Bush's Eulogy for John McCain," *New York Times*, September 1, 2018, https://www .nytimes.com/2018/09/01/us/politics/george-w-bush -john-mccain-eulogy.html.

3. Shirley Halperin, "Aretha Franklin Funeral: Read Clive Davis' Eulogy to the Queen of Soul," *Variety*,

August 31, 2018, https://variety.com/2018/music/news/aretha-franklin-funeral-clive-davis-eulogy-1202923282.

4. Oprah Winfrey, "Eulogy for Rosa Parks" (eulogy, Washington, DC, October 31, 2005), American Rhetoric: Online Speech Bank, accessed May 6, 2024, https://www.americanrhetoric.com/speeches/oprahwinfreyonrosaparks.htm.

8.7 Team Presentations and Public Group Discussions

1. Isa N. Engleberg and Dianna R. Wynn, *Working in Groups: Communication Principles and Strategies*, 7th ed. (New York: Pearson, 2017), 224.

2. Thomas Leech, *How to Prepare, Stage, and Deliver Winning Presentations* (New York: AMACOM, 1993), 278.

3. Engleberg and Wynn, *Working in Groups*, 224.

4. Carl E. Larson and Frank M. J. LaFasto, *TeamWork: What Must Go Right/What Can Go Wrong* (Newbury, CA: Sage, 1989), 27.

5. PowerSpeaking, Inc., "Strategies for Terrific Team Presentations," LinkedIn, November 10, 2021, https://www.linkedin.com/pulse/strategies-terrific-team-presentations-powerspeaking-inc-/.

6. Marjorie Brody, *Speaking Your Way to the Top: Making Powerful Business Presentations* (Boston: Allyn & Bacon, 1998), 81.

7. Judith Filek, "Tips for Seamless Team Presentations—A Baker's Dozen" (presentation blog post), Impact Communications, Inc., June 1, 2014, https://www.impactcommunicationsinc.com/presentation-communication-skills/tips-for-seamless-team-presentations-a-bakers-dozen/.

8. Engleberg and Wynn, *Working in Groups*, 224.

9. Deborah Harring-Makin, *Keeping the Team Going: A Tool Kit to Renew and Refuel Your Workplace Teams* (New York: AMACOM, 1996), 88–89.